AGAINST NATURE?

Against Nature?

*Types of Moral Argumentation
regarding Homosexuality*

Pim Pronk

Translated by John Vriend
Foreword by Hendrik Hart

WILLIAM B. EERDMANS PUBLISHING COMPANY
GRAND RAPIDS, MICHIGAN

Copyright © 1993 by Wm. B. Eerdmans Publishing Co.
255 Jefferson Ave. S.E., Grand Rapids, Michigan 49503

Printed in the United States of America

Library of Congress Cataloging-in-Publication Data

Pronk, Pim, 1948–
[Tegennatuurlijk? English]
Against nature? : types of moral argumentation regarding homosexuality /
Pim Pronk ; translated by John Vriend.
p.   cm.
Translation of: Tegennatuurlijk?
Includes bibliographical references.
ISBN 0-8028-0623-6 (pbk.)
1. Homosexuality — Religious aspects — Christianity.
2. Homosexuality — Moral and ethical aspects.
BR115.H6P76613   1993
241'.66 — dc20   93-4929
CIP

Contents

Foreword

Some issues are so controversial that confronting them is too painful. Rather than discussing them in an emotionally charged atmosphere, we prefer not to discuss them at all. Other issues are so important that confronting them is necessary even when this is unavoidably painful. We prefer to find an approach to them at almost any cost, including the risk of pain. The issue of homosexuality is, at present and generally speaking, in the first category in the churches and in the second category in society.

At its core, the issue of homosexuality in our culture has to do with the importance all of us attach to our sex and our gender and how these affect our very self-identity. By means of the categories of sex and gender, which are categories of, respectively, our reproductive roles and our socialization of these, we can make some sense of many threatening problems we have come to experience as a result of women's emancipation. But homosexuality cannot even be adequately dealt with in terms of these categories. In almost every respect, a gay person is a male capable of playing the same reproductive role of which males are capable and is socially a man the way men are men in our culture. Similar things are true of lesbians. For gays and lesbians we use, therefore, a third category, namely that of sexual orientation. Orientation is, as such, not the same as sex or gender. But it affects both, since homosexuals often do not play a sexually reproductive role and sometimes do accept certain gender traits not traditionally associated with their sex.

Given the immense significance of all this for our identity, heterosexual people tend to be deeply affected by the confusing picture of homosexuality and often find it threatening, whether emotionally, socially, morally, religiously, or even more deeply in the core of their personhood. Especially men in our culture experience this threat, in part because being a man is connected with issues of power and domination. Whatever tends to question or undermine this power can be perceived as threatening. In this context men's sense of manhood requires them to be different from all that is womanly. Thus they are confused by the idea that men can be men even if they are gay. In their minds, a gay man is an effeminate man, a femalish male.

This sense of fear around the issue, resulting in the rejection of homosexuality or of homosexual behavior because it forms a threat on some level, is today often called "homophobia." Originally homosexuals introduced this term to counteract a psychiatric theory that homosexuals were heterophobic. In this theory homosexuals were said to engage in same-sex behavior because of their fear of heterosexual behavior. Homosexuals then suggested that heterosexuals must, by analogy, behave the way they do because they are homophobic. Today, however, the term "homophobia" is used to describe the phenomenon of experiencing some anxiety around the acceptance of homosexuality, for whatever reason. The term does not mean, as some think, hatred of homosexuals. Many people claim not to be homophobic because they claim not to hate homosexuals. The real issue, however, is that people feel anxious about acceptance of homosexuals for many different reasons. Minimal acceptance may be tolerated by many heterosexuals; full acceptance is difficult for most.

Homophobia is, as can easily be seen, at least a moral issue. It has its focus in accepting or rejecting another human being. It also has a double edge: if accepting homosexuality is immoral, the rejection of another human being also seems immoral. Christians could possibly take homophobia to an even deeper level than that of morality, namely to the core of biblical religion: the love of God and neighbor. Homophobia deeply affects a Christian's ability to love a homosexual neighbor.

This homophobia is very widespread in our culture. But it is probably strongest in the churches. There the threat posed by relativizing sex/gender identity is increased by a perception that the Bible uniformly condemns homosexuality. Homophobia is, as I here describe it, not a self-consciously adopted attitude of rejection out of hatred but a moral-religious fear of condoning something terribly important that is also terribly wrong, because it is so "different" from what seems "natural." And this fear goes so deep that, in the light of the love Christians know they should have toward others, the topic of homosexuality becomes undiscussable. It is too controversial, too painful. There is a conflict of guilt — guilt toward homosexuals whom believers should love rather than condemn, guilt toward God who seems to condemn homosexual behavior. The conflict manifests itself tellingly in the difficulty heterosexuals have in acknowledging their homophobia on some level.

In society outside of the church the same fears play a role. Homophobia remains widespread here too. But there is a difference. The demands for public justice and the negative pressures on oppression and discrimination are so universal and powerful in our time that it becomes unavoidable to explore the meaning of justice for the public position of homosexuals in our culture. So among legislators, journalists, TV script writers and news people, novelists, filmmakers, and others we find leaders who have taken up this cause very openly, lately spurred on by the horrors of AIDS. They present this issue, they hope, in ways that help the public to have more informed opinions. But since the church is not a public forum, it is less vulnerable to this pressure and more likely to be shielded from it by tradition. Hence the church avoids the pain of confronting the issue, while the public is made to endure it.

Strangely enough, there was a time, quite recently, when the situation was the other way around. Society was basically closed to tolerance for homosexuals, but churches discussed homosexuality and created what they believed to be a tolerant combination of expressing love and not condoning evil. In the 1970s many major denominations debated and adopted official positions on homosexuality. The reason was that many governments had recently taken homosexuality out of the criminal code. This enabled homosexuals in western nations to speak out for themselves without fear of incrimination in the most literal sense of the term. The churches soon realized they needed to study and discuss the matter and did so. The result was what seemed a very enlightened approach. Most began by saying that homosexuals are God's children and need to be loved. And since they are now rejected, the church has a task in learning to love and accept the homosexual person. But homosexuals are also, like the rest of us, sinners. And one of their sins is that they are inclined to give expression to their sexuality in same-sex behavior. Such behavior is sinful, said the church, because it is *against nature* according to the Bible. It must, therefore, be rejected. It also disqualifies the evildoer for official positions in the church.

Today, however, the churches have exchanged roles with secular society in the acceptance of homosexuals. Once churches had taken the two-pronged position of love for the person and condemnation of the practice, it was the condemnation that most deeply influenced Christian behavior. Homophobia became identified with what seemed obedience to God. In the church, too, however, there have been many requests to reopen the discussion and to review the official position of two decades ago. This has been the result of many new developments. One is the ongoing research into the nature of homosexuality as well as renewed study of the relevant texts in the Bible. Another is the now widely available testimony of gay and lesbian Christians to the authenticity of their faith. Although their sexual practices may still be controversial to many, they are in every other respect recognizable as genuine followers of Christ according to the Scriptures. Yet another development is the ongoing growth of civil rights legislation that guarantees public justice for homosexuals, and the slow but steady increase in social acceptance. But so far almost no major North American denomination has been able to articulate a position of full acceptance for homosexuals in the church, one that could receive the approval of a majority in major assemblies. All the new information and all the growth in goodwill has so far seemed insufficient to occasion a serious reconsideration by the majority of church members of the condemnation of same-sex practices, no matter how they are conceived.

Why this resistance in the churches? This is not because no arguments or material have been advanced that throw new light on the issue. It has been argued that the Bible does not condemn, because it does not know, what we refer to as homosexuality. Homosexuality as a phenomenon of sexual orientation, such arguments go, is modern. Literature of premodern times can therefore hardly be expected to comment on an attempt to find a Christian morality for actively experiencing this modern orientation. Same-sex activity between homosexual adults who seek a moral expression for their sexuality is not a term of reference in the Bible. From this point of view, if informed analysis of texts in the Bible concludes that the Bible does refer to such sexuality, the links have been made by extrapolation.

It is widely recognized, even by pro-gay students of the Bible, that no Bible text is positive about homosexual behavior. But it is argued that, even if we could establish intended links between the negative Bible texts on homosexual behavior and the intended moral sexual practice of modern Christians of homosexual orientation, most churches can now make use of legitimate and accepted hermeneutical approaches to the Bible that would enable them to consider that these texts do not directly apply to our modern situation. In my own denomination, the Christian Reformed Church, recent decisions toward opening the church's offices to women has created a need for the hermeneutics behind such decisions to be identified as Reformed. Centrist theologians in Calvin Theological Seminary, such as John Cooper and John Bolt, have argued in published writings that if history has moved us to a different understanding of a phenomenon, the Bible cannot be directly applied to it according to principles of Reformed hermeneutics established by Calvin. Both also make it very clear, though without argument, that in the case of homosexuality this principle does not apply.

In the wider ecumenical context of my denomination, the

Reformed Ecumenical Council, a report has been produced on hermeneutics and ethics, especially because that relationship needed to be clarified with regard to the consideration of homosexuality. That report, written by Albert Wolters, unambiguously declares that in matters of morality the Bible does not have direct authority but only indirect, partly because the Bible's own focus is not ethical, partly because of the historical variability of ethical positions, including those of the Bible itself.

Quite consistent with such a position, the report on homosexuality adopted by the Christian Reformed Church in 1973 considered the possible healing effects on homosexuals of approval for same-sex behavior. But it concluded at the time that "there is no evidence that a person will in fact and from a long range perspective be helped" by this. Such evidence is now available. But its availability has not made any dents in the conviction that the Bible condemns same-sex behavior of all kinds.

There exists no widely accepted literature today that unambiguously demonstrates that the negative passages in the Bible directly apply to modern homosexuality. There is also no such literature that demonstrates that claims to the effect that the negative passages do not relate to today are simply and clearly mistaken. There is literature today that announces as Reformed the hermeneutical principles that take historical changes into account and require an indirect approach to the Bible's dealing with issues of morality. There is also literature with plausible alternative exegesis, literature that is perhaps not conclusive but that also is not conclusively refutable.

What is the upshot? It is that we have an authoritative text, but no authoritative reading of it. People can take various positions and root these positions in certain readings. Many of these readings can have the character of being honest, plausible, fitting a wider biblical context. But in and of themselves, none of these readings are the obviously right reading. Many of them just simply compel us to say that various sides of the issue are defended with biblical integrity. Traditional readings leading to rejection of homosexual intimacy remain plausible. But it is not these traditional readings that can authoritatively show other readings to be demonstrably mistaken. Such a demonstration must be directly based on the text, not on some other reading of the text.

Why, then, do churches remain so opposed to considering the morality of same-sex behavior? Since most churches want to be perceived to emphasize the need for loving homosexuals and for fully accepting them in the church as persons, what prevents them from legitimately interpreting the Bible on homosexuality the way they also went with usury, slavery, and women? It seems that the strong influence of an extrabiblical factor is used to explain this situation. And the factor that suggests itself is the widespread cultural condemnation of same-sex behavior, connected with the homophobia that is, in turn, related to the threat perceived to male power and identity in our culture. The Bible is primarily used to explain, give ground to, and excuse our own attitude to homosexuals. But a need for that attitude can in no way simply be derived from or be read in the Bible.

Normally Reformed people would not be tempted to derive their sense of what is "natural" straight from the Bible, nor would they use the Bible to become informed and knowledgeable about homosexuality. Reformed Christians have a long tradition of regarding the Bible as book of faith and not as text for geology (the flood), biology (evolution), hygiene (purity code), economics (jubilee), or whatever else. The Bible gives us our ultimate perspective, our fundamental orientation for our lives, but does not provide us with data and concepts we can simply and directly use in our time. Its concrete morality is not and cannot be ours. It is not a moral text. Christian faith is not moralistic. This attitude is rooted among others in the advice Jewish Christians give to Greek Christians in Acts 15. It is understood that the tradition is peculiar to the Jews and that the Greeks will have to mold one of their own, with the help of the Spirit. The above mentioned Reformed Ecumenical Council report makes this all abundantly clear. The Bible's moral rejection of homosexuality cannot simply be taken that any and all homosexual behavior is forbidden for us.

One fear in applying this general approach to homosexuality is said to be a fear of undermining the Bible's moral authority. But such a fear is without ground. For just as jubilee laws have authority for our confessional perspective on economic life, without requiring us to obey them as they are, moral prohibitions in the Bible also have orienting authority for our morality without demanding we follow them literally. The way the Bible roots the morality of its time in God helps us struggle with how to root our contemporary morality in God. The morality we adopt must be experienced by us as a morality God gave us. But that does not, in principle, differ from experiencing our children as given to us by God. That does not mean Christian couples do not make love or struggle with when, how, and how many children to have. It means they struggle with that in biblical light. Just so, they must also see their morality as their own responsibility, though in the light of the Bible.

This is, in effect, our practice and has been for centuries. There is no major western moral tradition that is not also the morality of the church. There have been no major moral shifts in our culture that have not also become shifts in the church. It is to be feared, however, that the church often greets such shifts with fear and suspicion, lets the world work it out, and then adopts it wholesale without deep biblical input. Instead, we would do better to regard shifts in our culture, with its secularized *Christian* roots that pervade it throughout, as opportunities for contributing to such a shift with biblical reflection. I will return to this theme below.

What could be done to activate the churches into more actively considering a practice of visible love for homosexuals such that homosexuals themselves would feel accepted? How could churches be influenced to practice the other side of their two-pronged approach? Today this practice is virtually non-existent and the absence of it is actively justified by appeal to the dark side of the classical two-pronged approach: if you do love the sinner, hate the sin. The ostracism of homosexuals is, in fact, exceptional. No other practice toward which there is a strongly condemnatory attitude in the church, such as stances and practices that are pro-abortion, pro-war, or pro-nuclear arms lead to the sort of exclusion that is practiced in the case of homosexuality. Both within and outside of the church homosexuals are indiscriminately discriminated against. AIDS is unfairly linked to homosexuality. Because of the fear of discovery in the gay community, it is the only infectious disease in our society that, for political reasons, is non-reportable. But we tolerate the danger this implies for all of us rather than let up on endangering homosexuals who come out. People are routinely abused, harmed, and even killed in every segment of our culture for no other reason than their noticeable homosexual identity. No major denomination that condemns homosexual practice shows that its professed love for homosexuals is real by actively protesting this persecution of homosexuals. The church here runs the risk of being fairly accused of injustice by neglecting to advocate on behalf of its homosexual members.

It is widely agreed that cultural situations of this kind, where members of a society are condemned because they are different, exist as a result of widespread prejudice and ignorance rooted in irrational anxiety. It is also widely agreed that only education, information, and advocacy can change this situation. Hence this foreword to a book that is fairly unique in Christian literature on homosexuality.

In writing this foreword I will be perceived to recommend this book. I acknowledge this perception as valid. But in the climate surrounding discussions of homosexuality I need to point out that recommending differs from endorsing. In my view it is too early to establish any approach to homosexuality as the universally shared or, for the present, final position of our culture, or of some society, or of Christianity. No discussion on any aspect of homosexuality is complete whether in the heterosexual or in the homosexual community. This does not mean, of course, that individuals or groups, including for example Pronk or myself, do not, over time, develop positions that are firmly held and defended and that can be justified with good arguments and solid evidence. However, the theological, ethical, legal, social, emotional, and medical understandings of homosexuality are all in a state of flux. Therefore, a practically universal position, one that makes further discussion superfluous, is not now available and moving toward it may be too early. Discussions of homosexuality are not the same as discussions of slavery would be in our time. It has also not yet reached the stage in the church where discussions of evolution are today. For that very reason the Christian community is under obligation to become well informed and to contribute to the discussion with insight and with compassion. And in such a context this book deserves a wide reading and serious consideration, not primarily for endorsement or rejection but for growth in understanding. Anyone in the Christian community concerned about the situation surrounding homosexuality and therefore interested in stimulating, in-depth study and widespread discussion as I am will need to wrestle with this text.

The most unusual aspect of this study is that its author, Pim Pronk, has developed enough expertise to be able to deal with homosexuality from three perspectives, namely, as a biologist, as an ethicist, and as a theologian. Such multilevel approaches by a single competent and qualified author are rare, if not absent, in the field. In the case of this study, which originated as the author's dissertation for the PhD degree defended at the Vrije Universiteit in Amsterdam, the work on each of the three levels received the scrutiny of a reputable scholar in the field, H. M. Kuitert in theological ethics, J. Lever in biology, and J. Veenhof in systematic theology.

Pronk's main theme is that same-sex behavior is a moral issue. Hence he rejects approaches that consider homosexuality mainly from a biological or from a theological point of view. Even if biological factors are relevant, and he does not deny this, they cannot by themselves determine what is moral. Organically rooted dispositions must give way to moral responsibility. Pronk's discussion is limited to the morality of male homosexuality, since he considers female homosexuality sufficiently different to require treatment of its own. He says that even if a man's biological makeup would totally disincline him to any sexual behavior except homosexual, he would still have to accept responsibility for acting on his inclination. And such a decision is primarily a moral decision that must be evaluated on moral grounds.

A similar position on relevance for biological factors holds for theological considerations. They may be relevant, but they are not moral or ethical in kind. Theology and confession do not give us a morality but provide ultimate perspectives that, in addition to other factors, give shape to our moral outlook. But in and of themselves they cannot solve moral problems. Hence it is mistaken, in Pronk's analysis, to expect the Bible to be the one and only or even sufficient ground for accepting or rejecting an ethic for homosexuality. If an ethic is to be biblical, and it should be, then it is not because it is an ethic found in the Bible but because the Bible's confessional perspective comes through in the ethic.

I can illustrate this with Romans 1 as example. No specific moral code in the Bible includes acceptance of homosexual behavior. But that does not mean the morality of same-sex behavior is identical throughout the Bible. The confessional perspective on the condemnation of homosexual practice in the specific moral code of Leviticus is related to purity laws, to the holiness code. That is definitely not the case in Romans, where it has to do with a morality of what is natural and where "natural" has a meaning specific to that text. The condemnation of Romans is contextualized by Hellenic-Jewish perspectives found, for example, in the Book of Wisdom. That Paul has deeply understood the meaning of what happened at the synod described in Acts 15, however, is evident from his own clear relativization in Romans itself of the condemnation of chapter 1. He refers to that condemnation after he has announced that he has a gospel of a new justice of God (1:16, 17). He explains that this condemnation would, rather than deal redemptively with sin, not help any of us but doom us all (2:1ff.). That exactly fits Paul's reorientation of life-in-Christ to the Spirit of the new covenant, as distinct from life oriented to the law and condemnation of the old covenant (2 Cor. 3:7–18). Richard Hays is a widely respected New Testament scholar who is concerned to protect Romans 1 from an agenda-driven pro-gay exegesis. But on more than one occasion he makes clear that there is a similar agenda-driven exegesis that uses Romans 1 to say that the Bible calls us to condemn homosexual behavior. In his view such a call to condemnation, however, cannot survive with an appeal to Romans 1.

If we would have to ask ourselves about an articulation of the New Testament's confessional orientation for an ethic, we might well go with what John Bolt calls the "sweep" of Scripture. That sweep could be taken as moving us from an Old Testament context of holiness as exclusion, separation, and condemnation to a New Testament direction toward inclusion, acceptance, and redemption. No more law as dividing wall of hostility (Eph. 2:11–22), no more male-female, Jew-Greek, slave-free division (Gal. 3:28). If the peculiar wording of the "neither male *and* female" (rather than the neither . . . *nor* of the other references) indeed points to Genesis 1 (Richard Longenecker and Herman Ridderbos), then an appeal to the creation order to limit a New Testament sweep might well be relativized by Paul's famous formula. In any case, such a sweep loses its very character of sweep when we try to hem it in with the warning that it applies only in cases where Scripture itself gives clear indications in specifics where God allows us to move our moral beacons. That is Bolt's own interpretation, taking with the left hand what he gives with the right. In that way he can assure us that the sweep does not include homosexuality. But he thereby removes an important characteristic for the sweep of the Spirit, namely our restoration to (moral) responsibility (Acts 2:14–21).

Traditional Christian believers will, by now, have understood the uniqueness of Pronk's book. The argument that the biological factors are not determinative will please them. But the consistency in applying it to theological arguments as well will seem puzzling. The pattern here is not what we have come to expect. The puzzle becomes more intriguing when Pronk, in addition, turns out to have appreciation for constructivism in the debate about the "nature" of homosexuality. He does not uncritically follow the line that there is such a thing as a biological homosexual nature over which a man has no control. That line of argument has been very influential in getting a hearing for homosexuals in the church. Pronk does not totally accept it. He is more inclined to see homosexuality as, at least in some aspects, a social construct of recent origin. He has the courage to forego the political leverage of essentialism.

At the same time, he does not conclude from this what many Christians conclude, namely that homosexuals must change. Apart from the fact that a social construct differs considerably from a purely individual choice, he also considers this question from a moral point of view. And he concludes that when neither "nature" nor faith provide the final or sole criterion, we need to consider seriously that if sexual behavior *meets moral standards,* it should then also be considered to *be moral,* regardless of the sex or gender of the partners and in spite of the Bible's condemnation of same-sex behavior in a *given* moral context of its own. For sex and gender are not moral categories. And a confessional perspective is not such a category either. Morality must be discussed from within. Biological or theological factors must display their relevance, therefore, from within a properly moral perspective that cannot simply be derived from biology or theology.

Again, there are lines here that do not follow the traditional patterns. But as the discussion opens up and advances, sound conclusions require our taking note of considerations such as Pronk advances. In the case of Christians, this is especially true for his approach to the Bible. Reading his text should make it impossible, I believe, any longer to consider carefully just what same-sex activity means in the Bible, as well as just what sort of ethical framework is in place. Let me illustrate what sorts of questions need to be raised here. The examples are mine.

One set of questions concerns the issue whether the Bible always means any and all homosexual behavior or only specific kinds. It has been argued that the Bible's Old Testament focus is on same-sex behavior as cultic. Others have identified it as prostitution. A case has been made for the prohibitions in Leviticus being limited to anal intercourse. Yet the opposition continues to suggest that the Bible indiscriminately refers to private intimacy of all kinds. So here lies one set of important questions that influence our conclusion whether the biblical injunctions are directly relevant for Christian homosexuals in pursuit of a morality of sexual intimacy.

There is another set that concerns the issue of whether the Bible is written in terms of a concrete ethical code it intends to be observed for all times or whether it sheds light on ethical codes that are themselves specific and historical for their time. Some say the Bible's morality in this matter was focused on rejecting pagan cults, others that it was related to the special regard for semen as life-bearer. It has been argued that it all has to do with the focus of fruitfulness for bringing forth the Messiah. If we have different moral perspectives, could they nevertheless still be biblical? If so, does a different morality require the same specific rejections?

A crucially important consideration in evaluating this book is that the author is a homosexual. To say that he is therefore prejudiced is not only too easy, but it undermines arguments against homosexuality by heterosexuals. Not only is there no evidence that homosexuals are incapable, as homosexuals, of serious and valid moral analysis, but there also is evidence that making far-reaching moral decisions affecting people whose experience we cannot share and whose participation in the process is not invited is, as such, morally inadequate. If the church, which is largely heterosexual, is to make morally binding decisions on homosexuality, it would benefit in its moral authority from including homosexuals in the deliberations. We have hopefully learned from the moral insufficiency of male councils deciding about women's roles without women's participation. The same holds for decisions by heterosexual assemblies about homosexuals without their participation. This is certainly true for churches who have already decided that a homosexual orientation is not a sin and who, for that reason, would be more prepared for openly accepting the presence of such people in their deliberations.

Many people still argue that we also do not make legislation concerning murder, theft, or drunk driving with the active participation of murderers, thieves, and drunk drivers. But it is then forgotten that no significant body of people in our society disputes our judgment that murder, theft, and drunk driving are evil, harmful, and destructive. Yet murderers, thieves, and drunk drivers are often treated with more compassion than homosexuals. But does anyone argue for a biblical morality of murder, theft, or drunk driving? Is there any desire on the part of murderers, thieves, or drunk drivers that their practices become socially accepted? If we neglect these things it will be lost on us that Christian homosexuals are a unique group of people. Their devotion to God in Christ is, in fact, so genuine that all over the world homosexuals have participated in the formation of a church, a denomination, in which homosexuals are free to worship God fully. In these Metropolitan Community Churches God is praised for the gift of homosexuality by people who, in every other respect, are believers like any other believer. In those churches their lives are celebrated as gifts from God.

It is clear, therefore, that Pronk's study offers perspectives that are unique, needed, and of value. It merits a careful study. In our North American context his work may seem overly radical or controversial because he was free to write without fear. In his native Holland there is roughly 90 percent social acceptance of homosexuality, and in his own Reformed church, partnered gays are ministers. His style and language do not, therefore, diplomatically need to respect the feelings of those who condemn him or even to be tactful toward people who still feel uneasy about homosexuality. This is not because he is rude or lacks the proper respect or understanding but because these are no longer the most relevant factors in his situation.

This study was written in a climate with the possibility for drawing conclusions because they are good conclusions rather than because they fit a confessional or political climate. Many of those who will read this translation are not in such a climate. For them there may be barriers to overcome. But in spite of that, and for the sake of supporting an in-depth discussion of homosexuality in the church, we can at least give Pronk a hearing.

Hendrik Hart
Toronto, January 1993

Introduction

The focus of this study is the moral evaluation of homosexuality, primarily as it developed in the Netherlands in the period following World War II. In view is the situation in Protestant Christian churches and, to a lesser extent, in the Catholic Church. Since the atmosphere in the Netherlands, also in the churches, is reputed to be extremely tolerant toward homosexuals, a secondary concern of this study is the question of how far the situation in the churches in the Netherlands differs from that in a number of other countries.

This tolerance in the Netherlands is of relatively recent origin. The past three decades have seen a massive change in societal attitudes toward homosexuality. This development did not leave the churches untouched; in part it was initiated there. Before World War II homosexuality did not exist as a moral problem. Both inside and outside the churches, one could take condemnation for granted. Polls have indicated, however, that from the sixties on, tolerance toward homosexuality increased and is still increasing today. For numerous people in the Netherlands, the moral permissibility of homosexual relations is no longer an issue. In the churches, however, it is still very much in discussion. Since this is also the case in churches elsewhere, this would seem to be sufficient warrant for an ethical study.

There is, however, an additional reason for this study.

R. Tielman, the historian who has mapped out the history of homosexuality in the Netherlands, has described the development of social attitudes since World War II as moving from "incomplete acceptance" (up until the early sixties), through "complete acceptance" (the seventies), to "past acceptance" (the eighties).[1] One must ask, however, whether this shift is based on moral arguments or on something else. One cannot always avoid the impression that the goodwill of today has more to do with the power of numbers than the force of arguments. In the Netherlands and in several other Western nations, homosexual emancipation has become a political issue that no political party can ignore with impunity. Emancipation nevertheless remains embattled. To furnish a few unrelated examples: In the tolerant country of the Netherlands an equal rights bill (for hetero- and homosexuals in socioeconomic situations, among other things) passed only with great difficulty. In Germany the notorious article 175 has still not been removed from the Penal Code. Since 1987 England has on its books "Clause 28," which makes punishable the teaching of the acceptability of homosexual acts ("in any maintained school"). In the United States the army still dismisses soldiers with a dishonorable discharge on the ground of homosexual activity. By comparison with these relatively more tolerant societies, countries in which homosexuality is legally prohibited stand out in stark contrast. Homosexuals who flee their countries are often not considered political refugees elsewhere. Even Amnesty International does nothing to change the fortunes of homosexuals.

Politically, in the Netherlands and several other countries, tolerance is grounded in the constitutional right to conduct one's sexual life in accordance with one's own preferences, provided one respects the corresponding right of all others. Hence, in that sense, homosexuality is no longer a societal problem. For numerous homosexuals, that is all they care about. To their minds, to raise ethical questions is to moralize and to set arbitrary limits of permissibility. They therefore expect little from ethical discussions.

1. R. Tielman (1982, Chapters 12 and 13).

That attitude, as I hope to demonstrate, is based on a misunderstanding. But it is fostered by the way discussions on homosexuality are usually conducted. Until recently, in the Netherlands, they were discussions by and for the benefit of heterosexuals. They did not focus on the value of homosexual behavior but on what "straights" thought permissible for "gays." To the degree this became more clearly the case, even in well-intentioned conversations, homosexuals found participation in them less tolerable. People hold up to others rules from which they themselves are exempt, at the very least creating an appearance of unfairness.

No wonder homosexuals preferred to focus on securing and expanding their political rights: for example, better police protection from gay-bashers, vigilance with regard to job application procedures, and sound sex education. In time, however, such pragmatism does not satisfy a person. Political rights, too, are based (in part) on the fundamental moral convictions of political majorities. Consequently it makes sense for homosexuals not to avoid participation in moral discussion. This study, as stated earlier, focuses on one particular social sector of the Netherlands. The shifts in attitude there are illustrative for goodwill that run aground on faulty argumentation. Accordingly, analysis of these shifts is also a contribution to the field of ethics. The results obtained can be used subsequently to analyze and assess the viewpoints of churches elsewhere in the world.

In my opinion the key concept in the discussion was, and is today, the concept of "nature." That concept is the funnel through which elements that have nothing to do with ethics have slipped into the moral discussion of (homo)sexuality. "Nature" has many meanings that are not only unclear but also function in differing contexts. In antiquity already the term "nature" was used in a *normative* sense. Plato, Philo, and Paul all condemned homosexuality by calling it "unnatural," and Christian tradition has repeated the word after them. The content of the *scientific* concept of nature, on the other hand, is very different. Here nature is "the sum total of things that can be observed." Within this concept we again find an assortment of distinctions, such as the natural versus the cultural, the healthy versus the diseased, biological and social factors, the inherited and the acquired, etc. Depending on the meaning assigned to nature, homosexual behavior is then called natural or unnatural. The context is here descriptive in kind. Finally there is the *religious* context: nature as originally created good, versus nature as corrupted by sin.

Obviously, the several meanings of "nature" in these different contexts can easily be confused one with another. The first question, then, is whether we can prove the existence of this conceptual confusion in the discussion of homosexuality. Is this important? Indeed it is, for it helps us to discern when a given appeal to "nature" is ethically valid and when not, however well-intentioned the appeal. In earlier times homosexual behavior was viewed as "the wrong choice" and condemned as "unnatural." Today many people view homosexuality as a natural given in which no choice is involved and which, therefore, cannot be forbidden. Still others regard an appeal to a deterministically conceived "nature" as a curtailment of their freedom to live by self-chosen standards. So it seems as though an appeal to "nature" still allows us to go in all directions and arbitrarily to derive from it either approval or disapproval of homosexual relations. When each of these viewpoints is then accorded theological legitimacy, the confusion is complete and the discussion seems interminable. Roughly speaking, this is, in fact, the state of the discussion, as we shall see.

The question as to the meaning of the appeal to "nature" also plays a role elsewhere.[2] It is involved in the choice of scientific models in so-called "homo-studies," which are being conducted at various universities in England, the United States, the Netherlands, and elsewhere. The controversial character of the appeal to nature is therefore by no means characteristic only of the prevailing ethics in the churches. Conversely, it is perhaps the case that many uncertain-

---

2. Cf. the discussion on "essentialism" and "constructionism" in the social sciences (homosexual studies); see Chapter II § G. This was one of the issues that received much attention at the International Congress "Homosexuality — Which Homosexuality?" held in December 1987 at the Free University in Amsterdam. See D. Altman, et al. (1989).

ties and opposing opinions on homosexual behavior within the Christian orbit are due to the vagueness and polyvalence of the concept of nature. That is the issue we plan to examine, especially within those situations where "nature" is used to indicate a moral norm.

By "ethics" I mean systematic reflection on morality. This entails the analysis of the grounds on which the normative viewpoints held in a given society are based.[3] The goal of ethical analysis is, therefore, not primarily the establishment of normative guidelines. Morality, hence also the sexual morality that will engage us in this study, is not made by ethicists. Ethics presupposes the existence of morality. To the extent that analysis and criticism of morality lead inescapably to the formulation of moral guidelines, ethics is also a norm-setting discipline. I define morality as the entire complex of the motivations, attitudes, feelings, and actions that are considered basic to communication within a group or society and are justified in terms of being permitted or not permitted. This definition is broad enough for us to regard as "morality" everything we encounter in the literature on homosexuality in the way of existing or proposed rules relating to sexuality.

From this definition it follows that we can speak of multiple moralities, hence also of the morality of homosexual lifestyles, in distinction from the morality of groups of homosexuals. Now we face the phenomenon that the differences among these codes are always interpreted, back and forth, as morally relevant differences. Of interest to our subject in this connection is the fact that not only the differences in sexual behavior are viewed as such (e.g., differences in the pattern of relating or differences in the number of partners) but also that the sex of the partner is regarded as morally relevant. How that can be is the first question I want to answer. That requires, in the first place, an accurate description of the phenomena being judged and an analysis of the concepts used in that description. Only after that has been done can we ourselves arrive at an appraisal of the different moral viewpoints concerning homosexuality. Our focus will be the attempt to distinguish cor-

3. Cf. W. K. Frankena (1963; 1973).

rectly the different concepts of "nature" employed because, as we stated earlier, *there* lies the source of the most important misunderstandings about homosexuality.

In Chapter I I first present an analysis of the traditional condemnation of homosexuality in terms of its being "against nature." Then I show that assumptions associated with this term are also implied in today's tolerant and approving arguments, not only in the Netherlands but also elsewhere.

Since arguments derived from the (biological and medical) sciences regularly play a large role in the moral discussion of homosexuality, various scientific descriptions and explanations of (homo)sexuality are examined in Chapter II in terms of their "image of nature" and tested by whether this image is merely descriptive and explanatory or normatively "loaded." I also broach the question in what way scientific information is needed to form moral judgments.

Chapter III deals with the sense and possibility of using the term "natural" in a moral context. This gives me "a place to stand" with regard to (the moral evaluation of) homosexuality.

In Chapter IV I discuss the religious arguments used in the evaluation of homosexuality. Central here is a question that is not exclusively tied to the moral discussion of sexuality but that is characteristic for the treatment of all ethical issues in the context of the Christian faith: the relation, namely, between universal human or rational arguments and religious, in this case biblical and theological, arguments.

Homosexuality, in this study, is the homosexuality of men. The pronoun "he" in this book cannot simply be replaced by "she." For homosexual women the issues are, at least in part, different. The position of women in society is different from that of men and relations betweeen women are different. Also, women are in a better position to make their own situations an object of study.

Unless the discussion requires another term, I consistently use the word "homosexuality" and not the euphemism "homophilia." The problem is sexual practice, not friendships as such. "Homosexuality" sometimes refers to sexual behavior, sometimes (also) to sexual identity. The context will show what is intended.

Chapter I

The Traditional Appraisal

A. Introduction: framing the question

Recent publications of the Gereformeerde Kerken in Nederland (GKN)* alone offer a spectrum of viewpoints regarding homosexual behavior. A few examples follow. The pertinent synodical decision of 1979 asserts that discrimination against homosexuals (the churches consistently speak of "homophiles") must end in the church and admonishes the members, also in view of the different standpoints regarding the scriptural data,

> to bear in mind that — out of respect for one another's right to privacy and one's own responsibility before the Lord, and in the light of God's justification of our common humanity — we do not have the right to condemn our fellowmen on account of their homophile predisposition and practice,** since also in this matter the last word is up to the Lord himself.[1]

* The GKN is the result of a merger, organized in 1892, between two evangelically oriented dissenting groups who left the NHK (the Netherlands Reformed Church) in 1834 and 1886 respectively.

** The Dutch original *beleving* refers to a way of understanding, experiencing, and living — hence practicing — *Translator.*

1. In *Instaan voor elkaar* (1982: 70–71).

The synod describes the decision as "pastoral-ethical": it is not a moral judgment concerning homosexual practices but an appeal to accept one another and to leave judgment to the Lord.[2]

A related "Report on the Use of Scripture in Questions Relating to Homophilia" (1982), failing to arrive at a unanimous conclusion, offers four positions, which run the gamut from strong condemnation to complete acceptance of "homosexual relations in love and fidelity." The report refrains from offering the synod a recommendation for a more specific pronouncement on the ground that this would be arbitrary and not in the interest of "the homophile neighbor who is unintentionally different."[3]

A third example comes from a pastoral booklet called *Fidelity in Love (In liefde trouw zijn)* that, among other things, deals with homosexual love. The opinion expressed here is that when it meets a number of criteria derived from the biblical idiom of covenant, a homosexual relationship has the same ethical value as that which is called marriage between a man and a woman.[4]

The examples show that one Reformed person views the biblical condemnation as normative, a second finds the norm in a pastoral approach (permission as a makeshift solution), a third in the fact of being "unintentionally different," and a fourth in the quality of the relationship. The synodical majority, meanwhile, abstains from making a judgment: judgment belongs to the Lord. For the homosexual — and not just for him — such a multiplicity of views is a jungle or, perhaps, a supermarket.

But in any case it also suggests a situation of discomfort. Nowhere, after all, are we given an answer to the question concerning the value of homosexuality as a general human form of behavior. In the best case, what we have is "moral permission for a minority to conduct itself in accordance with its own 'nature.'"[5]

---

2. *Instaan voor elkaar* (1982: 73).
3. Report: *Homofilie* (1982: 48, 75).
4. *In liefde trouw zijn* (1983: 42ff.).
5. Th. Beemer (1982: 54).

That means there is room for people who are different ("homophile") but certainly not for homosexual behavior in general.

Just what is objectionable here? In an analysis of recent church pronouncements A. Dekker observes that the churches cannot resolve the issue because they have gotten themselves stuck in a number of fields of tension: between nature (disposition) and conduct (practice), love (relationship) and sexuality, form (marriage) and content (fidelity), pastorate and ethics. At least in the synodical decision of the GKN he sees a breakthrough in principle: "the limits of ethics are here made visible from within the perspective of the pastorate."[6] Is that true? Dekker means that the one pole must not be played off against the other. It is not acceptable to tolerate pastorally what is considered inappropriate ethically, and that also applies to the other dichotomies. But one who says this, as Dekker does, should not then want to impose restrictions on ethics, as Dekker does, but ask for a better ethics than the sexual ethics of the church.

In this chapter I plan to show that all these dichotomies hinge on two not mentioned by Dekker: those of *natural* vs. *unnatural* and *ethical* vs. *religious*. The reason why these, in any case, are important is easy to demonstrate. In the first place, when homosexuals are given permission by others to conduct themselves in accordance with their own "nature," this not only pins a group down on its own particular predisposition but also keeps heterosexuals from questioning their own heterosexual group norms. That, ethically speaking, is not satisfactory. It is what whites often do to blacks. Further, if a given judgment is a moral judgment, it applies to everyone. A crime is a crime even when committed by a person of a special kind of disposition. The appeal to a special homosexual nature as an ethical argument therefore immediately raises questions. These are all the more interesting because the tradition also continually appeals to "nature" but it does this to condemn homosexuality as being "contrary to nature." The way the appeal to "nature" has functioned as ethical argument is the subject of this chapter.

6. A. Dekker (1982: 91–92).

The second fundamental distinction, that between ethical and religious arguments, plays a role in all moral discussion conducted by Christians. Morality is not, after all, the same thing as religion, even though every religion involves a morality. We cannot, therefore, simply assume that a good religious (in this case, biblical) argument is also a good moral argument.[7] In each case that has to be argued and demonstrated. In practice, for Christians the appeal to the Bible and to the Christian tradition always plays an important role, also in the case of the Christian authors I plan to discuss. Because this chapter is descriptive-ethical in kind, I will, when necessary, also include the appeal to Scripture insofar as it relates to the distinction "natural-unnatural." But the evaluation of religious argumentation intended as ethical argument is reserved for a later chapter.

It is not necessary to write a history of the ethical evaluation of homosexual behavior. It would be endlessly repetitive because the same arguments continually recur. My concern is rather to describe types of argumentation, beginning with the *contra naturam* argument. For a systematic overview of the successive types of argumentation, it is enough for us to concentrate on the post-WWII period. In that period the traditional condemnation is first continued, then yields to more tolerant approaches. I address the arguments employed in the circle of Protestant Christianity, mainly that of the Netherlands. Where necessary I also take notice of Catholic and non-Dutch sources. The conclusions we are able to draw from the analysis of the Dutch situation are finally used in a critical discussion of documents of churches elsewhere in the world. Successive sections will describe:

- elements in the traditional condemnation (B);
- the origin of these elements (C);
- the (more) tolerant handling of these elements (D);
- the role of these elements in ecclesiastical discussions outside the Netherlands (E).

7. See Chapter IV; for the distinction between religion and ethics, see Little and Twiss (1973).

B. Elements in the traditional condemnation

Accordingly, we take the situation in the Dutch Protestant churches after World War II as a paradigm for our ethical analysis. A good starting point is W. J. Aalders whose *Ethical Handbook* appeared still in the war years. In it he devotes a brief passage to homosexuality in which the argumentation proceeds along classical lines. Homosexual acts are wrong because they are *contrary to nature*. All sexual acts outside marriage are wrong, but a distinction can be made between natural and unnatural acts of transgression. The first are "corruptions of that which is good in itself," like premarital sex, adultery, and incest. The second are "reprehensible as such" and self-condemned "also because they are inherently unfruitful and therefore meaningless and senseless." To this category belong onanism, homosexuality, and bestiality. Their occurrence is a sign of moral decay and perversity. But also "pathetic and distasteful pathological instances" occur.[8]

The brevity of the passage indicates that for Aalders homosexuality is not a problem. The *contra naturam* argument is sufficient and the Bible (Rom. 1) supports it.

This is typical for the tradition. In the next section we will find that the argument already occurs in this form in Thomas Aquinas. A difference is that Aalders supports his ethical judgment with a reference to the physician's standpoint: homosexuality is perverse and pathological. In this statement we already encounter the first building blocks: the unnatural is pathological.

But how must we construe the meaning of "unnatural"? Aalders offers two meanings: on the one hand, "natural" is "that which is given with the nature of things" or "that which belongs to being human"; and on the other, "that which agrees with the impulses which are viewed as natural needs and thus have a claim to being satisfied" (p. 226).[9] Sexuality is "natural" in the first sense. That which is "natural" in the second sense must not be

8. W. J. Aalders (1947: 223–26).
9. One encounters such arguments in the literature of the emancipation movements of that time. Aalders, however, does not mention them.

allowed to surface: it is "to live it up," "to indulge oneself." One then crosses a line that has to be imposed on nature. Without it a human being sinks into the subhuman, Aalders thinks.

"Natural" thus clearly has a double reference: an empirical-biological (that which is given with humanity) and a normative (that which may or may not come out in the open). But what is the criterion for what may rise to the surface? That is not clear. Of course, Aalders makes his judgments on the basis of what he takes to be a biblical image of man. But the argument for that is, in part, derived from biology. The existence of the sexes and the manner of the propagation of the human race indicate what is natural sexuality (p. 226), and therefore all that falls outside this is sterile and senseless.

Here we face our first problem, for how can a biological judgment (which Aalders offers) be a criterion for a moral judgment (which he intends to offer)? In a moment I will return to this question but first I wish to discuss the resemblance between the moral and the medical evaluation of homosexuality, a resemblance Aalders mentions almost casually.

On this point we are informed by F. J. Tolsma, a Protestant psychiatrist who, in his study on homosexuality and homoeroticism, devotes a chapter to the moral evaluation.[10] To him homosexual behavior is pathological because it is usually not rooted in a congenital predisposition. That is the conclusion of his evaluation of the then-current medical theories of origin. For a person to be directed by his instincts is undeniably pathological, for "as a spiritual being he can characteristically raise himself above those instincts." When he is no longer able to do this, he is sick. Sexual behavior always requires an act of the will. Also the homosexual continues to have the higher spiritual capacities at his disposal. But "an appeal to these higher layers can only be accepted when there has been no expansion in the direction of

10. F. J. Tolsma (1948). He serves as an interesting figure to illustrate the changes in the moral assessment of homosexuality because fifteen years later the second edition (1963) of his study presented a very different picture. See § 4.

12

the deviant (unnatural) sphere of sexuality characteristic of the homosexual," because that again impacts the other spheres of his personality, "seeing the homosexual person is disturbed" (pp. 146–48). Tolsma evidently does not view homosexual behavior as an act of the will but as a sign of illness and sees only resistance to homosexual desires as a sign of the freedom of the will. In this way, he can dismiss the argument of the "proponents of homosexuality" who appeal to a natural base to justify homosexual behavior. Homosexuality is always an illness, certainly also when it has organic roots. Nor is the appeal to homosexual love correct because, according to his information, the purpose of this love is always sexual, and also a homosexual friendship has a sexual root (p. 149).

But why is homosexual behavior morally wrong? Tolsma offers two arguments. The first is that homosexual behavior involves an unnatural use of the sex organs and constitutes the "negation of a biological purpose." That is morally reprehensible, all the more because it implies the "unnatural use of a fellow human being" (p. 151). But his main argument is that, according to his observations, real love and faithfulness are always lacking, even when there is the intention to be loving and faithful, and the search for partners among younger men and married men never stops. Homosexuality is therefore an inadequate form of being human. Hence also the Bible is opposed to it. Conversely, the natural sex act is "creative"; it creates higher values and is therefore meaningful. The homosexual act is simply deficient in that respect. And no wonder: "it would be remarkable indeed if a perverted form of sexuality associated itself with the highest form of being human as we know it in love" (pp. 151–54).

Tolsma undoubtedly made his judgments on the basis of his experience as a psychiatrist if he never encountered solid homosexual relationships and regarded seduction as a great danger. But there is another reason why he could hardly think otherwise: his medical and moral judgments are mutually interdependent. His moral judgment was codeterminative of his medical viewpoint. The core of Tolsma's reasoning, after all, is that homosexuality is morally wrong because love is lacking, while love has to be lacking because homosexuality is pathological. That comes close to begging the question. How must we explain this? Well, the problem is present already in the term "unnatural." From ancient times it was used to condemn certain forms of behavior, but in the medical world it was interpreted biologically to denote "disease." Not only Tolsma does this; it is characteristic for the medical world as a whole.[11] Hence Aalders can mention the moral and the medical judgment in the same breath. At the decisive moment medical description and moral judgment coincide. From an ethical point of view, that entails a *"naturalistic fallacy."*

Just what is this fallacy? The term "unnatural" or the phrase "contrary to nature" is used, as we saw, to render a judgment, i.e., evaluatively.* "Nature," then, is something prescriptive. But often the word "natural" is used in a non-evaluative ("value-neutral"), descriptive sense; for example in the statement: "the courtship behavior of bantam cocks is natural," or in the phrase: "a natural death." When the word "natural" is used to qualify a human action each of these two meanings may be intended; namely the action as it ought or is intended to be (on account of human destiny) or as it is described by the biological sciences. But between the two there is a big difference. The natural sciences exist to describe the attributes, inclinations, motivations, etc., that characterize humanness. Now there certainly is a relationship between having these characteristics, etc., and human morality. One can say that because human beings possess certain tendencies and lack others, rules need to be followed to counter the "natural tendency for things to go very badly"[12] (the *that* of morality). But it is a very different matter to say that a human being, because he is endowed

11. G. Hekma (1987) shows the connection between what he calls the social prevention of what was considered antisocial homosexuality and the rise of homosexuality as medical syndrome.

* Note: In his *Studies in Words*, 1960, C. S. Lewis writes: "Anything which has changed from its sort or kind (nature) may be described as *unnatural*, provided that the change is one the speaker deplores. Behaviour is *unnatural* . . . when it is a departure for the worse" (p. 43) — *Translator.*

12. This approach, which goes back to Th. Hobbes, is presented by G. J. Warnock (1971: 23).

with certain tendencies, ought to follow them. In that case a norm or prescription, hence the *what* of morality, is *derived* from a statement of observation, in this case from a biological datum. That is a naturalistic fallacy. I have in mind the phenomenon of deriving a norm from a state of affairs. Because this is logically impossible (no "ought" can follow from an "is"), it is a fallacy. Normative conclusions (value judgments) can only be derived from a normative premise and one or more factual premises (descriptions).[13] These conclusions are correct only if the premises are true. Factual conclusions are drawn from factual premises alone.

A complication is that, while factual assertions can be recognized by the descriptive terms in which they are couched, normative assertions are far from being always recognizable by the normative terms in which they are couched. We have to distinguish between the meaning of terms and that of assertions. The cry "Fire!!" is a description intended as a warning or incitement, hence as a prescription. For such assertions, prescriptives in short, an obligation to take a certain attitude or to follow a certain course of action is laid on the hearer.[14] In such cases we use descriptions as a command, request, prohibition, etc., hence as evaluation. Involved here is a convention, agreement, or norm that both speaker and hearer know and *endorse*. In normal usage such acts of description-as-evaluation are common. Granted, the assumption underlying this practice is a certain unity of lifestyle between speaker and hearer, for otherwise they will not both subscribe to the pertinent norm.[15] When that is no longer the case or when a person doubts the correctness of the judgment made — as in the case of the term "unnatural" as applied to homosexuality — such description-as-evaluation is no longer meaningful. In such a situation description and evaluation have to be separated and we have to begin by describing *without* evaluating.[16] One can then extricate the value judgment from the descriptive assertion in order to ex-

---

13. See, for example, H. G. Hubbeling (1971: 43ff.).
14. V. Brümmer (1975: 31ff.; 111ff.).
15. Cf. H. M. Kuitert (1980: 25ff.).
16. As in the case of self-murder and suicide; see H. M. Kuitert (1983).

amine the grounds on which it is based. The naturalistic fallacy as the exposure of a pseudo-argument then constitutes a criterion for judging the logic of a given line of argumentation.

Back to our discussion. One may object that since Tolsma was no ethicist but a physician, one cannot hold a naturalistic way of thinking against him. Theologians have generally been very conscious of the naturalisms implicit in the work of non-Christian authors. A case in point is the Kinsey reports, which encountered much criticism in Christian circles. Kinsey concludes that homosexual behavior belongs to the "basic capacities of the human animal."[17] His conclusion is that it need have no harmful individual or social consequences. On the assumption that homosexual behavior is natural, he pleads for a relaxation of the prevailing moral and legal norms (pp. 201; 666). That suggestion has not been well received by theologians[18] (who are not alone in this regard[19]). Their criticism is that in this way a statistical norm has been made into an ethical one. Kinsey is a naturalist and depicts human beings as merely a pleasure-oriented animal. The question is whether theologians themselves do better or whether they also tend to adopt a naturalistic stance.

We certainly do not expect this from Karl Barth, the archenemy of all natural theology. As is well-known, for him the covenant between God and man has theological precedence over the creation of man. From the fact that, and the manner in which, God became man (the Incarnation) he wants to infer how man is intended. Barth wants nothing to do with the notion that God's will can be known from nature or from certain ordinances — the so-called creation ordinances — and this applies also to sexuality. Man was created for covenant; he is "capable of entering into covenant with God," not because of his own fitness but because of God's grace.[20] The basic form of humanity has its criterion in

17. A. C. Kinsey et al. (1948).
18. See J. M. Van Veen (1949: 380); cf. R. Niebuhr (1954) with reference to Kinsey's report on the sexuality of women.
19. Cf. H. Schelsky (1957: 59ff.).
20. K. Barth, *C.D.* III, 2, 224.

the humanity of Jesus. In him it is evident that humanity is never an abstraction but always humanity in conjunction with a fellow man. A human being is not an "I," a personality in opposition to others; he is human only if at the same time he says "you"; in that relationship he becomes human. "Humanity absolutely, the humanity of each and every man, consists in the determination of man's being as a being with others, or rather with the other man" (*C.D.* III, 2, 243). That is Barth's "natural" man: man as God intended him. Barth does not mean that man's being created for and adapted to the other is something psychological; it is true in virtue of God's command: by grace God made man twofold.

The basic form of this twofoldness Barth finds in the relationship between male and female. Human beings are not created merely as human but as woman *or* man and at the same time as man *and* woman. These two will be one, not because of a natural will in that direction but because of God's grace (*C.D.* III, 4, 116–18). Barth derives this viewpoint from his biblical anthropology,[21] more specifically from his exegesis of Genesis 1:27. For him, man's being God's image consists in sexual differentiation. Barth's reason for putting it this way is to say sexuality is not incidental or secondary. It does not hang in the air. It is essential to humans, not something lower, nor is it something autonomous. Its place is at the center of the totality of life-relationships. Thus Barth creates more space for sexuality than the tradition did before him.[22]

But life-relationships between whom? Between man and woman, says Barth with emphasis. A human being must be either

---

21. K. Barth, *C.D.* III, 1, 183.

22. He was not, however, the first to do this. In the thirties the sexual ethics of O. A. Piper (1941) attracted attention. For him the meaning of sexuality lay not in procreation, nor in marriage, but in "becoming one flesh" with one's partner: an essential unity between two people of different sex that comes into being as a "divine miracle." In sexual intercourse humans discover the inner meaning of being sexual. A person is never simply human but always man or woman. Hence there is no room for homosexuality; Piper dismisses it as something like onanism, which "contradicts the very meaning of sex": becoming one with one's partner. Cf. H. Ringeling (1968: 219).

man or woman and in that context man and wife; that is God's command (= God's grace). Hence the word is: Accept it![23] One who blurs the distinctions between the masculine and the feminine as God created them touches the very roots of fellow-humanity and therefore of humanity as such (*C.D.* III, 4, 154). Accordingly, to be a man or a woman is a dispensation of grace and at the same time a duty.

It follows from this that Barth would not stop to think long about homosexuality. Homosexuals, says he, decline to be either men or women. Consequently, homosexual behavior is inhuman. It is a result of the fact that men withdraw from the company of women.

Hence arises "the physical, psychological and social sickness, the phenomenon of perversion, decadence and decay, which can emerge when man refuses to admit the validity of the divine command. . . ." From the refusal to recognize God there follows the failure to appreciate man and thus "humanity without the fellow-man"[24] (*C.D.* III, 2, 229ff.). And since humanity as fellow-humanity is to be understood in its root as the togetherness of man and woman, as the root of this inhumanity there follows the ideal of a masculinity free from woman and a femininity free from man.

> And because nature or the Creator of nature will not be trifled with, because the despised fellow-man is still there, because the natural orientation on him is still in force, there follows the corrupt emotional and finally physical desire in which — in a sexual union which is not and cannot be genuine — man thinks that he must seek and can find in man, and woman in woman, a substitute for the despised partner. . . . (*C.D.* III, 4, 166)

23. It is important "to recognize that each man and woman owes it not only to himself but also to the other always to be faithful to his own sexual characteristics. Fellowship is always threatened when there is a failure at this point either on the one side or the other" (*C.D.* III, 4, 154).

24. That is Barth's exegesis of the word "unnatural" in Romans 1:26–27. Much later Barth, then eighty-two years old, stated in a letter that he was no longer satisfied with that passage in the *C.D.* In a conversation with A. Dekker he said he now preferred the designation "problematic humanity" instead of "inhumanity." Cf. J. Van Veen (1977).

This condemnation is painfully sharp. Not only the homosexual act but also the very inclination is clobbered. It is also denigrating: a homosexual, in his desire for his partner, is actually seeking a woman. Barth could have known better. What is worse (for him) is that his reasoning is totally naturalistic. Here too the condemnation is implicit in the idea of the "unnatural," defined by Barth as humanity without fellow-humanity. Against this latter point there is no objection. But Barth does not define the meaning of sexuality in light of the norm of humanity but in light of the structure of the human body. Moral condemnation does not follow a demonstration that homosexual relations fall short of the fundamental norm of humanity, but conversely Barth infers a lack of humanity from the form of sexuality. Factually, the focus on the opposite sex continues, says Barth. That is to say: it does not fit, therefore it is not allowed. The fact that Barth believes he has weighty theological grounds for his condemnation in no way detracts from the untenability of his argument.

There are echoes of Barth's view in the writing of the contemporary theologian J. Douma (1978; 1984). "Natural" to him is that which corresponds to the originally created nature. One must not attempt to infer from empirical nature what is natural or unnatural, he believes, for that is using the biological key. Hence he tries to avoid the naturalistic fallacy. On the other hand, he says, the Bible teaches us what is natural in a normative sense. Here we learn that God has united man and woman; only these two will become one flesh. *That* is natural. Equipped with this knowledge one can then observe the wisdom of the Creator as it is manifest in the structure of the sexual organs. Now, then, in the Bible homosexual behavior is labeled "unnatural." For that reason it has at all times been forbidden. Granted, what at one time was "not nature" can in the course of history become "nature": from aversion to God comes inversion. This leads Douma to call the homosexual inclination ("homophilia") a "creaturely degeneracy," a sinful sickness.[25]

In Douma two contradictory theses run through each other.

---

25. J. Douma (1973: 81). In the reprint of 1984 this has become "a disturbance or distortion" (p. 94).

The first is that man does not learn from nature (the biological key) but from Scripture what is natural and what is unnatural (sin). Not the testimony of tradition or the witness of biological nature is decisive but that of Scripture (1984: 96). The second is that only Scripture is the right source for knowing that unnatural acts are wrong. Homosexuality is not wrong because it is contrary to nature but because unnatural acts are against the will of God. That homosexuality is against nature is simply presumed by Douma. How else can we interpret his definition of "homophilia": "a condition in which a person lacks the natural sex drive and feels attracted only to persons of the same sex" (1984: 9).

Evidently a person can also know on his own what is (un)natural. And by implying this, Douma makes his reasoning vulnerable. To the extent that he conceives "(un)natural" as a religious value judgment (sin) we are dealing with theology, and that falls outside the scope of this chapter. But Douma does not just use theological arguments; he has no objection whatever to biological arguments; the only requirement is that they can be found in the Bible. Why the Creator's wisdom should only come to expression in the structure of the sexual organs and not, say, in the happiness and security sexuality offers the partners is obviously no question for him. The argument based on anatomy (or: Douma's prejudice regarding homosexuality) already settles the issue. In other words, the appeal to Genesis masks the fact that in reality we are dealing with the naturalistic fallacy. In this manner the ethically unacceptable is accorded theological legitimacy. And that, of course, won't wash.

Last to be mentioned here is the Reformed ethicist G. Brillenburg Wurth. He is of interest for our subject because in his work one senses a hint of understanding — perhaps even more than that — for homosexuals. But only for the homosexual person, not for his sexual behavior: we are looking at the basics of the disposition/behavior distinction. Wurth picks up on Barth's view that human differentiation as man and woman is paradigmatic for all other differentiation in human life: without a woman a man is incomplete.[26] But as neo-Calvinist and in contrast with Barth, he

26. G. Brillenburg Wurth (1951 II: 63).

believes that the meaning of sexuality is implicit in the creation order. It belongs to the sphere of marriage between a man and a woman. For his evaluation of homosexuality, Wurth leans on Tolsma's study. One who understands the meaning of the two sexes knows that homosexual behavior is abnormal, for meaningful encounter and creative love is possible only between the two sexes. That which falls outside of that arena is external and sterile. Wurth expressly adds here that, in addition, homosexual behavior violates the divine order at one of its most important points, that of the relation between the sexes. Thus he adds a religious argument to the ethical argument: even if it should be the case that homosexual behavior is not contrary to the order of nature, it is in any case against the order of God.

For the authors we discussed earlier, that settled the issue. But Wurth takes a further step.[27] Says he: even though homosexuality is disgusting to a normal person, the fact is that there are people physically and psychologically so constituted that their desire involuntarily goes out to members of the same sex. We are not now talking only of seriously pathological cases; among them are highminded people who sincerely fight their unnatural desires. Meanwhile, such a disposition does not warrant expression or practice. Homosexual behavior only brings false happiness and suffering to those who engage in it. The struggle is therefore hard and lonely and, sometimes, lifelong. But — and here understanding breaks through — in this struggle homosexuals are entitled to respect and do not deserve contempt. The condition exists through no fault of their own but is a sign of the devastating effect of sin. It must be borne, not as a fate, but as a cross. Since sin has its effects in everyone's life, the problematics of the homosexual concern the entire Christian community. And the homosexual may be assured that he can accept his cross in faith; despite his lifelong struggle, in the gospel he has been given "a principle of victory."

Winsome — yet distressing! Here we see the reason why the distinction between the condition and the behavior was introduced into Christian ethics: it was from a well-intentioned pastoral mo-

---

27. G. Brillenburg Wurth (1951 II: 104-8 and esp.: 1953).

tive. Wurth's concern is to find a solution to the problem posed by Tolsma: how can a person be held responsible for a pathological, degenerative predisposition? One must not call a homosexual "sick," contends Wurth, for in so doing "one deprives him of his last remaining nobility as a human being."[28] But a person can retain his dignity when the condition is viewed as the effect of original sin.

In this manner one can maintain the ethical condemnation without necessarily assigning an inferior status in the church to the homosexually disposed person. In 1951 it created room for dialogue in the church. It is, however, a dubious construction. On this assumption we now no longer know whether we are dealing with sin or with sickness. Sin demands condemnations; sick people require help. On top of this, no room is left for something that is neither sickness nor sin.[29] But, as we saw, Wurth does not want to speak of disease; "disposition" or "orientation" is the word. Disease takes away a person's responsibility; apparently orientation or disposition does not.

Is that true? In ordinary usage we encounter "disposition" in the sense of "prevailing tendency." A disposition toward homosexuality in this connection usually means that some people are more inclined to engage in homosexual acts than others. That is a fact of experience. This, however, has nothing to do with the (moral) evaluation of the behavior in question but with its explanation. An orientation or disposition, in the sense of a lack or deficiency, is not something one can hold against a person. That is what Wurth means: a homosexual disposition is something one cannot help. And it is true, a person so "inclined" cannot help it and therefore can be excused. That was a gain in 1951. But it had the far-reaching consequence that in this way *the status of being a voluntary intentional act* was denied to homosexual behavior.

In my opinion this is one of the essential points in the discussion of homosexuality. Why is it so important? Although the

28. G. Brillenburg Wurth (1951 II: 88).
29. H. M. Kuitert makes this point (1980: 59). The same objection applies to Douma's construct of "creaturely degeneracy."

tradition had regarded homosexual behavior as immoral, it nevertheless viewed it as voluntary and intentional — hence as the "wrong choice." Wurth and many later ethicists (see § D) oppose this. At the same time they uphold a person's responsibility for his sexual behavior in order to be able to maintain their strong condemnation of homosexual behavior. How? By asserting that a sexual act always requires an act of the will but that the desire for homosexual acts is the consequence of a deviant and determining disposition or inclination. Consequently, though a person may not want to yield to a homosexual inclination, a homosexual act itself is not an act of the will. Accordingly, one only has the (asymmetrical) choice between saying no and being an involuntary homosexual. Thus two things have been achieved: the condemnation remains intact while at the same time a measure of understanding has been realized for the homosexually inclined.

For a number of reasons this construction is mistaken. Later we shall examine these reasons at length, but at this stage I merely want to point out that the question "Why does a person do it?" is answered by Wurth with a reference to the causes of the behavior, while completely ignoring the intentions of the person who engages in it. The "why" question is conceived as a question concerning the causal explanation of the behavior instead of one concerning the intentions (reasons) of the actor himself. The result, despite the good intentions, is that the traditional condemnation is reinforced. "Unnatural" used to mean: there is *never* a good reason for it. "Determined by a natural orientation" means: a person has no reasons, and certainly no good reasons, for his behavior, because his behavior is not a deliberate act.[30] However, in this manner, by means of the disposition-behavior distinction, one has seemingly provided justification for not having to take homosexuals seriously as acting individuals with their own intentions, so disqualifying them in advance as partners in the moral discussion.

---

30. "Act" denotes a conscious, deliberate deed; "behavior" refers to everything a person does willy-nilly (e.g., shivering). I will later deal at length with the essential distinction between "intentional act" and "behavior determined by causes."

The moral discussion on homosexuality thus remained a discussion by heterosexuals about homosexuals.

It was certainly not Wurth's intention to disqualify homosexuals. How could he nevertheless do this? Because, in his case and that of numerous others, the assumption is that man has "by nature" been created heterosexually. This is the reason why homosexual relations are "unnatural" and therefore morally inferior. The problems are therefore traceable to the prevalence of the word "nature." So far we have encountered at least three meanings; a biological, a moral, and a religious meaning. On top of this, all these meanings are vague. An illustration of this follows.

"Natural" can be a synonym for "biological." That produces new problems for two reasons: this term is also ambiguous; besides, biology knows no specific concept of nature.[31] "Natural" in all the meanings of the word "biological" is, however, consistently non-moral. Biology teaches us what people usually do and why but not whether they ought to do the things they do. In its moral meaning, however, "natural" refers to human acts as they ought to be, specifically to denote the destiny of man or the purpose of human acts. Biology cannot say a thing about this. One cannot, as the above authors all did, use "unnatural" to condemn (the moral meaning) and at the same time act as if one is simply recording a fact as a biologist or doctor might. In that case one commits the naturalistic fallacy. Finally there is the religious meaning of "nature," meaning the creation as God intended it to be. This meaning is non-biological and non-moral. Creation is not the same as (biological) nature, and theology, therefore, has no concept of nature of its own. The question is how do we know when we are dealing with creation (= nature in the religious sense)? Do we know this apart from our moral judgments? Thus, the adoption of what one takes to be a Christian, or biblically based, view of what is "natural" and what is not leads inevitably to the question whether such a Christian viewpoint can count as a moral judgment — valid for

31. Accordingly, there is no definition of the concept "(human) nature" in biology. It is not a scientific concept, though a biologist may write a book entitled *On Human Nature* (E. O. Wilson). See further Chapter III § E.

all — or whether it presupposes a moral judgment (made in advance).[32]

It is the confusion of these meanings of "natural" that causes all good intentions to misfire. For that matter, also intentions less positive misfire, as can be demonstrated by citing the argumentation of the Catholic Magisterium for its completely negative viewpoint. With that I shall conclude this section.

The Declaration of the Sacred Congregation for the Doctrine of the Faith on "Certain Questions Concerning Sexual Ethics" (*Persona humana,* 1975) states that man's dignity cannot be promoted unless the essential order of his nature is respected. The reference here is to the moral order, the so-called natural moral order. The subject, then, is "nature" in the moral sense, but this is known from the order of human nature, i.e., his biological nature teleologically conceived. The document asserts that for all the changes that occur, the real nature of man is subject to "immutable principles." These are contained in "the divine law — eternal, objective, and universal — which man can know by the exercise of his reason." Now the reference is to the religious meaning of "nature."[33] The church preserves and interprets the "principles of the moral order which have their origin in human nature itself." These principles also exist in the domain of sexual ethics. Sexual acts must be judged by objective criteria that are based on the nature of the human person and his acts. These are "mutual self-giving and human procreation in the context of true love." Hence the sexual act has a double finality. This finality only comes into its own in marriage. Homosexual relations are always wrong. Although *Persona humana* states that homosexuals must be treated with "understanding" and their culpability must be judged with "prudence," nevertheless "homosexual relations are acts that lack an essential and indispensable finality" and "can in no case be approved."[34]

32. "Moral" means: "what is right, permitted, or required of all people." "Christian" means: "what only Christians are obligated to do."

33. Th. Beemer (1983: 36) remarks that church documents tend to speak of the "natural and divine law" in the singular.

34. *Declaration* (1975: §§ 3–5, 8).

The increasingly more tolerant interpretation of this document caused the congregation to send a special "Letter to the Bishops of the Catholic Church on the Pastoral Care of Homosexual Persons" (1986). It repeats the teaching of *Persona humana* and even reinforces the condemnation by saying that "homosexual activity is not a complementary union, able to transmit life." Hence biological nature is here frankly used as moral argument. True, homosexuals can often be generous and self-giving, "but when they engage in homosexual activity they confirm within themselves a disordered sexual inclination which is essentially self-indulgent."[35] The church, "in rejecting erroneous opinions regarding homosexuality, does not limit but rather defends personal freedom and dignity realistically and authentically understood," states the Letter.

Hence also in Catholic ethics the three senses of the word "nature" play an important role. We will attempt to unravel the confusion among them. This will take several chapters but for a start we will examine how the different elements have entered the discussion. This occurs in the following section.

C. The origin of the elements

It is not so strange that until now the different senses of "nature" have been confused. For on the classical, teleological concept of "nature" of antiquity and the middle ages, the empirical and moral senses were one. "Nature" referred to a concept of being that included the norm. It was, therefore, a normative entity. Since the seventeenth century that has changed. The change can be well illustrated by what Thomas Aquinas and Immanuel Kant respectively understood by "nature." That choice of names is not arbitrary. Thomas systematized the preceding tradition; his system became the model for later (Catholic) generations; and Kant's influence in Protestantism has been extensive. In his ethics, Kant

35. Congregation for the Doctrine of Faith *Letter* (1986: 38).

emerged as a strong opponent of natural inclination as moral imperative. Thomas, on the other hand, many people say, saw the biologically conditioned inclination as moral imperative. Nature taught him what is good. In this section we will find that this is not the case but that such an inference is plausible if Thomas's concept of nature is replaced by that of Kant.

In the *Summa Theologica,* to which I will limit myself, Thomas speaks about homosexuality[36] three times, each time in connection with "nature." I will first reproduce his arguments (1), then discuss a number of interpretations (2), and finally offer an evaluation (3).

(1) According to the first and most familiar argumentation, homosexual behavior is *against the order of nature.*[37] Here, in his treatment of the virtue of moderation, Thomas makes the distinction that, by now, is well-known to us, that between natural and unnatural sins. Homosexuality, like a number of other types of actions, is contrary to nature because this sexual act excludes the possibility of procreation. Why does Thomas select this criterion? Acts are morally just, he believes, when they possess a natural order, i.e., are ordered to their own end (*suum finem*). A human being ought to use things, including his body, in accordance with the purpose for which they exist, because that purpose is good. Acts that meet this standard are "natural." Now natural acts do yield a good, indeed, a *bonum excellens:* offspring.

Sexual intercourse is, therefore, a good thing when it occurs with a view to the preservation of the human race and in accordance with the right order. This order can be slighted in two ways: by not pursuing the good purpose in the right way — e.g., in extramarital relations — or because the purpose pursued is itself not right. In the first way the *ordo recta rationis,* the order of right reason, i.e., the order of the intellect, is disregarded. That is a

---

36. Using the word "homosexuality" in this connection is, in the nature of the case, anachronistic: "sexuality" and "homosexuality" are nineteenth-century concepts. The matter to which Thomas is referring is, however, the same as what today we call "(homo)sexuality": same-sex relations.

37. *S. T.* IIa IIae Qu. 154, Art. 1, 11, 12.

"natural sin." In the second way, also the *ordo naturae* is violated. That happens in the case of "unnatural sins." That is worse, for the *ordo rectae rationis* is a human order but the *ordo naturae* is God-given.

But how do we humans know this order? Answers Thomas: the violation of the order of nature is the violation of the "first principles of the intellect." Knowledge of these principles is given to man naturally: they are "infused" by God. Thomas offers no further definition of these principles, nor a definition of "nature." It is clear, however, that unnatural acts are sins against God-given reason. In such sins a person refuses to use his intellect. In committing them, adds Thomas, a person sins against his generic nature and not only against another individual of that nature (Q 154, 12).

In another part of the *Summa* Thomas seems, quite surprisingly, to define these matters differently. There he says: for some individuals unnatural acts can, in a certain respect, be natural (*connaturalis*), i.e., in agreement with an individual nature.[38] What have we here? Thomas as the inventor of the "homophile orientation"? Not really. The context in which he posits this thesis is the question whether a person can derive pleasure from unnatural acts. The fact is that pleasure is a natural feeling. A human being delights in that which is typically human, in contemplating truth or practicing virtue, and in the things men have in common with other creatures, such as eating, drinking, and sex. How can the experience of a "natural" pleasure be consistent with unnatural acts? That, Thomas believes, can happen when "the principles which are natural to the species as a whole" have broken down in certain members of the species. In them something that is against the generic nature of man may have become their individual nature. Thomas does not develop this idea and presumably he has in mind the principles given in the intellect we mentioned above. But he does give an example. Water is normally cold. But the nature of warm water is that it gives out heat. A departure from the normal state can therefore bring about the opposite of the "natural" effect. That can also occur in the case of people. Such a change, to be

38. *S. T.* Ia IIae Qu. 31, Art. 7.

sure, is *connaturalis,* but it is nevertheless a departure.[39] A sick person may find sweet things bitter! Following this exposition one is no longer surprised to find that Thomas mentions homosexuality in one breath with other forms of "dispositional disorder" *(complexia mala):* bestiality, coprophilia, and cannibalism. Accordingly, we can conclude that not everything that belongs to the nature of a person is also natural in the sense of in accordance with nature.

Thomas, finally, comments on homosexual behavior in the well-known exposition of "natural law."[40] He bases this moral law on the principles that "the good is what all things seek after." The most general precept that flows from this is "that good is to be sought and done, evil to be avoided." All concrete directions for behavior can be inferred from this formal principle, though Thomas is very sparing in his inferences.[41] Good is that toward which man has a natural tendency. The good has the character of being an end. Consequently, all the things toward which man has a natural tendency are naturally good and, therefore, worthy of being pursued. All that is contrary to this is bad and to be shunned. "The order in which the commands of the law of nature are ranged corresponds to that of our natural tendencies." In three ways man has a natural tilt toward the good: (a) in what he has in common with all natural beings; viz., the urge to self-preservation; (b) in what he has in common with other animals; viz., the thing which nature teaches all animals,[42] heterosexual intercourse and the care of children; and (c) in what belongs only to man; viz., the inclination to seek truth and to live in society.[43] In this last instance, a right action is directed toward a social good. Also in the case of actions that seem to be solely directed toward self-interest, as in eating or drinking and sexuality, the ultimate goal is the "com-

39. "Propter aliquam corruptionem naturae in eo existentem," *S. T.,* loc. cit.

40. *S. T.* Ia IIae Qu. 94, Art. 3 ad 2.

41. A. G. M. van Melsen (1983b: 64/5).

42. Ulpianus's concept of nature: "Ius naturale est, quod natura omnia animalia docuit." See J. Boswell (1980: 313).

43. *S. T.* Ia IIac Qu. 94, Art. 2.

mon good *(bonum commune)*."[44] Homosexuality, according to Thomas, is in conflict with the nature man and animals have in common.

(2) Undoubtedly in this reference to the concept of nature Thomas's argumentations show differences in emphasis, and one can attempt to use them in the interest of reevaluating homosexuality, as Boswell (1980) and van de Spijker (1968) attempt to do. Boswell wrote a historical study, the thrust of which is that Christianity is not the inventor of the aversion to homosexuality but followed the ethos of the surrounding culture. Thomas also did this; according to Boswell, he capitulated to the growing popular disapproval that in his day, along with the rise of urban culture, gained ascendancy. He is said to have yielded to the zoological notions of Ulpianus. However, had Thomas been consistent, he would not have pronounced his disapproval of homosexual behavior.

Boswell's arguments focus on Thomas's second argumentation. When Thomas concedes that homosexuality is *connaturalis,* it is perhaps a defect but not for that reason immoral. Boswell does not find Thomas convincing when, in the third argumentation, he appeals to nature in its manifestation as reason: it is precisely by the appeal to reason that modern homosexuals defend themselves against the charge that homosexuality is contrary to nature. And the condemnation in the first argumentation has little weight because in it Thomas fails to furnish a definition of "nature," and nature "simply means the moral" so that the condemnation entails a circular argument.[45] Boswell makes no attempt to find a deeper unity behind Thomas's concept(s) of nature. In fact, he drives a wedge between "nature" as a purely descriptive term (reason and biological nature) and "nature" in its normative sense. And it is true: if Thomas had sometimes used the term nature as an empirical term and then again as a synonym for "morally acceptable," he would have been inconsistent. But the meaning of "nature" as a

---

44. *S. T.* Ia IIae Qu. 94, Art. 3 (ad primum).
45. J. Boswell (1980: 318–28). He strongly emphasizes the naturalness (in a biological sense!) of homosexuality. For a critique, see: De Cecco and Shively (1984: 3/4).

normative term escapes Boswell.[46] So whereas Boswell separates moral evaluation and empirical descriptions and plays them off against each other, in Thomas they are one.

Van de Spijker, a Catholic moral philosopher, also points out the difference in argumentation in Thomas. According to him, Thomas speaks in his first argumentation about the metaphysical nature of man but in the second primarily about his actual nature. But what does he mean by "actual nature"? The distinction plays a large role in the Catholic tradition. Metaphysical nature here means

> The reality which has to exist for us to be able to speak of "humans," regardless of the historical situation and the individuality in which this humanity is real.[47]

We are dealing here with the immutable essence of man. An act is natural when it is in accord with the human essence. Actual nature here means the biological-physiological human structures. To act "in accord with nature" is to be in congruence with the biological-physiological structures.[48] In line with this distinction van de Spijker interprets Thomas as follows: In terms of the metaphysical nature, homosexual acts are generically bad. But in terms of the actual nature such an act can be natural (*connaturalis*) for an individual, even though it does not correspond with the generic nature of man. Van de Spijker then accuses Catholic moral philosophers of having totally overloaded Thomas's second argument. It is this argument that offers us a possibility of arriving at "a dynamic view" of homosexual behavior, namely "to ascribe more legitimacy to the actual nature when it has been determined that it does not tend to the detriment of the community, but remains within the individual domain."[49]

---

46. J. Boswell (op. cit., 13) distinguishes the "real" and the "ideal" concepts of nature. In the course of history the ideal conception (Plato!) prevailed over the realistic. Within the "ideal nature" concept the word "unnatural" is "a vehement circumlocution for 'bad' or 'unacceptable.'"

47. J. Fuchs, citing F. Böckle (1966: 127).

48. F. Böckle (1966: 139).

49. A. M. J. M. H. van de Spijker (1968: 110).

In the next section I will return to this subject. Here our concern is solely the Thomas interpretation. Is van de Spijker correct?

In a discussion of the development of the Thomistic concept of nature, F. Böckle asserts the following. From Late Scholasticism onward, the metaphysical concept of nature predominated. Alongside of it various other conceptions developed in the tradition, which we do not need to consider now. Important is that for Böckle the actual concept of nature is a "mistaken development." It is inspired more by the desire to make abstract connections clear to people than by the results of moral philosophy. Even more important is that, in his opinion, neither the metaphysical nor the actual concept of nature is that of Thomas.[50] In Thomas nature is innate in human knowledge. Reason as the human capacity for knowledge is not merely the organ for interpreting an already existing order. It has a self-ordering function: "Man is, and gives himself, his own law."[51] In other words, natural law, in the form of the basic principles of morality, is "known naturally," a priori. That is to say, man knows by nature what is good for him and if he does that which he has come to believe is a good for him, he acts (morally) well. "Natural" here means "non-discursive," without a prior process of investigation. The first principles are fundamental institutions,[52] which, granted, depend for their interpretation and definition on human experience, hence on the activity of discursive reason.

Now Catholic moral philosophy has made of this that man has knowledge of the original natural order created by God. And if he follows this, regardless of circumstances, he acts correctly.

---

50. F. Böckle (1966: 122–23).

51. Thomas's nature-concept is that of *ratio ut natura* (reason as nature). Cf. J. Th. C. Arntz (1966: 91; 100) who says that the core of Thomas's natural law theory is "Lex naturalis est aliquid per rationem constitutum" ("Natural law is something established by means of reason"). He concludes: "Natural inclinations present themselves to a person only as the [raw] material in which he himself has to create a rational order." Natural law is given as an assigned task.

52. A. G. M. van Melsen (1966: 79).

In this manner the (metaphysical) nature of man becomes the norm and his cognitive capacity plays a subordinate role, viz., merely that of an organ that reads this reality.[53] From a teleological ethics, in terms of what is beneficial for man, we have come to a deontological ethics, in terms of preserving the natural order to which it is oriented.[54]

Corresponding to the abandonment of Thomas's nature-concept there is still another change, namely the equation of the *lex naturalis* (natural law) with the *lex aeterna* (eternal law) and the latter with the *lex divina* (divine law). But Thomas makes distinctions between them.[55] The eternal law is the eternal law of God, the conception of the order of the universe existing in God as architect. The divine law is the redemptive-historical law, hence the law as it relates, among other things, to reconciliation. Thomas defines natural law as nothing other than "this sharing in the eternal law by intelligent creatures."[56] Says Th. Beemer: natural law radiates and reflects the wisdom of God, the eternal law. Following Böckle, he criticizes the ecclesiastical pronouncements that speak of "the natural and the divine law" in the singular. This betrays a divinization of natural law. Divine law (*lex aeterna*) and natural law are equated for the purpose of supporting the idea of a transcultural, immutable moral order.

> In philosophical terms one can say that the natural (moral) law was metaphysically upgraded. It is no longer an intelligent order designed on the basis of empirical indications but acquires the status of an order based on what is called the immutable nature of man, his *natura metaphysica,* or his esssence.[57]

Here lies the reason why, in my opinion, we must not adopt van de Spijker's interpretation of Thomas's nature-concept. It is

53. J. Th. D. Arntz (1966: 99).
54. F. Böckle (1977: 315ff., specif. 318).
55. See D. J. O'Connor (1974: 139).
56. *S. T.* Ia IIae Qu. 91, Art. 2.
57. Th. Beemer (1983: 36); cf. following in his footsteps, R. Houdijk (1986).

not true that one moment Thomas appeals to the metaphysical nature and the next to the actual nature, as moral norm. Add to this that, in both cases, a nature-concept is attributed to Thomas that he does not use.

It is not necessary for us to explore further Thomas's understanding of the relation between the eternal law and the moral natural law. I want to repeat, however, that the Catholic tradition is clearly familiar with the three uses of "nature" we encountered in the previous section — albeit in its own way, viz., as the actual-biological nature, as metaphysical nature, and as the participation of reason in the eternal law in God — and that, like Protestant ethics, it fails to keep them distinct.

(3) But then how does Thomas use the term? There are, to my mind, three questions: According to Thomas, how does man know the good? What is the relation between "nature" and "the good"? How does Thomas know what is good?

The first question has already been answered: through his reason man knows by nature what is good. The second question is more difficult. To answer it we have to examine the Aristotelian origin of Thomas's nature-concept. Every bit of reality, every substance, carries within it a principle of movement. It has a natural tendency to move toward an end (*telos*). That end is always a good. The good is the substance in its completed form.[58]

This teleological nature-concept is totally other than that of our time. Between Thomas and us stand the scientific revolution of the seventeenth century. We will return to the implications of it in Chapter III. That difference goes beyond the fact that we do not, and Thomas does, believe that nature works toward an end, i.e., purposefully. At issue is the nature of the nature-concept. For us nature is a descriptive term. Our modern concepts of nature, numerous and vague as they are, always express a condition or state of affairs. Assertions like: "The Great Lakes are part of nature"; "sexuality is natural," etc., are statements of the same type as the assertions "Thomas was a Dominican" or "it rains." The word "nature" has a *referential* meaning. In Thomas it also has a *dispositional* mean-

58. For this, see J. A. Aertsen (1982: 331–48).

ing.[59] A disposition is a capacity or tendency things display under certain circumstances. Example: "fragile" describes a thing that, under certain circumstances, has a tendency to break. In Thomas "natural" has the same meaning: the tendency of every substance to move toward its end (*telos*) or completeness. That is the natural inclination of every substance. For us, however, a natural inclination is an innate or biologically rooted inclination: something that is inherent in man. Such a natural inclination can yield either a good or an evil. But not in the thinking of Thomas. In other words, in his thinking the naturalness (in a modern, empirical sense) of an act is not the criterion of its being good but vice versa: the good is criterion for its naturalness. With that the question becomes what is the good?[60] That is the really problematic point.

Thomas is an intuitionist: he believes that the commands of natural law are self-evident in the same way as the principles of logic.[61] In terms of its first principles, natural law is necessary. All secondary commands can be inferred from it; if necessary, the latter can be changed. It is not clear how Thomas conceives this (logical) derivation or in what the change can consist. Does the development of morality more clearly bring to light the implications of the first principles (as mathematical development does those of mathematical axioms), or does historical development entail changes in human nature and, therefore, in human obligations? On this issue Thomas is not clear.[62] This means that his

59. Cf. V. Brümmer (1975: 54ff.).

60. According to Thomas, as a result of "dispositional disorders," wrong pursuits may become "second nature" (*connaturalis*). Then we have to do with "sins of nature," exceptions that confirm the rule (J. A. Aertsen, op. cit.: 343). That, thinks Thomas, is the case with homosexuality. So an appeal to his views may occasion a "more dynamic view" of homosexuality, as van den Spijker thinks, but offers no ground for approval of homosexual intercourse, as Boswell (op. cit.: 328) claims: ". . . Aquinas admitted . . . that homosexual desire was the result of a 'natural' condition, which would logically have made behavior resulting from it not only inculpable but 'good.'" Boswell uses "natural" in the biological sense.

61. For this, see D. J. O'Connor (1974: 144ff.).

62. D. J. O'Connor (op. cit.: 158).

attempt to ground the good in self-evident truths is not very successful. The consequence is that, ostensibly by an appeal to what (empirically-speaking) people find natural, Thomas gives normative content to what is good (are the goods) for man but in so doing turns his normative thirteenth-century image of man, including the prejudice of a static, immutable (human) nature, into a norm for all times.[63]

Hence the real problem of Thomas's ethics is not that one moment Thomas uses "nature" in the empirical sense ("realistic" in Boswell) and another time in the normative ("idealistic") sense. Nor that one moment he appeals to the metaphysical nature as norm and another time to nature as a biological given, the actual nature, as van de Spijker thinks. Thomas says that the good that nature has put into man will also come out, i.e., as a natural inclination, and if — Heaven forbid! — something else should emerge, that is unnatural. Whatever questions the notion of "natural inclination" may evoke, "unnatural" in Thomas does not mean "in conflict with the biological structures in man" but a normative something.

Remarkably, we do find the biological definition of "unnatural" (in the sense of "contrary to nature") in Immanuel Kant. Did he not make a sharp distinction between "counter-causal" moral motivation and motives proceeding from natural inclinations? That is true; but this in no way leads Kant to disapprove of unnatural acts *because* they are unnatural.

Like Thomas, Kant knows of a teleology of nature. But it is not that of "all things seeking goods." In Kant's day a new concept of nature had arisen, viz., as "the sum total of all the objects of experience,"[64] which are accessible to the senses and thus an object of study for the new natural sciences. (I will return to this later.) From this time on, human "nature" primarily meant man's biological nature. Kant was well acquainted with the biological discussions of his day.[65]

63. Cf. H. M. Kuitert (1983: 49).
64. Cf. I. Kant, *Critique of Pure Reason* (Preface BXIX). Cf. W. Stoker (1980: 142ff.).
65. See J. Lever (1973) for the origins of the concept of species in

According to Thomas, nature — in *his* sense — works teleologically through natural inclination toward the good. According to Kant, nature — the world of empirical phenomena including the phenomenon of man — works toward an end but not intentionally. At least intentionality cannot be demonstrated scientifically. On the other hand, Kant thinks that the idea of nature as a functional whole must be the starting point in the study of *animate* nature. He is opposed to a "bad teleology" that is content to point out functional connections such as "a horse is meant to ride on" or "grass exists to feed cattle with." That is not science. Science demands explanations in terms of mechanically operative causes. Now, in Kant's opinion, this manner of explanation breaks down when it comes to animate nature. There we are at the limits of causal explanation. We cannot even explain the growth of grass. The reason is that living things display an organization in which every part is involved in the whole and vice versa. Therefore, organisms display themselves to us *as though* they were directed toward an end *(Zweck)*. An animal eats food in order to survive. An embryo develops purposefully. Etc. Such organization is present only in animate nature but then in *all* of life. Although Kant, in very modern fashion, does not rule out the advent of a theory of evolution — "a bold adventure of reason" — for him the boundary between the animate and the inanimate is absolute. One could perhaps lengthen the chain of causal explanations far beyond where it is now, but one always dead-ends on the differences between the animate and the inanimate. Life is regulated by the end products it produces; non-life, by antecedent causes.

The idea that nature conducts itself as though it were working toward an end is not a judgment based on empirical knowledge but an a priori judgment.[66] This Kant calls a regulative principle;[67]

---

biology. See I. Kant, *Critique of Judgment* (§§ 80, 81) for a discussion of epigenesis and evolution.

66. I. Kant, *Critique of Judgment* (Introduction: BXXVIII. AXXXVI).

67. "The example that nature offers us in its organic products justifies us, indeed calls upon us, to expect nothing from it and its laws except what is purposive in [relation to] the whole," Kant, *Critique of Judgment* (§ 67).

we cannot study animate nature except by *attributing* a purpose to it. That is a heuristic but indispensable principle of investigation.[68] Now this applies also to sexuality.

> . . . the organization of both sexes in relation to each other for the propagation of their kind; for here, as in the case of the individual, one can always still ask: why did such a pair have to exist? The answer is: this first of all constitutes an organizing whole, although not an organized whole in a single body.[69]

Accordingly, on the basis of the idea of organized wholes Kant knows of only one purpose or function of sexuality, a biological one, namely reproduction. This is a "natural end" (*Naturzweck*); not a practical goal but "objective reality."[70] One who acts contrary to this end acts in a way that is contrary to nature. In Kant the word "unnatural" is *descriptive.*

In his *Metaphysics of Morals* sexuality is discussed under two headings: "legality" (in the section "doctrine of law") and "morality" ("doctrine of virtue"). In the "doctrine of law" he makes the, by now familiar, distinction between natural and unnatural sexual intercourse. By this he means (not very thrillingly!): "The mutual use which one person makes of the sexual organs and capacity of another."[71]

Hence, for Kant, sexuality is genital. In his book, homosexuality and bestiality are "unnatural";[72] masturbation, which clearly

---

This principle "is regulative and not constitutive. . . ." Cf. G. J. Warnock (1964: 316).

68. W. Windelband (1880 II: 160): "The teleological view of organisms is not a constitutive principle of knowledge, but a heuristic principle of research." The controversy between a teleological and a causal-mechanistic interpretation for a long time continued to have impact in biology, e.g., in the twentieth century between mechanists and vitalists. See J. Lever (1973: 106ff.).

69. I. Kant (*Kritil der Urteilskraft:* B381, A376).

70. I. Kant (*Kritik der Urteilskraft:* B295, A291).

71. I. Kant (*Metaphysik der Sitten, Rechtslehre* §§ 24–25).

72. This is Kant's term. But he means "crimes of the flesh against nature," hence what I call "unnatural."

belongs in this category (see the following) is not mentioned here. In the case of natural sex acts, Kant distinguishes between the acts that are "according to a purely animal nature" and those that are "according to law," i.e., exclusively within marriage. This distinction also is purely descriptive. All sexuality is, as such, "animal-like" because man, as a "natural" and "sensuous" being, has this property in common with animals. But "naturalness" does not make an act legal, let alone morally justified. In the "doctrine of law" Kant offers a rather remarkable argumentation to make clear that only marriage legalizes sexual acts. He says sexual intercourse is a pleasure. In the process, a human being gives a part of himself away, so making himself into a thing (*Sache*), and that is in conflict with "the right of human beings to their own persons." There is only one circumstance in which this is permitted, viz., in a permanent mutual covenant when "the one person is acquired by the other as a possession and vice versa; for so the person again acquires himself and reconstitutes his personhood." Hence the well-known definition of marriage: "the union of two persons of different sex for the lifelong possession of their sexual attributes."

Unnatural acts are not only in conflict with the rights of man but form "a lesion of mankind in our own person."

Why is that? As is well-known, Kant makes a sharp distinction between an act issuing from natural inclination and an act based on duty. The assumption of moral action is that it can be in conflict with natural desires.[73] A person may try to derive a moral principle from "the special natural disposition of humanity" but that only yields a maxim for oneself, never an objective, universally binding principle.[74] In various forms Kant formulates such a principle, i.e., a "categorical imperative." We are here concerned with one of them, "the Principle of Personality":[75] "So act that you treat humanity in your own person and in the person of everyone else always at the same time as an end and never merely as means."[76]

---

73. H. B. Acton (1974: 322ff.; 337); W. Windelband (1880 II: 136).
74. I. Kant (*Grundlegung zur Metaphysik der Sitten:* B60/A60).
75. H. B. Acton (op. cit.: 341ff.).
76. Kant (*Grundlegung:* B66/A66).

Accordingly, a person may not use himself merely as a means either. And here, for Kant, lies the core of the issue. In the "doctrine of virtue" of *The Metaphysics of Morals* Kant asserts that a human being not only has obligations toward others but also toward himself; the latter he even considers the more basic. A human being can use himself as a means because he is human in two respects, as a "natural" or "sensuous" being and as a "purely rational" being, i.e., a being endowed with inner freedom. The latter

> is susceptible of obligation and, indeed, of obligation to himself (to humanity in his own person). Thus man (taken in these two different senses) can consistently recognize a duty to himself for "I can recognize that I am under obligation to others only in so far as I, at the same time, obligate myself."[77]

Now what are unnatural sexual acts? Those that are "a violation of duty to oneself." Kant only discusses "carnal self-defilement," which was viewed for centuries as a "common disease." He adds, however, that the argument applies to all unnatural use of the sex organs.[78] Self-gratification is unnatural because lust is aroused by an imagined object. That is contrary to the "natural end" *(Natursweck)*. Sexuality is for the preservation of the species. But why would a person act contrary to a duty to himself? One can say such a violation is not even mentioned by name (= the unmentionable crime *[crimen netandum];* also used with reference to homosexuality), or it does not occur among animals, or a person feels shame when he engages in it. All this, says Kant, is true; but none of these is a reason for moral rejection. One who makes unnatural use of sexuality, hence in violation of the purpose of reproduction, has made himself "a means to satisfy his animal instincts" instead of an end. That is, he fails to respect the humanity in his own person. Because the preservation of the species is a suprapersonal end, unnatural sexuality is even worse

77. I. Kant, *Metaphysik der Sitten* (Tugendlehre § 3, resp. § 2). Cf. *The Doctrine of Virtue,* trans. Mary J. Gregor (University of Pennsylvania Press), pp. 81 and 80 resp.

78. I. Kant, *Metaphysik der Sitten* (Tugendlehre § 7). Cf. 4.80.

than suicide. Suicide, after all, requires courage; this is merely loathsome.

This condemnation is surprisingly sharp. But, please note, masturbation and homosexuality are not wrong because they are lustful or contrary to the purpose of reproduction but because they are violations of the moral law. A person cannot at the same time want to be human, i.e., moral (man as end), and refuse to uphold morality (by making oneself into a means). With unnatural sexuality one lapses into a *logical* contradiction. Whereas Thomas grounds his rejection in the divinely infused natural inclination toward the good, Kant offers a transcendental ground. That is the difference; for the rest, the argument comes down to the same thing.

But is Kant's argumentation cogent? Only if we share his presuppositions. Hegel, in discussing Kant's argumentation regarding why we have to keep our promises, already brought out one of them.[79] Says Hegel, Kant is right when he thinks that a world in which people break their promises is *logically* incompatible with a world in which they keep them. But Kant neglects to show that the first world is inferior to the second; he simply assumes this. His assumption is that it is good to keep one's promises.

We can now apply this argument to Kant's idea about sexuality. True, it is contradictory to desire to be moral and not to will the maintenance of morality. But the idea that one can only promote the maintenance of morality by actions that do not exclude reproduction is an assumption Kant regards as self-evident. In other words, Kant's reasoning rests on a *petitio principii* (begging the question).

The fact that Kant regards this as self-evident is linked with his image of human sexuality. I have already said that for him sexuality is genital; at issue is the correct use of the sex organs. Further, Kant's sexual ethics, like his ethics as a whole, is a personal, not a social, ethic.[80] Kant and many generations after

---

79. For Hegel's argument, see W. H. Walsh (1974: 402/3). Kant's argumentation occurs in *Grundlegung*: B54/A54.

80. W. H. Walsh (op. cit.: 392): "Being moral was for Kant primarily

him neglect to take account of the social aspects of sexuality.[81] On the basis of his scientific knowledge, Kant thought that only reproduction was a universalizable aspect of sexuality. We know better.

Linked with Kant's scientific insights is a third assumption. The entire project of a transcendental grounding of morality is an attempt to show that views concerning man as object of science and man as moral subject are totally independent of each other.[82] Science concerns man as "natural" being — causes and consequences. Morality relates to the intentions and acts of man as person. That is and remains an important distinction. In addition, Kant could not do anything in ethics with man as a natural being, man as pictured by the science of *his* time. He had still another reason for thus opposing nature and morality: he believed that all natural inclinations are selfish.[83] Modern ethology and sociobiology have shown that there are also social, "altruistic," natural inclinations. Of this Kant knew nothing. Hence, now that in our time it is no longer necessary to oppose the self and the social, it is also no longer necessary to treat sexual pleasure and morality as opposites, as Kant does.

In short, in his condemnation also Kant proceeds in part from normative and in part from factual assumptions about man. Like Thomas, he makes his judgments on the basis of a normative view

---

a matter of personal concern." Cf. Windelband (op. cit.: II: 136): "Kant's ethics is an individualistic ethics which limits the duties of the individual to personal relationships and is incapable of understanding the moral value of institutions."

81. See Chapter II. A modern writer can say: "Sex modifies strongly or weakly whatever social relationships . . . ," in: J. van Ussel (1975: 148 n. 13).

82. G. J. Warnock (1964: 312).

83. "Kant, in addition to his worries about determinism, refused to locate moral motivation in the realms of desire because he was strongly tempted to subscribe to some simple version of psychological egoism, i.e., to believe that if a person acts to satisfy his own desires, then a person is acting selfishly. Seeing clearly that morality is not a matter of mere selfishness, Kant thus had an extra reason for removing it from the realm of desire entirely," J. G. Murphy (1982: 75).

of man. It is one we need not endorse. His condemnation is, by no means, naturalistic, but his view of human sexuality is one-sidedly biologistic. "Unnatural," for Kant, is a descriptive term that gets its content from the biological knowledge current in his day. The tragedy that now unfolds in the course of history is that this meaning of "unnatural" takes the place of the original ethical meaning found in Thomas. In the process the naturalistic fallacy became a fact.

To illustrate this point I will give a couple of examples of naturalistic interpretations of Thomas and Kant. In a discussion early in this century between a homosexual (Commutator et al., 1927) and a Dutch professor of theology (H. Y. Groenewegen, 1923, 1928), the former appealed to Hirschfeld's "transitional forms of sexuality" to justify homosexual behavior. Hirschfeld viewed homosexuality as a transitional form of sexuality between men and women. Groenewegen, on the other hand, saw only pathology, for to be either man or woman can only mean that "in virtue of their physical structure they are able, destined, and inclined to take part in reproduction in one of two possible ways."[84]

For — with an appeal to Kant! — sexuality can only be grasped in terms of the utility of the structure of the sex organs. So the — naturalistic — conclusion is that a state of affairs in which a human uses his or her sex organs unnaturally is morally inferior. Tolsma (first edition), whom we discussed in § B, cites Groenewegen with approval (which is lacking in the second edition in which Tolsma adopts a more tolerant position; see § D).

A second example comes from the congress of Dutch Catholic physicians on homosexuality held in 1939. There more theologians than men of science had the floor. The official representing the archdiocese of Utrecht, F. A. H. van de Loo, offered a solid exposition of the church's position with an appeal to natural (moral) law. The sex act, in virtue of its nature, which is evident from the structure and activity of the sex organs, is directed toward

---

84. H. Y. Groenewegen (1923: 35; 58; 99).

43

the procreation of new life. A biologically interpreted Kant fit beautifully into this argument and was accordingly cited with approval.[85]

D. Arguments in favor of tolerance

1. Backgrounds

The shift toward a more tolerant attitude in the churches originated in the pastorate. It is not unusual for ethical discussion to start because the pastorate has spotted a problem, as in the case of homosexuality. So, in the late fifties, as a problem of certain *individuals,* homosexuality became a topic of ethical discussion and, in the seventies, an item on church agendas. We will find that the arguments of pastors constitute the pattern that has shaped the discussion ever since.[86] We will subject it to critical analysis, but first we will have a look at the background against which the shift to a more tolerant approach has to be understood.

1. During the fifties people could no longer deny that were among Christians also there were homosexuals. This fact, as we saw earlier, was made discussible on the ground that as human beings with a deviant orientation they are entitled to pastoral understanding. Accordingly, the starting point of the discussion for the pastors was the condition/conduct distinction.

2. As a result, a need arose for more information about homosexuality, and for this purpose people turned to the results especially of medical science. In the same period medical professionals gradually moved toward another view, particularly on the basis of a more extensive study of homosexual life patterns,

---

85. J. A. J. Barnhoorn (1941: 88). Compared to these statements from the thirties, the recent pronouncements of the Catholic Magisterium (discussed in § B) offer little that is new.

86. Within the churches one may pick up much more radical sentiments, but the official position has remained indecisive. See the conclusion of this section.

hence of the social aspects of homosexuality (Chapter II). An example is the changed view of Tolsma (in 1963). Decisive for the change in him was the meaning of seduction. He now recognized that in a great many cases homosexuality develops without any form of seduction. The seduction of children not disposed to homosexual behavior need not cause permanent or profound damage. He also now thinks that it is irresponsible to force homosexuals into a heterosexual direction. Although he still calls a homosexual relationship "sterile," he admits that it can certainly have its own values when the sexuality is integrated into a relationship of love and mutual responsibility. The idea of medical professionals that homosexuals, too, are capable of permanent relationships played an important role in the changing views of pastors. A strong contribution to that end was the growing self-awareness of homosexuals and the increasing visibility of homosexuality.[87]

3. In place of the idea that homosexuality is a disease, the view that it is a deviant and practically unchangeable condition or disposition slowly broke through in society as a whole. Initially the condition in question was always viewed as *deviant*, a deficiency, hence not a variant, as e.g., Hirschfeld held in his theory of genetically determined "transitional forms" *(Zwischenstufen)*. This view, as we will see, plays a key role in the attitude of tolerant pastors.

How can we explain that a medical line of thinking should have so much influence among pastors and in pastoral ethics? The motive, as we saw in § B, lay in the desire to help. We must look for the explanation in the fact that from the start there was a link between the moral condemnation of homosexual relations and medical involvement. In the nineteenth century doctors began to take an interest in the roots of socially deviant behavior. They believed that immoral behavior was the result of a (mental or physical) *defect*. For defects in the sexual domain they used the term "perversion." In that way the traditional condemnation acquired a (quasi-)scientific base.[88] And ethicists again used that base to support their judgment.

87. See K. Tielman (1982: ch. 11).
88. G. Hekma (1981) calls it "the medical foundation of an air castle."

45

"Perversion" is not easy to define. It always applies, in addition to whatever else it may apply to, in any case to the subversion of social norms.[89] Hence it implies a moral viewpoint. "Perversion" therefore corresponds with a disease-concept that regards disease as a disturbed relation of an individual to his environment. That is sometimes called a "normativistic" disease-model. Others speak in this connection of an "open" disease-model. Today, however, doctors usually employ a *naturalistic* disease-model, also called the medical model. In it the sick person is presented as the bearer of a disease.

According to the "normativistic" (value-laden) model of disease there is a fluid line between sickness and health. The individual himself is not sick but his relation to his environment. There is no such thing as "disease," only sick people. According to the naturalistic model there is a sharp line of demarcation between sickness and health. Diseases exist independently of the context. They are objectively ascertainable. Disease is an entity.[90]

Within the "open" model of disease, (some) diseases can be interpreted as the reflections of social and political ideologies operative in the diagnoses of physicians. According to I. Ilich, this is especially true of mental illnesses.[91] The deviations physicians

---

Physicians sometimes called the new psychiatric category "insania moralis," bad moral health.

89. See M. Dannecker (1981: 112). Th. Nagel (1971) offers a theoretical analysis; for reactions to this, see S. Ruddick (1971), R. Scruton (1986: 348ff.). For the history of the concept, cf. article by Fasznacht in A. Hertz *et al.* (1978: II: 177ff.).

90. H. ten Have (1903: 289ff.). The normativistic model harks back to the classic theory of miasmatism. A miasma is an infectious influence emanating from the environment, which can affect entire groups of people simultaneously. It is not communicable in the sense of being transferable from person to person (p. 58). That is the distinguishing feature of a contagion. Contagionism is the theory that certain illnesses are transmitted by specific infectants from individual to individual (p. 41). This theory is the forerunner of the naturalistic disease-model. The purity laws of Leviticus are the most ancient indication of contagionism. Hippocrates is the founder of miasmatism. In later periods the distinction between the two streams disappears.

91. H. Achterhuis (1979: 170ff.).

describe as perversions also fall in this category. In the medical model, on the other hand, only disorders that can be placed in an anatomical and physiological context are considered disease. The notion of homosexuality as a "condition" belongs in this category.

In a "normativistic" model of disease the disturbed behavior is the disease; in a "naturalistic" model the disturbed behavior is the result of disease. An important difference between the two is that the first implies a *value judgment* on the individual by his environment; hence the designation "normativistic" model of disease. The second does not. Here *objective* medical criteria apply and one who is not a medical professional cannot say a word.

Pastors and ethicists took over the doctor's representation of homosexuality as a deviant "condition." In addition, there is now a movement among them, based on the authority of science, away from the "normativistic" to the "naturalistic" concept of disease. However, as the medical understanding of homosexuality-as-disease began to mean also to ethicists that homosexuals are the bearers of a disease-as-entity, there was an added possibility of being tolerant toward the person without having to endorse the behavior. Disease-as-entity, after all, is clearly something other than sin, more so than perversion, because perversion always includes a connection with disturbed relations. With that a further step became possible: when it became clear that homosexuality is not a pathological but a natural constitutional abnormality, a specific condition, people could also regard the consequent behavior as permissible. That is precisely what we are going to see happen among tolerant pastors and ethicists.

While this line of reasoning is understandable, it is based on an absolutely mistaken premise. From the nineteenth century on, ethics' appeal to medical science was attributable to the superficial resemblance between the moral judgment ("unnatural") and the medical ("perversion"). People did not see, however, that a disturbed relation to the environment in the sense of perversion is something other than a morally misguided relation. In other words, people overlooked the fact that in passing from a medical category to a moral position they had committed a naturalistic fallacy.

However, as we shall see, this mistaken attachment to the medical and biological sciences continues to this day.

2. Tolerance in the pastorate

Initially pastors indeed wanted to be helpful but did not know how. Writing in 1950 Trillhaas stated that it is the task of pastoral care to help these people live with a good conscience. The most advanced advice pastors could offer was to live in abstinence. However, in the case of constitutive, congenital homosexuality the pastor was practically helpless:

> whether God nevertheless blesses this pastoral care in the lives of such people is something that can in any case no longer be decided from the position of the pastoral care-provider.[92]

Roscam Abbing (1959) likewise sees no alternative for homosexuals except the way of sexual abstinence. His ethical reason for this is that, in his opinion, God wants no life-encompassing covenant between likes but only between unlikes. God wants to make only the relation between man and woman fruitful,[93] says he, echoing Barth and Wurth. The pastor's duty is to help the homosexual bear his heavy cross as "God's prisoner."[94] To honor God's command one has to accept the fact that in a broken world being fully Christian cannot always bring with it the full development in all external respects of our humanity. Pastors need not counsel homosexuals to avoid friendships, however, despite the great danger this entails for their continued chastity (pp. 154ff.).[95]

A note that was new to the Dutch Protestant world was struck in the writing of S. J. Ridderbos (1959, 1961, 1973), who rejected

92. W. Trillhaas (1950: 190, 197).
93. P. J. Roscam Abbing (1959: 152).
94. Title of a book by Wilma, a friend of the homosexual poet De Mérode.
95. Roscam Abbing later revised his position. See Ridderbos (1973a).

the absolute prohibition.[96] His reasoning was that when the psychic nature of a person does not correspond to his physical nature, sexual contact with the opposite sex is unnatural for him. In view of the fundamental structure of the biblical ethos, the love-commandment, love of neighbor has to take account of the different nature of the homosexual. This love can exist just as well between homosexuals. A homosexual relationship must, therefore, be allowed but only when a firm conviction exists "that for this fellow-human every other door is closed; in other words, that he possesses an unalterable homosexual structure" (1961:40). A homosexual relationship does, however, thrust a person into a disharmonious situation because his body does not function in the way indicated by nature (idem: 39). But the physical structure does not always have to take precedence over the psychic structure. The compromise in which the psyche does not come into its own is not always preferable over the compromise in which this applies to the body (idem: 42).

Ridderbos was later followed by pastors like A. Klamer and A. J. R. Brussaard and a number of Catholic priests who, in this way, demonstrated their respect for homosexuals.[97] His idea concerning the homosexual relationship as a "compromise" in the form of a "disharmonious harmony" was widely accepted as a model, in many cases as a "makeshift solution" to be tolerated pastorally. Today this viewpoint feels condescending. But at the time this was the best one possible. For, following psychiatry's lead here, Ridderbos saw homosexuality as a deviation, as "an essential discongruence between the physical and the remaining structure" (idem: 41). Actually, at that time, also for homosexuals themselves, the sense of being "different" was especially a sense of *not* being something.[98]

On the one hand, Ridderbos's view constitutes a striking

96. On the origins of the volume "De homosexuele naaste" (1961), see J. Goossensen and M. Sleutjes (1985). Ridderbos expressly intended this publication to come out of the circle of the Free University. Two of its professors (A. L. Janse de Jonge and H. Bianchi) collaborated in it.

97. Also to be mentioned here are the physicians C. J. B. J. Trimbos (Catholic; gave radio talks on the K.R.O. in 1961) and C. van Emde Boas (1965).

98. R. Tielman (1982: 121).

break with the past and, on the other, it is continuous with the condemnation: the appeal to nature. That dichotomy comes to expression in his compromise solution. It seeks, on the basis of neighborly love, to take account of the homosexual's "dissimilar" nature and recognizes that homosexuals can maintain love-relations. The absence of this recognition in the past, we remember, was always a reason for complete rejection.

Ridderbos's magnanimous conclusion: "Love your neighbor — and feel free to sort things out yourself"[99] does not alter the fact that even he, in my opinion, does not escape a naturalistic form of reasoning, granted that he is thoroughly aware of the problems associated with the appeal to nature. He thinks that in ethics one can and may operate with the concept of "natural obviousness." By this he refers to insight that precedes experience and is common to all humans. On the basis of this immediate sense of obviousness and human experience we know as the nature of man "his continuing end-oriented basic structure which is his destiny" (1973b: 143ff.), in the form of those structures that cannot be changed except to the detriment of his humanity. "Unnatural" is that which is not congruent with it. To this basic structure belongs the fact that the male body and the female body are oriented to each other. But also the desire for a partner belongs to it. The refusal to take this aspect into account also produces an unnatural — and bad — situation. Therefore, while a homosexual partnership has an unnatural element, the road of solitariness has it no less. If someone opts for a homosexual relationship there is so much that is natural in this relating that it may not be disqualified as "unnatural."[100]

99. S. J. Ridderbos (1973a: 133). He still calls the homosexual "way" a "makeshift" solution, because of what he thinks he finds in the Bible about "unnatural" (idem: 132). In some tension with this stands his view of Paul's statements in Romans 1; see the following note.

100. S. J. Ridderbos (1973b: 136–56) speaks of natural "obviousness or patency," instead of natural revelation (creation ordinances), in order thus to create room for a theological reinterpretation of Rom. 1:26, 27. In his opinion Paul is not speaking here in virtue of a special revelation but from his sense of patency. We, on our part, may speak differently. For Ridderbos's theological opinions, see further Ch. IV.

Accordingly, when he refers to "the nature of man," Ridderbos has in mind a norm: not what people do or do not do at all times and in all places, but what they ought to do. That is correct. I do, however, question his grounding: that which presents itself to collective human experience as self-evident. To this must be added: "which always applies in the context of the situation in a given society." Ridderbos means that ultimately the norm called "nature" rests on necessity. That is correct, but also the necessary is not an immutable datum for us human beings. In the days when Ridderbos's articles appeared, homosexuality was still generally regarded as a deviation. In such a situation the argument that only the man-woman polarity belongs to the established basic structure of man holds true because that reality is considered a given: it cannot be otherwise. It is wrong, however, to deduce human destiny from the basic biological structures, as Ridderbos still does to some degree. The destiny of man indeed depends on meeting the intent of basic structures because they constitute the necessary conditions for the realization of his destiny and consequently have moral value. But the man-woman polarity does not constitute the destiny of man because it is a basic structure. The reverse is true. This polarity is a basic structure because it makes a contribution to the destiny of man, i.e., because of its directedness toward the good life. In other words, the fact that man and woman are oriented to each other is a biological given concerning sexuality, but its moral value lies in its contribution to human destiny. The latter cannot be derived from the former, for that yields a naturalistic mode of reasoning. Accordingly, Ridderbos takes a sufficient reason to be a necessary one and that is understandable in terms of what was then thought to be a known fact about sexuality.

In those years Ridderbos's articles set the tone for the discussion. The same double-track approach — homosexual relations in part do, and in part do not, meet the "intent" of nature, or answer to the destiny of man — can be found among Catholic priests, but their tolerance tends to be based less on ethical than on pastoral considerations. (I call a position "pastoral" when, having originated in involvement with a person, it is intended as the "solution" that offers the best prospects to the person in question.) Thus J. Vermeulen, a teacher of

51

moral theology, stated in a pastoral booklet on homosexuality, which appeared in roughly the same period,[101] that among Christians there is no difference of opinion on the norm, for that is abstinence. But pastorally one is faced by the problem of the "conscience invincibly prone to error" (*conscientia invincibiliter erronea*). Then one may apply as guideline the standard of tolerating what is unavoidable for the moment. Homosexual acts are permissible as long as they are not intentional (1963: 70). In the same publication one encounters the statement by H. Ruygers that not the homophile friendship but the unalterable inclination is the "proximate cause" (*occasio proxima*), meaning that homosexuals do not choose their relationships; they are the consequence of an unalterable condition. Friendship as a means of avoiding enforced loneliness is the lesser evil *(minus malum)* by comparison. But abstinence remains the norm (idem: 76). J. B. F. Gottschalk (1967), addressing the pastorate, offers the following rules of thumb: (1) never try to break a friendship; (2) never recommend marriage as a solution; (3) never force anybody to take the way of abstinence; (4) help homophiles build a stable relationship and (5) stress the importance of fidelity.

J. van Kilsdonk, S.J., goes beyond pastoral considerations when he says (in a sermon):

> The few very creative homophile friendships I have witnessed and know down to their silences and depths actually seem to me models for a dynamic marriage, a kind of perpetual revolutionary model."[102]

The work he and other pastors have done for the "naturalization" of homosexuality in this period — the sixties — both inside and outside the churches, is to my mind of inestimable value. As stated earlier, their efforts were aimed especially at giving help to individuals. The norm — the "natural" orientation of men to women and vice versa — was not at all or hardly in dispute. The

---

101. I consulted the reprint of A. F. C. Overing et al. (1963).
102. Quoted from: *Twee Dominees* (1971: 159). He repeatedly criticized the official Catholic position on the ground that its composers were unfamiliar with the practice of the pastorate.

goal was to foster understanding for the homosexual neighbor in his "otherness." The idea was to break down prejudices regarding the homosexual, not those concerning the way western people practiced and viewed sexuality in general.[103] As a rule homosexuals remained anonymous[104] and where they identified themselves publicly their intent, like that of the pastors, was to make clear that homosexuals, too, can live by moral standards. These, then, are consistently the same ones that apply to heterosexual relations.

In sum, "steady friendship" is now the ethical ideal among homosexuals[105] and the guidelines used by progressive pastors. Legitimation is based on pastoral considerations alongside the ethical argument of the relation as a dignified form of human existence. Theologically the appeal to the love-command was decisive.[106] Accordingly, the viewpoints of the pastors, specifically the Protestant, were certainly not only pastoral but pastoral-ethical: i.e., they not only looked for a practical solution but tried to ground it ethically.

103. For this see H. Bianchi in A. L. Janse de Jonge (1961); G. Th. Kempe in A. F. C. Overing (1961).

104. Thus in A. L. Janse de Jonge, op. cit., and in a report of the Dutch Center for Dialogue (*Nederlands Gesprek Centrum,* 1966). The latter, to which S. J. Ridderbos also contributed, breathes the same cautious spirit as the Christian brochures. In the interest of those involved a "peripheral homosexuality" should be corrected. "Core homosexuals" — the terminology is that of C. van Emde Boas, chairman of the ad hoc N. G. C. committee — have a different orientation. That makes it hard for homosexuals and heterosexuals to understand each other's relationships. Many homosexuals, says the report, have the feeling "they do not totally meet the criteria for being human." It posits that, for both, the same commandments ought to apply, specifically with reference to the love-command. Love does evil to no one. Still in 1971, a small book appeared, whose authors, both of whom are ministers, remained anonymous (*Twee Dominees,* 1971).

105. Cf. R. Tielman (1982: 173ff.).

106. Among the adherents of the "New Morality" in the sixties, in the wake of the publications of the controversial bishop Robinson, the love-command was the only criterion for sexual behavior ("Love does evil to no one"; "what happens in love cannot be wrong"). See, e.g., the critical response, "Sexuality and Morality," a report presented to the British Council of Churches (1967): the concept of love, which is open to many interpretations, offers no guidance for action unless it is further defined.

3. Ethics as pragmatic solution

The ethical question is this: what is wrong with homosexual relations? We will find that this question was avoided and thus implicitly answered by this: they are not permissible. The question that
was answered — reluctantly — in the affirmative was whether
sexual behavior is morally permissible for homosexuals, i.e., for
people with a "deviant" orientation. As examples for this approach
I will mention the ethics of Thielicke and Trillhaas.

Thielicke's *Theological Ethics* (Engl. 1964) is the first full-
fledged Protestant ethics that sounds a more tolerant note.[107] In
Thielicke's opinion, the theologians of past generations were too
much guided by "doctrinaire prejudices" and conveniently dis-
missed homosexuality as pathology (Barth!). The sciences, however, have now demonstrated that homosexuals have a specific
predisposition. This creates a new ethical problem because homosexual behavior can no longer be equated with indulging a
corrupt physical desire.

From a theological perspective, says Thielicke, homosexuality is a disturbance in the order of creation. It is contrary to God's
intention for man. But all human beings live and share in a broken
world. God has adapted his ordinances to this disordered creation
as it exists since the Fall. The order of creation is not an ideal
order but an "emergency-ordering" of it, a "compromise."[108] In
that context the homosexual predisposition may not be depreciated
more strongly than the status of existence we all share (Engl. p.
283).

This is not to put homosexuality on a level with normal
sexual relations. The homosexual has fallen from the framework
of the order of the sexes. He must therefore "be willing to be
treated or healed so far as this is possible" (idem: 283). Should
healing be impossible, this must not be viewed as a "fate" but as
a "talent that is to be invested" (Luke 19:13ff.) (idem: 284). Con-

107. H. Thielicke (1964: 282–304).
108. The idea of "emergency-ordinances," or "Noahitic ordinances"
as the will of God for the fallen creation is a specialty of Thielicke's theology.

cretely this means that if a homosexual is unable to live in abstinence, he "has to realize his optimal ethical potentialities on the basis of his irreversible situation" (idem: 285). What this entails cannot be stated with precision, for we are here dealing with "borderline situations" for ethics. The homosexual needs to "structure the man-man relationship in an ethically responsible way" (idem: 284–85). In view of the great dangers that threaten, such as promiscuity, and thus "sabotage even that relative 'order' which the homosexual *could* achieve even on this basis" (idem: 286) pastoral care will, in the main, have to focus on the sublimation of the homosexual urge. This may for example be found in teaching: "therefore the goal of this sublimation will be found precisely in the actual danger zones" (idem: 287).

Accordingly, Thielicke's *ethical* answer is a *pastoral* solution. His views follow a double track: that of the traditional condemnation (homosexuality is sin) and that of scientific insight (homosexuality is unalterable). The link between the two is the theological thesis that all humans share existence in a broken world;[109] therefore every order is only relative (in relation to the norm: marriage!). But because a relative order also has a right to exist, there is room for an order adapted to the potentialities and realities of homosexuals. However, in view of the dangers, abstinence is the safest road to take.

A less ambivalent, but not more tolerant, answer is that of Trillhaas.[110] The starting point has to be, according to him, the recognition that homosexuality as an unalterable given is an abnormality based on "irregular genetic formation." An abnormality, not a variant. There can be no doubt about this, considering the use and meaning of the sex organs and the biological infertility associated with it. Only after this fact has been recognized does ethics have anything to do with it, i.e., in the evaluation of the different modes of homosexual behavior. One cannot forbid homosexuals to form relationships; where possible, these relation-

109. An "ontologically generalized understanding of sin." H. Ringeling (1987a: 21).
110. W. Trillhaas (1969: 63–79; 1970³: 331–36).

ships should be lasting. Basically, we do not ask anything from a homosexual we do not ask from a normal person; maintain a disciplined lifestyle, do not abuse dependents, avoid prostitution, seduction, etc. (1969: 75).

Accordingly, instead of sin (as it still is in Thielicke) homosexuality is here an abnormality; not "unnatural" in the moral but in the biological sense. But this viewpoint fails to take homosexuals seriously. We read, for example, that homosexuals need to avoid occupations in which they come into frequent contact with minors (idem: 70), for

> his psychic weakness all too easily causes a homosexual to seize opportunities in which he can yield to his inclinations, particularly with respect to dependents. (1970: 335)

We read further that homosexual relationships that have not been institutionalized can always be broken up and in reality often break up because such relationships constantly demand a new decision in favor of fidelity.

This is more than most homosexuals can handle, for

> The yearning to stray is unceasingly at war with the fidelity of the homosexual. . . . [These are simply] the unmistakable characteristics of the abnormalcy. . . . Sadness and despair are part of its very constitution. (1969: 73)

That surely is an easy "explanation." Other things, such as the oppressive anti-gay legislation in Germany, are not even considered.[111] But even if this explanation were correct it is ethically unacceptable. When all the problems of homosexuals are reduced to being the consequences of biological abnormalcy, this means that the refusal of homosexuals to act in accord with the reasons Trillhaas considers correct is explained as their inability to act on the basis of reasons. We encounter here the consequence of rea-

---

111. For an account of the wretched situation of homosexuals in Germany in the sixties, see T. Brocher et al. (1966). Cf. "Homosexuelle und Kirche" (1988, 1991).

soning we already found in Wurth, viz., that homosexual behavior is not human. Only on that basis can homosexuals not be forbidden to enter into relationships that are in keeping with their nature. Trillhaas's solution is, therefore, neither pastoral nor ethical but purely pragmatic: one cannot forbid such relationships in view of the "vitality" of the sex drive!

Still, as late as 1987 H. Ringeling regards Trillhaas's view as representative for the state of the theological debate in Germany.[112] He bluntly endorses Trillhaas's opinion of homosexuality as "irregular genetic formation."[113] On this basis he judges that the normalcy of the knowable order of nature yields a normative indication for the construction of a scale of goods. This finds confirmation in the theological interpretive system of the creation ordinances. Homosexuality and bisexuality, too, can be regarded as "wholesome" and "natural" forms of sexuality due to their "symbolic fruitfulness," but real fruitfulness in marriage and the family deserves precedence (p. 96). The church must, therefore, adopt a strong position in favor of the "supreme validity of marriage." Other forms of relationship can be subjectively meaningful but should not be institutionalized by the church. Homosexual ministers (if I understand him correctly) need to live in abstinence (pp. 100–101). This reasoning is based on Ringeling's denial that

> The 'naturalistic fallacy' is already present when the ethical assessment of sexual conduct cites the naturally-given sexual structure in all its functions. (p. 94)

But that is precisely the case here. For the *natural* sequence or the normalcy of knowable nature — the author neglects to say how this can be ascertained — is said to be the *normative* sequence, not on the basis of an additional argument, but based on the thesis that the normal equals the creation order, which equals the will of God, which is normative. The polyvalence of the con-

112. H. Ringeling (1987a: 33).
113. H. Ringeling (1987b: 98).

57

cept of nature as we sketched it in § B escapes Ringeling. Without any arguments he makes the transition from a concept of normalcy (nature) to normativity (creation order). That is not a possibility.

The Catholic moral philosopher A. M. J. M. H. van de Spijker (1968), whom we encountered already in the preceding section, offers us a much more careful phenomenology of homosexuality. His premise is that it is the nature of generic man that he stands in the world as a person — i.e., a unity of spirit, soul, and body — of sexuality, eroticism, and love. This applies as much to the homosexual as to the heterosexual person. He is not only physically oriented to the other but totally. To give expression to this totality van de Spijker introduces the terms homo- and heterotropism,[114] the orientation of a person to persons of the same or the opposite sex. For that reason, one must not, as Catholic moral philsophy tends to do, judge the homosexual only in terms of the nature of the sex act. The personalistic, "totalistic" approach van de Spijker advocates requires one to take account of three aspects, viz., the position, situation, and condition of a person. "Position" refers to the freedom of man, "situation" to his social-psychological circumstances, and "condition" to the biological rootage of his behavior, i.e., his actual nature. Now, a human becomes whole when his *condition* and *situation* are incorporated in love as his choice of *position* (p. 167).

That is a much more acceptable approach than we encountered in Thielicke and Trillhaas because van de Spijker views the homosexual as a person, hence as someone who, in his situation, has reasons for his actions. But does he keep this up? In the past, he says, moral philosophers have overestimated the freedom of man at the expense of the aspects "situation" and "condition." The correction of this construal leads us to other conclusions than the tradition. Ontologically, i.e., on the basis of a normative anthropology, heterotropism is the ideal. Complete harmony, as the highest form of human existence, is attained only in the man-woman polarity. "In light of the ontic ideal," homotropism is,

114. A. M. J. M. H. van de Spijker (1968: 25). "Tropism" denotes an "involuntary orientation." These terms have not found acceptance elsewhere.

therefore, "a deficiency, a diminution in being, a reduction of existential possibilities" (p. 198). That is also the case from a theological point of view. According to the Bible, heterotropism is the unique and "complete" form of human existence and therefore, from a metaphysical point of view, homotropism is an "existential deficiency *(Existenzmanko)*." It is not a variant but an abnormality (p. 160; just as color blindness is not a variant but a visual abnormality says van de Spijker). Homotropism is to be regarded as an effect of original sin. That is not anyone's fault personally, but conversely for the heterotropic person, it may be a reason for gratitude that he is equipped with better possibilities for living a full life (p. 200). From a moral point of view, therefore, only sublimation (abstinence) is completely correct.

But humans, who are fundamentally capable of discerning the demands of the creation order and natural law, are in fact hindered in this by original sin. Now, for the homotropic person, the factors of "situation" and "condition" form a hindrance to arriving existentially at a correct insight into the order of creation, i.e., at a correct position. Hence "the personalizing of the homosexual predisposition" can be considered a step toward the fulfillment of the command to sublimate, for in a love-relationship homotropic persons realize the "measure of human dignity possible to them" (pp. 201–2).

Fundamental to this argument is van de Spijker's base in normative anthropology. This means that as person, hence with his whole being, a human is oriented to another person. An ethical assessment, therefore, always has to take into account causes (condition), the actual circumstances (situation), as well as the reasons for the behavior in question (position). Therefore a homosexual relationship can, to a certain extent, be ethically justified. That is genuinely tolerant by comparison with Trillhaas and Thielicke and an outcome similar to that of Ridderbos.

"To a certain extent" — be it noted! For homosexuality is here "an existential deficiency," a departure from the ideal, from the ontic ideal and the creation order, and is therefore unnatural, the term van de Spijker employs as well. But that can be tolerated because homosexuality is a deficiency in the sense of deviancy,

abnormality, and incapacity. That prevents homosexuals from arriving at an objectively correct insight into the creation order. That
can be excused, however, if and insofar as they commit themselves
to a homosexual relationship in love and fidelity.

The pattern of the reasoning is the same as that followed in
the traditional condemnation. Approval applies to relations "in love
and fidelity"; homosexuality remains a "moral deficiency." This
approach applies to all the tolerant positions. There is only one
correct position, the heterosexual norm, which van de Spijker
elevates to the level of "ontic ideal." The factors of "condition"
and "situation" play only a role, given this starting point. Van de
Spijker treats them as determining causes; he therefore discounts
the homosexual's freedom of choice by limiting it to the choice
for or against personalizing the sex drive. In the end that does not
differ too much from the scheme we already encountered in Wurth.

Van de Spijker is clearer about what the factors "situation"
and "condition" determine. As already stated in his or her orientation, a human being is a unity of condition, situation, and position. In addition, he views the sexual as a unity of *sexus, eros,* and
philia. The two sets of description now prove to be interrelated,
as one can infer from his definitions (pp. 24–37). "Sexuality"
denotes the realm of physical drives; "eroticism," the sensuous
and sensory; *philia* the spiritual-emotional aspect. Sexuality produces physical desire, eroticism joy, and *philia* happiness and
personal responsibility (p. 37). We may therfore conclude that
sexuality embraces the aspect of the condition, eroticism that of
the situation, and *philia* that of the position. Thus, by means of
his division into components, van de Spijker has in fact furnished
a rational account for saying that human freedom of choice is
limited to spiritual love and that everything else is a consequence
of causally operative factors. But does the argument stand up? Van
de Spijker pretends to offer a purely descriptive account of the
sexual. But, as we shall see below, there is no denying that norms
are involved as well.

That is also the case in the approach of the Reformed (*Her-
vormd*) theologian H. W. de Knijff (1987), whose position is akin
to van de Spijker's model and whom I mention as a contemporary

representative. He, too, works with the distinctions of *sexus-eros-philia-agapê* and fits them into a polarity of "nature" and "spirit," the (in his opinion) decisive anthropological components of western spirituality. *Sexus* is the bare biological given, *eros* the cultural articulation, *philia* the personal relation. In their concurrence they are embraced by *agapê,* the God-given love that is marked by self-denial.[115]

In de Knijff's opinion homosexual relations are acceptable, but the highest form of *philia* is married love. He grounds this view by conceiving the relationship between marriage and sexuality as *entelechy,* the Aristotelian term for the intrinsicness and teleology of the sex act (p. 303).[116]

"Fertility and the will to procreation belong essentially to marriage and are an implicate of the sex act" (p. 301).

This continues to be true also where the separation of sexuality and reproduction is viewed as a gain. For we are still dealing with "a composite unity of meaning," even in cases where people are not fully conscious of it. In this regard, homosexual relations are deficient. But that is true also of many marriages. Hence, says de Knijff, the homosexual, too, is entitled to experience his orientation as an opportunity to live a moral, human life (p. 305).

4. A characterization of tolerance

What is it that distinguishes the tolerance-argument from the traditional attitude of condemnation? On the one hand, there is a big difference: homosexual intercourse was wrong on account of its unnatural character; now it is considered permissible because, and insofar as, it takes place in love. On the other hand, we note that the norm, heterosexuality, is not in question. Also, proponents of tolerance simply continue to repeat that heterosexuality is the divinely willed order among humans and homosexuality is not. They view this norm as Bible-based (creation order). In that per-

115. H. W. de Knijff (1987, spec. pp. 262–310).
116. On "entelechy," see Ch. III.

spective, homosexual relations can be pastorally permitted (Thielicke), or not very well prohibited (Trillhaas), or — a further step — be acceptable on the basis of love as the personalization of sexual desire (van de Spijker; de Knijff), or, as the optimum realization of human destiny, granted that an unnatural element continues to adhere to them (Ridderbos). So we see tolerance, even acceptance, on the one hand and the retention of the norm on the other — all at the same time. How can that be? The key is the confusion of "natural" in the moral (and religious) sense with "natural" in the biological sense. Homosexual relations are now called "natural," meaning natural in a biological sense: the abnormal constitution is natural. On account of the given unalterable predisposition, these authors no longer see a reason for disapproval but a reason for tolerance. In this way homosexuals are upgraded from being *morally deviant* to being *biologically deviant.* From being a wrong choice, homosexual behavior now becomes a form of behavior in which a person does not have to make a choice. Where, in the traditional condemnation a biological argument was the compelling reason for condemnation ("unnatural"; see § 2), a biological argument now furnishes a compelling reason for a more tolerant attitude ("natural"). Consequently, also the argument for tolerance rests — at least in part, see Ridderbos — on a *naturalistic fallacy.* In other words, the tolerance concerns a love-relationship other than marriage and hence a homosexual relationship but not the homosexual element in the relationship.

How come? It is related to the prevailing view of the meaning of the word "sexual." In numerous instances sexuality was (is?) synonymous with what relates to the sex act. From within an anthropological viewpoint people viewed sex as a natural, physical need issuing from the sex drive that has to be channeled into and through the marriage relation.[117] Thus the "sexual" is given a place as the physical expression of a love-relation in which "love" constitutes the spiritual, the "higher," aspect of the relation. We explicitly encountered this hierarchical and dualistic model in van de Spijker in the form of the trio: sex (= drive = physical desire);

117. E.g., H. Schelsky (1957: 18ff.); cf. M. Dannecker (1978: 50ff.).

eros (= sensuousness = pleasure); *philia* (= the spiritual = responsibility). We also find it in so many words in de Knijff and Trillhaas and implicitly in others.[118] It is, however, a misleading, impoverished, abbreviated model. Of course, if people so desire, they are free to distinguish various centers of gravity in the various aspects of the complex called "sexuality," as long as they do not mistake a division in components for a division of the reality itself. *Sexus* and *eros* and *philia* always produce a series of physical responses *and* numerous emotional reactions *and* have a relational aspect. Undoubtedly the idea is that only the desire to nurture the other person in a permanent relationship is a good reason for sexual behavior. That is a norm. But sexuality also *creates* relationship. Also what people call purely sexual relations or even fleeting sexual contacts have communicative and relational aspects. Therefore, that which presents itself as a descriptive-anthropological, empirical model is in fact a *normative* model. For that reason it is misleading.

Add to this that it is impossible to make a sharp distinction between "sexual" and "non-sexual." The boundary between them is not fixed. In Chapter II I will come back to this matter at length but have to make a number of remarks about it now. The model described above suggests that human behavior can be divided up into parts. One of these is sexual behavior. The reference here is to all the acts in which the sex organs are involved. Sexual behavior is rooted in a drive or instinct. Specific stimuli mechanically release such behavior. This leads to the satisfaction of the instincts. The instincts have a vagabond-like character. They are not focused on, but at best directed toward, another human being. Instincts are promiscuous. Accordingly, they require social regulation. The sex organs indicate the direction in which the sexual instincts are to find satisfaction. This model is linked with the call to reproduction and the demand of an exclusive love relationship within marriage.[119] According to van Ussel, this is the foundation of the

118. W. Trillhaas (1969); *Liefde en Sexualiteit,* a pastoral aid (1972); S. P. de Roos (1964), H. W. de Knijff (1987: 262ff.).

119. J. van Ussel (1974) calls this the negative, narrow sexual model:

prevailing sexual morality.[120] I call it the *static-mechanical* model. *Static,* for it furnishes an unambiguous criterion for determining whether a person's behavior is sexual or not, viz., the involvement or non-involvement of the external sex organs. Male friendships, accordingly, are non-sexual and homosexual relations are sexual; a hug on a soccer field is not, but the kiss of lovers is. And *mechanical,* because the relation between the sex drive and sexual behavior is like that between the wound-up alarm clock and its going off.

This model is partly incorrect and partly one-sided. For in this conception, sexuality is reduced to a biological phenomenon whose explanation — along with the theory of drives — rests on a dated biology.[121] Sexuality, indeed, has aspects that biologists and medical researchers study. But they only inquire into the causes of behavior, not into its intentions, purposes, and associated feelings. Accordingly, the study of sexuality as a biological phenomenon only brings to light those aspects that belong to the domain of the biological sciences, i.e., the sexual as the field of operative causes. There is no objection to this provided the medical-biological accounts of sexuality are not taken for the full and always appropriate description of sexuality. When that happens, sexual behavior is isolated from the human reasons and motives informing it and, thus, not actually appreciated as human action. Then, indeed, the only alternatives are either the control or the indulgence of the drive, and all motives other than love fall under the heading of "giving free rein" to it.

Accordingly, the static-mechanical model of sexuality is seemingly descriptive but in fact prescriptive and, therefore, mis-

---

negative, because sexuality is pictured as something dangerous that has to be restrained, suppressed, or sublimated; narrow because sexuality is isolated from the whole of being human in all its relations. For a lengthy discussion of his views, see Ch. II, § D.

120. J. van Ussel (1974: 80). See further Ch. II, §§ D and G.

121. The mechanistic view of human (sexual) behavior is comparable to the stiff way in which the reproductive behavior of the stickleback occurs. Such rigid behavior, released by signal-stimuli (Lorenz), is an exception rather than the rule in the animal world.

leading and one-sidedly biological, partly based on dated biology. This model, nevertheless, was present in the thoughts of all the ethicists discussed above when they evaluated homosexuality. And it served them well. They assumed, after all, that there were no good reasons for homosexuality, and a further step is that there are no reasons for it at all.

But there are *causes!* With the aid of the biological drive–theory of sexuality they could present the fortunate and less fortunate aspects of homosexual lifestyles as the consequences of deterministically operative *causes* of *behavior* without having to ponder this behavior as the (intended and possibly anticipated) *result* of human *choices*. In this way the norm — the heterosexual love-relationship — could remain outside of the discussion and at the same time homosexual relations could be accepted. In Chapter II I will return to this confusion of reasons and causes.

A second objection to this model concerns the one-sided accent on the *private* character of sexual relations.[122] It pictures sexuality as an individualized property, as an entity one carries with him like one's head or feet. Consequently all the problems surrounding homosexuality are reducible to the problems someone has with "his" homosexuality and society has with the recognition of this "fact." In this connection no attention is paid whatsoever to the fact that tolerance toward certain forms of sexual behavior depends not only on morality but also on ideas of what is sexual and what is not. Our culture has a biologistic view of sexuality and that has to do, in part, with societal relations in western culture, as we will see in the next chapter. To a large degree such societal notions shape the individual consciousness. In our culture a person *is* a homosexual or a heterosexual or perhaps a bisexual. And people experience themselves as such. The prevailing communal ideas of what is sexual and what is not form the programs that explain, at least in part, why a person is a homosexual or a heterosexual.[123]

This view of sexual behavior has one great advantage. It

122. J. van Ussel (1974: 117).
123. J. van Ussel (1975: 130ff.).

enables one to view homosexual relations as a personal choice belonging to the sphere of privacy. In that way it has played an important role in liberalizing laws against homosexual behavior. A person's sexual behavior is now regarded as a matter of personal morality, not of social morality and, therefore, not of the law. Despite its shortcomings, therefore, and the static-mechanical model of sexuality underlying it, this view has been of decisive importance.[124]

> The most interesting discussion of this issue took place in England. It was triggered by the Wolfenden Report (1957) which proposed a liberalization of the legislation regarding homosexuality. It took place between Lord Devlin, a judge, and Hart, a philosopher of law. Over against the recommendations of the report Devlin defended the thesis that the role of the penal code is to protect society against the subversion of its morality. In his opinion the morality of a society, including the sexual, forms "a single seamless web." One who deviates from one part of it will probably deviate also from other parts. Hart, on the other hand, denied that a society is coextensive with its morality. For the continued existence of a society there has to be a measure of shared morality but it is not society's task to punish "private immorality" by way of the penal code. Devlin later retreated from his negative position.[125]

Still, this privacy view of sexuality also has an important weakness. It fails to do justice to the social dimension, the role aspect of homosexuality.[126] Homosexuals called attention to this

124. For the Netherlands that was the abolition of Art. 248, again in 1971. Cf. R. Tielman (1982: 77ff.). For Germany, T. Brocher et al. (1966), H. Thielicke (1966: 300ff.).

125. P. Devlin (1959); H. L. A. Hart (1962). See also B. M. Leiser (1979: 10–30). His view is that sexual behavior is a matter for a person's private morality, not of positive (social) morality. If homosexual behavior were damaging it would be so only for the persons involved. A system of a maximum number of liberties ought to be the moral norm for a society that is proud of its tradition of liberty for all, including minority groups (p. 60; Leiser is an American). "Society has better things to do than to enforce private morality" (p. 71).

126. "Private" and "personal" are not always synonymous. Sexuality is certainly a personal matter and therefore a private matter. But a personal

issue in the slogan "the personal has become political." To this subject I will return as well.

We noted that the more tolerant attitude toward homosexuality is based on a naturalistic argument that assumes a biologistic view of sexuality. Within this framework, just what does tolerance mean? It may be defined as "a posture of not taking action against behavior of which one disapproves." In a pluriform society this posture is morally necessary as one that recognizes the right of another person to arrive in his situation at different decisions than we would. We are not talking about those moral issues about which society believes that the individual has to settle them himself.[127] Tolerance, therefore, expresses the recognition of moral pluriformity in a society. It is based on the principle of respect for the autonomy of persons. In that situation homosexuality is a matter of *personal* choice. But it is not tolerance in this sense that is at issue in the case of the tolerant Christian ethicists we discussed above. By and large Christians are still far from viewing homosexuality as a matter of personal choice.

What is the difference? We need to make a distinction between respect for those who do not want to do anything other than what they are doing because they believe they have good reasons for it and tolerance toward those who cannot do anything other than what they are doing. In the second case we are talking about the *exoneration* of behavior that, judged by moral standards, is considered wrong. We forgive children their impudence, the aged their forgetfulness. Tolerance then consists in refraining from applying a moral standard because the people in question do not meet the criteria applicable to a mature, moral person. It is this form of tolerance that is virtually always in play toward homosexuals. People do not bother them and excuse them — a form of tolerance based on the naturalistic fallacy. In the first

---

relationship also has impersonal aspects, if one means by "impersonal" acting in a role. That is not a private matter. Conversely, the impersonal teacher-pupil relationship, for example, also has personal aspects. For the several meanings of "personal," see R. S. Downie (1971: 121ff.).

127. A. W. Musschenga (1980: 71; 1984).

instance the assumption is the equality of everyone as partners in the discussion on the basis of an equal standing as moral subjects. In the second, some people decide for others. In virtue of certain empirical characteristics some people are excluded from the moral discussion: because they are children or . . . homosexual. Sometimes there may be compelling reasons for excluding them. But that situation always presupposes a disease-model of behavior, a model we have to be very careful with. Applied in all cases other than illness, it fails to take people seriously. This may even happen in an inherently tolerant love-ethics (as in the case of Ridderbos and van de Spijker), when homosexual relations are accepted (by the heterosexual majority) because of their resemblance to heterosexual relations. That still does not mean more than the recognition of monogamous relations not of homosexual relations.

Dominant in the ethics of the churches is the mindset of tolerance in the sense of not-holding-guilty (exoneration). The first to point this out, and to demonstrate the condescending character of this tolerance, was C. O. Jellema (1977). In fact, says he, this tolerant opinion of homosexuals does no more than assign them a separate little corner in the social order. That gives the "normal ones" a sense of security. At best, this leads to the view that others must accept homosexuals and they must accept themselves (Sengers' thesis). But acceptance has to do with deficiency and shortcoming. Acceptance implies exoneration: "sorry, that is how I am." In the case of acceptance, causes have become excuses. Society accepts homosexuals as long as it can recognize causes. But that is not a moral solution. A solution can come only when homosexuals present their lifestyles as *the way they have chosen to live.* "Chosen" does not mean that there are no causes; it means homosexuals have assumed responsibility for those causes and not left it to the authority of the church, the psychiatrist, or society. Only when this is the assumption, the assumption of autonomy (i.e., deciding for myself instead of another making the decision), can a judgment be fair. A meaningful lifestyle, in any case, is one that has been consciously chosen, though the significance of the lifestyle does not coincide with the prevalency of the choice.[128]

This is a well-argued objection to the ethics of exoneration, the best I know. But for the churches there exists a big problem that has precedence over possible objections to such exoneration, viz., how to justify this more tolerant attitude theologically (biblically). This can be illustrated by a consideration of the difficulties experienced in this area by the mainline (Protestant) churches.

5. Tolerance inside the churches: "ethical" and "pastoral"

In the seventies the discussion inside the churches expanded.[129] We already encountered the completely negative position of the Catholic Magisterium. There is no "elasticity" in that position. The report of the Catholic Council for Church and Society (1979) attempts to tone down the sharpness of the church's judgment by referring to the naturalness of homophile sexual expression. The core of the problem, says the report, lies in "the stability of the relationship between predisposition and behavior" (p. 18). Cautiously it states: "There is a growing insight that homosexual behavior can be the natural expression of a typical and irreducible homosexual predisposition" (p. 21). The connection between predisposition and behavior must not be conceived too stringently, as the Magisterium does, but on the other hand it must not be too much disconnected so that the predisposition is, and the behavior is never, acceptable. In view of its peculiar predisposition, homosexuality poses no threat to the values of marriage and family. Similarly, an appeal to the Bible to condemn homosexuality is to

128. C. O. Jellema here opts for the only — in my opinion — correct premise: that the homosexual needs to be taken seriously for his reasons instead of those of the heterosexual majority (which speaks of causes).

129. Among the positions held within the churches I count not only the official pronouncements but also publications of work groups and individual reactions to them, etc.

misuse Scripture. Scripture knows of no such peculiarity of pre-disposition. Therefore the churches and homophiles must "com-munally search" for a responsible lifestyle, says the report. This is a typical example of the tolerance-pattern: exoneration based on a naturalistic fallacy. In the "Letter" of the Congregation for the Doctrine of the Faith, exoneration is rejected without qualifi-cation as "an overly benign interpretation . . . of the homosexual condition."[130]

In 1972 the General Synod of the Netherlands Reformed Church (NHK) released a booklet of "pastoral help" written by P. J. Roscam Abbing.[131] By comparison with his earlier position this offers no new theoretical perspectives but he *is* more tolerant. It is a "sober observation" that homosexuality is an aberration, both from a statistical point of view and as measured by the standard of nature. Decisive, however, is only the theological standard "that God the Creator created man after his image as man and woman, in mutuality, with (in general) the calling to be fruitful and to multiply." The rejection of homosexuality is "based on deep theological grounds" (Romans 1). But in contrast with his earlier position, he does not stop here. Now Roscam Abbing says: As in so many other areas of life, so here too compromise cannot be avoided. A "situation of distress" exists here for the homophile person and "necessity knows no law." The homophile can, there-fore, "consider himself responsible if he lives lovingly with a member of his own sex. That remains, in a sense, a makeshift solution; it is a solution, however, for which he himself bears no responsibility" (p. 75). Accordingly, one can "understand and appreciate a homophile person who considers himself justified in not letting himself be frustrated by the duty of abstinence as he puts his talents to use in the service of God" (p. 76).

A. Dekker calls this position one of "repressive tolerance." For after the condemnation has been pronounced, "the pastorate

130. "Letter to the Bishops of the Catholic Church on the Pastoral Care of Homosexual Persons," § 3. For developments in Catholic thought in the Netherlands, see P. Luykx (1980).

131. *Liefde en Sexualiteit* (1972: 26ff., 70ff.).

is given permission to patch up the person who has just suffered a knock out blow from the side of ethics." Still it could be said: "For an official church position, it was a big step forward" (Kuitert).[132]

A second publication of the NHK, "The Pastoral Ministry to Homophiles" ("Het pastoraat aan homofielen," 1978), starts out from a different perspective, the pastorate. Here we read: "With some exceptions, every human being finds himself or herself either a homosexual or heterosexual. It is his (her) responsibility to give responsible shape to this reality" (p. 5). By starting out on the side of practice, the publication initially avoided the theological issue. It nevertheless cropped up, however, when the appeal to Scripture came up. Then it was said that Bible texts may not be torn from their context and directly applied to the homosexuals of today; the law may not overrule the gospel. How, then, the appeal to Scripture *should* function requires "further in-depth study." The result of this study appeared in a memorandum for discussion called *Confusion and Recognition* ("Verwarring en Herkenning," 1984). Precisely when it came to Bible proofs there was no consensus. Positions ranged from a pronounced yes (in the line of liberation theology) to an absolute no. From an ethical point of view, the memorandum offered no new viewpoints. What *was* new is that the theological grounding proved to be as richly diverse as the ethical viewpoints. Says the memorandum: "We have to acknowledge that though study of the texts did serve the conversation, it did not yield a conclusive answer. Finally what proved decisive was the kind of authority one attributes to the text. This showed the problem to be also a question concerning the authority of Scripture, and not only one concerning an ethical or moral order" (p. 12). This clearly demonstrates how the discussion shifts from the moral issue to a very different one, that of the authority of Scripture, which then proves to be the reason why people cannot come to a position. In any case the outcome can only be viewed as a pseudosolution.

The Gereformeerde Kerken (the GKN), despite a very prom-

132. A. Dekker (1982); H. M. Kuitert (1984).

ising beginning, did not do much better. The Report to the General Synod *Concerning People Who Are Homophile* ("Over mensen die homofiel zijn," 1972) — presented by the Synod to the churches as study material — also consists of separate contributions, but here the authors did succeed in arriving at a common approach. In the introduction it is stated that homophilia is not an aberration or abnormality. And it anticipates the conclusion: the pastor has to value the relationship as "the way to go." The homophile need not be thrust back on his personal decision. The Old Testament contributor concludes that the Old Testament condemnation is not the last word. Says the New Testament contributor: We are familiar with a bit of nature that was unknown to Paul. There is no reason, therefore, to advise a couple of male or female friends to live in abstinence. The pastoral chapter extends this line of thought toward admission of homosexuals to the offices of the church. The chapter on ethics, written by G. Th. Rothuizen, states: the church has the privilege and duty to know better than the apostle [Paul]. The reason is that we know of an unchangeable predisposition; Paul did not.

This report consistently pleads for approval of homophile relations, albeit on the basis of a naturalistic argument. Approval applies to the sexual behavior in love and fidelity of homophiles, not to homosexual behavior in general, the argument being that homophiles have no choice (p. 5, etc.). All this does not alter the fact that the pastorate is here given well-founded and clear guidelines.

Expectations raised by this study report were not borne out by what followed. Granted, in 1979 the synod pronounced itself in favor of respecting one another's right to privacy as well as one's own responsibility in the matter of giving physical expression to one's homophile orientation, but — as is evident from the accompanying explanation — that decision was meant as a pastoral-ethical guideline.[133] That is a step back (by a synod) compared to the position taken (by a study committee) in 1972. Positively the decision means more arguments can be advanced than

133. For the literal text, see § 1.

only the biblical. But negatively it means it is not permissible to derive moral approval for homosexual relations from the pronouncement, let alone for homosexual intercourse outside a stable relationship.[134] Just as in the case of NHK, so here further study of the "hermeneutical presuppositions in the use of Scripture as it concerns questions relating to homophilia" had to furnish a definite answer. This in turn resulted in the "Report on the Use of Scriptural Data in Questions Relating to Homophilia" (1982). And here also the GKN committee, far from arriving at a homogeneous position, presented four "differently shaded perspectives," a euphemism for an irreconcilable difference of opinion, because the positions run the gamut from condemnation, through tolerance, to approval.[135]

The assessment of the theological argumentation lies outside the scope of this chapter. But it is most significant that both churches ended up with the same antithetical positions, which they then describe as the pastoral versus the ethical. Whether that is the correct description of the dilemma is a question to me. By "pastoral" the churches (also) refer to what I call "ethical" (arising from the discipline called ethics); and "ethical" is for them a reference to "church ethics," i.e., religious. The real question seems to me the following: are the various ethical (the churches: "pastoral") positions based on different theological ("ethical") perspectives — regarding the authority of Scripture, biblical exegesis, etc. — or is the reverse true, i.e., are the various theological perspectives based on different ethical positions, which precede the theological? I will return to this issue at length in Chapter IV. We can

134. Accordingly, I regard as incorrect the interpretation of A. Dekker (op. cit.: 92) that with the decision of 1979/80 the churches moved from tolerance ("possibly peculiar to the pastorate") to acceptance ("an ethical matter").

135. H. M. Kuitert (1984) has pointed out the inadequacy of the positions (here discussed) of the Protestant churches. An ethic of exoneration, which fails to take the homophile and his disposition seriously, is as far as they go. A facile appeal to Scripture, which is applied without any knowledge of homophiles, is still current. And the kind of pastorate that first states that homosexuals are cripples and then urges them to run jauntily with the flock is offensive, says Kuitert.

in any case say that in the churches there has been a two-track approach: a religious, which in the churches is called the ethical, and another which I call the ethical (arising from the discipline of ethics) and the churches the pastoral. Now, basic to this situation is what proved to be the fundamental problem in this chapter. The churches are caught in the problematics entailed in the concept of nature: the tolerant ethical judgment that is based on the biological naturalness of homosexuality is at odds in their thinking with the biblical condemnation inherent in the word "unnatural." That is the same complex of problems we laid out in § 2. So in thirty years of discussion the framing of the issue has remained the same.

We are dealing with a situation of "double entry bookkeeping," one religious, the other ethical. This fact can be well-illustrated by an analysis and comparison of two theologically related works: van Gennep's "People Need People" (*Mensen hebben mensen nodig*) and "The Redemption of our Body" (*De verlossing van ons lichaam*) by Hirs and Reeling Brouwer.

F. O. van Gennep's book (1972) is the depository of what was originally the majority position of the study committee that prepared the 1972 pronouncement of the NHK synod; this position was rejected in favor of the minority position formulated by Roscam Abbing. Central in van Gennep's Barthian line of thought is the biblical idea of covenant. The most important elements in this idea are choice and fidelity. If sexuality constitutes the expression of a covenant, i.e., a relationship of love and fidelity, there is no reason not to judge homosexual friendships the same way one judges marriage relationships. The meaning of sexuality is embedded not in procreation but in covenant. Since homosexuals have not freely opted for their orientation, there is no objection against regarding their relations as a form of the covenant (pp. 102ff.). However, homosexuals may not be obligated to live in a permanent friendship-relation. After all, there is no obligation to marry either. Sexuality is also permitted outside of a covenant on account of the pleasure, relaxation, and security it affords the partners, as long as relations meet the conditions of affection (coexistence), respect for the other person's covenant, and voluntary consent. Since the Bible does not know the modern situation of non-marriage as an option (pp. 122ff.; 143ff.), it does not offer any direct guidance in this situation.

These are very liberal conclusions — even though with respect to homosexual intercourse van Gennep does not get beyond the ethics of exoneration. Now one can criticize his conclusions on theological grounds. Not everyone, after all, shares his Barthian principles. The danger is then, first, that a discussion of homosexuality will turn into a discussion of Barth.[136] But, second, van Gennep's theology is not enough for him. With regard to sexuality-within-the-covenant the biblical argument is decisive but with regard to extra-covenantal sexuality van Gennep takes his cues from a general human morality. Hirs's comment is correct:[137] van Gennep uses an uncritical ideology of equality; he considers acceptable what a bourgeois morality considers acceptable. In this way the distinction between a covenantal theology and a relational ideology disappears. In other words: van Gennep reads in the Bible what he already knew from his morality.

It is specifically this ideology of equality that calls forth the opposition of F. J. Hirs and R. Reeling Brouwer. In their book (1985) they propose to furnish what they call "a theology of gay liberation." Van Gennep, they believe, turns the covenant into a timeless idea called "marriage," of which all other covenants, such as homosexual relationships, are reflections. But thus, one of the biblical images of God's faithfulness to his people becomes the only image. Homosexuals do not wish to be measured by an idea that weds fidelity to matrimony. To be troth-ful is to be trustworthy, and "one who openly shares his body with many, could very well be trustworthy" (pp. 82ff.; p. 85). The object of the authors is to break out of the naturalistic-ethical view of homosexual behavior, and they think they can manage this with the help of purely theological arguments: theological ethics must remain theology and decisions have to be made theologically (p. 9). That can be done only if Scripture is read well (p. 20), i.e., in the manner of liberation theology (p. 45). Then one acquires room to view homosexuality as criticism of the potent

136. W. H. Velema (1979). On different theological grounds: W. Speelman (1974).
137. F. J. Hirs (1982: 183).

male-power of all ages (pp. 32, 99), and as a calling of homosexuals to witness to this inside the church (p. 71).

Here, too, the assessment of the theological argumentation has to wait for Chapter IV. But I do want to point out how remarkable it is that Barth finds in the Bible the conservative morality of his time, van Gennep the morality of his generation, and Hirs/Reeling Brouwer that of their group. But both van Gennep and Hirs/Reeling Brouwer know their indebtedness to Barth. Remarkable? The conclusion is inescapable: in the churches people operate with a double-entry system of bookkeeping: one moral, the other theological. This is not, of course, intentional, especially in the case of Barthians: no double-entry system, but law *and* gospel; dogmatics *and* ethics, etc. That is certainly a respectable stance but one of a dogmatic nature, i.e., belonging to a subdivision of the discipline of dogmatics. What one can do with it in matters of morality is another issue. Still, ethics is also a discipline, one that is distinct from that of dogmatics. And because people refuse to practice it as a distinct discipline or to acknowledge the difference, they do precisely what they do not want to do. Because the double-entry system has been officially abolished, it no longer exists (for these folks). Consequently, the question of the soundness and consistency of an ethical argument is equated with the question whether the argument is acceptable in light of the theological system adopted. In this way a given position is immunized against all criticism except that which arises from one's own theological point of view.

But is van Gennep wrong when he says that sexuality outside a covenant may be valued on account of the relaxation, pleasure, and security it affords? No, but is that a discovery he makes only after he has established that the Bible furnishes no direct instructions for that situation? Are Hirs and Reeling Brouwer wrong when they believe that a person can be trustworthy even though he shares his body with many others? No, but do they derive that insight from the Bible? Or from their moral intuition and do they get that from the Bible only after they have first read it into the Bible? In § 2 we witnessed Barth in full swing reading the book of nature. Ridderbos does it too, but according to him that is the thing to do, and according to Barth it is not. That is a theological difference.

Despite this, both follow a comparable naturalistic line of reasoning and arrive at diametrically opposite conclusions! Accordingly, in order to contest reasoning based on a naturalistic ethics, something more needs to be done than challenging "natural theology," as Hirs and Reeling Brouwer think.

With this we have completed our "ethical" (arising from the discipline of ethics) analysis. What conclusions can now be drawn from the ecclesiastical discussions of homosexuality? First, that the attempt at theological legitimation of the tolerant position adopted within Protestant churches blocks one's view of the incorrect (because naturalistic) line of reasoning on which the tolerance is based. Accordingly, it does not illuminate but rather obscures it, the reason being that, in fact, theological argument simply cannot take the place of an ethical argument. Second, that the churches' exclusive focus on a biblical grounding of moral positions is more a hindrance than a help because a tangle of theological issues then crowd into the picture as well. A development of this point must wait till the fourth chapter. There, for that matter, we will arrive at the same conclusion, but then from a theological rather than an ethical perspective.

E. The positions of churches in other countries

In this section we will examine differences from and similarities to the Dutch discussion in churches elsewhere. I will refer to the development of these positions only in passing and discuss some samplings of a number of — especially recent — church documents from England, Germany, North America, and of documents issued by a number of supra-national church organizations.

1. England

Discussion of homosexuality began in the churches with a view to the law reform that followed the acceptance of the Wolfenden

Report (1957; cf. § 4.4). According to this report it is not the task of the law "to enforce morality."[138] In this period hardly any theological reflection occurred, the exception being the work of D. S. Bailey (1955).[139] In 1967 the Anglican church appointed a study commission that reported in 1970. The report embraces two opposing positions. According to the one, homosexual praxis is sin; according to the other, a homosexual relationship, though "not as fully human" as a heterosexual marriage, may be the best solution for a person with "an exclusive and fixed homosexual disposition."[140] In 1974 a "working party" was appointed to study the theological, social, and pastoral aspects of homosexuality. The resulting report, *Homosexual Relationships* (1978), presented a unanimous position that was, however, amended by the body that commissioned it, the Board of Social Responsibility. The report states that

> there are circumstances in which individuals may justifiably choose to enter in a homosexual relationship with the hope of enjoying a companionship and physical expression of sexual love similar to that which is to be found in marriage.[141]

Still, marriage constitutes the Christian norm. Besides, in the homosexual relation biological complementarity is lacking. A stable relationship may be the best option for a given person because he has no choice with regard to his sexual orientation. So says the report. It encountered sharp criticism of the chapter on biblical proofs and the chapter on ethics and was given the status of "material for discussion" (1981).[142] Thus the report refrains from giving approval but opts for what I earlier called the pastoral approach. This also comes to expression in the stipulation that the option of a homosexual relation is not permissible for priests. They need to adhere to the Christian norm. This is still the official

138. See § D above and at length J. Weeks (1981a: 239ff., 260ff.).
139. "Towards a Quaker view of sex": in E. Batchelor (1980: 135–38).
140. P. Coleman (1989: 215ff.).
141. *Homosexual Relationships* (1979), the Gloucester Report: § 168.
142. P. Coleman (1980: 269, 271; 1989: 90, 153).

position of the Anglican church. Further polarization occurred at the synod meeting of 1987 when a motion opposing all homosexual intercourse was adopted.[143] The Church of England is, therefore, seriously divided.

How the church leadership should deal with it is the issue addressed in the Osborne Report, a confidential report to the bishops published only in the form of an extract. This report makes no (new) prescriptive pronouncements on homosexuality but takes stock of the positions current in the church, analyzes them, and stresses especially the points of agreement. I will discuss this material at somewhat greater length because it seems representative of the different positions held in the Church of England and makes possible a good comparison with the situation in the Netherlands.

In keeping with the Anglican tradition, Scripture and tradition on the one hand and contemporary experience on the other are viewed as the two poles of Christian thought. In the first chapter ("On Scripture and Tradition") the report sees the positions diverge in the exposition of *phusis* (nature) in Romans 1. The question is: does Paul here condemn all homosexual intercourse as contrary to "the natural order of God's creation" or does he have in mind only homosexual intercourse between people who are otherwise heterosexuals (§§ 10ff.)? However, the diverging opinions agree in that, for them, exegesis alone cannot settle the issue. The exegesis has to be interpreted in the framework of the theological themes of "sin, creation, and redemption" (§ 17). That cannot be done without relating contemporary experience to the biblical witness. The church has not done this adequately: "a new formulation of the tradition is necessary" (§ 31). The chapter ends with a summary, without comment, of the different positions that the interpretation of Scripture and tradition in the Anglican church has produced (§ 33):

(1) The full preservation of the tradition: a "no" to all homosexual intercourse. (2) The preservation of the tradition but with a recognition of the necessity of pastoral care for homosexuals.

143. P. Coleman (1989: 164ff.).

79

(3) The accommodation of the tradition in the light of present-day scientific knowledge of homosexuality. (4) The acceptance of homosexual relations characterized by love and fidelity; a correction of the tradition.

The second chapter treats contemporary experience. It refers to the big changes in lifestyles, to the role of the women's movement (not to the gay liberation movement!), to the power structures in society that also affect the church. Then comes a lengthy address to the issue of the aetiology of homosexuality. The focus on methods of treatment is striking.[144] According to the authors it has not yet been sufficiently determined whether homosexuality is a (changeable) developmental disorder or an unalterable orientation. It is suggested that the position one adopts with regard to the causation of homosexuality has to be a factor in determining one's moral position: "(. . .) the ethical questions which arise out of these models vary from one to the other. If we are faced with an unchangeable condition the questions are bound to look different than if this is not the case" (§ 69).

The issue of personal responsibility is central here. The chapter is concluded with a description, by way of brief biographies, of the choices homosexuals themselves have come to: a celibate lifestyle, a stable relationship, a communal lifestyle. No evaluation is offered.

The third chapter is the theological, having as its theme: God as Creator, Redeemer, and Sanctifier, the God of grace in a fallen world. The theme of creation is relevant to the question whether the homosexual "nature" is part of the diversity of the good creation or a sign of nature as distorted by sin. Many homosexuals recognize themselves in the first interpretation. To this the authors object that the natural in the sense of the human experience of the good does not simply coincide with the natural order God intended for creation. Those who are too quick to appeal to the creation order are told that in Scripture itself the meaning of "natural" varies. However, though "it is tempting to assume that to describe something as 'natural' or

144. The authority here is the psychologist E. Moberly (see Moberly 1983/88). For her theory, see Chapter II § 3.

'unnatural' is sufficient to foreclose the debate" (§ 115), Christians cannot stop with what they view as natural. The Christian faith speaks of the necessity of redemption for all that is natural. In a fallen world God is Redeemer by his gracious love, and Sanctifier in a dynamic process that transforms us into life-in-union with Christ. Homosexuals also experience this growth in Christ, but in different ways: one in the form of healing, another as acceptance of his/her feelings, a third as happiness in a homosexual relationship. The report emphatically points out that each person's choices, including his/her moral principles, are imbedded in the reality of sin. This is also true of the traditional, often homophobic and discriminating, judgment of the church regarding homosexuality. Consequently, one may not easily judge or condemn — judgment belongs to God. One has to ask to what extent it concerns Christians what others do, and one has to realize that such differences of opinion were also present in the early church (e.g., in Rom. 14). "The Church is called on to decide . . . whether the issue of homosexuality is one on which conscientious difference of opinion may be held" (§ 137) and "only a broad understanding of human sin and of the fallenness of the world and a wider vision of the grace of God in creation and re-demption can rescue us from such misconceptions," like the dispro-portionate attention given in the past to sexual morality (§ 143).

The subject of the fourth chapter ("Human Sexuality") is actually the chapter on ethics. The Christian faith sees sexuality as having three purposes: enjoyment, mutuality, and creativity, this last category encompassing both the relational and the procreative aspect. On this there is no difference of opinion among Christians. Except for the procreative aspect, homosexual relations can meet those goals. However, in sexual matters also one has to take account of the "corrupting effect" of sin: "genital relationships thus have a meaning over and above the intention of the couple, however casual they may be about them" (§ 160). This meaning cannot simply be read from what we ourselves experience as enjoyment or creativity. The Christian tradition recognizes two modes of expression as legitimate: marriage and celibacy. Also it has always linked the relational aspect to the procreative. This, however, is not all there is to say about homosexual relations for

(1) the church has to respond to the culture in which it lives, and (2) all people are "embodied persons" and maintain relations with others as sexual beings, and (3) it is not good, according to Genesis 2, for a human being to be alone. On these points Christians agree (§ 171ff.). They differ in the assessment of homosexual relations. The report sees the discussion on this subject move between two extremes. One line of thought assumes that homosexuality is a part of the good creation and regards an involuntary homosexual orientation as God's creation gift. In the context of a personalistic (relational) ethics, marriage and celibacy are no longer viewed as the only acceptable expression of sexuality (§ 176ff.; § 185). The other line of thought is that the homosexual condition is part of the disturbance caused by sin. The creation stories not only tell of psychological complementarity but also view the man-woman differentiation as essential. Homosexual intercourse constitutes a denial of this complementarity. Therefore a relational ethics is inadequate as a Christian sexual ethics (§ 180ff.).

The chapter ends with a summary of the ethical positions found in the Anglican church: (a) affirmation of the tradition: homosexual intercourse is always wrong; it is a sign of fallen human nature. However, homophobia and discrimination need to be avoided; (b) rejection of the tradition: a homosexual relationship is in accord with the will of God by the same standards as the heterosexual; (c) a series of intermediate positions: a homosexual orientation as such is not culpable but homosexual intercourse is "objectively" sinful. However, in a sinful world acceptance of a homosexual relationship may be the best solution (§ 190).

The report abstains from making a judgment of its own and observes that the church still has a long road ahead of it (§§ 191, 352).

The remaining chapters treat a large number of related issues (upbringing[145] and the ordination of homosexual priests[146]) along the

145. In England the social climate is less tolerant than in the Netherlands. Clause 28 of the Local Government Act reads: "A local authority shall not promote the teaching in any maintained school of the acceptability of homosexuality as a pretended family relationship."

146. Positions on this show the same variety as the ethical. Here, too, the report refrains from making a judgment.

lines of the chapters discussed here. In the conclusion, under the heading of "the forming of a theological framework," the bishops — the majority of whom assume a conservative attitude to the tradition — are told: "to agree on method would be a major step forward" (§ 309). Accordingly, the significance of this report lies in its methodology: the clarification of the patterns of argumentation employed.

It is a question whether in this regard the report goes far enough. A new feature is that it seems to view the diversity of insights as something to be accepted in the church rather than a temporary phase in the discussion. I question whether this diversity has not been accepted too uncritically.

First let me make a few remarks in general. By comparison with the Dutch situation it is striking that the more radical positions such as those of gay liberation theology[147] are absent from the report. This is all the more remarkable because in the British churches there is an active Christian homosexual movement.[148] For the rest we recognize as familiar the positions sketched in the report: the traditional condemnation (§ 190a), the relational ethics (§ 190b), the ethics of exoneration (§§ 190b, c), and the pastoral approach (§ 190c). It is remarkable, in the second place, that the section on aetiology, while it relies heavily on the medical model of homosexuality, pays no attention to modern sociological insights (on this, see the next chapter). This is significant, as I will demonstrate below.

The report presents the various positions relating to exegesis and those concerning ethics in different chapters, arguing that between them falls the evaluation of contemporary experience, specifically the scientific data on homosexuality, and the theological discussion, specifically the themes sin, creation, and redemption. The report expects greater unanimity as greater clarity is achieved in these areas. Hence it has high hopes for a continuing *theological* discussion. The report is not clear, however, about the manner in which it should be conducted. With reference to the relationship between Scripture and

147. M. Macourt, *Toward a Theology of Gay Liberation* (1977).
148. The Lesbian and Gay Christian Movement. For the Dutch situation, see specif. Van Gennep, Hirs/Reeling Brouwer and "Verwarring en Herkenning."

tradition it says: "We reject both a simple moving from the text to the moral answers and an uncritical acceptance of the experience." Then how does one proceed? "The difficulty of the task in this particular issue is the apparent distance between the poles" (§ 18), the reason why at this point the church cannot make definitive pronouncements (§ 19). So a report that stresses the importance of method defaults at the very point of method! This fact alone makes one doubt the feasibility of the course recommended: continuing theological discussion. But while in this chapter I will not yet evaluate the theological discussion, I can say a little more about the method. The authors of the report in fact take as their starting point the normative question: what weight should Christians give to the positions of Scripture and tradition in the determination of their ethical viewpoint? On the idea that this has to occur by way of theological discussion while also weighing the factor of contemporary experience their minds are made up; the only question is how. But we can also raise the *empirical* or analytic question: in reality how determinative are the theological positions (based on Scripture and tradition) for the ethical? Since the report presents the two types, the exegetical and the ethical, in separate chapters, it is not possible for us to explore the way the connection was actually made in the church discussions. Still, something of it can be tracked down.

In all the chapters we have discussed, the concept of "nature" plays a decisive role. Each time the positions diverge at the point of the interpretation of this concept. In Chapter I it occurs in the context of the question whether Paul is referring to the normative order of creation or to normal — universally familiar — sexual intercourse. The reference is either to "natural" in the religious sense or to "natural" in the empirical sense. In Chapter II, it occurs in the context of the question whether homosexuality (in a biological sense) is "natural" or pathological. Accordingly, this focus on "nature" explains the amount of space the report devotes to the biological-medical view of homosexuality at the expense of the sociological. In Chapter III, it occurs in the context of the problem of the relativity of nature (in all senses) and grace. In Chapter IV, in the context of the question whether the homosexual orientation is a gift of creation and, therefore, "natural" (i.e., moral) and hence a good or — on account of its disregard for the man-woman polarity — a sign of sin and, therefore, unnatural, i.e., evil.

From this perspective we may assume that the confusion of nature-concepts, as I have repeatedly laid it out, also plays a role in this report. The report does not explicitly discuss the concept of nature. Implicitly, however, this confusion can be shown to be present because we can reconstruct its reasoning as follows: "to take account of experience means that concerning homosexual relations more arguments can be advanced than only those furnished by Scripture and tradition. These are the arguments arising from medical-biological science. The self-experience of homosexuality illustrates these data. Is the condition of homosexuality biologically natural? If so, then there is reason to amend the traditional condemnation. After all, Paul does not know of this orientation. However, we are not yet completely sure whether homosexuality is biologically natural or not."

So for the reconstruction of the argument. Again, it is a naturalistic line of reasoning that plays a role alongside of and in the theological arguments of the report. So here, too, we run into "double entry" bookkeeping (§ 4.5). It is this naturalistic reasoning — note the ethic of exoneration that comes with it — that undoubtedly shaped the account of the scientific data with its accent on disease and healing. It is not, then, an objective statement of facts but one that rests on an antecedent, more specifically a naturalistic, ethical premise.

2. Germany

Up until the decade of the sixties, Christian ethics paid little attention to the problems of homosexuals. The discussion began in the fifties, as it did in England, with the debate on penal reform (§ 175).[149] Handbooks of ethics treated sexuality in the context of

---

149. K. Bochmühl (1965; 28ff.). The infamous § 175 is still officially on the books, though the German government has declared its intent to abolish it. See the periodical "Homosexuelle und Kirche" (1988).

marriage.[150] As in the Netherlands, so here tolerance had its origin in the pastorate. Already at an early stage the Swiss psychiatrist Th. Bovet pleaded for acceptance of homosexual relationships (on the ground of an unchangeable disposition).[151] Another example is the theologian van Oyen.[152] There were also counter-reactions.[153] Sometime later homosexuality appeared as a topic in books on ethics. We have already discussed the most important work, that of Thielicke and Trillhaas (§ D.3).

One of the earliest standpoints to arise from the churches is that of the Evangelische Kirche in Rheinland (1970).[154] In retrospect it also turns out to have been one of the most tolerant. Homosexuality is defined as an "inculpable disposition," "relatively incorrigible," that is neither perversion nor sickness. Ideas that homosexual intercourse as such is wrong, or a disturbance of the creation order, or a sign of the fallen world are rejected. It is sinful only when practiced in an immoral manner. It cannot be inferred from the biblical witness that same-sex relations are fundamentally wrong. The dilemma "marriage or celibacy" is false. Citing Bovet, the report pleads for the acceptance of homosexual relations.

The "Research Paper on Questions of Sexual Ethics" (*Denkschrift zu Fragen der Sexualethik*) issued by the Evangelische Kirche Deutschlands (1971),[155] on the other hand, in an argumentation reminiscent of Barth's, regards marriage as the sole legitimate place for sexuality. Consequently, a homosexual orientation is a "developmental disorder," not culpable but sick. Granted, homosexuals do have the capacity to love. For that reason, a relationship may sometimes be the best solution. At this point the report is in agreement with Thielicke.[156]

150. H. Bolewski (1966: 87).
151. Th. Bovet (1959), among others.
152. H. van Oyen (1964).
153. E.g., W. Eichrodt (1963).
154. "Kirche und Sexualstrafrecht" in: G. Roosenboom et al. (1970).
155. "Denkschrift zu Fragen der Sexualethik" in *Tutzinger Studien* 2 (1977: 56–54).
156. Cf. S. Keil, in *Evangelische Akademie Iserlohn* (Hrgb.) (1966: 76).

The position of the VELKD (1980)[157] — a cooperative body of a number of Evangelische Kirchen in Northwest Germany — broadly agrees with this. It regards the homosexual as a victim of his orientation. Much life potential is denied him (p. 69) even when he is capable of a lasting relationship because the "experiential scope" of the sexual relationship between a man and a woman is much greater (p. 64). This (unexplained pre-) judgment — the reference is to reproduction — is grounded in a theology of creation ordinances. Homosexuality is a disturbance of the creation order and a homosexual relationship "falls short of the creation mandate" (p. 66). To the extent that he is able, a homosexual must give responsible shape to his life. That may mean looking for help. Sometimes a stable relationship may be the best solution. Here the report agrees with Thielicke: the pastoral approach as ethical solution.

In the churches of what used to be East Germany, the discussion did not start until the eighties. It came about especially as a result of pressure from homosexuals themselves who questioned the traditional pastoral approach and asked for public recognition in the church.[158] Soon an impasse developed between those who favored a disease model of homosexuality — basing themselves on the work of the Dutch therapist van den Aardweg — and those who believed that homosexuality "neither calls for therapy nor is it capable of therapy."[159] Theologically these two positions correspond, respectively, with that which appeals to marriage as the creation order and that which views homosexuality as a creation gift.

The only East German synod to have studied the homosexual problem up until now is that of Sachsen (1984).[160] The brief report submitted to the synod states that, while in the Bible homosexual intercourse is condemned, we must listen to the Bible in a changed

157. In: H. Kentler (Hrgb.) (1983: 62–79).
158. See "Homosexuelle in der Kirche?" (1985: 4ff.).
159. M. Punge, in: A. Grau (Hrgb.) (1987). On the theories of van de Aardweg, see Chapter II § C.
160. "Vorlage der Kirchenleitung: Stellungnahme zur Frage der Homosexualität" (unpubl.).

situation. While the tolerant social climate of today is not a reason to change the traditional assessment, modern scientific insights *are*. The issue is this: is homosexuality a disease or a changeable condition? Science makes clear that there are people who cannot voluntarily change their homosexual orientation and enter a heterosexual relationship. For that reason the biblical condemnation cannot be applied to them. The report calls for dialogue "to reflect on an ethically responsible life style for such people."

In recent years the issue has been focused on how openly ministers and other office-bearers in the church should be allowed to conduct a homosexual lifestyle. In the church of Hannover, to mention one, this issue has led to conflict.[161] H. Hirschler, bishop of the church of Hannover, speaking as a private person, explains the prohibition by the church leadership of homosexual relations in the case of pastors in terms of the modeling function of pastors. Recognition would imply ethical legitimation and that would be contrary to a Christian-based ethic, he says. Granted, homosexuals must, as much as possible, be recognized "as a minority having a special status," but this status, says he, can only be viewed — and this is not discrimination — as a "lack," a "limited life potential." In this perspective the homosexual relationship is "the lesser evil" by comparison with "casual sexual contacts." Homosexual groups in the churches should accept this position, as well as the incomprehension displayed in the churches toward homosexuality. When they propagate another point of view — as they did at a *Kirchentag* in Düsseldorf in 1985 — "we as church leaders are not particularly enchanted with the existence of groups called 'Homosexuals and the Church.'"[162] Homosexuals and their cohorts, writes Hirschler (pp. 6, 29), are mistaken when they take the position that the only thing that counts ethically is the love-command regardless of the form: hetero-, homo-, or bisexual. The argument they have for this is that, according to science, man is by nature bisexual and this bisexual nature, as a result

161. For a critical response, cf. H. Kensler, op. cit.
162. H. Hirschler (1985: 39/40).

of certain developments, goes either in one direction or another or in both directions at once. Adherents of this position accuse the church of "sexism," "biologism," and "pharisaism" (p. 19).

So the discussion is polarized and then the chances of arriving at a rational and relevant judgment are zero. One of the reasons is that a number of arguments are confused.

First, it is interesting to see with what arguments Hirschler undergirds the positions. They clearly illustrate my thesis that both the disapproving and the approving arguments stem from the same mistaken reasoning, i.e., that of the naturalistic fallacy. In short: the question "sickness or not?" — therefore that of "natural" in the empirical sense — is confused with that of "sin or not?" — hence with that of "natural" in the religious/moral sense. To Hirschler and his associates homosexuality is a "lack," etc.; or (biologically) unnatural and therefore wrong.[163] To his opponents homosexuality is (biologically) natural and therefore good. The charge of biologism — if its object is a naturalistic line of reasoning — strikes at both sides in the debate.

Second, and connected with the preceding, is the fact that though Hirschler and all the German reports recognize the problems of homosexuals in church and society, they are invariably attributed to their "non-normalcy" and "special status." Homosexuals are saddled with the role of victim (also the seduction-theory is regularly referred to). The assumption, therefore, is that the causes of the problems of homosexuals are identical with the causes of homosexuality. The idea that the attitude of society could be a more important cause is not even considered. Thus homosexuality is viewed as a problem of individuals, and the task of the church is defined accordingly: it is a pastorate to homosexuals.

Third, there is the theological assessment. How decisive are the exegetical and the theological-ethical arguments? It is interesting to compare the report submitted to the synod of Hannover

---

163. Hirschler (op. cit.: 33): "Surely it is not good when a person is only focused on his own sex and for him the transmission of life does not come into the picture. Or is it wrong for me to think that way?" Accordingly, the "transmission of life" and "reproduction" are equated.

(1983)[164] and that of Westphalia (1989).[165] Both reports display a phenomenon we also encounter in other countries: no unanimity exists; there is a majority and a minority position. I will first present a summary.

In the Hannover report both sides seek "a biblically-based ethical assessment of homosexuality." They agree that in the Bible homosexual intercourse is condemned but also say that the Bible's authors were unfamiliar with the homosexual disposition and with stable homosexual relationships. However, the texts concerning homosexual relations alone are not sufficient for forming a theological-ethical judgment. For that purpose the scientific data also have to be weighed, say both sides. Both sides also agree on the core of their Christian ethics: i.e. — in typically Lutheran fashion — it is justification in Christ by faith alone that gives freedom. For a Christian this freedom is, therefore, always freedom within limits. With regard to sexual freedom the biblical witness clearly excludes the possibility of understanding homosexuality as a creational variant and thus as a self-evident form of sexuality. But is a homosexual relationship always wrong?

At this juncture the two sides separate. One says that according to science certain forms of homosexuality cannot be treated. There is no possibility of a heterosexual partnership for those so fated. Celibacy is the best solution. But that can only be realized as a voluntary choice. Many, "because of the vitality of their sex drive," are unable to take this course. A lasting, stable relationship is then a better solution than lifelong inner conflict and a troubled conscience. Not as an alternative to marriage but because, "on account of their genetic formation, marriage is not an option" (p. 7). We here recognize Trillhaas's position: the pragmatic solution. This line of thought is then extended to the position on homosexual church workers: to spare the church conflict and division, they

164. *Aktenstücke der 19. Landessynode no. 179. Homosexualität kirchlicher Mitarbeiter.*

165. *Verhandlungen der 11. Westfälischen Landessynode 1989, Bericht der Arbeitsgruppe an der Kirche, "Zur Situation homosexueller Menschen in Kirche und Gesellschaft."*

must not go public with their homosexual relationship. This position respects their moral choice and recognizes a person's right to a private life, but open discussion of this matter in the church is unacceptable (p. 9).

The other side upholds the traditional condemnation of homosexual relations. Granted, in light of an autonomous ideal of self-realization abstinence from sexual intercourse is considered an "unfair hardship and a missing out on realizing one's identity," but "according to a Christian understanding of life and liberty, this recommendation embodies a completely reasonable expectation" (p. 15). One who is not able to forgo homosexual praxis cannot, therefore, hold an office in the church. It is this last position the church leadership (Hirschler) adopts.[166]

Again we have an illustration here of the large role the concept of "nature" plays. The essence of the unanimous theological judgment is that homosexuality is not a variant of a good creation and therefore not "natural" in a religious sense. But the ethical stance finally arrived at has still another ground, viz., a value judgment concerning the homosexual disposition, argued in the same incorrect manner just described in connection with the first point.

By contrast with the Hannover report, the Westphalian report does arrive at unanimous recommendations. The difference here is located on another level, that of the exegesis. According to the first position, exegesis has no more arrived at unambiguous conclusions than science. Does the Old Testament prohibition apply to all people? Is marriage, even if it lies outside a person's potential, the only legitimate place for the expression of one's sexuality? Does not Paul expressly say in Romans that all are without excuse? Arguing that judgment belongs only to God and that sexuality is a part of everyone's total humanity, the majority of the reporters want to leave the decision to the individual — a position reminiscent of that of the GKN in 1979. The other position agrees with that of the exegetical-theological part of the Hannover report. In the Bible homosexuality is condemned as being contrary to the

166. H. Hirschler, op. cit.

creation. Accordingly, Christians are "basically" unable to approve of homosexual praxis because outside of marriage and celibacy there is no way to God. However, in the cautiously worded common part about the homosexual in the church, this last viewpoint is not explicitly repeated. Here, reflecting obvious unanimity, the report states that sexuality belongs to our created nature. There has to be room in the church for homosexuals and both homosexuals and heterosexuals must again think through what it means that sexuality pervades the whole of human life. The issue is how to give responsible form and expression to human sexuality and that may imply forgoing a sexual partnership. This viewpoint allows for a variety of options. The position of the Westphalian report is, therefore, most reminiscent of that of the NHK (1972), which speaks for a "makeshift" solution (§ 4.1).

As I summarize the data concerning the role of biblical and theological arguments in the German discussion, I come to two conclusions, both of which emerged also in the Dutch situation. First, in the search for a biblically based ethical judgment, not only biblical-theological but also extrabiblical arguments play a role. Second, we find that agreement or disagreement in the exegetical position adopted does not simply lead respectively to a like or an unlike ethical position. The implications of this fact for the usefulness of theological arguments, in this case for the usefulness of biblically derived arguments in the discussion of homosexuality, is a subject I will save for the fourth chapter.

By comparison with the Dutch discussion, it is striking that in most church reports the more liberal positions are not mentioned. The reports reflect a conservative mentality. One does not get the impression that homosexuals themselves are partners in the discussion. Sometimes individual theologians take positions that go much further.[167]

167. E.g., H. G. Wiedemann (1982, 1983a); D. Sölle/S. A. Cloyes (1984).

3. The United States

Church life in the United States, as we know, is enormously diverse. Of the more than 1,200 religious groupings, the Catholic church has by far the largest membership, followed by the Baptists, Pentecostals, Methodists, Lutherans, Mormons, Presbyterians, and Episcopalians — to mention only the largest church families. To obtain a somewhat trustworthy overview of attitudes toward homosexuality would require extensive research. Besides this, there are distinct differences in the social climate; some states still have rigorous laws against homosexual intercourse on the books.[168] Included in the overall picture is a fanatic anti-gay movement (remember the "moral majority," Anita Bryant) as well as the phenomenon of churches whose membership is primarily gay or lesbian (The Metropolitan Community Churches). Loosely connected with a number of denominations are lesbian and gay organizations, such as *Dignity* for the Catholics, *Integrity* for Episcopalians, *Affirm* for Methodists, and *Aware* for the Christian Reformed.

Up until the decade of the seventies, the churches as much as possible remained silent on the subject.[169] Among the first to plead for the acceptance of homosexual relations toward the late sixties were the Methodist pastor H. Kimball-Jones and the Episcopalian process-theologian N. Pittenger.[170]

The literature I am familiar with contains pronouncements issued by the Mormons[171] (disapproving); the Lutheran Church of America (1970)[172] (disapproving but not a matter for the judge); the United Church of Christ (1977; accepts homosexual relations;

168. P. Coleman (1980: 192ff.); N. Leiser (1979); D. F. Greenberg (1988: 455ff.).

169. According to S. Hiltner (1980). On the sociological backgrounds of religious opposition to acceptance of gay rights, see D. F. Greenberg (1988: 467ff.).

170. H. Kimball-Jones (1967), N. Pittenger (see in M. Macourt 1977). See P. Coleman (1980: 250ff.; 1989: 136ff.).

171. W. Müller (1986: 60).

172. W. Müller (1986: 88); S. Hiltner (1980: 224).

93

for more information see below);[173] the United Presbyterian Church[174] (1978; homosexual relations not acceptable in the case of clergy); the Episcopalian church[175] (comparable to the Church of England; for more information, see below). The National Association of Evangelicals condemns homosexuality on biblical grounds; God approves of the union only of man and woman. It opposes the idea of an inborn and unchanging orientation. Homosexuality is a departure from the creation plan, but in the name of Christ there is hope of forgiveness and healing. Laws establishing gay rights are viewed as an unwarranted legitimation of homosexuality.[176] Also the Pentecostal Fellowship of North America deems homosexual practice unacceptable for Christians.[177]

The same is true for the Christian Reformed Church in its synodical report of 1973 — the official stand of this church to this day.[178] In this report the concept of "disorder" plays a crucial role. The report first discusses the medical-biological data and concludes that homosexuality "often is a condition which is rooted deeply in biological and psychological aberations that create a disorder for which the individual can be held only partly responsible, if at all" (p. 623).

In the exegetical section one conclusion is that the man-woman differentiation is an essential part of the created order. Therefore homosexuality must be viewed as a "disordered condition," the consequence of sin (pp. 615–16). According to Paul, homosexual relations are contrary to nature. In so speaking he is not referring to a "natural law" theory but to "a distorted use of the increated sex-differentiation" (p. 623).

173. R. Scroggs (1983: 2). In 1983 the United Church of Christ declared that homosexuality is "not a moral issue" (Source: *Equal Time,* May 22, 1990).

174. R. Scroggs (1983: 3); S. Hiltner (1980: 225); W. Müller (1986: 93, 96, 105).

175. W. Müller (1986: 115, 116); P. Coleman (1989: 178ff.).

176. Resolutions adopted in 1985, National Office.

177. "This has been the position from the origin of our church, and I fully anticipate that it will continue to be so," personal letter of M. J. MacKnight, President of the Pentecostal Fellowship.

178. Acts of Synod 1973. Report 42: 609-633.

In the theological-ethical part the question is considered in how far the biblical condemnation is applicable in the light of modern knowledge of homosexuality; "what we have learned of creation itself through modern science" (p. 622). Now, homosexuality (in the sense of condition) must be considered "a disorder, a distortion of the sex differentiation implanted in the human race." The homosexual "bears the disorder of our fallen world in his person" (p. 623). Homosexuality is not just an "accidental variation," like left-handedness. "Scripture clearly teaches that man was originally created 'male' and 'female.'"

> The fact that a male homosexual can only fully experience his maleness in relation to another male . . . is therefore a reversal of the created order. (p. 624)

When this assessment of homosexuality is then placed in the broad framework of the biblical view of sexuality, there proves to be room only for marriage and celibacy. The New Testament repeatedly refers to the creation order of Genesis. Accordingly, as "condition," homosexuality is a "disorder of human nature and more than a mere variant" (p. 624). Homosexuals, therefore, ought to seek help and to recognize that their "sexuality is subordinate to their obligation to live in whole-hearted surrender to Christ" (p. 632).

The reasoning of this report, which bears some resemblance to that of Brillenburg Wurth and Douma (§ A), leaves a somewhat confused impression. Again, the reason for this is that the three meanings of "contrary to nature" or, as the report has it, "distortion" are confused. It also confuses the normal with the normative. The premise is that we know from Scripture what is "unnatural" (i.e., not belonging to the creation order). This is how Paul views homosexual relations, says the report, expressly adding that the reference is not to "natural law," that is to the moral meaning. So the reference is to the religious sense. The next step in the report is to ask whether the judgment applies to homosexuality in the forms in which we know it today. The answer is that science, from which we also learn about creation, makes clear that homosexuality (as condition) is a "distortion." Hence: distortion, sickness. Now the reference is to the empirical meaning (I am not now commenting on the correctness of the conclusion). Sickness or sin? Both! It brings to mind Douma's description: "creaturely degeneracy" (cf. my criticism of this point in § B of this chapter). That is the first "knot."

This knot is drawn tighter when in the theological-ethical part homosexual relations are condemned by saying that they are not a variant of nature (like left-handedness) but a "distortion" of the *normative* order of creation and therefore wrong. Now the reference is to "unnatural" in the moral sense. Of course, it is not Scripture that has made clear to us that left-handedness is a variant, but science. We therefore have to read the report to mean that science — which also teaches us about the creation — demonstrates that homosexuality is not a natural variant but a distortion. From this, however, it certainly does not follow that homosexuality is morally wrong. Does the normative order of creation coincide with the normal? The report states that homosexual intercourse is a reversal of the creation order and therefore wrong: a male homosexual can only fully experience his 'maleness' in relation to another male (p. 624). But that is simply a psychological version of the "naturalistic" (derived from anatomy) argument we found in Barth: it is not good because it does not fit. The report thus creates an impression that modern science supplements and confirms Paul's moral judgment; but in reality its logic is the reverse: ethical arguments are derived from biology and via a naturalistic fallacy read into Scripture as normative creation ordinance. There need be no objection to "reading something into" Scripture (see Chapter IV) but it is something other than "inferring from," which is the premise of the report.

The Episcopal Church USA (Anglican) has repeatedly issued pronouncements on homosexuality. Its earliest position is liberal (1976): for homosexual relations the same norms apply as for heterosexual relations. The position of 1979 is more restrictive: no ordination to the priesthood for practicing homosexuals. In 1989 the General Convention called for open discussion and continuing study. The result is the report of the Commission of Human

Affairs of the Episcopal Church USA (1991).[179] At the very outset
it refers to the importance of the question of the causes of homosexuality: ". . . responsible ethical decision making requires
that we consider evidence that bears on intentionality" (p. 1).

Now then, says the report, it has become clear that homosexuality is not a voluntary, self-conscious choice and that this orientation
is hard to change. Thus it opens the door to the ethics of exoneration.
The theological section that follows mentions as sources for possible
ethical guidelines: Scripture, tradition, and reason. The report states
that, while it is true that the authors of Scripture condemned homosexual relations, they did not know the homosexual orientation.
At stake in Scripture, in imitation of Jesus, is self-giving love. As to
the implications of these guidelines in the light of the biblical teaching
concerning marriage, procreation, and the various functions of sexuality, only further study can bring them out.

In its recommendations the Commission did not reach a
homogeneous position. It agrees that marriage is the Christian
norm but that the homosexual orientation as such is not culpable.
Further, "it is not good that man should be alone." These considerations cause a majority to support the decision to

> fully support marriages of men and women. . . , without withhold-
> ing support and blessing from persons of the same sex who are in
> faithful, committed relationships. . . .

It is recommended that liturgical forms be developed for
such unions. Further, there is no objection to ordaining homosexuals as officebearers: the church has unwittingly(!) done this with
men for centuries and of late also with women. The recognition
of homosexual priests puts an end to hypocrisy, according to this
realistic argument.

A minority has strong objections to these recommendations:
only a heterosexual marriage is in accordance with the will of God.

179. The Episcopal Church dealt with homosexuality in 1976, 1978,
and 1989 (P. Coleman, 1989; 178–80). For this most recent report I used an
excerpt provided by Bishop G. N. Hunt, Rhode Island, chairman of the
commission.

In brief: this is a (partly) liberal and pragmatic report, which does not, however, get past the ethics of exoneration; with respect to a homosexual relationship it leaves the decision to the individual and with regard to the ordination of priests, to the different dioceses (p. 7).[180] Whether it really helps the homosexual thus remains to be seen, the more so since it shows the same dividedness we have found elsewhere and offers no other solutions than continuing study: "This commission believes that our Church is engaged in a long and ongoing process on the issues" (p. 7). This belief is undoubtedly correct, considering the resolution that was adopted:

> General Convention affirms that the teaching of the Episcopal Church is that physical sexual expression is appropriate only within the lifelong, monogamous "union of husband and wife" . . . and That this church continue to work to reconcile the discontinuity between this teaching and the experience of many members of this body; and That this General Convention confesses our failure to lead and to resolve this discontinuity . . . and That this General Convention commissions the bishops and members of each Diocesan Deputation to initiate a means for all congregations in their jurisdiction to enter into dialogue and deepen their understanding of these complex issues; and That this General Convention directs the House of Bishops to prepare a Pastoral Teaching prior to the 71st General Convention using the learnings from the Diocesan and Provincial processes and calling upon such insight as is necessary from theologians, theological ethicists, social scientists, and gay and lesbian persons. . . ."

The most radical report that has come to my attention, and was moreover written from a clearly different perspective on homosexuality, originated in the Presbyterian Church (U.S.A.).[181] It is much more broadly based than most of the others because it has "Human Sexuality" as its subject, and homosexuality here only

180. The majority position comes down to "neither allow, nor disallow, but could allow," says Hunt in an oral explanation.
181. Keeping Body and Soul Together: Sexuality, Spirituality, and Social Justice (1991).

constitutes a small, though important, subdivision. In view of this fact I will only discuss the relevant parts of the report.

It seeks to speak "a fresh word" to the church in a time of change in family relations and of crisis and conflict in society (lines 112ff.). In its diagnosis of the crisis, the report immediately points to the cause: "the unjust patriarchal structure built on dehumanizing assumptions, roles, and relationships" (201ff.). To this Christians cannot react with "a return to a romanticized past of cultural homogeneity" (293), nor with a "sexual permissiveness" whose only norm is mutual consent (312ff.). People expect "creative moral leadership" from the churches. That can emerge only if the churches take a stand for "sexual justice" and want to be a church of and for the marginalized (401ff.) because "solidarity is the prime Christian value today" (435). "Human flourishing . . . is a sign of divine blessing in our lives" (479). That is God's intention for the creation (504), also with regard to sexuality, for sexuality is a divine gift. This demands — the predominant ethical guidelines in the report: "seeking justice-love or right-relatedness with self and others" (506). Justice-love can occur only when we listen to the voice of the marginalized, of blacks, women, and homosexuals.

Sexuality as the longing for an intimate relationship is an indispensable element in Christian spirituality (599ff.). Eros is not a foreign power outside ourselves (646). "To embrace the erotic as a moral (sic!) good" (651) is necessary for us "to be lovers of God's world" (654).

> Sexual justice calls us to acknowledge and respect the diversity of age, gender, sexual orientation, color, body size and shape, families, and custom. Such diversity enriches rather than diminishes our life together. Justice requires us to promote such diversity. It questions elitist cultural assumptions and stereotypes. (700ff.)

In the church the division is not between homosexuals and heterosexuals, between men and women, or between white and black, but between justice and injustice (740ff.).

The report has listened well to feminist theology and liberation theology: "Clearly, the test of our theology, our ethics, and

99

our ministry is whether they represent faithful responses to God's activity in human liberation, love, and justice" (791ff.).

For sexual ethics the report demands a two-way street: Scripture and tradition on the one hand and experience on the other. Therefore we must not have a theology of sexuality designed solely from within the Bible — which has no single clear sexual ethic — but a dialogue with experience such that we escape subjectivism, and the Bible does not become irrelevant. To that end — but without much in the way of grounds — the report offers a criterion:

> Whatever in Scripture, tradition, reason, or experience embodies genuine love and caring justice, that bears authority for us and commends an ethic to do likewise. Whatever in biblical tradition, church practice and teaching, human experience, and human reason violates God's commandment to do love and justice, that must be rejected as ethical authority. (1019–23)

In light of this, standard Christian sexual ethics must be reformed. God's intention with us as sexual beings lies not only in procreation but more especially in "loving companionship." Traditional sexual ethics focused too much on the form (marriage) rather than on the moral quality of the relationship. "It no longer makes sense to grant uncritical religious and moral legitimation to heterosexuality and heterosexual relations simply because they are heterosexual" (1467). "Justice-love or right-relatedness, and not heterosexuality (nor homosexuality for that matter), is the appropriate norm for sexuality" (1482).

Sure — but do these assertions refute the traditional condemnation? The report posits its theses but does not argue (any more!). Its intention comes out clearly in the following quotation:

> All persons, whether heterosexual or homosexual, whether single or partnered, have a moral right to experience justice-love in their lives and to be sexual persons. Being sexual includes the right and the responsibility to explore our own sexuality tenderly, to enjoy our capacity to give and receive loving touch, and to honor our commitment to deepen self-respect in relation to others. The church

100

must actively promote and protect this right for all persons, without distinction. (1743ff.)

Hence no theological ethic for homosexuality (no "morality on the basis of sexual orientation," 3854), but ethics on the basis of the neutral empirical fact that homosexuals and heterosexuals simply exist. The argument is not: it is unnatural and therefore wrong, nor: it is natural and therefore good; but: there is this ethically neutral reality. In Chapter III I discuss this further.

However, are we here really so far removed from an ethics of exoneration? After the general section on human sexuality, the special chapter on homosexuality is somewhat disappointing. Granted, the customary part about the causes of homosexuality does not occur; in line with the report as a whole, a refutation of stereotypes is given in a section entitled: "Dispelling the Myths." One of these myths is that "the Bible consistently and totally condemns homosexuality." In reply the report here first repeats what has already been said in the general section, viz., that the gospel "frames a theology of sexuality that affirms sexual expression which genuinely deepens human love and promotes justice" (3853). Viewed from this perspective, "the pressing moral problem . . . is not homosexuality, but rather the unjust treatment of gay and lesbian persons and their devaluation in our midst" (3870).

Then follows a brief discussion of the related Bible passages. The conclusion is: the Bible knows no homosexual orientation and consequently views same-sex relations of persons, who are always assumed to be heterosexual, as abnormal (hence in the non-normative meaning, in contrast with, say, the report of the Christian Reformed Church). So here, too, the exegesis is made to say what the authors already discovered from other sources: general human knowledge. Homosexuality is an established orientation (not a preference, expressly states the report, 3694); it cannot be helped. So the sexual behavior of homosexuals is accepted — again, read: exonerated!

Now then: not everyone will be able to share the theological conclusion of the report for exegetical, hence "scientific" (scholarly) reasons. But if the Bible should prove to hold to a certain notion about homosexual orientation, would that falsify the ethical viewpoint? Accordingly, here too the exegesis is potentially divisive. In response to this, what is to be expected is a discussion about the relationships between the command (justice-love) and the commandments, as we are seeing it emerge in the Dutch situation. So one who endorses the premises of the report that (1) sexuality, whether heterosexuality or homosexuality, is a gift of God's creation; and that (2) the only criterion for what is good and what is evil is what does, or does not, promote liberation and justice; and that (3) the traditional church ethics is unfair to homosexuals — will find in the report a theological, ethical, and exegetical confirmation of his viewpoint. But the demand for a further undergirding of these premises irrevocably presents itself. In this sense the report serves as a good illustration of the fact that the churches are operating with a double-entry system of bookkeeping: on the one hand the position on homosexuality is a result of a theological line of reasoning and, on the other, a theological legitimation of the position one already had, in this case that of the gay rights movement.

The report was rejected by an overwhelming majority of the members of the General Assembly of the Presbyterian Church (U.S.A.).

While the issue of homosexuality divides people within the churches, one can count on this to be the case when this issue is debated between churches. I have in mind the position of the National Council of Churches of Christ in the USA with regard to the Fellowship of the Metropolitan Community Churches, which had a membership (in 1990) of approximately 75,000 divided among some 300 congregations and consisted of gays, lesbians, friends, and family members. In 1981, this denomination applied for membership in the National Council. According to its Statement of Purpose, this Council is a "community of communities" of different churches of Protestant, Orthodox, and Anglican persuasion, each with its own theology. It has, for that reason, not formulated a position on homosexuality. It did adopt a resolution "on civil rights without discrimination as to affectional or sexual preference" (1975).[182] The application led to lengthy discussions. In 1983, it agreed "to postpone indefinitely" a decision on the membership of the Fellowship of the Metropolitan Community Churches. Following a number of conferences in 1986–87 the process was on hold for some time. But the dialogue will be continued. Points of discussion fall in the area of Bible interpretation, anthropology (the biblical view of humanness), and, especially, that of ecclesiology, the question of what makes a church a church. Proponents view the emergence of churches along the lines of "gender preference" as "part of the unfolding story of American Church history," just as in the past churches merged along the lines of doctrinal, class, and racial differences.[183] Others view the Metropolitan Community Churches as "single issue" churches, with homosexuality as the — too restricted — principle of organization. It is not yet clear whether the central issue on which the member churches are divided is homosexuality or ecclesiology. Some member churches have no problems with membership; for others it is a "breaking point."

Among the individual denominations, the United Church of Christ, generally known for its liberal views, decided in April 1990 to extend membership to the congregation of the "Spirit of the Lakes Community Church."

4. International

The discussion of homosexuality occurs especially in the churches of the West. In at least some parts of the world it is not experienced as a moral and religious problem.[184]

182. Documentation from the National Council of Churches of Christ, New York.

183. See A. Smith (1987).

184. The bishop of Seoul, S. S. Kim, president of the Anglican Convention, wrote me as follows: "To date this Church has neither discussed homosexuality publicly, nor made any pronouncement on it. It is not a pressing matter in our society" (Feb. 1991). Coleman (1989: 160) writes that the Lambeth Conference of Anglican bishops observed in 1978 that in parts

The bishops of the Catholic church adhere to the positions of the Vatican. "Revisionist" ideas of individual theologians in line with those of the Dutch report "Homophiles in Society" (§ 5) also occur elsewhere.[185]

The World Council of Churches (WCC), headquartered in Geneva, has never made a pronouncement on the subject.

The Reformed Ecumenical Synod (now: The Reformed Ecumenical Council), a confessional counterpart to the WCC, in 1988 discussed a report[186] that had been written in opposition to the tolerant position of the Dutch Reformed Churches (GKN). It led to a break in the Synod. This "Report of the RES Committee on Homophilia" actually carries the wrong title. It is in reality an exegetical, hermeneutical, and ethical critique of the theology of the GKN, carried out against the background of their position on homosexuality as expressed in the "Report on the Use of Scripture in Questions Relating to Homophilia" (1982) (= "Homophilia" from here on) to which I referred in § D.5. Never more clearly than in this case do we see how the position on homosexuality one takes becomes the criterion for one's orthodoxy. "In Reformed ethics, the creation order and moral law function as objective norms that give continuity and constancy to moral life" (IV B14). That is the subject of the report, and its position on homosexuality is simply derived from it. At issue is the doctrine of an a priori moral order that, as law, has authority for all times, and that is disclosed in Scripture as the creation order, and begins in Genesis 1 and 2 (III A5 and 6). Chapters 1 and 2 of Genesis lay the moral groundwork for human sexuality. "A major component in these foundations is the male-female polarity. This polarity forms the moral as well as biological basis of marriage" (III A6). From this one can tell from the start that for Christians only marriage and

---

of the Anglican Communion homosexuality "has not emerged as a problem." He refers to the Church of Africa.

185. E.g., W. Müller (1986), D. Mieth (1989), J. Callagher (1985), A. Kosnik (1977); cf. R. R. Ruether (1989). As a rule, the ethic of exoneration is the issue. See also J. H. McNeill (1976), the American priest who had to leave the Jesuit order because of his ideas concerning homosexuality.

186. *Acts of the RES, Harare,* 1988.

celibacy are legitimate possibilities. The assessment of homosexual relations has thus been established at the outset.

A theology of creation ordinances is an embattled theology. However, here I will only discuss the ethical argumentation and then, of course, particularly the use of the word "nature."

(1) According to the authors of the report, Paul in Romans 1, in his mention of the word "unnatural," refers to the unchanging moral order. Accordingly, it has normative significance here (III C1c). The report on "Homophilia" (GKN) says: Paul is referring to the moral order known to him. It has an empirical meaning.[187] Which is correct? That is a question for exegesis. Hence it would seem that here, too, the interpretation of the biblical texts is the cause of division. Something must, however, be added to that statement. The question I wish to raise is: Is the teaching of Scripture really decisive for ethics in this report, as the authors claim, or does the exegesis serve to legitimate an a priori ethical position? The RES report at least creates a suspicion that the latter is the case.[188] In its response the GKN also takes that to be the situation.[189] If that is true, the a priori ethical position should be verified before it is given theological legitimacy, and that does not happen. Thus the report's position on homosexuality retains its character as prejudgment.

(2) That prejudgment is again rooted in a confusion of the various concepts of nature. The most important point of the RES criticism of the GKN report is that the latter replaces the classic Reformed ethics of the moral law with an ethics in which the accent is on usefulness, intentions, and dispositions. Act (condemned by the moral law) and character (the disposition of the

---

187. On "normal" and "normative," see Chapter II § C.

188. "This first section (the teaching of scripture) has as its main purpose not an exhaustive exegetical study, but the presentation of *sufficient* biblical material to *adequately* address the . . . GKN approach to homosexuality" (IIB; emphasis added).

189. ". . . It means that in the RES report too, as in our own report, the exegetical approach to the Scriptural texts is marked by a specific ethical model and a specific hermeneutical method" (*Acts Harare,* Supplement 3b, I3).

homosexual) are played off against each other. Thus, for "Homophilia," room is created to accept the relations of homosexuals on account of their disposition toward love and fidelity. But by that token, says the RES report, the link with the unchanging moral (creation) order has been severed. That, namely, is a "natural order" and not a "historical" one (which would leave room for a judgment in terms of usefulness as the GKN report does).

I will not now comment on whether this criticism (which says that Christian ethics has to be deontological rather than teleological, or a disposition-ethics) holds water. Instead, I want to show that this is not the issue and can limit myself to pointing out how the term "disposition" is used in the report.

"That the problematics of moral being and doing, disposition and practice, have become a major part of the moral debate regarding homosexuality is understandable" (IV B4).

Here the reference is to a moral disposition, e.g., the disposition to love and to be fruitful. However:

> Homosexuality, even as all sexuality, pervades the totality of a person. This means ethically and morally that the dispositional and deed aspects of homosexuality are both very significant. What aspect churches consider most significant comes to expression in their final pronouncements. The GKN . . . resolves the tension between disposition and deed in favor of disposition. The homosexually-oriented person is granted freedom "as to how he/she is going to live with his/her disposition." Other churches have resolved the tension between disposition and deed in homosexuality on the side of deed. Homosexual practice is declared a sin and the dispositional dimension is left somewhat indefinite in moral significance. (IV B4)

However, the GKN does not mean moral disposition but biological disposition! It accepts the homosexual condition as naturally fixed, i.e., a biological datum, and accepts the homosexual relationship on account of its intention, hence the moral disposition to love and to be faithful, and not because the homosexual disposition is biologically natural and therefore good. An exoneration ethic may not be sound, but it is not the same as a disposition-ethic.

The reason why the RES fails to distinguish between a biological and a moral disposition is its own concept of nature. That concept does not allow for the distinction: the "natural order" is the moral order; and this is the creation order, which is identical with the biological order. The three distinct uses of the word *nature* are here confused.

This argumentation regarding homosexuality is most reminiscent of Douma's thinking (§ A). But I have again described it at some length because it shows all the more clearly how a complex problematics — in the form of questions: May a Christian ethic be teleological? Can it base itself on moral dispositions instead of acts? — arises when one neglects to make careful distinctions between the various concepts of nature.

F. The situation outside the Netherlands: a summary

(1) Lines of division relative to the assessment of homosexuality run squarely through the churches, not between churches. Perhaps on the average Anglicans (or Episcopalians) are a trifle more tolerant than Lutherans, or Presbyterians than the Reformed, or Protestants than Catholics. Perhaps, but even then we are only speaking of the church leadership, not of the opinion of individual church members. But insofar as my research permits me to draw a trustworthy conclusion, it has, I think, become clear that despite large differences in theology, the same type of questions are raised everywhere and the same type of answers are given.

(2) Comparison of the Dutch situation with that of other countries has not brought out other approaches. The conclusions reached with regard to the Dutch situation — namely, that the discussion turns on two dichotomies: the ethical-religious and the natural-unnatural — proved to be valid also for the situations elsewhere.

(3) In the case of each position an attempt was made to get the Bible on one's side. The exegesis and interpretation of the related Bible passages everywhere have a divisive effect.

(4) Besides, and because of, the appeal to Scripture (Rom. 1), the appeal to nature plays a large role. The ethical question in relation to homosexuality is almost always (an exception being the Presbyterian Church (U.S.A.) framed in terms of the dichotomy natural vs. unnatural. The kind of errors pointed out in our discussion of the Dutch situation, both in the case of disapproving arguments (§ B) and in that of the arguments favoring tolerance (§ D), occur in precisely the same way elsewhere: they are naturalistic arguments.

(5) These arguments, in each case, assume a biologistic and deterministic model of sexuality that focuses on the causes of, but not on a person's reasons for, (homo)sexual behavior.

It is, of course, no accident that medical-biological concepts of nature have played an enormous role in ethical discussions of homosexuality. In the following chapter we will, accordingly, take a look at the various scientific accounts of the phenomenon.

Chapter II

A Look at the Explanations

A. Introduction: framing the question

One may well ask: If our interest is the moral assessment of homosexuality, why do we need a chapter that deals with the causes of homosexuality? We found, after all, that one of the reasons the moral discussion dead-ended is that it was interested only in the causes of the behavior and not in the reasons homosexuals themselves present for their conduct. In answer, I have three arguments.

(1) In Chapter I we discovered that the moral assessment of homosexuality in each case followed the pattern of a naturalist type of argumentation. What it came down to was that sexuality was not evaluated on the basis of a norm but that, conversely, the norm was derived from biological data concerning the structure and function of the human body. A characteristic example was the reasoning of Karl Barth who, despite his own fundamental theological objections to "natural theology," in his theological ethics made the structure of the human body the criterion for the moral norm: humanity. This approach does not commend itself. But are empirical-scientific data then of no concern to ethics? On the basis of the present status of the research J. D. Weinrich, a biologist, concludes that homosexuality is "biologically natural," but, says he, this gives us no indication whatever for the attitude

society should adopt. Both approval and disapproval are compatible with the datum that homosexuality is natural (in the sense that it occurs in the animal world) as well as with the opposite situation. No scientific research can, in any way, affect a normative judgment.[1] Is that true? Weinrich says he means what Hume and Moore meant with the assertion that no "ought" can be derived from an "is." But even when we assume the logical impossibility of deriving a norm from a biological datum, it remains interesting to ask whether a relation exists — and if so, what? — between the content of moral judgment and what is actually the case. If none exists, we are stuck with the position that moral judgments are arbitrary labels a society fastens on behavior. Then moral judgments are stripped in advance of cognitive value. To proceed on that assumption comes down to begging the question. So then we must, in any case, not start by putting aside the empirical-scientific information.

(2) The concern of morality is to assess human conduct. Not all behavior qualifies as conduct. That statement can mean two things. All that people do or refrain from doing is *behavior* in the empirical sense. That behavior can be studied without reference to intentionality, say, by ethology. If, however, we speak of "conduct" we are dealing with intentions and meaning. Actions are performed with a specific intention and with a view to a specific result. Accordingly, we must distinguish between human "behavior" in the empirical sense and human action in the intentional sense of "conduct." Not everything humans do or refrain from doing (*actus hominis*), however, qualifies as human action (*actus humanus*).[2] Reflexes, tics, addictions, etc. occur. This distinction is of great importance for the moral assessment of a person's behavior. To be able to judge one must know whether he is dealing with a muscle reflex or a deliberate act.

Important, then, is the kind of account that is given of behavior. Each behavior can be described in totally different ways.

---

1. J. D. Weinrich (1982: 211).
2. Cf. Thomas Aquinas, *S. T.* Ia IIae Qu. 1, Art. 1. Cf. A. Fagothey (1972: 13–23).

Someone may describe his own behavior, or a researcher may do it; and for different disciplines different aspects of the behavior are relevant. The resulting accounts may all be equally correct but different because they were written from different perspectives. The purpose of the description may be explanation or clarification. In the case of a scientific explanation one searches for the *causes* of a behavior. A person other than myself then offers the explanation. However, I can also explain my behavior myself in the sense of giving an account of *my reasons* for behaving as I do. At issue, then, in any case, is behavior as action. Obviously, different accounts are needed for different types of explanation. Is one type better than another for the explanation of homosexual behavior? Is one type useful, and another not, in the case of moral issues? These are questions we need to consider. In any case, actions are also behavior in a moral sense and as such they are objects of causal-scientific explanation. Thus, though there is a difference between an explanation in terms of reasons and one in terms of causes, having reasons for one's behavior does not exclude an explanation in terms of causes.

(3) Value judgments, which themselves are no longer scientific, are often linked with scientific explanations, even by academics. Numerous — especially older — churchly publications on homosexuality suffer from this fact. People acted as if they already understood the phenomenon when science — usually in the person of a psychiatrist — had explained what caused it. And they acted as if in this explanation they were dealing with objective truth. On account of a kind of respect with which they viewed science, they paid no attention to the question in how far certain normative positions had already been built into the presentation of the scientific data. Now the pursuit of scientific objectivity is one I deem correct. But precisely for that reason I want to examine whether the conclusions these scientific folk draw from their data concerning homosexuality are of a purely scientific kind or also bear a normative character. That is *one* issue.

But there is another. That is the issue of the ideology behind a specific type of scientific explanation. Today, as a result of discussions of "value-neutral" science, we are more aware than in

111

the past that empirical science and values are related. Duintjer,[3] a social scientist, lists as many as nine relations. Among them are values that are inherent in the scientific method employed. At the moment these are not the ones on which we want to focus; they belong to the competence of the relevant disciplines. However, every discipline is also subject to the influence of extrascientific values. In the first place every theory embraces a selective viewpoint. Sometimes that is so self-evident it seems unquestionable. In connection with the natural sciences, Feyerabend[4] speaks of "natural-interpretations" — ideas existing in the culture and so tightly intertwined with observation that they can hardly be isolated from it. Knowledge is always gathered from a selective viewpoint.[5] Even when it is correct, i.e., by the standards of the relevant discipline, its validity is limited to the theoretical perspective within which it was acquired. Duintjer even remarks that when the constituent values of a discipline change, it is possible the phenomena observed may cease to exist.[6] Entire branches of scholarship are constituted by societal values, e.g., economics, pedagogy, and medical science.

This is also important in the study of homosexuality. A familiar example of the influence of societal values on this study is the sickness model of homosexuality. In 1978 the American society of psychiatrists decided by majority vote to remove homosexuality from the list of mental disorders. Is that really how this should be done? Is it the case that homosexuality is not a sickness because an accidental majority no longer views it as such? Are there no arguments to prove that homosexuality does not meet reasonable criteria for establishing an illness? Thus it is important to ask whether the premises of the different accounts are normative (pre-)judgments or premises, such as methodological assumptions, that are meaningful and useful for the research in question. One

3. O. D. Duintjer (1974).
4. P. Feyerabend (1975: 69ff.).
5. Th. Kuhn (1970^2): paradigms.
6. The Aristotelian opponents of Galileo did not "see" what he "saw" through his telescope.

112

can also put it this way: in how far does the preference for specific types of explanation relate to moral values instead of values that have to be considered inherent in the scientific inquiry as such? Biology, as we saw earlier, is "in" with the churches, and sociology is "in" among those who favor the emancipation of homosexuals. How come? On what normative (pre)judgments is preference for or opposition to a specific explanation based?

In this chapter we will examine the problems defined under (2) and (3) in order to get into a good position from which to discuss problem (1) — the problem we are ultimately interested in and will discuss in the next chapter. As my point of departure I am here adopting a conventional division of explanatory models: psychological, biological, and sociological — terms by which I simply mean: explanations as offered by psychologists, biologists, and sociologists. It does not seem necessary to add to this list. I further give prominence to what I view as the three most important "normative problem areas" because they keep coming up in the discussion of homosexuality: (a) the relation between what is empirically speaking normal and what is normative; (b) the way sex-related ("biological") traits connect with current notions of "masculinity" and "femininity," and (c) the relation between homosexual conduct based on human choice and homosexual behavior that is causally determined. Explanations originating in each of the above-mentioned disciplines give rise to a position in each of the three issues but one linkage seems more natural than another. I, therefore, make a choice as to which "normative problem area" will be treated under which model of explanation. The first is discussed under the heading of psychological explanations (§ C), the second under the anthropological (§ D) and sociological (§ G), and the third under the biological (§§ E and F). We will start with the attempt to define homosexuality (§ B).

B. The problem of definition

Definitions of homosexuality exist in many kinds and are constructed for different purposes. In the sixties, the period when

113

homosexuality was "naturalized," a large number of concepts were in circulation: manifest homosexuality, constitutional and peripheral homosexuality, pseudo-, latent, and circumstantial homosexuality; further, also homophilia and homoeroticism, paedophilia, biphilia and bisexuality.[7] These distinctions had their origin in medical science: homosexuality was a medical term[8] and as such found its way into common usage. One gets an idea from Webster's Third New International Dictionary: "Homosexuality: 1. atypical sexuality characterized by manifestation of sexual desire toward a member of one's own sex; 2. erotic activity with a member of one's own sex . . . ; 3. the extent to which one's libido is fixated at a homoerotic level."[9]

It is not easy to write a good definition. Just to mention a few things: a couple of male friends living together will satisfy Webster's definition, but what about the married man who has fathered children but maintains homosexual contacts on the side or the school boy who prostitutes himself for pocket money? Under what heading do we put sexual contacts in all-male communities like the army or a prison or sexual experiments among pubers? Such questions assume one can tell "real" homosexuals from others. That was precisely the intention of the doctors, and this again is the background of the proliferation of concepts. My purpose is different. The definition I need must meet the following requirements: (a) it must satisfy the formal rules of definition, hence not be too broad or too narrow, too vague or unnecessarily negative; (b) it must not materially prejudge the questions raised in § A; (c) it needs to tie in with, at least not be inconsistent with, normal usage, or else it will fail to clarify.

Definitions may be analytic (descriptive) and synthetic (de-

7. In the Netherlands the doctoral thesis of W. J. Sengers (1969: 31ff.) established order in this chaos.

8. For the history of the attempt "to doctor" the homosexual male, see G. Hekma (1987).

9. Dictionaries tend to reflect changes in usage. Van Dale's *Groot Woordenboek der Nederlandse Taal* moved from "sexual desire toward members of one's own sex" (1976) to "homosexuality as a fixed orientation" in a medical sense (1984). This reflected the work of Lengers, op. cit.

scriptive). Analytic definitions establish the actual meaning (function) of terms: the *intension* of the concept (not to be confused with the intention of an act). Intension means an unknown entity *x* has the same significance as a known entity *c*. Such definitions add nothing to the store of information; their correctness depends solely on the meaning of the words used. They are linguistic conventions or agreements. To this category belong lexical and stipulative definitions. Synthetic definitions have empirical reference. They apply to concrete things. Their truth depends on facts. They establish the *extension* or denotation of a concept. Extension means: x relates to $c_1, c_2, c_3, \ldots$

Webster's definition is lexical: *x* (the *definiendum*) has the same meaning as *c* (the *definiens*). A stipulative definition is a definition of the form x means the same thing as c. An example is the introduction of the term "homotropism" defined as: "The actual orientation to a partner of the same sex; on the sexual plane: homosexuality; on the erotic plane: homoeroticism; on the personal plane: homophilia."[10]

The distinction between analytic and synthetic definitions is not always sharp. That is especially the case with terms like homosexuality that originate in a given science and end up in common usage. Doctors are interested in making diagnoses and will, therefore, as much as possible operationalize their concepts. They work primarily with the extension of concepts, not with the question: What is homosexuality? (intension), but with the question: By what features can we recognize it? Diagnostic criteria, however,

---

10. By A. M. J. M. H. van de Spijker (1968: 25). A famous extensional definition is: man is a featherless biped. The *definiens* and *definiendum* here have the same extension and a different intension. Concepts in the (natural) sciences should have empirical reference (but mathematical concepts, to cite an exception, do not). For example, "centaur" (intension: a man with the body of a horse), though it is easy to define, has no empirical reference because such beings do not exist. As a result of scientific inquiry the meaning of terms may change. Today DNA has another (biological) meaning than before the discovery of its genetic function. Scientific concepts are also required to be operational (meaning-criteria have to be usable). C. G. Hempel (1966: 86, 103; W. J. van der Steen (1982: 6ff.).

are not "meaning criteria."[11] C. G. Hempel, a philosopher of science, offers the following illustrative example. Substances such as penicillin and testosterone can be characterized by molecular formulas. In this way biological expressions are extensionally defined in chemical terms. But this says nothing about the biological meaning, the intension of the terms in question, as antibacterial substance and sex hormone, respectively.[12] Or take a simpler example: "water" does not mean H_2O but does have the same extension. Now my thesis here is that in the reality of daily-life homosexuality, as it is experienced by members of the same sex, is something different from what the medical term expresses. In ordinary usage the term has mistakenly acquired the medical meaning (as in Webster). What is intended as an extensional definition (for the purpose of making a diagnosis) is conceived as an intensional definition. I am looking for a better intensional definition that — because I do not accept the usage followed in daily parlance — will have the character of a stipulation but at the same time not clash with the definitions of the sciences.

Let us take a look at some definitions. The earlier term "sodomy" defined homosexual behavior in terms of human acts but at the same time expresses disapproval. The latter element does not belong in a definition. By comparison with it the more neutral term "homosexuality," which has dominated the discussion from the mid-nineteenth century on, is an improvement. However, what has happened here is not just a change of terminology. Involved is a transition from a moral and religious viewpoint to a scientific one that is interested in the causes of the behavior. Since that time the same-sex act related to the medical category "homosexuality" (extension) and meant a symptom of a psychopathology (intension)[13] or, more neutrally, of a fixed predisposition (Dutch: *gerichtheid*).

11. This confusion occurs often. The language-philosopher Searle speaks of "mistaken assumptions about the relation between our understanding of a notion and our ability to provide criteria of a certain kind for its application," quoted from J. M. Brennen (1977: 46).

12. C. G. Hempel (op. cit.: 103).

13. M. Foucault (1978: 43) says: "the sodomite had been a temporary aberration; the homosexual was now a species."

This is the background of the definitions of the great sexologists of the nineteenth and early twentieth century.[14] It also lies behind the definition of the psychiatrist W. J. Sengers (1969: 29/30):

> We speak of homophilia when a person feels attracted exclusively or almost exclusively to persons of his own sex. . . . "Homosexual" is the word which describes every form of physical contact between persons of the same sex that tends to, or results in, orgasm, regardless of whether that contact takes place in reality or in fantasy or dream. . . . By "feeling sexually attracted to" I mean the attraction to others, the motive force of which is the expected, originating, or existing feeling of sexual pleasure. [To experience such an attraction is one's "fixed predisposition":] the fact of feeling attracted in a constant and clear manner to certain categories of people as a sexually mature person.

The intent of such a definition is to operationalize the medical concept of homosexuality. In this definition it occurs with the "criteria of disposition": behavior, fantasy, and dream content. The real meaning is indicated with the (vague) term "disposition." This type of definition — in terms of disposition, condition, or nature — predominates, also in the writings of theological ethicists[15] and in common usage (Webster).

To this I have two objections. The first is that in this manner (by definition) homosexuals are not only distinguished from others (every definition does this) but also set apart as a special type of human being. Homosexuality, in this view, is a discontinuous state: it exists or does not exist in a person. Some people have recognized

14. Sexology flourished around the turn of the century. See G. Hekma (1985: 359ff.). I will reproduce only M. Hirschfeld's definition (1926: 563): "Homosexuality or 'same-sexedness' denotes a certain make-up, from which springs a certain sensibility, which expresses itself in certain acts. . . . It is here as in sexuality in general: the make-up comes first, the sensibility and inclination comes next, and the act is third."

15. If they define it at all. Barth, Wurth, and Thielicke do not. Trillhaas (1970: 331) defines the subject in terms of the degeneration of sexual relations. J. Douma (1984: 9) presents an unnecessarily negative definition: "a condition in which the natural sex instinct is lacking."

this objection. Kinsey (1948), in his well-known six-point scale, presents a continuum that runs from exclusive heterosexuality to exclusive homosexuality, based on the criterion of "overt activity and/or psychic reactions." For, in his opinion, the homo-hetero division is not present in nature but is of a conceptual kind.[16] For him homosexuality is a category of observable behavior. But that, too, is an (overly narrow — Sengers) operational criterion and not a criterion of meaning.

The second objection is the occurrence of "the fallacy of reification" (J. Stuart Mill). That is the false opinion that everything that has a name also exists as an entity. As a rule we do not do this in the case of other behaviors of people that cause them to stand out. Here is a person who is very fond of poetry — is she a poeticophile? Was Karl Barth perhaps afflicted with "amadeophilia," i.e., a person who in a constant and clear manner feels attracted to the compositions of Mozart? If we rightly find this absurd, why then do we do this in the case of sexual behavior? This is not to deny the possible existence of (biological, psychological, etc.) differences between homosexuals and heterosexuals. Such differences presumably exist between, say, lovers of poetry and readers of comic strips. But it is absurd to define these preferences in terms of such differences. For here the element of *intentionality* is missing. I mean that an intensional definition of every form of human action must give expression to the element of intention, i.e., of conscious intent. For otherwise the behavior in question is being robbed by the definition of its character as an

16. A. C. Kinsey et al. (1948: 637): "It is fundamental of taxonomy that nature rarely deals with discrete categories. Only the human mind invents categories and tries to force facts into separated pigeon-holes. The living world is a continuum in each and every one of its aspects. The sooner we learn this concerning human sexual behavior the sooner we shall reach a sound understanding of the realities of sex." Also the psychoanalyst I. Bieber defines in terms of behavior: "I do not diagnose patients as homosexual unless they have engaged in overt homosexual behavior" (1965: 28). Like Kinsey he denies the existence of a specific homosexual condition because "we assume that heterosexuality is the biological norm and unless interfered with all individuals are heterosexual. Homosexuals do not bypass heterosexual developmental phases and all remain potentially heterosexual" (1962: 319).

118

act. Disposition-definitions of homosexuality fail to distinguish —
and that is my objection — between behavior that happens to a
person and behavior he or she knowingly and voluntarily engages
in. And definitions in terms of observable behavior, such as Kinsey's, make no distinction between the various reasons a person
may have for that behavior. By way of comparison: the word
"pianist" is not defined in terms of observable behavior but in
terms of intention. A pianist is one who has the intention of making
music. For that reason, however useful the above types of definition may be for a special purpose, namely that of scientific research, they are unsuited as intensional definition.

In some definitions this element does more or less emerge.
Thus the psychiatrist J. Marmor concludes:

"A psychodynamic definition of homosexuality cannot ignore the element of motivation."

Senger's definition bears some resemblance to his:

I would characterize the homosexual person . . . as one who is
motivated in adult life by a definite preferential erotic attraction
to members of the same sex and who usually (but not necessarily)
engages in overt sexual relations with them.[17]

Motivation here, however, has a technical-psychological
meaning that is closer to disposition than to intention.

The report of the Dutch Center for Dialogue (NGC 1966)
simply says: "Homosexuality is a person's desire for total communion with someone of the same sex."

To clarify this statement it adds: the word is "desire" rather
than "urge" so as "to highlight the personal and human dimension."[18] The definition is probably too narrow because not every
homosexual contact is intended as "total communion." Still, this
definition is the best I have come across. It indicates what homosexuality means, not what causes it. The sequel however makes
plain the desire referred to is that of "the homosexual person
marked by total orientation (Dutch: *gerichtheid*) to persons of the

17. J. Marmor (1965), unchanged in J. Marmor (1980: 4, 5).
18. *Homosexualiteit.* Nederlands Gesprek Centrum (1966: 4, 5).

119

same sex." In this way homosexual disposition, inclination, orientation, motivation, and desire become practically synonymous, viz., as a determining causal "force."

To escape this problem some sociologists have proposed a series of other definitions. In these definitions homosexuality is viewed either as a social role, or as a specific identity, or as the special meaning an actor assigns to his behavior. M. McIntosh (1968) views the homosexual rather as a person who fulfills a special role than as one with a specific disposition. The latter conception unnecessarily restricts the research to aetiology. "Role" includes more than the description of sexual behavior. Roles, after all, can more easily be dichotomized into those of homo- and heterosexual than sexual patterns of behavior. In her opinion, a specialized homosexual role has existed in England since the end of the seventeenth century. With "specialized role" she is referring not only to the role-related ideas existing in a culture but also to the institutionalized orders that reinforce these ideas. These include the institutions of heterosexual relations such as marriage but also "labeling processes," like gossip, psychiatric diagnoses, and judicial indictments, as well as homosexual subcultures and networks.[19]

Shively and De Cecco (1977) and De Cecco (1981) see the distinctiveness of homosexuals as lying in their identity or identities. This embraces four components:

(1) the biological sex, which includes the physical, physiological, and genetic characteristics on the basis of which a person is male or female;

(2) the gender-identity.[20] This is a person's basic conviction relative to being a man or a woman. It constitutes part of a person's self-knowledge;[21]

19. M. McIntosh (1968/1981: 38ff.).
20. M. Duyves et al. (1984: 11). J. de Wit and G. van der Veer (1984: 146ff.), in surveying psychosocial sexual development, distinguish the following: (1) the development of male/female identity; (2) the development of the sex role; (3) the development of partner-preference; (4) the development of sexual behavior in relation to a value-system; and (5) the process of integrating sexuality into a personal lifestyle. 1–3 coincide with De Cecco's 2–4.
21. According to psychologists gender-identity is firmed up at two or

(3) the gender-role (or social sex role), which concerns the characteristics a given culture associates with masculinity and femininity;

(4) the sexual orientation. This refers to the partners one feels sexually attracted to. Here three subcomponents come into play: physical sexual activity, personal affection, and erotic fantasy.

The authors view the purpose of this rather complex theoretical model as lying, among other things, in a distinction between social sex role and sexual orientation. Failure in most discussions (medical and lay) to make this distinction gives rise to the misconception that the sexual orientation is dichotomous and permanent. But the degree of masculinity and femininity — the authors mention no fewer than ten independent variables — is independent of a person's sexual orientation. Accordingly, the latter must not be understood in terms of the social sex role.[22]

J. Marshall also starts from the idea of "sexual identity." But his division is different. Instead of "sexual orientation" he presents two categories: sexual behavior and sexual meaning. The latter is the way the actors themselves experience the sexual activity. In Marshall's opinion, in our culture, past and present, four forms of identity can be distinguished. For men they are as follows:

sexual identity	**A. hetero-male**	**B. male invert**
sex:	male	male
gender identity:	man	man-woman
gender role:	masculine	feminine
sexual behavior:	heterosexual	homosexual
sexual meaning:	heterosexual	"heterosexual"

---

three years of age. When at the time of birth a mistake has been made in the identification of the sex of the child this decision can be reversed without negative consequences up until the eighteenth month; after that this can no longer be done without harm. Stoller (1965); Money and Ehrhardt (1972).

22. De Cecco (1981: 61). As categories within the male/female distinction Shively and De Cecco (1977) mention inter alia the degree of aggressiveness, hobbies, interest in ornaments, mannerisms, and habits.

sexual identity	C. hetero-male	D. homo-male
sex:	male	male
gender identity:	man	man
gender role:	masculine	masculine
sexual behavior:	homosexual	homosexual
sexual meaning:	heterosexual	homosexual

Model A represents the "normal" male. B represents the conceptualization by sexologists in the nineteenth and early twentieth centuries (Krafft-Ebing's "psychic hermaphrodicia," Hirschfield's "intermediate or transitional sexual stage," a "third sex," etc.) and basically says: the homosexual looks for the same a normal person looks for: a man for a woman, a woman for a man. C represents "circumstantial" homosexuality: sexual contacts in male communities where no women are present. D, finally, concerns the ordinary homosexual of our days.

The difference between D on the one hand and A and C on the other is the *meaning* that the actor assigns to his sexual behavior. The difference between B on the one hand and A and D on the other concerns the difference in *gender identity*; according to the nineteenth-century theories (B), homosexuals were disturbed in their sense of manhood.[23]

The tenor, in these social-science models, is to say that the dichotomy homo-/heterosexuality (or the trichotomy homo-/hetero-/bisexuality) must be understood on the level of social roles (McIntosh), sexual orientation (De Cecco/Shively), or the meaning of the sexual behavior to those involved in it (Marshall), and not on the level of biological sex or psychological gender. So, then, must we now define homosexuality in terms of roles or identities? I would think not, if for no other reason than that these concepts

23. Marshall's indiscriminate use of the terms "sexual meaning" and "sexual orientation" is confusing. G. Hekma (1987: 221), on good historical grounds, combats Marshall's thesis that initially homosexuality was especially conceptualized as gender-deviation and not until much later as sexual object-choice. He affirms his opinion that not until recent decades were modern views on homosexuality (Model D) widely accepted. Hekma takes Marshall's models to be descriptive; I take them to be conceptual (analytic).

themselves require definition. "Identity" has several meanings[24] and "role" is a complex social-science concept. The difference between "orientation" and "disposition" is unclear; the criteria for a "disposition" in Sengers resemble, like peas in a pod, the sub-components Shively/De Cecco distinguish in sexual orientation, while Marshall uses the terms "orientation" and "meaning" interchangeably.

Have we then made no progress at all? Yes, we have, and the key to it is a later article by De Cecco and Shively in which they already distance themselves from the notion of "sexual identity." Their argument is that, at bottom, this is a biological concept based on the anatomical difference between male and female. But their intent had been to examine sexual relations from a vantage point such that the "motivations, attitudes and expectations of the partners" might come into their own. For this purpose biology is unsuitable. Biological explanations have an "aura of determinism" and biology "hardly provides a context broad enough to account for the complexity and consequences of choices that are conceived and exercised in sexual relationships."[25] What they are saying, therefore, is that what homosexuality actually means cannot be explained by biology because that discipline is too deterministic (in their eyes). Social science, not being deterministic, can explain it.

What they should be saying, in my opinion, is homosexuality includes more than either biology or sociology can explain. De Cecco/Shively, in their attempt to offer a better definition of the concept of homosexuality (attitudes, expectations, and choices — notions biology does not know what to do with — belong to it too, they think), do this by at the same time changing the *extension* of the concept: from a biological to a social-science definition. In so doing

24. The concept has been developed by the psychoanalyst E. Erikson. Concept-analysis has shown that he used it in a variety of senses. Cf. De Wit/van der Veer (op cit. 192/3). The idea of "homosexual identity/identities" was popular in the seventies. But one can pin homosexuals down on it in the same way as with "predisposition." We may consider it a catchword in a particular phase of gay-liberation: that of "gay pride." See M. van der Heyden (1983).

25. De Cecco and Shively (1984: 2; 15/6).

they anticipate the outcome — which is a social-science explanation. And so they end up in the same pitfall as that of the disposition-definitions: they intend to establish the meaning *(intension)* of homosexuality — i.e., as a form of human action — but do it by incorporating in their definition only those aspects of the action that can be studied by the social sciences. So a sociological definition replaces a medical one. By contrast with biologists, sociologists indeed study processes of meaning-bestowal. But the question: Which aspects of human behavior can be explored by which discipline? is a different question from that concerning the aspects that belong in a definition. Certainly, we do not define other human activities — making music, fighting, playing tennis, etc. — in terms of roles or identities. These activities may be elucidated with the help of these concepts — but that is something else. The fallacy here is that homosexuality has to do with choices in relations; these are the things the social sciences study; therefore, biology cannot say a word about it. Or, homosexuality has to do with freedom, whereas biological explanations are deterministic; therefore, biology cannot say anything about homosexuality. From the fact that homosexuality can be defined as an object of social-scientific inquiry, it does not follow, however, that this phenomenon could not also be defined as an object of biological research. From a definition, which is a linguistic convention, no empirical conclusions can be drawn. It is an a priori of these sociological definitions that homosexuality does not *exist* on the level of genes or hormones simply because genes and hormones do not belong — true! — in an intensional definition of homosexuality.

Accordingly, my conclusion is that the conceptualizations of social science rightly seek to express the element of intentionality. This is done by means of the terms used: "meaning," "choice," "attitude," "expectation," "relation." But they wrongly reduce the question concerning the definition of homosexuality to one concerning what homosexuality is as object of social-scientific inquiry.

I have stated that definitions of every form of human behavior that is more than an *actus hominis* must convey the element of intentionality. That is a norm. But can homosexual behavior be viewed as *actus humanus?* Are there empirical grounds for this position? From the broad stream of books that appeared since Kinsey (1948) broke the "conspiracy of silence" (A. Comfort) and society began to take an interest in homosexuals and their worlds,[26] I will mention a few. Ford and Beach (1951) mapped out forms of sexual behavior in various cultures. This showed clearly the multiformity and polyvalence of homosexual behaviors.[27] The first full-fledged sociological study that broke with the habit of studying homosexuality by way of populations of exclusively psychiatric patients or of prisoners was that of M. Schofield (1965). In a comparison of three groups of homosexuals (patients, delinquents, and "normal" homosexuals) with corresponding groups of heterosexuals, the differences among the three groups of homosexuals proved greater than those between each group of homosexuals and the corresponding group of heterosexuals. The group of homosexuals showed the same distribution as the population as a whole. This conclusion corroborates the largest study undertaken thus far, that of the Kinsey Institute (1977) in the San Francisco Bay area, which correctly bears the title "Homosexualities."[28] The researchers encountered various lifestyles, which they subsumed under four categories: "close-coupleds," "open-coupleds," "functionals" (jolly bachelors), "dysfunctionals" and "asexuals." They found no difference in self-esteem between heterosexual males and "functionals," nor between heterosexual males and the homosexual "close-coupleds." In the Netherlands Sanders (1977) found a link among young people between self-esteem on the one hand and the acceptance of homosexual feelings and their manifestation on the other. Relationships proved very important in the life of homosexuals. That is also the conclusion of the Kinsey Report. And Reiche and Dannecker, on the basis of their broad study in West Germany (1970/3), concluded: "All promiscuous homosexuals have a tendency to engage in a stable friendship (at some time) and all firmly attached homosexuals have a tendency to be promiscuous."

26. An early contribution is that of E. Hooker (1959).
27. But also, e.g., see already E. Westermarck (1906: 456ff.).
28. A. P. Bell and W. S. Weinberg (1979).

On the whole, viewing them as a social group, they found homosexuals well-adjusted, with a greater tendency than other groups to be above average in the occupational group to which they belonged.[29]

Our conclusion can only be that, even though there are differences between homosexuals and heterosexuals as a group, these differences are not absolute or even sharp. Individually there are huge differences, but that is true for heterosexuals as well. It is correct, therefore, to define homosexual behavior in the same way as heterosexual: i.e., in terms of intentions.

A careful definition of homosexuality must also define "sexuality." I have no weighty objection to Senger's definition of the word "sexual": "every form of physical contact that tends to, or results in, orgasm, regardless of whether that contact takes place in reality or in fantasy."[30]

I offer the following definitions:

An act is *intentional* when (1) the actor is conscious of performing the act, and (2) he performs it as an end in itself or as a means to an end, when the act is performed deliberately.

Homosexual *behavior* (in a descriptive sense) is sexual behavior between members of the same sex.

Homosexual *acts* are intentional sexual acts in which sexual contact with a member of the same sex is desired as the result of the sexual act, for whatever reason.

A *homosexual* is a person who performs a homosexual act or desires to perform it as the goal of his sexual behavior.

Homosexuality is (a) the phenomenon of homosexual behavior; (b) the phenomenon of being homosexual.

Since the term "homophilia" was introduced as a euphemism for homosexuality, I will not attempt to define it.

With reference to the definition of a "homosexual" I want to point out that it does not say that homosexuals are always "gunning" for sex but that in their sexual contacts they are seeking

29. R. Reiche and M. Dannecker (1977: 35–53). (The quote is on pp. 40–41.)

30. W. J. Sengers (1969: 29/30).

contact with a member of the same sex, for whatever reason: lust, love, or total union, etc., and in whatever form: manual, oral, anal, without a partner or with one or more partners simultaneously.

These definitions tie in with common usage but do not anticipate an explanation or rule out any type of explanation. They do not prejudge any "normative problem-areas" (§ A) and do not divide humanity into two or three groups. Finally, they do not contain terms that are open to more than one interpretation. They, therefore, meet the demands I have posed for a definition.

C. Homosexuality as psychological phenomenon

Beginning with this section we will deal with explanations as given by different disciplines. Our purpose, let me repeat, is not to judge the correctness of these explanations but to track down the normative components they may contain. With regard to the psychological explanations, I especially pay attention to the psychoanalytic because these in particular are associated with the sickness-model of homosexuality. Here the question is whence are the criteria on the basis of which the judgments "sickness," "disturbance," or "psychopathology" are pronounced.[31]

For this purpose we do not have to make a thorough examination of psychoanalytic views. That would not be a simple matter in any case, because even Sengers, himself a psychiatrist, believes he can give no more than a summing up, not a systematic exposition. But for our purpose his conclusion is enough. On the basis of our present knowledge, he says, it cannot be determined whether homosexuality is a sickness or a developmental variant.[32] That, however, remains to be seen. Can this conclusion be drawn *solely* from a factual state of affairs? That is the question. In this section

31. Not to be confused with disease-models, see Ch. I §§ D. "The disease-model of homosexuality" states that this is disease but it does not say according to what criterion it is a disease.
32. W. J. Sengers (1969: 79–91).

I will limit myself to the psychoanalytic view of sexuality as inter-human (individual) phenomenon. The tie-in with societal relations comes up in the next section.[33]

Surprisingly enough, we do not find the sickness-model of homosexuality in S. Freud, though later theories do link up with him. In the "Letter to an American Mother" (1935), who was worried about her homosexual son, he writes: it is certainly no advantage to be homosexual, but neither is it anything to be ashamed of; it is not a vice, nor degeneracy, let alone a crime; and "it cannot be classified as an illness; we consider it to be a variation of the sexual function produced by a certain arrest of sexual development."[34]

What Freud means by this becomes clearer from a footnote (added in 1915) to his "Three Essays on the Theory of Sexuality" (1905). Here he opposes the ideas of Hirschfield et al. that homosexuals can be set apart from the rest of humanity as a group of a special character, a "third sex." Freud stresses the common psychic structure of hetero- and homosexuals. All people are in principle capable of the homosexual object-choice and have also made that choice in the unconscious. Homosexuality is a facet of all human sexuality, not a separate category applicable only to homosexuals. Humans are psychically bisexual, as is apparent in childhood. That is the original situation from which, "as a result of restriction in one direction or another," the two types develop. Neither of the two developments are self-evident and both require explanation. "A person's final sexual attitude is not decided until after puberty." It is "the result of a number of factors, not all of which are yet known; some are of a constitutional nature" but others are social in character. Freud does not deny that qualitative differences in the end products exist but "the differences between their determinants are only quantitative."[35]

"Blocked development" is the result of the restriction of the "partial instincts" of childhood. Freud subsumes homosexuality

33. For the distinction, see N. Drayer (1984: 212).
34. Cited from M. Ruse (1981: 271).
35. S. Freud (1905, 1920/1983: 21–25); M. Dannecker (1981: 46–49).

("inversion") under the "perversions," adult sexual behaviors in which the sexual *object* (the person from whom the sexual attraction emanates) or the sexual *aim* (the aim toward which the instinct strives) deviates from the normal, viz., heterosexual genital satisfaction.[36] A child is born "polymorphously perverse"; it is subject to a series of "partial instincts" that independently and separately tend toward — not only genital — gratification. In a normal development toward adult sexuality these are subordinated to the primacy of the reproductive function. Accordingly, adult sexuality is the result of a specific organization of the instincts. Perversions — a psychiatric category[37] in Freud — are fixations in adulthood of these partial instincts; they are "fixations" of or "regressions" to the partial instincts (component impulses) of childhood.[38]

This last statement suggests that Freud, while not regarding homosexuality as sickness, certainly viewed it as a deviation, a disturbance caused by an abnormal organization of the instincts. The picture as a whole feels deterministic and mechanistic. On balance Freud seems to replace the genetic determinism of Hirschfield, "innate" homosexuality, by an equally drastic psychic determinism. We must, however, be careful with this conclusion. According to a modern interpretation,[39] it was Freud's consistent aim to show the normal in the abnormal and vice versa. He distinguished himself from the sexologists before him by no longer

36. S. Freud (1905/1983: 13, 26). Here he seems to use the term perversion only for changes in the sexual *aim* (e.g., fetishism), not for those in the sexual *object* (e.g., inversion). Freud (1917, Lecture XXI) states that the essence of perversions does not consist in the extension of the sexual aim nor in the variant choice of the object "but solely in the exclusiveness with which these deviations are carried out as a result of which the sexual act serving the purpose of reproduction is put on one side" (translation by James Strachey). Where Freud uses the term "act," I speak of "behavior" (in the descriptive sense).

37. "Perversion," therefore, has no moral connotation in Freud. It is true that the indulgence of the perversion in practice brings with it a conflict with morality (Freud, 1983: 129).

38. S. Freud (1905/1983: 69; 1917, Lecture XX).

39. J. Mitchell (1974: 16–30).

viewing sexuality as a monistic "essence" on the model of biological instincts but as a composite whole (the "partial instincts").
Freud humanized sexuality by seeing that, on account of its mental
character, it is a typically human phenomenon. This is also clear
from his definition of the sexual instinct in the "Three Essays":[40]
as the psychic representation of an endosomatic, continuously
flowing source of stimulation. Throughout his life Freud remained
uncertain about the nature of these instincts, but he consistently
viewed them as *psychic* entities. Granted, Freud's formulations of
sexual development are sometimes strongly reminiscent of the
succession of biological phases. In his later life, however, Freud
increasingly distanced himself from biological associations. He
thought, to be sure, that the instincts are rooted in physiological
processes, but his psychoanalytic interest lay emphatically in the
mental representation of the instincts, hence not in their origin but
in their aim and object. The instincts have no *natural* object. What
is considered normal sexuality is always a combination of "partial
impulses." In each of them fixation (perversion) or regression
(neurosis) may arise, but none of them is totally absent from
normal sexuality.[41]

Accordingly, the normal is not synonymous with the natural.
Then in what respect is the abnormal, which is not a sickness,
deviant? Perversions are not neuroses (illnesses), thinks Freud,
though perverts can be neurotic.[42] Health and normality are different things. The criterion for health, says Freud in his Lectures

40. S. Freud (1905/1983: 43).

41. There has been much discussion about whether unconscious motives must be viewed as (determining) causes or as psychological meaning
bestowals. J. Habermas (1968/1973: 300–332) thinks that initially Freud
planned to design a psychology on the model of a mechanistic brain physiology but changed his mind. He does retain a mechanistic diction but more
closely resembles an archeologist than a mechanistic physicist. The object of
psychoanalysis is to uncover "the causality of fate, not of nature" as was the
case in the life of Oedipus. Empirical connections are simultaneously intentional. See Th. de Boer (1980: 134ff.) and J. D. Hencken (1982: 134ff.).

42. "A neurosis is, so to speak, the negative of a perversion," Freud
(1905/1983: 41). P. C. Kuiper (1966: 219) is critical of this thesis; in his
opinion, perverse acts are also defensive in character.

(1917)[43] is: "the possession of a sufficient degree of capacity for enjoyment and active achievement in life." That can also be applied to homosexuals; see the Letter cited above. What then is the element of deviancy in homosexuality? In the Lectures — intended for an educated Viennese lay audience — Freud called homosexuality "a fateful peculiarity," a "pathological form of sexuality," and "an abnormal manner of achieving gratification." But here he is speaking the language of his audience. For he subsequently makes clear that he regards homosexuality as "a regular type of offshoot of the capacity to love" (*General Introduction to Psychoanalysis,* 1943, p. 270): "The differences between manifest homosexuality and the normal attitude are certainly not thereby abrogated; they have their practical importance, which remains, but theoretically their value is very considerably diminished."

And somewhat further:

> You are making the mistake of confusing sexuality and reproduction with each other. . . . It is indeed one of the most important social tasks of education to restrain, confine, and subject to an individual control (itself identical with the demands of society) the sexual instinct when it breaks forth in the form of the reproductive function. . . . Without this the instinct would break all bounds and the laboriously erected structure of civilization would be swept away. . . . At bottom society's motive is economic; . . . the eternal primordial struggle for existence, therefore, persisting to the present day. (p. 273)

Normal, in other words, is what agrees with the demands of civilization. It is, therefore, a *normative* term. Abnormal is the unusual, the statistically deviant *and* that which is in conflict with the demands posed by civilization. Please note, however, that Freud does not say homosexuality is in conflict with them.

Freud's theory, I conclude, is a *gender-theory,* a theory that explains a person's sexual orientation, his social sex role, and their sexual meaning in terms of events that occur in childhood. Ho-

---

43. S. Freud (1917, Lecture 28); cf. idem (1905/1983: 37).

mosexuality is a departure from the normal development, i.e., the development the majority undergoes. Humans are psychically bisexual. Freud is very careful not to impose a biological interpretation.[44] Homosexuality is not a normal expression of sexuality. Why is it not? It is due to social regulation in a society that considers it contrary to its demands.

Freud's pupil, S. Rado,[45] vigorously resists the idea of psychic bisexuality. In biology there is no such thing as bisexuality. In nature we always find sexual dimorphism. Sexual cells are differentiated in terms of their function in the process of differentiation, and the structure of individuals is adjusted accordingly. "Sex in its entirety refers to the differentiation in the individuals as regards their contrarelated action systems of reproduction" (p. 180). One cannot lift a single component, the psychic, from this entirety and have it serve as a criterion for normal sexuality. Then it is detached from the functionality of the system as a whole, which is the individual. Psychoanalysis now faces the question: "Must we abandon the dictum of biology that sex is a matter of the reproductive action system?" (p. 183). His answer is negative. Also in humans "The masculine" and "The feminine" refer exclusively to the reproductive system. The presupposed bisexuality must be interpreted in that context. Now all biological indication for its existence is lacking. Biologically speaking it is absurd to say that every human also possesses a homosexual component — that, says Rado, would then be a component of the other sex — as though manifestations of behavior typical of the other sex pointed to a constitutional component of the other sex. The fundamental challenge for psychoanalysis, therefore, has to be: determine which causes lead individuals to "aberrant forms of stimulation of the standard genital equipment" (p. 186).

That is clear language: homosexuality is a pathological aberration. The ideas behind it are these. First, Rado defines human

44. Freud calls the biological duality of the sexes "a great mystery." J. Mitchell (op. cit.: 42ff.) shows that Freud does not interpret the notions of "maleness" and "femaleness" biologically.

45. S. Rado (1940/1965).

sexuality in terms of the then-current knowledge of biology, then poses this *biological* norm as criterion for health and normalcy. A reductionistic biological sex theory has now come in the place of a gender theory. Among sexuality as reproduction, sexuality as experience, and sexuality as social role, there is no difference here.

I. Bieber also bases his position on the consideration that there is no biological support for the existence of bisexuality. In 1962 he published one of the first systematic studies of homosexuals (patients only) and is an adherent — alone with other prominent psychoanalysts — of the "phobic" or "adaptation" theory of homosexuality. According to this theory, homosexuals are men with an impaired sense of maleness, which originated as a result of parental attitudes in early youth. This impairment expresses itself in fear toward and aversion from the genitalia of the opposite sex. As a reaction to this, homosexual behavior develops as an adaptation, "as a consequence of immobilizing fears surrounding heterosexual activity."[46] This is the reason why Bieber diagnoses(!) a person as homosexual only when he actually behaves as such. All homosexuals have "a potential for heterosexual excitatory response" but this is suppressed. In contrast to the popular notion that many men are latent homosexuals, Bieber thinks that all homosexuals are latent heterosexuals. "Homosexuals do not choose homosexuality. The homosexual adaptation is a substitutive alternative brought about by the inhibiting fears accompanying heterosexuality" (p. 254).

An objection advanced against Bieber's viewpoint is that from research done among patients he draws conclusions for all homosexuals.[47] Under this setup we no longer know whether the causes he cites (the parental constellation) are causes of the patient-status of the homosexual or of homosexuality itself. For Bieber, however, there is no problem here:

46. I. Bieber (1965: 253).
47. W. J. Sengers (1969: 90): "there is the obvious hypothesis that the factors of which one assumes that they led to the homophile orientation are those which actually in this way — that is as homophile — caused the person to become a patient."

Where in nature can a group of males be found with manifest aversion to the genitalia of the female of the species? In no other species in which reproduction depends on male-female sexual coupling have deviant types appeared that fear or abhor heterosexual matings and engage in homosexual behavior consistently, exclusively and in highly organized patterns. Fear and aversion to female genitalia, in themselves, demonstrate the pathology of the homosexual adaptation. (pp. 253–54)

Here reproduction is the criterion for naturalness (in the biological sense) and naturalness as criterion for health. Apart even from the question whether the psychological category of "fear" is applicable to the animal world and apart from Bieber's deterministic view of sexual behavior, it is clear that we are far removed here from Freud's criterion of illness.[48] Bieber's theory, too, is a gender theory but one that uses indiscriminately psychological ("fear") and biological (reproduction) arguments.

E. Moberly, a psychoanalytically oriented psychologist, holds to a view that resembles Bieber's theory.[49] It is based on her own evaluation of the psychoanalytic position (p. 2). In her opinion, the underlying principle that explains homosexuality is that in his or her youth the homosexual "has suffered from some deficit in the relationship with the parent of the same sex and that there is a corresponding drive to make good this deficit — through the medium of same-sex or homosexual relationships" (p. 2). Homosexuality is not an independent condition caused by this deficit but "is itself a deficit in the child's ability to relate to the parent of the same sex which is carried over to members of the same sex in general" (p. 5). "What the homosexual seeks is the fulfillment of these normal attachment needs, which have abnormally been left unmet in the process of

48. I would not deny that "unconscious dread of the female genitalia" can be called an "illness." This causes non-reproductive homosexual behavior, says Bieber. But with reference to the animal world Bieber suddenly takes the opposite tack: all of them mate heterosexually, hence the dread does not exist there. Homosexuals do not mate heterosexually, therefore they are afraid, therefore they are sick.

49. E. Moberly (1983: 1–56).

growth" (p. 9). He seeks such fulfillment in homosexual love but "the homosexual condition is one of same-sex ambivalence, not just same-sex love" (p. 17). "The capacity for same-sex love presupposes an underlying pathology . . . , but it is not itself pathological" (p. 10), because "homosexuality involves both a state of incompletion and a drive to completion" (p. 21). The latter consists in heterosexuality, "to become complete members of their own sex" (p. 23). "Homosexuality (same-sex incompletion) has a goal beyond itself, and that goal is heterosexuality (same-sex completion)" (p. 23). "The homosexual condition does not militate against male-female complementarity but rather provides a paradoxical confirmation of such complementarity by confirming the need for the normal means of attaining complementarity" (p. 29), namely the need for same-sex love as condition for a complete development into a heterosexual.

Thus far Moberly. Hence, in her view, the abnormal development of the homosexual is an illness that can be cured. "Abnormal" here means "sick." But how does she know? She does not present evidence arising from research. Her position arises rather from her Christian view of life. She seeks to convince Christians that the homosexual condition is not an unchangeable (biological) given but the normal need for love from members of the same sex that is here met in an abnormal manner: by homosexual contact. That homosexual intercourse is wrong she does not leave in doubt. The Bible condemns homosexual intercourse and "the need for reassessment is not to be found at this point" (p. 27). Accordingly, for her the man-woman polarity is a *normative* datum. So, even if Moberly is right in saying that homosexuality is caused by factors in the relation to the parent of the same sex, we still have to reject her reason for calling this different (statistically divergent) development wrong (pathological), for that reason is her moral-normative starting point. That does not hold water: the homosexual condition is not an illness because the behavior is said to be sinful. What we have here is confusion between a medical and a moral norm.

A comparable kind of reasoning as Bieber's occurs in P. C. Kuiper's much-used and frequently reprinted work on the theory of neuroses: *Neurosenleer* (1966). Homosexuality may arise when the negative oedipal complex in the development of a boy predominates. True, that is always present, but a strong sexualization of feelings, used as a defense against the heterosexual disposition, is pathological. In this connection castration-fear plays a decisive role.[50] Manifest homosexuality in adulthood is discussed in the chapter on perversions; Kuiper here follows Freud's definition of perversion. He thinks, for that matter, that this is not simply an expression of the "partial instincts" but, like the neurotic syndrome, always has a defensive component. In some cases there could also be a primary disturbance in the organization of the instincts. Kuiper thinks that the answer of psychiatry to the question of what motivates perverts is one of its most important results: i.e., perverts cannot accept the sexual difference. They cannot accept a being without a penis as a sexual partner. The most essential motive for this is the fear of castration or the castration-complex (pp. 219–20). Granted, Kuiper does not want to put homosexuality on a level with bestiality and necrophilia and he is also willing to admit that some perverts find a more or less stable adaptation, but for him homosexuality is, nevertheless, a pathological phenomenon. Here is a strong resemblance to Bieber's fear-adaptation model. The difference is that Kuiper employs as his criterion for illness the sexual difference that homosexuals cannot accept. Freud also puts it in that way — in the twentieth lecture of the series we have extensively quoted earlier: some perverts have, so to speak, eliminated the sex-difference from their program. The big difference, however, is that Freud intended this descriptively whereas for Kuiper a norm is at issue: one who eliminates this is sick. That is his premise.

Kuiper clearly sensed this because in his 1984 edition he presents another view. Now homosexuality is dealt with in a separate chapter. In it Kuiper makes a distinction between a person's sexual identity and his or her sexual orientation. As his definition shows he is dealing with what in § B was called respectively gender identity and sexual orientation (p. 193). Now, commenting on the negative Oedipus-complex, Kuiper says: "Sublimation of the ten-

50. P. C. Kuiper (1966: 51–59).

dencies and feelings belonging to the negative Oedipus-complex — sexual orientation to the opposite sex — is *usually* regarded as the *optimal* end-stage" (p. 76, italics by P. P.). He goes on to say, "It is not what the sexual orientation is but whether life is disturbed by unresolved childhood conflicts that decides the answer to the question: healthy or neurotic?" (p. 80).

For that the criterion is now: "the capacity to love, work, and play" (p. 193) — Freud's criterion! Now Kuiper believes that homosexuality *can* have defensive functions — but that is true for every psychic phenomenon — and that one must distinguish from these disturbances the manner in which society reacts to homosexuality (pp. 203–23). I want to add that for the rest Kuiper still maintains a deterministic view of the origin of homosexuality (he distinguishes, though not sharply, an active and a passive type, each with its own genesis).

An extreme example of how a normative view of homosexuality is brought into scientific research is the work of the psychologist G. J. M. van den Aardweg (1967, 1981, 1984). For years he has been the advocate of the theory that homosexuals are neurotics. In his opinion, a distinction has to be made between the social adjustment of homosexuals and their psychological adaptation. The first is not a measure of the second because neurotics can be socially well-adjusted. He spots a similar confusion in Schofield's research (mentioned in § B). The tests he used are not neuroses-tests. Over against them van den Aardweg posits:

> The neurotic instability (immaturity, lability) of homophile men has been demonstrated in all studies in which their scores on 'neurosis-tests' were compared with those of heterosexual control groups which were otherwise the same in age and training.[51]

Such a conclusion makes one curious. It is, however, incorrect. To support his conclusion van den Aardweg cites fifteen references. Only one of them, says he, points in another direction. In large part

---

51. G. J. M. van den Aardweg (1967: 111). The quotation occurs in van den Aardweg (1981: 174).

it is the research classics that are at issue. A good number of them were discussed by J. C. Gonsiorek (1982). For methodological reasons he considers them inadequate. The method of sampling, for one, is inadequate. The control-groups have not been carefully made up. The definitions of homosexuality are not careful enough. In many cases the samples are too small to support statistically reliable conclusions. Van den Aardweg, however, nowhere pays attention to these methodological questions. Gonsiorek concludes that since then it has become clear from the research that homosexuality as such is no sign of deficient psychic adaptation. In a survey article on the test-literature of the period 1900–80 B. F. Riess (1980) highlights this conclusion: no tests exist that reliably distinguish homosexuals from heterosexuals. Further, the most-used neurosis-tests show no difference in pathology between hetero- and homosexuals. Van den Aardweg in part cites the same literature as Riess but comes to the opposite conclusion. Finally, M. Siegelman (1972, 1978) concludes that homosexuals of a more masculine type in some respects displayed a better psychological adaptation than a heterosexual control group. He suggests that the tests in which homosexuals emerged as more neurotic than heterosexuals measure femininity rather than neuroticism. Van den Aardweg — of all things! — also mentions these two studies as confirming his position! Accordingly, he does not allow even scientific findings to dissuade him from the idea that homosexuality is an illness. Why is this? We read:

> . . . homosexuality as the dominant sexual orientation is already as such a neurotic phenomenon because this sexual variant is inefficient. . . . Development toward heterosexuality is a universal law and can therefore only be explained by a biological or a genetic predisposition.

And after he has rejected genetic and endocrinological interpretations as inadequate — it is a disordered development, not inborn — he says:

> Accordingly, there is really little that argues for, and much that argues against, the notion of a bisexual constitution. A final argument *against*

it is of a theoretical kind. Everywhere in nature we see the expression of the principle of utility or appropriateness. This means that living organisms and functions possess meaning, purpose. . . . Given the fact that bisexuality is already a biological monstrosity, one can never maintain that homophilia could be intended by 'nature.' . . . Accordingly, homophilia is a disturbance of the sexual function whether one wishes to regard this disturbance as good or bad.

The term "disease," in his opinion, is the best way to describe this disturbance; it is a disturbance in the ability to function appropriately and purposefully. Homosexuality is unnatural: that is van den Aardweg's normative (not moral[52]) premise. From within this perspective he defines homosexuality as "illness." Sexuality has but one healthy, normal function: reproduction. That which fails to satisfy this end is illness. His starting points here are the static-mechanical sexuality model and the naturalistic concept of illness (Chapter I). But van den Aardweg does not demonstrate their correctness; instead he adapts his research material to his starting points. Bieber and Kuiper (1966) draw normative conclusions from their scientific results. Van den Aardweg does the reverse: that is the difference.

The issue continually in debate is that the abnormal and unusual is not synonymous with illness. Freud knew this and Kuiper (1984) followed him. But one may ask, is not Freud's viewpoint as much a normative one as that of those who link sexual health with the criterion of reproduction? Our answer is: Yes — but a better one, as we will see.

First I need some definitions. The conceptual pair "normal-abnormal" is used in three distinct contexts:

(1) in relation to the *frequency of occurrence* of a trait. "Normal" is what occurs with great frequency; "abnormal" that which deviates from this pattern. I propose that in this connection we use the neutral term *variation:* a given trait's form of occurrence. Hence, an abnormal variant is a form that occurs with low statistical frequency;

52. G. J. M. van den Aardweg (1981: 168–79).

(2) in relation to *health.* "Normal," in this (western) context, means healthy (cf. normal eyesight). "Abnormal" now means *disease,* disturbance, deviation.

(3) in relation to *social acceptance.* "Normal" here means that which conforms to *prevailing social norms;* "abnormal" that which does not. Non-conformity with social norms I designate with the term (social) *deviation.*

In all three contexts it takes empirical research to determine what is normal and what is abnormal. This research is possible only when we know which criteria we must employ. To know if something diverges from a statistical standard we must have at our disposal a criterion of measurement. To know if someone is sick we need a criterion for health and illness. To know which behavior is deviant we must know the prevailing norms. However, we can also subject the existing criteria to a critical inquiry in order to test their soundness for the context in question. Then we are posing the question of *normativity.* This question is of a different order from that concerning the normal. The two may easily be confused. So the question whether homosexuality is an illness may be intended to mean: does homosexuality show the characteristics referred to in a given definition of illness? Empirical study must supply the answer. But the question can also mean: does the definition of illness according to which homosexuality is qualified as such hold water? Is it sound? Here conceptual analysis has to provide a solution.

In cases where the different contexts of the normal are confused — with each other or with normative questions — we are dealing with *fallacious* reasoning. We saw it in all the above-mentioned authors except Freud. From a given behavioral phenomenon's frequency of occurrence one cannot draw any conclusion about the actors' state of health nor about social acceptance from a medical assessment.[53] Earlier in this section I noted Senger's

---

53. S. Ruddick (1971: 94) rightly says: " 'Natural' sexual desire is for heterosexual genital activity, not for reproduction. The ground for classifying that desire as natural is that it is so organized that it could lead to reproduction in normal physiological circumstances. The 'reproductive' organization of sexual desires gives us a *criterion* of 'naturalness,' but the *virtue* of which it

conclusion that at this stage one cannot yet tell whether homosexuality is a variation, a deviation, or an illness. My definitions of the normal have made this question meaningless: all three may be the case without any logical inconsistency.

But this does not yet settle the question whether homosexuality is an illness. I do not now mean this as a question concerning the characteristics of homosexuals but concerning the defining characteristics of the concept "illness." Why is Freud's criterion of health (the ability to love, work, and play) better than the reproduction criterion (employed by Bieber et al.). In Chapter I I offered a general characterization of a couple of disease-models: the naturalist "medical" model and the normativist "open" model. Biological dysfunction was the criterion of the former; social and subjective valuation the criterion of the latter. M. Ruse indicates the difference with the aid of two words the English language has for sickness: "illness and disease." "Ill" indicates the subjective awareness of not being well, while "diseased" indicates a state of biological dysfunction.[54] A function is "biologically appropriate" when it contributes to survival and reproduction. Now the adherents of a naturalist illness-model believe that "disease" and "illness" are *independent* entities. This is to say that even when a person is not dissatisfied with his or her physical situation, the physician in attendance may still diagnose it as diseased, i.e., when the disorder restricts appropriate biological functioning. Accordingly, a sharp distinction is made here between sickness as an

---

is a criterion is the 'naturalness' itself, not reproduction." But when it becomes evident that in the case of animals not every sexual activity is directed toward reproduction, the reproduction-criterion has to be abandoned. Animals are by definition incapable of unnatural behavior.

54. Cf. the discrepancy between the medical assessment of the use of alcohol and its social acceptance. An extreme example is the assessment of bilharzia (=schistosoma) among African people. This disease in one of its forms results in blood in the urine. Red urine so often occurs in children that parents consider it abnormal when that is not the case. To the people here red urine is normal in all three senses; to a Western physician only in the first and third sense. The normal can also become rare — think of the disappearance of normal plant and animal species as a result of environmental pollution.

objective datum and its subjective valuation. Adherents of a normativist sickness-model view "illness" as a *consequence* of "disease" and "disease" as *cause* of "illness." If someone did not view
himself or herself as "ill," and if feelings of discontent were not
to be expected, even in the future (a person might be coming down
with a disease), he or she is neither "ill" nor "diseased." In this
model "proper functioning" always presupposes *social* norms.

It is clear that on the basis of the naturalist model[55] (exclusive) homosexuality is usually considered a disease and on the
basis of the normativist model it usually is not. Bieber, in view of
his reproductive criterion, is an adherent of the first; Freud is rather
an adherent of the second model.[56]

Can we make a choice? The pivotal point is the way in which
the phrase "biologically appropriate functioning" is interpreted.
Also in the case of "the ability to work, play, and enjoy oneself"
appropriate functioning is at issue. Now — again — the word
"function" is also used in several different senses. For our purpose,
three of them are important:

(1) function as the value or utility of a thing; the reference
then is to the intended effects;

(2) function as the set of effects a thing has on the whole of
which it is a part; the reference then is to more than only the
intended effects;

(3) function as the contribution an entity as part makes to
the preservation of a whole.[57]

When biologists talk about the "functions of x" they usually
have in mind the third meaning. "Functional" is that which has
adaptational value. An attribute x is present because it has been
"accepted" by natural selection in the process of the evolution of

55. M. Ruse (1981: 247ff.; 1988: 203ff.).

56. This depends on whether homosexual behavior is viewed as act or
as something that "happens" to a person.

57. Examples: the function of a hammer (1); the function of methadone
in the treatment of drug addiction (2); the function of red blood cells in the
body (3). See E. Nagel (1961: 522ff.), who distinguishes six meanings of the
word "function." Sometimes three meanings may be intended simultaneously,
as, say, in speaking of the function of a political party in a democracy.

the behavior. "Function" then means something like "those effects that are responsible for the evolution of the attribute."[58] In § D I will return to this issue. The point here is that in this manner biologists give *functional explanations* of sexual behavior, explanations in terms of functions such as copulation, couple-bonding, social cohesion, etc. Medical professionals are interested especially in dysfunction; hence their concept of function is (3) or (2).

In the context of human conduct, hence of intentional behavior, we use the word "function" especially in sense (1). The reference then is to the *meaning* of the behavior. Some people think that the meaning of sexual behaviors lies in the fulfillment of biological functions. When they do this they are assuming a *normative* viewpoint. Others entertain a different normative viewpoint. However this may be, in the context of intentional behavior "appropriate functioning" always means: functioning meaningfully and therefore social norms are involved. Accordingly, we have to make a sharp distinction between function in the sense of meaning, utility, which presupposes purposeful action on the basis of norms, and function in the other two senses. These have to do with "cause-consequence" relationships.

Now the naturalist disease-model is most useful when we are dealing with the functions of organs. But applied to human sexual behavior this model tends to confuse the several meanings of "function." Within this model it will have to be made clear why for health reasons conduct in accordance with the reproduction-criterion deserves preference. That, precisely, is what Rado, Bieber, and Kuiper (first edition) neglect to do. They assume it.[59] But the moment one argues that one (biological) criterion deserves preference over another, the naturalist model ceases to be a naturalist model and changes into the normativist (which says, we remember, that sickness always implies social norms).

---

58. Cf. W. J. van der Steen (1982: 70–72).

59. A similar objection applies to A. Kinsey's (1948) naturalistic health-model. Says he: homosexuality is part of the normal repertory of mammal behavior and is, therefore, not a disease. Even then a biological concept of function has been upgraded into a normative criterion.

Accordingly, we would have to conclude that the normativist model is the more correct of the two. But that is not an attractive solution; for then we can no longer tell disease and social deviation apart. If homosexuality is a disease when a society (or group of individuals) finds it to be so, the door is wide open to arbitrariness. But this need not be the case. A. Flew shows us that the mistake of equating social deviation and disease already occurs in Plato's *Republic*.[60] One of the underlying ideas is that ultimately social deviation is as much to a person's disadvantage as disease.[61] But that is incorrect. Violation of social norms (crime) can be very rewarding while a disease is always to a person's disadvantage. The big difference between the violator of a norm and a sick person is that a violation is a conscious act and in the case of disease one is a victim. For "act" Flew uses the term "moving" *(actus humanus)* and for behavior resulting from illness he uses "motion" *(actus hominis)*. Therefore the criteria for crime are *logically* different from those for disease. Accordingly, he is critical of the normativist model of disease. That which is really painful and produces "uneasy sensations" (J. Benthan) has nothing to do with cultural preference. In addition, pain and unpleasant sensations are not the correct criteria for sickness and health. Painful experiences are often associated with the fulfillment of certain social roles. *They,* and not the pain, are culturally conditioned. To give birth to a child is painful but not a disease. And circumcision, which in many nations is normal, has a mutilating effect, but it is not a disease. The aristocratic Chinese girls whose feet were bound when they were little were indeed deformed, but they were not diseased. The ability to fulfill a role thanks to such handicaps often made a person unfit for another role. But the inability to fulfill certain roles does not make a person sick!

So pain and physical unfitness are not sufficient conditions

---

60. A. Flew (1973: 10ff.). Vice is a kind of disease of the soul, thinks Plato's Socrates. ". . . Justice and injustice 'are in the soul what health and disease are in the body; there is no difference'" (p. 18).

61. In some developing countries children are sometimes deliberately kept abnormal so that they can function as breadwinners (disfigured beggars).

for the designation "disease." Nor is pain a necessary condition for the presence of disease. Now Flew, like the adherents of the naturalist model of disease, posits dysfunction as the main criterion of disease but assigns another meaning to it than they do:

(1) "It must always be presumptively and in itself bad for the sufferer" (p. 44). These last words imply that the sufferer, and not the people around him, has to assess his situation negatively.

(2) "It must be defined not in terms of actual behavior but in terms primarily of capacities and incapacities" (p. 50).

Now these criteria apply not only to physical but equally to mental diseases: "The disease, if it is to be a disease, must be defined: not in terms of the mere inclination of the disfavoured behavior; but in terms of an inability to inhibit that inclination" (p. 66).

Accordingly, not the deviant behavior is the criterion, nor deviant inclinations, but the inability to resist them. In other words: not the fact that *others* find my behavior or desires strange is critical but the fact that *I myself* cannot resist them. Kleptomania is a disease because the person in question cannot view his own behavior as desired. From this vantage point, neither homosexuality nor heterosexuality is a disease. The homosexual is not irresistibly inclined to engage in homosexual coitus but like the heterosexual he is able to control his inclinations. Only if "mental disorder" were defined as "non-conformity in preference and behavior," hence as social deviation, would homosexuality be a disease (p. 67).

Accordingly, Flew corrects both the normativist and the naturalist model of disease. His criticism comes down to saying that the normativist model fails to distinguish correctly between dysfunction and incapacities having to do with role-fulfillment. The naturalist model fails to distinguish between undesirable behavior and irresistible behavior. Or more briefly: the normativist model fails to distinguish disease as disturbance from deviation, and the naturalist fails to distinguish behavior resulting from an intentional act from reflexive muscular movements that happen to a person. At bottom, both disease-models confuse "function" in its biological-medical meanings with "function" as utility and purpose.

145

After this analysis we can, on good grounds, reject the reproduction-criterion as a standard for sexual diseases: it applies the standard too much to external observable behavior and fails to do justice to the intentions of the actors.[62] That element should be kept out of a good definition of disease. Not what comes out in the way of behavior, not what are the consequences or causes of the behavior, but whether the behavior is "moving" or "motion" is a correct criterion for the absence or presence of disease. Only after it has in this way been determined whether a disease is present can the question concerning the causes of this disease be discussed. But from the demonstrability of causes or from the occurrence of certain effects one can never infer that a given phenomenon is a disease. Freud had a keen eye for this because for him a divergent development (which he himself viewed very deterministically) and good health could very well go together. The capacity to love, work, and play — that is the issue. Consequently, Freud's view is more correct than that of Bieber, Rado, or Kuiper (first editon). Homosexuality as such does not meet rational criteria for disease.

D. Sexuality and the societal relations of the sexes

Today society no longer views homosexuality as a disease. What has remained, however, is the notion that we are dealing with a distinct form of minority behavior. People now speak of a variation or a social deviation; not sick but deviant.

Just as in the case of diseases, so one can present causal explanations for deviations: biological, sociological, etc. In the following sections we will discuss these explanations because it is simply a fact that homosexuals differ in some respects from those who live heterosexually, and where there are differences there are also causes.

But first a preliminary question: why does the homosexual-

62. Bieber is indeed consistent because (in § B) we also saw him define homosexuality in terms of externally observable behavior.

heterosexual distinction strike people? And in such a way that it has become a categorical difference? People differ from each other in practically every imaginable respect. Also in sexual preference: blond or brunet, younger or older, stout or slim, monogamous or promiscuous. But such differences strike most people as less than the difference between a homo- and a heterosexual preference. The differences among heterosexual preferences are minimalized; there is room for these differences and "it is no use arguing over taste." But many people feel that homosexual preference should not really be allowed and there is much argument over this "taste." The matter even calls for equal rights laws.

Why? There are only two sexes and only their physical conjunction is biologically functional. That is the opinion held by psychoanalysts such as Rado and Bieber, just as it is held by numerous traditional ethicists. In Chapter I (§ D) we described this idea under the heading of the "static-mechanical model of sexuality" and rejected it as inadequate. According to this model, it is ultimately an anatomical difference — the difference in the type of sexual organs — that is the decisive factor in the determination of what is normal and what is abnormal sexuality.

In the preceding section we noted that from this distinction, based as it is on concepts derived from biology, no conclusions about the health value of "abnormal" sexual behavior may be drawn. But what value can we assign to a biological argument as criterion for normal and abnormal sexuality? That value seems self-evident, but is it? We can answer this question by tracing how our culture came by this *naturalistic* model of sexuality. "Naturalistic" here has the same meaning as it did in relation to the disease-model because in this model biological functions serve as criterion for normal or abnormal sexuality.[63] Also the static-mechanical model of sexuality is a naturalistic model.

In this section I will discuss a number of theories about how our culture came by the biological reproduction-criterion for normal sexuality. They constitute a relatively arbitrary selection, but,

63. "Function" in the sense of "effects"; "normal" in the sense of "statistically normal." See the previous section.

of course, my agenda here is not to write a history of sexuality-models in western culture. I just want to demonstrate that, hidden behind the apparently descriptive notion of sexuality — defined in biological terms — there are certain normative elements. They are the reason why, in our culture particularly, the difference between homo- and heterosexuality is so striking to people.

In his "Eros and Civilization"[64] H. Marcuse establishes a connection between Freud's psychoanalytic theory and the social theory of the Frankfurt School. He believes that psychoanalysis has been made into a kind of happiness-therapy for the self-realizing personality (among others, by E. Fromm). As a result, the immense influence of society upon the development of the individual has been underestimated. That was not Freud's intention. Individual situations are derivations from the common lot and common societal repression forms the individual down to his most personal traits — as Freud also viewed it. In Marcuse's views "repression" is a key word. The idea of civilization implies the restriction of the instincts (repression) and their historical modification. Human history is the history of the repression of instincts. In their uncontrolled form the most important instincts, *eros* and *thanatos,* are dangerous; only in their transformation can humans be human. A transformation of the "pleasure principle" into the "reality principle" is needed; this is to say that delayed gratification has to replace immediate gratification. In the place of play and pleasure alone, there must also be control; besides joy also toil; besides receptivity also productivity. That is a precondition for culture; hence culture presupposes a degree of repression of the instincts.

At th's point Marcuse launches his attack on Freud. Freudian concepts he says, are ahistorical. Now, in order to capture the historical dimension of the transformation of the instincts, Marcuse introduces two concepts: "surplus-repression" and the "performance principle." "Surplus-repression" is a repression that comes on top of the repression needed for civilization and the "performance principle" implies the historical form of the "reality principle." Now in

64. H. Marcuse (1955).

our society the rationality that demands that the instincts undergo a certain measure of repression (reality principle) has been turned into irrationality because the performance principle (work) has become dominant, partly as the result of the development of science and technology and of rising bureaucratization. The resulting surplus-repression especially concerns sexuality, the most unruly of the instincts. In order to protect labor, the body was desexualized; sex was limited to genital achievements and banished to the private sphere of leisure time. This serves people exclusively as a rest-period to get ready for the work of the next day. For the same reason love and sexuality were welded together in a tight unity. Sexuality was sublimated in "love." The private world of the family and the public sphere of society were increasingly separated and subjected to different kinds of rules. In the world of work, the exchange of products and labor power was now central; in the sphere of the family, the divine and moral law. The idea of a human being as an end and never merely as a means (Kant) applied almost exclusively to the second sphere. Consequently, the full force of morality was mobilized against sexual expression: the body was not permitted to be an object and instrument of pure pleasure because that was the dubious privilege of prostitutes, degenerates, and perverts. Particularly in their experience of sexual pleasure, people were thought to be devoted to high moral ideals. Hence sexuality needed to be the expression of love within monogamous marriage. Marcuse, accordingly, views this situation as the consequence of surplus-repression. But this is not our only option. When the division of labor is oriented to the fulfillment of individual needs and the body is not the exclusive instrument of work, humans can be re-sexualized. Marcuse calls this a "spread of the libido." It expresses itself in "a reactivation of all erotogenic zones, and, consequently, in a resurgence of pregenital polymorphous sexuality and a decline of genital supremacy" (p. 201).

This will lead to a breakdown of the institutions in which sexuality is presently organized. Marcuse certainly does not mean an explosion of presently repressed sexuality. That would only have a destructive effect. But he does see a "transformation of libido" on the horizon:

from sexuality constrained under genital supremacy to erotization of the entire personality. It is a spread rather than explosion of the libido — a spread over private and societal relations which bridges the gap maintained between them by a repressive reality principle. (pp. 201–2)

In such a society the perversions also, insofar as they are compatible with civilization, can find a legitimate place. Specifically this applies to homosexuality as a return to the polymorphously perverse sexuality of childhood. If, at present, homosexuality still expresses itself in a destructive manner, this must be viewed in the context of the general perversion of human existence in an oppressive society, writes Marcuse.

Accordingly, his thesis is that current western ideas on sexuality can be grasped only in light of an analysis of *modern* society. Whether Marcuse's analysis is correct is not our concern, anymore than his utopian prescription. But we do want to note that the fixed center of his analysis lies in the idea of the instincts as supratemporal and transcultural entities. In other words: Marcuse criticizes western sexual ideas in light of a *naturalistic* model of (homo)sexuality, viz., that of the psychic drives or instincts.

G. Rubin (1975) also bases her position on this psychoanalytic premise. She, however, analyzes western sexuality in light of past society — a society based on kinship relations — by drawing a parallel between the psychoanalysis of Freud and the anthropology of Lévi-Strauss. The resemblance between them is that both theories describe the transition from a "natural" mode of human existence to a "cultural" one. Freud does this for the individual, whose ups and downs are described in terms of the transformations that occur during the liquidation of the Oedipus complex, while Lévi-Strauss describes the break between animal and human culture.

Lévi-Strauss conceives social reality as a process of exchange. The basis of human culture is the gift. The definitive break between animal and human culture is that the exchange now occurs in a controlled manner. This may consist in an exchange of words (language), of goods and services (economy), or of people (kinship). In all cultures these are the women[65] and the exchange is controlled by the men! For that reason the essential relation in the kinship-system is always that between brothers-in-law. In it the basic elements are the relations of brother-sister-father or of spouse-son (in place of the father-mother-child relations in the "biological nuclear family"). The elementary forms of human society are the relations between families and not those within the family.[66] Exogamy, therefore, becomes the rule. Coupled with the law of exogamy is the prohibition of incest. That is the cornerstone of society, because it forces exchange. Lévi-Strauss calls the incest-taboo "the rule of the gift *par excellence.*"[67] Rubin adds that the incest-taboo presupposes an antecedent taboo of homosexual relations: the prohibition of some heterosexual relations implies a prohibition of all non-heterosexual relations. She therefore thinks that humans pay a price for access to culture: the abandonment of all incestuous and non-heterosexual relations.

Now Rubin finds this anthropological conclusion confirmed in Freud's conception of the development of a child (i.e., a boy). In the resolution of the Oedipus complex the child abandons the "natural" incestuous relation with the mother because it has been confronted by the "law of the father" (Lacan). By way of the Oedipal phase a human child gains access to culture; with it his entry into humanity begins. In this phase the child assimilates the rules concerning sexuality; the psychological differences between the sexes and the heterosexual orientation originate. This development precisely fits the demands the kinship-system imposes on the members of society!

Rubin points out that according to psychoanalysts the Oedipus complex is a universal problem. Only the form in which it arises is culture-dependent. Freud described the Oedipal drama for the Viennese bourgeoisie around the turn of the century, but

65. The exchange of women is a defining characteristic of human, in distinction from animal, culture, says Mitchell (1974: 372).

66. J. Mitchell (op. cit.: 374).

67. The incest-taboo serves to prevent kinship from coinciding with blood-relationship (A. Mooy 1975: 27–37; cf. J. Mitchell, op. cit.: 370–76).

the theory of the Oedipus complex has universal validity. Once the child has passed through the Oedipal phase, his or her libido and sense of gender is usually shaped in accordance with the rules of his or her culture.

The conclusion Rubin draws from the strong resemblance between the theories of Freud and those of Lévi-Strauss is that also in our culture sexuality is still organized according to the principles of the kinship-system, while it is precisely here that such big changes have occurred. The family has lost its former economic and political functions, and in the bourgeois nuclear family, which emerged since the eighteenth century, the figure of the mother's brother, the key-figure in the kinship system, no longer plays a role. Says Rubin:

> The organization of sex and gender once had functions other than itself — it organized society. Now, it only organizes and reproduces itself. The kinds of relationships of sexuality established in the dim human past still dominate our sexual lives, our ideas about men and women, and the ways we raise our children. But they lack the functional load they once carried. One of the most conspicuous features of kinship is that it has been systematically stripped of its functions — political, economic, educational, and organizational. It has been reduced to its bare bones — sex and gender. (p. 199)

But in our society this manner of sexual socialization is no longer necessary because it has become functionless. A "resolution in kinship" could, therefore, be pursued and obligatory heterosexuality eliminated: "Women are not only oppressed as women, we are oppressed by having to be women, or men as the case may be" (p. 204).

When this oppression has stopped — and in this connection psychoanalysis can help the feminist and gay movement — a new "androgynous" society, in which the primary object-choice would be the bisexual one, would come into being.

Central in Rubin's argument is that heterosexual socialization in the kinship-system did not have the function of stressing the biological differences between the sexes but of stretching them

152

and blurring the resemblances in the interest of the *societal* function of the sexes. Their roles were mutually exclusive and mutually complementary. In today's society this is no longer the case.[68]

We need not agree with Rubin's dream of an androgynous society to conclude that the function of the prohibition of homosexuality in a society based on kinship relations is different from what the contemporary argument — couched in biological terms — against homosexuality conveys (homosexuality as biological dysfunction). We may accordingly, suspect that this biological argumentation is the scientific rationalization of an ancient taboo rather than a rational argument. In any case, the biological view of (homo) sexuality (specifically, its contraction to the reproductive function) arose at some time in western culture. Such a view says as much about a culture as it does about human sexuality. On this point, despite their different theoretical frames of reference, Rubin and Marcuse are agreed.

Rubin, too, makes use of an objective, universally valid criterion for sexuality: Freud's theory of the "polymorphously perverse" instincts of childhood, hence a naturalistic (psychological) model. The authors we will now discuss, M. Foucault and J. van Ussel, demonstrate, however, how *normative* this model actually is. According to them, social conceptions are constitutive for what is viewed as sexuality.

Says M. Foucault (1976):

> Sexuality is the name that can be given to a historical construct:[69] not a furtive reality that is difficult to grasp, but a great surface network in which the stimulation of bodies, the intensification of pleasures, the incitement to discourse, the formation of special knowledges, the strengthening of controls and resistances, are linked to one another, in accordance with a few major strategies of knowledge and power. (pp. 105, 106)

68. For this see also I. Illich (1982).

69. The French term "dispositif" is hard to translate. One English translation reads: "interlocking historical mechanisms." Foucault displays a strong preference for metaphors derived from technology.

This intertwinement of knowledge and power is much more characteristic for what is called "sexuality" in the West than the fact that it is subject to repression. That also exists but knowledge of sex must not be analyzed in terms of repression but of power, for sexuality is not a "stubborn drive" that resists being regulated but "a transfer point for relations of power" (p. 103). Power is a central theme in Foucault's work. He rejects a concept of power that is all one-way from above (the powerful) to below (the powerless). True, this form of power exists but it is only one of many. Power is omnipresent and is produced everywhere at every point and in every relation. It comes from above but also from below. Power also everywhere produces resistance, a counter-force that in turn can be a source of power.

> Power is everywhere; not because it embraces everything, but because it comes from everywhere. And "Power," insofar as it is permanent, repetitious, inert, and self-reproducing, is simply the over-all effect that emerges from all these mobilities, the concatenation that rests on each of them and seeks in turn to arrest their movement. One needs to be nominalistic, no doubt: power is not an institution, and not a structure; neither is it a certain strength we are endowed with; it is the name that one attributes to a complex strategical situation in a particular society. (p. 93)

In the process of generating power, language plays a central role, i.e., in naming and categorizing the invention of new terms and the creation of various kinds of discourse. In this context scientific discourse has a special function. It is not only guided by the unprejudiced will to knowledge but also serves as part of the power-strategies. According to Foucault, it is impossible to divorce the knowledge from the power exerted through it; they are two sides of the same coin: power-knowledge (pp. 98–99).

Knowledge of sexuality has, since the eighteenth century, become the object of power-relations. The background was the population problem. Sexuality proved a very suitable means of control over people through the medium of their bodies. The reason for this is that in the West the truth about sex was increasingly viewed as the truth about "man," as the road to self-knowledge. Sex was interrogated for the truth about "man." Foucault traces this development back to the time when oral confession became obligatory (1215) and people had to confess everything, put everything into words, especially their sexual acts and yearnings.

In the eighteenth and nineteenth century the "strategies of discipline" were given a "scientific" foundation. Foucault describes this development as the "entry of life into history" (p. 141). Life was no longer simply a natural given that the sovereign can take or leave but became the object of power-strategies, power over life, biopolitics. Foucault distinguishes four great power strategies:

(1) a "hysterization" of women's bodies; (2) a "pedagogization" of children's sex (the masturbation discourses); (3) a "socialization" of procreative behavior (family planning); and (4) a "psychiatrization" of perverse pleasure.

A series of new personality types made their appearance such as the sadistic husband, the frigid wife, the precocious child, the perverse homosexual, etc.,[70] "the combined figures of an alliance gone bad and an abnormal sexuality" (p. 110).

What was it this "sexuality-construct," in which one component was scientific knowledge, had to accomplish? Says Foucault: "It is no longer a matter of bringing death into play in the field of sovereignty but of distributing the living in the domain of value and utility" (p. 144). Power no longer "draws the line that separates the enemies of the sovereign from his obedient subjects; it effects distributions around the norm." To that end it is necessary "to qualify, measure, appraise, and hierarchize" (p. 144). In this context, "the notion of sex made it possible to group together, in an artificial unity, anatomical elements, biological functions, conducts, sensations, and pleasures, and it enabled one to make use of this fictitious unity as a causal principle, an omnipresent meaning, a secret to be discovered everywhere" (p. 154).

This knowledge acquired an appearance of being "scientific" because some of the contents of biology and physiology bordered

70. In §B of this chapter I already referred to the difference between "sodomy" (aberrant behavior) and "homosexuality" (personality type).

on it. Accordingly, some of their concepts could be used in what is no more than an analogy, "as a principle of normality for human sexuality" (p. 155). The individual and his sexual practices are caught in this web. Do not think, warns Foucault, "that by saying yes to sex, one says no to power" (p. 157). In saying this he does not deny that the concept of sexuality, couched in biological terms, also had a function in the emancipation of homosexuals. The discourse on sexuality also enabled homosexuals to start a "reverse" discourse. Homosexuals began to speak in behalf of its "naturalness," using the same medical categories that were used to disqualify them (p. 101). But now sexual liberation is no longer enough; we need to liberate ourselves from the medical-biological-naturalistic concept of sexuality itself.[71]

Hence, for Foucault "sexuality" is a collection of heterogeneous elements gathered into one word, written in biologistic language with the intent to discipline sex by subordinating it to norms. Although he seems to assume a minimum biological basis of "sexuality," the precise point on which the sexuality-construct seizes remains in the dark. This is not the focus of Foucault's interest as evidenced by his thesis that knowledge of sexuality is "power-knowledge." Too little attention is paid to the truth-claims of this knowledge.

On that subject we are better informed by the historian and ethicist J. van Ussel. Although his work displays numerous parallels with that of Foucault,[72] he expects more from rational opposition to existing prejudices. Van Ussel (1968), in contrast with Foucault, does interpret sexuality in terms of repression and thinks that the cause of what he calls "the anti-sexual syndrome of the West" lies in the rise of the bourgeoisie and its principles, in the "bourgeois conditioning of society." The burgher represented a new mindset: its most important principles are abstinence, delayed gratification, parsimony, the rejection of useless leisure time, and strong control over the passions. He combines "the fear of pleasure" with a "morality of performance." Van Ussel shows how

71. Interview. See L. Dullaart et al. (1983: 14).
72. See the various contributions in: J. Kruithof et al. (1979).

156

sexuality was increasingly restricted to the intimacy of the bedroom and how sex slowly became the greatest evil and a pathological and fear-inducing thing. Along with this came the sexualization of perception. The burgher looks at life through "sexual glasses," i.e., the sexual aspects of human relations strike him most. In van Ussel's opinion, increased sexual repression also occasions greater sensitivity to the sexual.

In his later work van Ussel points out that it was not until the nineteenth century that the term "sexuality" acquired its present field of meaning and is itself a product of the anti-sexual syndrome. Accordingly, he wonders whether the term is useful as a scientific concept. We tend to indicate sexual behavior by referring to the organs involved, usually only the primary sex organs. This betrays our "genital view" of sexuality. That is remarkable because we do not describe other kinds of behavior by referring to the organs involved: kissing is not oral behavior, nor is eating; why then is an erection "sexual"? Is a person homosexual because the genitals of the partners are of the same sex? Sexologists think that way, says van Ussel, and thus resemble painters who do not get beyond a grasp of materials and technique. From the visible reactions of "sexed" organs (erection, orgasm, etc.) they conclude that "sexuality" exists and that from them one can tell whether a person is highly sexed or not. If sexuality could be equated with "gender," there would, in his opinion, be no objection to the term. It would then denote the fact that plants, animals, and human beings come in two sexes, what van Ussel calls the phenomenon of "being-sexed." But then also the difference between the sexes in handkerchiefs, dress, bicycles, etc. is sexual. So in one way "sexuality" is broader and in another way it is narrower than "being-sexed," but the criteria in terms of which this is the case are unclear. Sexologists — including the drive-theoreticians of the Freudian school — argue from what is in fact a combination of functions of behavior to the existence of a functional whole, thinks van Ussel. Accordingly, his conclusion is that the necessary and sufficient conditions for calling a given area of reality "sexual" are lacking.[73]

73. J. van Ussel (1975: 115–27).

157

Then with what *are* the different functions of sexual behavior linked up? With a person's normative image of the human, says van Ussel. Some find the reproductive function very important, others the orgastic or sensual function, or the fulfillment of relational need. But a person's image of the human is a choice. It does not say anything about the "essence" of the human. On that score nothing objective can be said. Accordingly, nothing objective can be said about the "essence" of sexuality either.

> This means that all views of the sexual, all sexual-ethical systems, make a mistake when they base themselves on the 'peculiar nature' of 'man,' or nature, or whatever. When we say that 'man' can go in all directions, and that all images of the human are based on choices, this also applies to the sexual.[74]

For the rest van Ussel believes that humans possess a "bisexual or supra-sexual nature," and bases this claim on the early embryonic development. The sharp division between men and women, maleness and femaleness, is the consequence of a *normative* reproductive view. The idea is to overcome this division by putting more emphasis on "intimacy" (in distinction from "sexuality"). Accordingly, van Ussel considers exclusive homosexuality just as problematic as exclusive heterosexuality. It is the result of self-programming in one of the two directions, based on the desire for certainty about one's identity. But it betrays a sexualized view of human relations.[75]

Thus far van Ussel. We need not agree with his overly facile assessment of sexology or his (seemingly?[76]) relativistic ethics. He writes and judges on the basis of a strong conviction. But as a result — or in spite of this — the problematic character of the naturalistic model of sexuality that he opposes does become clear. The "kink" in this model lies in its use of the word "function."

We discussed a few of its meanings in the previous section.

74. J. van Ussel (1974[4]: 11–27; the quotation occurs on p. 26).
75. J. van Ussel (1974: 71; 1975: 130–37).
76. On this see H. van den Enden (1979: 221–55).

The most important distinction concerned that between "function" as value, utility, or meaning and "function" as effect. In biology "function" is *not* used in the first sense. The problem is that sexology ostensibly uses "function" in the biological sense but in reality uses it in the first sense, that of utility or meaning. Why is that? We saw how the naturalistic sexuality-model makes the biological functions of sexual behavior the standard for normal sexuality. But the phrase "biological functions of the behavior" is ambiguous. The phrase can refer to: (1) an analysis of human action (conduct) in terms of the contribution it makes to the occurrence of certain "biological functions"; and (2) a manner of approaching human *behavior* as this is customary in biology, by the application of ethological methods of animal research, in the context of which no reference is made to intentions, feelings, and thoughts but only to causes and functions.

Reproduction is sometimes called a "biological" function of sexual behavior in distinction, say, from its "religious" function. This means there is a function of sexuality (function in the sense of use or utility) that is examined by biologists, medical researchers, or students of religion. But "function" in the sense it has in biology is something very different. "Functional" there is a given trait, e.g., an element of behavior, when it makes a contribution to the maintenance of a whole, viz., the individual himself, his descendants, or a group (species). "Biological" here means a special manner of approaching animal behavior, including the human, i.e., without referring to feelings or intentions. From this angle biologists may also try to approach religious behavior (biologists will assume that religion has functional significance). The confusing factor is that reproduction is "biological" in both senses. But the fact that representatives of discipline *x* do research on phenomenon *y* does not make it an *x*-like phenomenon![77]

Now sexologists are interested in the biological "functions" of behavior in the first sense. But they make it appear as if they are studying "functions" in the second sense, hence as though sexology were a biological science of human behavior alongside

77. B. Voorzanger (1986: 31).

of ethology as the biology of animal behavior. That is not the case because sexologists study human sexual behavior. Thus confusion arises between "functions" as human meaning-bestowal on behavior in the sense of act (conduct) and a biological concept of "function" that relates to behavior in the sense of externally *observable* behavior.

Functions like meaning-bestowal (use, utility) have to do with norms. Functions in the biological sense have to do with descriptions and explanations. Now the concept of sexuality, as conceived in a naturalistic model, is intended descriptively: sexual behavior as biologically functional behavior. But actually it establishes a *norm:* functionally sexual behavior (function as meaning-bestowal) is biologically functional. Thereby a term intended as a *characterization* of certain behavior (sexuality) also acquires the character of a *norm*. This also explains why discussions of abnormal sexuality (in the statistical sense of abnormal) so easily turn into discussions about disease, social deviation, and immoral behavior.

Even by the standard of a naturalistic sexuality-model, western homosexuality is not necessarily less normal than western heterosexuality. That is demonstrated by Marcuse and Rubin. The latter also gives a (functional) explanation of the restriction of sexuality to sex and gender. But van Ussel and Foucault demonstrate how normative (in a disciplinary sense, says Foucault) the concept of sexuality is in western sexology.

Must we now join van Ussel in "taking leave of sexuality"? No, on closer scrutiny van Ussel only proves to have in mind a farewell to *regulation* by means of the sexuality concept. In its place he proposes the notion of "intimacy." His objection, as it is mine, is that sexology normativizes the average, makes it the criterion of good sexuality by means of which people determine what is and what is not deviant. But to say this is not to say anything to the disadvantage of a *biological* (ethological) approach to human sexual behavior. This is what van Ussel fails to understand; Foucault does not express himself on it.[78] The preceding

78. Van Ussel, for that matter, does say (1975: 102): "the importance

section demonstrated that homosexuality is definitely not a disease. The disease-model of homosexuality is based on a confusion of act (motion) and reflective muscular movement (moving). This section shows that sexology distinguishes the normal from the abnormal on the basis of a confusion between *act* (conduct) and *behavior*. But a person is not biologically deviant because his sexual intentions are directed toward something other than the biological function (utility) of sexuality, even though thereby he deviates from the social norm of western culture. In that regard van Ussel and Foucault are correct. This does not mean it is senseless to speak in any way about the biological dysfunctions of human behavior, but then we are talking about human behavior, not conduct. For that we must not go to sexology but to ethology and sociobiology. Behavior is either *intentional*, and then it is called conduct, or it is *non-intentional*. One excludes the other. But behavior can be examined by way of two distinct methods of approach: from the perception of function as meaning-bestowal and from a biological perspective. That is the difference.

E. Biological explanations I: ethology and endocrinology

No conclusions can be drawn about the biological (physiological, endocrinological, etc.) functions of human behavior from classifications of that behavior in terms of its meanings. The essence of Foucault's and van Ussel's objections to sexology is that it does not see this clearly. Van Ussel's position is that the average westerner is heterogenital in his behavior, primarily heterosensual in his feelings, often bi- or homoerotic in his need for intimacy and security, usually homophile in his friendships, largely homocultural in his social contacts, and particularly homosocial because,

---

attributed to the sex organs arises not so much from biology or psychology as from factors of economic, social, and political power." Foucault (1976/1984: 152) refers to the merely general analogy between biological and sexological concepts.

for the most part, the sexes live in separate worlds. In his opinion, to consider only the sex of the sexual organs is to have a rather dull view of human relations.[79] With some exaggeration he concludes that the necessary and sufficient conditions for calling an area of reality "sexual" are lacking. He is, however, correct when he asserts that one cannot arrive at true insight into the sexual behavior of human beings from the vantage point of sexology. But that assertion says nothing about the value of the biological approach to the knowledge of human sexual behavior.[80]

Often the medical-psychiatric approach to sexual behavior and the biological, in this case the ethological approach, are lumped together. That is a mistake. Ethology describes and explains animal behavior, including the human, without reference to the subjective contents of consciousness and intentions. It is based on careful observation. This is not because the first approach would not yield information but because, being colored by the prejudices of the informants, this information is inexact. Accordingly, the ethological approach does not replace the introspective but operates alongside of it.

The ethologist is not interested particularly in human behavior. For him Homo sapiens is one species among many. Human behavior is even more complex than animal behavior. The results of animal research can, therefore, never be directly applied to humans, although they do yield data that can be tested for their applicability to humans. They have made clear that in general the construction of human and animal behavior is the same as to organizational structure.[81] The large differences in behavior between animal and man are not thereby denied, but this indicates that the study of animal models makes sense for the acquisition of information on human behavior, including the sexual. The question of which animal model is suited for this purpose is a difficult one and I will come back to it later.

79. J. van Ussel (1975: 135).
80. G. P. Baerends (1973: 288) lists as the advantages of the biological approach: (1) an objective type of research that does not make use of subjective data provided by informants and (2) viewing behavior as adaptation rooted in evolution.
81. G. P. Baerends (1973: 288ff.; 321).

The ethologist can be interested in the functions, as well as in the causes, of the behavior. Those two are not the same. In the case of functions we are interested in tracing the factors responsible for the origination and continuation of the behavior patterns of a species. The background here is the evolutionary theory according to which all life-forms are adapted to their life-environment. Functional factors, however, are not causal, nor is a functional explanation a causal one,[82] granted that approaching behavior as a functional adaptation rooted in evolution presupposes a genetic, hence a causal, basis for the behavior. The organizational structure of the behavior originates in the interaction between environment and genes.

Behavior arises from the presence of a specific external and/or internal *stimulus-situation* and the presence of a specific *motivation*.[83] In the case of a difference in motivation a same stimulus-situation evokes a different response (behavior). The study of motivational factors is performed by branches of biology other than ethology, such as behavioral physiology, neurophysiology, and endocrinology (the theory of hormones). Hormones that

82. A clear example of the difference between the function and the causation of behavior is the following. Banana flies (drosophila) always emerge from the pupa at daybreak. This is an adaptation to prevent dehydration to which in the first few hours the tender wings are especially vulnerable and humidity is at its highest in the morning. But high humidity is not the causal factor. Experiments proved that the pupa cannot even register humidity. The causal factor is the rotation of day and night in the pupa-stage, which brings about irreversible biochemical reactions (J. J. A. van Iersel 1973: 2b).

83. When a series of connected behaviors that succeed each other in time increase or decrease in a given time, ethologists postulate a common motivational mechanism underlying the pattern. Motivation in ethology means: "the complex of factors responsible for the variable readiness of an individual to react to a given situation with a certain response" (L. de Ruiter 1973: 113). This concept replaces the old "instinct" or "drive" concept employed in "animal psychology." By contrast, the motivation-concept is "a set of problems, not a thing" (R. A. Hinde 1974: 25). This implies that nest-building, courtship, flight behavior, and the like are not explained by reference to a presumed nest-building, or sexual, or flight instinct; instead they demand further (physiological, etc.) research into the causal factors that together influence these behaviors.

circulate in the blood are important motivational factors. Depending on their concentration they increase or decrease the motivation for a specific behavior pattern. For that matter, the motivating function of hormones is not the only one involved. To that subject, too, I will return in a moment. In brief: on the basis of the observation of behavioral elements and their succession, the ethologist arrives at hypotheses concerning the existence of specific motivations — this in distinction from sexology. Physiology and endocrinology attempt to unravel their background.

Now the question is whether animal research gives rise to the assumption of a specific homosexual motivation (hence in the ethological, not the psychological, sense) and how hormones play a role in it. At that point, then, biological research links up with sexology, whose central concern was always the search for hormonal differences between homosexuals and heterosexuals.[84]

Every answer to that question, however, must be placed in the context of what ethological research can and cannot do. One who wants to know why in our culture one person becomes heterosexual and another homosexual must not turn to ethology. The reason is that ethologists make assertions about differences and similarities between human behavior and animal behavior. These assertions relate to the behavior of the human species and have no direct bearing on differences between groups of people. In the ethological approch such diverse phenomena as classic pederasty, initiation rites in Polynesia, shamanism in Africa, western homosexuality, and homosexual pedophilia, and possibly also transsexuality all fall under the single heading of homosexuality. A person interested in the differences between them — hence in differences between groups of people — ends up not with ethology but with the human sciences. What ethology can do is furnish information about the comparability of human and animal (homo)sexual behavior.

84. Sexual hormones were discovered at the beginning of this century. Deviations in (neuro) physiological processes in the case of homosexuals were already presupposed by nineteenth-century sexologists like Krafft Ebing ("psychic hermaphroditism").

The fact that ethology does not serve to explain the differences between groups of people does not mean, however, that such differences are therefore environmentally (and not genetically or hormonally) determined. From time to time people draw this mistaken conclusion. They then — wrongly — think in terms of dichotomies: nature vs. culture, innate vs. acquired, genetically vs. environmentally determined, or biological vs. sociological. That is the pitfall of the so-called "nature-nurture issue" in which the members of dichotomies are opposed to each other as mutually exclusive alternatives.[85] But the statement (by a biologist) that "behavior x in the human species is genetically determined" is not inconsistent with the statement (by a sociologist) that "behavior x in people is not genetically determined." The biologist is making a comparison between man and animal, hence between different species; the sociologist is talking about differences between groups of people. Biology does not make the distinction between "environmentally determined" and "biologically determined" characteristics.[86] Accordingly, the nature-nurture dichotomy does not have a basis in reality. Still the issue persists. One reason is that sometimes people prefer explanations in terms of "culture" — by which sociological explanations are meant — because they attribute "an aura of determinism" to biological, specifically genetic, explanations (as, e.g., De Cecco [§ B] does). The fact that this is erroneous will be discussed in the next section. Such a viewpoint in any case precludes the possibility of a precise description and decoding of the program underlying the behavior.[87]

It is often difficult to determine, in behavioral research among social animals, when one is dealing with sexual behavior. In many social contacts, a category that includes the sexual, multiple motivations — such as those of aggression and flight — play a role. Conversely, elements of the repertory of sexual behavior have a function in other contexts as well, e.g., the presentation of

85. Thus in a discussion of biological explanations of homosexuality Th. F. Hoult, a sociologist, states: "If the social factor is determinative, it is unnecessary to posit an unidentified and unmeasured biological 'component.'"

86. See B. Voorzanger (1982).

87. As G. P. Baerends (1980: 454) correctly posits.

the genitalia with a view to greeting or threatening another animal. Males mount each other in dominance-submission relations, in situations of play, or to reinforce the social coherence of the group.[88] Sexual behavior is a category of behavior that is hard to distinguish from other social behavior. But even when one takes account of this in the research, one finds same-sex sexual behavior throughout the animal world. Observations of such behavior, especially among males, have been made in such divergent groups as fish, birds, reptiles, and numerous groups of mammals, including primates (apes, anthropoids, man). No hormonal or other structural abnormalities are involved and heterosexual mating behavior is normal. The same-sex behavior usually has a circumstantial character. It may be related to special social circumstances, such as abnormal population density. But usually it is part of the learning behavior of young animals and serves as a sign of submission or affection (apes). We are dealing here with observations in natural settings. Our conclusion has to be that all animal species naturally display same-sex behavior under certain circumstances. It usually, but not always, occurs without seminal discharge.[89]

In how far is comparison with homosexual behavior among humans possible here? Some see great resemblance. They point out that all forms of homosexual behavior that occur among humans are, to some degree, also found among animals, both among males and females. Of some individuals it can be said that their behavior is bisexual. Homosexual behavior as the expression of dominance-relations in the pecking order of social animals is reminiscent of the "circumstantial homosexuality" that occurs in prisons and also of forms of homosexuality that occur in the Arab world. Also homosexual pairing has been observed, for example, among birds that live very monogamous lives (like humans?). Sexual (= mating) behavior among young males during their learning period resembles the homosexual experiments that take place among the young in the human world.[90]

88. F. Beach (1979: 128ff.); R. A. Hinde (1974: 293ff.).
89. R. H. Denniston (1980).
90. J. D. Weinrich (1982: 199ff.).

But "to resemble" is not the same as "to be biologically comparable." In reality the resemblance is superficial. Characteristic for western homosexuality is the sexual preference for members of one's own sex. That is a psychological given and has to do with intention and with reference to intention nothing can be inferred from observation of behavior among animals. But also on the level of the behavior itself there are differences. Sexual behavior in the case of animals can be analyzed in terms of three variables: the genetic sex, the sex-typical behavior, and the type of stimulus-pattern. The sexual behavior proves to be dependent both on the sex and the stimulus-pattern. That is to say, while males usually display male behavior and females female behavior, the male stimulus-pattern evokes a female response in females *and* males, and a female stimulus-pattern evokes a male response in males *and* females. Beach calls this phenomenon the principle of stimulus-response complementarity.[91] If this were the only determinant of sexual behavior, the result would be complete bisexuality. That, however, does not exist because the readiness of a male to react to a female stimulus with male behavior is, as a rule, much greater than his readiness to respond to a male stimulus with female behavior. For females, *mutatis mutandis,* the same applies. Built-in thresholds clearly exist. For that reason animals usually behave heterosexually and sometimes homosexually, but in the latter case they behave homosexually *in relation to their genetic sex,* not *in relation to the sexual stimulus-pattern.* Now that is different in human (read: western) homosexuality. Homosexual men are usually more attracted to male patterns of behavior and lesbians to female than the reverse.[92] Beach's conclusion is: in the case of human homosexuality, in contrast with animal homosexuality, stimulus-response complementarity is not present. In the case of animals homosexuality comes down to a temporary reversal of the

91. F. Beach (1976, 1977).

92. This is confirmed by the Masters and Johnson (1980) study of the physiological responses of homo- and heterosexual men and women: the sexual behavior of homosexual men resembles that of heterosexual men, not that of heterosexual women.

mating role; in humans it does not. Accordingly, there is no appropriate animal model for the study of human homosexuality.

For the explanation of animal homosexuality three factors are important: the external stimulus, the manner in which the brains are organized, and the concentrations of hormones circulating in the blood. According to the relevant theory, the sexual organization of the brains takes shape shortly before or after birth, and that under the influence of hormones. These effects are irreversible. Scientists speak at this point of the organizing effect of hormones in contrast with the motivating and activating effect of *the same* hormones in later life. The brains are potentially bisexual. Every normal individual, to be sure, develops either male or female genitals, but in an individual brain mechanisms for both female and male behavior can nevertheless be simultaneously present. While the development of external and internal genitalia is separate from the development of these brain-centers, both developments are subject to the influence of the sex hormones. In animals that are genetically male the development of male centers of behavior predominates, and in the case of female animals those of the female.[93] These brain mechanisms are organized early in life but only activated from the onset of puberty. In both sexes both male and female hormones are released in the blood but in a different ratio. In females the production from then on is cyclic and in males tonic. Male brain centers are activated by male hormones and female brain centers by female hormones. This occurs in both male and female animals, the difference being that in the case of females the female mechanisms respond to a lower concentration of female hormone than the same mechanisms in the case of males, and vice versa.[94]

Accordingly, the explanation for the predominance of hetero-

93. In rats G. Dörner (1979, for example) localized a male and female mating center in the hypothalamus and the adjoining pre-optic area. The development of genitalia and brains in a female direction occurs in the absence of the male sex hormone testosterone. This hormone is indispensable for a development in a male direction.

94. F. A. Beach (1976, 1977, 1979).

sexual behavior in animals lies in the predominance and greater sensitivity of the sex-specific brain mechanisms that are activated by the circulating hormones; this then leads to the appearance of sex-specific behavior. The explanation for the possibility of "homosexual" behavior in animals lies in the presence of brain mechanisms characteristic for the other sex.

Question: What are the similarities between this — generalized and roughly reproduced — animal model and human sexuality, specifically human homosexuality? Nowadays differences in prenatal exposure to sex hormones are increasingly brought to bear on differences in skills and behavior between boys and girls. These differences are not absolute and can be nullified in the socialization process, but they do indicate a tendency.[95] The theory that distinct neural tissues for male and female sexual behavior develop side-by-side in an individual is now generally accepted. This is not the case with the external and internal sex organs, which are normally always of one sex. Their differentiation occurs under the influence of prenatal hormones (as that is also the case with animals). According to M. Diamond, distinct (still unknown!) but closely connected sets of neural tissue are responsible for (1) the development of sex-related reproductive patterns; (2) the establishment of one's own sexual identity and knowledge of the other sex; (3) the sexual object-choice; and (4) the rise of sexual mechanisms.[96]

95. See, for example, E. E. Maccoby and C. M. Jacklin (1974), A. C. Peterson (1980), and E. H. M. Bontekoe (1984).

96. M. Diamond (1976). Reproductive neural tissues regulate the sex-specific secretion of sex hormones. These influence the capacity for erection and orgasm. Sexual identify is the awareness of belonging to one or the other sex (= gender identity, § B). The sexual object-choice is the preference for one or the other sex (= sexual orientation). The sexual motor patterns are the behavior patterns characteristic for men and women. Diamond agrees that these are markedly subject to cultural influence (= approx. the gender role). See further J. Money and A. A. Ehrhardt (1972), J. Money (1977), A. A. Ehrhardt and H. Meyer Bahlburg (1979). D. F. Swaab and M. A. Hofman (1988) describe a sexually dimorphous core in the pre-optic area of the human hypothalamus. *No* differences were found here between homosexual (AIDS patients) and heterosexual men. Accordingly, homosexual men display no female differentiation of the hypothalamus.

His position is "that nature sets limits to sexual identity and partner preference and that it is within these limits that social forces interact and gender roles are formulated — a bisocial interaction theory."[97] The implication of this theory is that homosexuals do not necessarily differ from heterosexuals in anything other than their object-choice. The preference, according to him,[98] is very likely prenatally programmed hormonally.

Is there any evidence for this theory? The investigation of differences in concentrations of hormones circulating in the blood in humans was originally undertaken on the basis of the simplistic given that in the case of animals hormones influence sexual behavior directly. That was assumed to be the case also in humans — hence the notion that homosexuality is a consequence of a hormonal aberration. But in the case of higher animals, already the connection between hormone-concentration and behavior is not always direct. In humans behavior is, to a high degree, independent of hormones present in the blood. In the seventies hormonal research gained new impetus when it became possible to measure hormone concentrations directly in the plasma rather than inferring them indirectly from degradation products in the urine. It may now be assumed as established that in the case of adult homo- and heterosexuals hormone concentrations do not differ significantly.[99] This is not the whole story because, as we remarked

97. M. Diamond (1982: 183).

98. How, in fact, the object-choice comes into being is unknown. Baerends (1980) thinks it is by imprinting, a genetically programmed learning situation that is bound to a certain developmental phase and has a once-for-all and irreversible character. This phenomenon has been well studied in birds (learning the species-specific song) but scarcely in mammals where, however, the phenomenon is also known.

99. See the bibliographic overviews of R. Niesink (1985), N. K. Gartrell (1982), L. Birke (1981), and the research-overviews of H. F. L. Meyer-Bahlburg (1977, 1980), and G. Tourney (1980). Some differences were found by a number of researchers. As a rule these can be explained better in terms of the limits of the research method employed than in terms of a difference between homosexuals and heterosexuals. Hormonal research can, in principle, still continue for a long time because the number of kinds of hormones involved in sexual behavior is very high.

earlier, sensitivity to the same concentration can differ among individuals. Consequently, the focus shifts to prenatal hormonal influences. In humans knowledge of these influences can only be gained indirectly from a number of clinical samplings. Ad hoc experiments can be undertaken in the case of animals. I will start with the latter.

Especially G. Dörner's experiments with rats have attracted attention. In rats the differentiation of the nervous system under the influence of hormones takes place a few days after birth and not, as in the case of humans, especially before that event. Males that were castrated immediately after birth and upon reaching maturity treated with female hormones displayed female mating behavior, preferably with normal males. Dörner describes these males as homosexual. However, when the animals were castrated only after a two-week delay, this behavior did not occur despite treatment with female hormones. With females treated after birth with male hormone and then again in maturity, comparable results were obtained. Dörner was able to localize the brain areas concerned and to distinguish a female and a male mating center. Surgical elimination of the female mating center in the case of castrated male rats treated with female hormone caused the heterosexual male behavior to return. The elimination of the male mating center in the case of the treated homosexual females similarly led to the return of heterosexual female behavior.

Now Dörner thinks his results are directly applicable to humans. In his view, homosexual men were exposed in the prenatal period to insufficient concentrations of male hormone, which could be a result of stress in the life of the pregnant mother. Surgical intervention here, just as in rats, could change the behavior. Unfortunately Dörner's suggestions found a hearing. A couple of ("East") German surgeons carried out the surgical interventions and the result was called successful.[100]

100. G. Schmidt and E. Schorsch (1981). The reference (between 1962 and 1976) is to 75 patients, two-thirds of whom were prisoners and other persons involuntarily institutionalized but who otherwise "voluntarily" underwent the operation. See further G. Dörner (1979: 82–83) and H. F. L.

However, Dörner's conclusions were critically received in the scientific community.[101] His comparison with homosexual men was based on castrated and hormonally manipulated rats. Ostensibly Dörner defined homosexuality in terms of preference for members of one's own sex (as is the case with humans). In reality he defined homosexuality in terms of the genetic sex because as a result of manipulation essentially female brains originated in animals that were genetically male, brains which reacted — in a way that is normal for females — to the female hormone with which they were stimulated. In other words: Dörner effected a permanent reversal of the mating role and mistakenly equates this with homosexuality in humans.

This conclusion is confirmed by research data pertaining to two deviations in humans, viz., the adrenogenital syndrome in girls and androgen-insensitivity in boys. In the first case there is a disturbance in the adrenal gland of the mother, as a result of which it produces androgens (male hormones) and these in turn influence a female fetus in a male direction. In the second case, there exists a genetic aberration in a male fetus in relation to sensitivity to androgens, which results in their having a diminished effect. As a result, children come into the world whose external genitalia do not, or do not completely, correspond with their genetic sex. When the aberration is corrected at an early stage (within about a year) by surgery combined with hormone therapy, there need be no

---

Meyer-Bahlburg (1980: 111-12). It is noteworthy that in homosexual men Dörner encountered the positive estrogen feedback effect characteristic for women. They react to the release of estrogen (a female hormone) in the blood with an increased secretion of luteinizing hormone (LH) by the hypophysis. This also occurs in animals; it never occurs in males. The male rats that had been castrated immediately after birth also showed this phenomenon but those castrated after two weeks did not. This points to the influence of the organizing male hormones. However, analysis of the data has revealed that the estrogen response of homosexual men is by no means uniform and is not evinced by all. Further, Dörner's reports are silent on the screening of the test persons; the research awaits replication (Meyer-Bahlburg 1977, 1980). For a theoretical critique of Dörner's ideas, see G. Schmidt (1984).

101. Discussion of Dörner's paper occurred at the Ciba-symposium (1979); see further Meyer-Bahlburg (1977).

permanent damage. In some cases, however, the aberration is not caught at birth and these children are reared in keeping with the sex of their external genitalia. Since the gender identity is established after about a year and can no longer be changed, surgical correction then takes place in keeping with the sex of rearing (the sex according to which a child is brought up as a boy or a girl).

The interesting feature here is that in their behavior such children display elements deemed characteristic for the other sex (in the case of girls preference for rough-and-tumble, tomboyish behavior; in the case of boys, preference for dolls, etc.: "sissy boys"). But sexual orientation proved to develop in keeping with the sex of rearing in an almost exclusively heterosexual direction. That was true both for individuals who were reared in keeping with their genetic sex and for those who were not. Accordingly, the conclusion of the researchers is that the influence of social factors in upbringing can compensate for the prenatal effects,[102] or more strongly: there is no question of a deterministic effect of prenatal hormones on sexual orientation and gender identity. Sexual orientation follows the sex of rearing.[103] Hence the majority of the victims of one or both of these syndromes develop heterosexually; and that in keeping with the genetic sex when the aberration is noticed at birth and the sex of rearing corresponds with the genetic sex; and heterosexually relative to the sex of rearing but homosexually relative to the genetic sex if the aberration has not been recognized in time. As for the latter group, though corresponding in a high degree hormonally to Dörner's manipulated rats, in view of their sexual preference we will definitely *not* call this group homosexual. To answer the question concerning the comparability of homosexual behavior in humans and animals, it is, therefore, important to note the point of comparison in terms of which behavior is *defined* as homosexual: the genetic sex (Dörner) or the sex of rearing (Beach, Money, Meyer-Bahlburg).

The data here indicate that the influence on sexual orientation

102. J. Money and Ch. Ogunro (1974: 204); cf. J. Money (1977).
103. A. A. Ehrhardt and H. F. L. Meyer-Bahlburg (1981); cf. R. Green (1979).

of upbringing is more decisive than that of prenatal differentiation (at least in the case of these aberrations). This does not, however, warrant the conclusion that, therefore, sexual orientation can only be explained in terms of social influences. In that case "nature" and "nurture" are mistakenly treated as opposites. It is possible, for instance, that an anomalous prenatal androgenization is coupled with greater flexibility and conditionability of later social behavior.[104] But it is completely unknown how many people with normal sexual characteristics were exposed in utero to abnormal hormonal concentrations, let alone the correlation between this fact and sexual orientation. How then could one compare in research the relative influence of social and biological factors? The complex nature of the *interaction* is evident from the following two studies.

(1) In a village community in the Dominican Republic, Imperato-McGinley et al. found that individuals who, on account of their ambiguous external genitalia, had initially been reared as girls, underwent a noticeable masculinization in puberty and then, clearly without problems, assumed a male identity. Their sexual orientation was heterosexual. Involved here is a genetically-determined aberration in a certain enzyme that causes normal androgenization in the fetal stage to lag behind. This aberration is so general that the population has a name for it: *"gueve doces,"* meaning "a penis at twelve." The researchers conclude that the sex of rearing obviously plays a lesser role than the masculinizing effect of testosterone, considering that an incomplete effect in utero is compensated for by a testosterone thrust from puberty onward.[105] Sexual orientation, for that matter, could still largely be a consequence of the effects of rearing: rearing might anticipate a possible sex-change in view of the high premium placed on maleness in Latin-American countries.[106]

104. The manner of prenatal androgenization is said to determine the degree of flexibility of the later behavior in the way "nature" and "nurture" interact. Anomalous androgenization could lead to greater conditionability (Diamond 1976: 54).

105. J. Imperato-McGinley et al. (1974). The enzyme deficiency in part renders the prenatal testosterone inoperative.

106. The sociologist Th. F. Hoult (1984), who rightly makes this comment, incorrectly concludes that postulating a hormonal cause is super-

174

From the three pathological situations discussed so far, all of them caused by hormonal aberrations, we can now, I think, conclude that they clearly show the influence of hormones on the development of the sex organs, some effect on behavior, less clearly an effect on gender identity, and even more ambiguously an effect on sexual orientation. The sexual identity corresponds with the sex of rearing, which is based on the sex of the sexual organs, and the sexual orientation is usually heterosexual in relation to the sex of rearing. An aberrant prenatal androgenization, therefore, has apparently no predictive value with regard to the ultimate sexual orientation.

(2) One can also start the investigation on the other side; i.e., with the existing sexual orientation. The largest study of this type is that of the Kinsey Institute (1981), which was based on approximately five hundred interviews, two-thirds of which were with homosexuals. This study shows that sexual preference is firmly fixed at the beginning of adolescence and is based more on feelings than on sexual experiences. Homosexual youth do not differ from their heterosexual counterparts in the number or kind of sexual experiences they have had but in the fact that they did not enjoy heterosexual experiences. In the case of males there are no, or scarcely any, differences in their relations with parents. In the case of homosexual women, on the other hand, there was often a bad family situation, particularly in relation to the father. The researchers found, however, that for both men and women there was a strong positive correlation between gender-nonconformity (the display in youth of behavior deemed characteristic for the other sex) and later homosexuality. This result has been confirmed by various other researchers.[107] That is a surprising result considering

---

fluous when a society anticipates and in fact prescribes such a sex-change. That is a non sequitur: from the fact that differences in rearing explain certain role differences, as Hoult believes, it does not follow that differences in hormonal exposition (in which Imperato-McGinley et al. are interested) are unimportant. In such cases one simply cannot study the influence of two variables simultaneously.

107. A. P. Bell et al. (1981). The correlation for that matter is far from being 100 percent. Half of the homosexual men did view themselves in child-

the fact that, as we saw, gender-nonconformity as a result of the adrenogenital syndrome and androgen-insensitivity shows no positive correlation with a homosexual orientation![108]

Hence for the following reasons the total picture is still by no means clear:

(1) There is little resemblance between homosexual behavior in humans and homosexual behavior in animals (lack of stimulus-response complementarity, Beach). (2) For the majority of people it is true that their genetic sex corresponds with the sex of rearing, the latter with gender-identity, which corresponds with sexual orientation, which corresponds with social sex-role. We may suspect, as Diamond does, that behind these correlations there is a causal connection.

(3) One can also posit such a connection and validate it by means of definition, as Dörner does. According to him, homosexuality in the case of males is due to the predominance of female brain mechanisms programmed prenatally by hormones. In taking this position he is indeed corroborating a current stereotype. Many researchers, for that matter, do not exclude a connection between such factors and sexual orientation.[109] But this does not explain — among other things — the fact that the behavior of most homosexual males is not feminine, nor the (few) data in which a deviant hormonal development has been established but where, in the majority of cases, the sexual orientation turns out to be hetero-

---

hood as being male and a quarter of the heterosexuals as "sissy" (p. 188). For an overview of studies pointing in the same direction, see J. Harry (1984: 118ff.).

108. Interesting in this connection is what R. Green (1987) found as a result of long-term study of boys with frequent feminine behavior ("feminine boys"). No less than three-quarters of the group still continuing after fifteen years (two-thirds of the original sixty-six) had developed a homosexual or bisexual orientation. In a control-group of "masculine boys" that was the case with only one. His conclusion is that neither biological factors nor socialization processes can independently explain this development. There are too many exceptions to every rule (p. 384). "There is too much variability in the lives of men who *also* happen to be heterosexual or homosexual" (p. 389).

109. So say A. P. Bell et al. (1981: 217) — with great caution, however — "If there is a biological basis for homosexuality, it probably accounts for gender nonconformity as well as for sexual orientation."

sexual in accordance with the sex of rearing, even when this is the opposite of the genetic sex.

When (differently than in Dörner) homosexuality is defined in relation to the sex of rearing, hence as sexual behavior between members of what is experienced as the same sex (gender), the influence of hormones on sexual orientation is totally ambiguous. In that case homosexuality in humans must be viewed as the result of a specific learning process, one that probably takes place between birth and puberty. This learning process could then relate to the acquisition of one's sexual identity (Money;[110] Baerends speaks of imprinting[111]), to sexual orientation alone (Mayer-Bahlburg), to the acquisition of a specific role (sociologists). Even if it concerned acquired behavior, the results of studies in gender-conformity in prehomosexual children can be explained biologically, i.e., on the basis of preprogrammed learning potential. Of course, as we noted earlier, social-scientific and biological explanations are not mutually exclusive.

Accordingly, the subject — the development of human sexual behavior — is very complex. But it becomes especially complex when it is contaminated by theoretical questions. I have already mentioned the most important one: the misguided dichotomizing of "nurture" and "nature." In the next section we will consider the alleged determinism of biological explanations. But here we must point out the thing that is rightly disturbing to

110. Time and again J. Money (1984 inter alia) underscores the importance for the learning processes of unambiguous nurture from the side of parents. In the absence of it, gender-ambiguity may occur. The development of the sexual identity, in his opinion, includes two components: identification of one's own sex ("gender copying") and complementation with knowledge of the opposite sex ("gender practicing"). A girl learns to dance from her mother but dances with her father or brother. Identification and complementation are each said to have their own representation or imprint in the brains. Money compares their acquisition with learning a language. When the development takes another course, there is what is called "gender transposition": homosexuality, transvestism, and transsexuality.

111. G. P. Baerends (1980: 456) believes that ethological insights concerning imprinting tie in well with Money's psychological views.

opponents of biological explanations: defining (western) homosexuality in such a way that it is, a priori, an aberration or disturbance, an example being Dörner's definition. See also § B. Perhaps hormones "determine" our behavior and explain why sexual development takes different directions in different people. However, we do not yet know this. But we do know that social/societal definitions decide whether the behavior is masculine or non-masculine. A value judgment is involved, something that should be kept out of the definition. I want to put it more strongly: the difference in biological factors that make people different in their sexual behavior are not necessarily the same as those that make a person masculine or unmasculine, sick or healthy, homosexual or heterosexual.

F. Biological explanations II: sociobiology and genetics

The idea that homosexuality is "genetically determined" already constituted the cornerstone of Hirschfield's emancipative designation of homosexuals as the "third sex." In our time this biological grounding of homosexuality again finds support from within sociobiology, a more or less new branch of biology. In the opinion of its founder, E. O. Wilson, "There is, I wish to suggest, a strong possibility that homosexuality is normal in a biological sense, that it is a distinctive beneficient behavior that evolved as an important element of early human social organization. Homosexuals may be the carriers of some of mankind's rare altruistic impulses."[112]

Sociobiology is the interpretation of the social behavior of humans and animals in evolutionary perspective. There is kinship here, therefore, with ethology. Since the publication of Wilson's *Sociobiology: The New Synthesis* (1975) it has occasioned much discussion among biologists and sociologists, one reason being the speculative comments of sociobiologists about the relation between the biological and the social sciences. Ethicists, too, have

112. E. O. Wilson (1978: 149).

entered the discussion in view of the normative undertones struck in sociobiology (e.g., in the quotation cited above: homosexuality is good because it is biologically normal; this type of naturalistic reasoning can be illustrated with numerous quotations). This side of the subject has, however, had enough attention.[113] The debate surrounding sociobiology has again raised the question concerning the relation between biology and the social sciences.[114] This sometimes leads people to use objections to specific sociobiological explanations — in this case of homosexuality — in order to demonstrate the non-desirability of a (socio)biological approach to human (sexual) behavior. Proponents of sociobiology do the opposite. These, however, are different issues. In this section I first wish to discuss the evidence for a number of sociobiological interpretive models of homosexuality and then the often-expressed objection of genetic determinism that is said to be part of this type of explanation.

Sociobiological and genetic explanations are here mentioned in one breath. The reason is that only those traits for which there is genetic variation can be subject to evolution. In the previous two sections we noted that biologists are interested in the function of traits, phenotypes, i.e., those effects (adaptations) that are responsible for their evolution. In biology there is a close connection between the function of a trait, its evolution, and reproduction. Adaptations after all would disappear if they were not passed on to posterity, and their transmission via genes in reproduction is an important means for the transmission of information. In sum: an evolutionary explanation of a (behavioral) trait is based on its function: the contribution it makes to the preservation and reproduction of the individual or the species. When such a contribution can be shown to exist it is legitimate to assume a genetic basis for the trait. Further genetic research can bring to light its precise nature.

113. On the naturalistic fallacy, see Ch. I, and on the difference between "normal" and "normative," § C of this chapter. For naturalistic arguments in the work of sociobiologists, see espec. A. W. Musschenga (1981: 172ff.).

114. For the discussion in the Netherlands, see F. M. de Waal (ed., 1981).

The question here is how a trait named "homosexuality," a behavioral pattern that seemingly decreases the chances of reproduction, has been able to persist in evolution. On the assumption that "genes for homosexuality" as well as "genes for heterosexuality" exist, the former will gradually be replaced by the latter when homosexuals have fewer descendants than heterosexuals. And that is not unlikely.

In the literature of sociobiology in the main three models are used to explain homosexuality.[115] Only the last two are typically sociobiological models. They are here simplified and discussed apart from their background in evolutionary theory.

(1) *Homosexuality as a function of heterozygosis or heterozygote advantage.* When a heterozygous individual, in this case an individual who has received a gene for homosexuality from the one parent and one for heterosexuality from the other, has greater survival or reproductive potential than either of the two homozygotes (individuals with genes only for homosexuality or for heterosexuality), this is referred to as "heterozygote advantage." Every manual on evolution offers multiple examples of it, also in the case of humans. Here genes for homosexuality are preserved in the population despite the lesser reproductive potential of homosexuals because heterozygotes serve the spread of these genes.

(2) *Homosexuality as the result of kin-selection.* The biological significance of reproduction lies in the transmission of genes. An individual can leave copies of his genes in his offspring by reproducing himself but also by helping relatives, who in part carry the same genes, increase their reproductive potential. Sociobiologists speak in this connection of "inclusive fitness" that can be increased by "altruistic" behavior. Even when a gene in a homozygous condition causes sterility but also the inclination toward "helping behavior" with respect to relatives, such a gene can spread rapidly in the population, even more so than when an individual would reproduce himself. Thus the genetic disadvantage of non-reproduction in the case of homosexuality would be more than compensated for by the help of homosexuals to relatives.

115. E. O. Wilson (1975, 1978), M. Ruse (1979, 1981b).

(3) *Homosexuality as consequence of parental manipulation.* In the preceding model homosexuality is presented as fitness-enhancing for the individual himself. In this model the reproductive interest of the parents is accented. Their interest is that their descendants in total should have as much offspring as possible, not that every child should reproduce himself. It can, therefore, be to their advantage to manipulate some of their children (e.g., those whose growth was stunted or a "late arrival") in such a way that, instead of taking part in reproduction themselves, they would assist their brothers and sisters with "altruistic behavior" to increase their reproductive potential. The capacity to manipulate has adaptive value and has, therefore, maintained itself in the evolutionary process. Both in this and in the previous model, homosexuals distinguish themselves by "altruistic" behavior. In practice it will be difficult to distinguish between causes (2) and (3).

If homosexuality has a distinct genetic basis, these models, developed within the biology of evolution and population genetics, furnish an explanation. What data argue for the assumption of such a basis? In any case, there is no correlation between chromosomal abnormalities in the number of sex-chromosomes and the occurrence of homosexuality.[116] In a study of twins, at least one of whom was homosexual, Kallmann (1952) found that among monozygotic twins (who are genetically identical) almost 100 percent of the other half was also homosexual (37 pairs) while for zygotic twins the correlation amounted to only 10 percent (36 pairs), not higher than the average according to the statistics of A. Kinsey (1948). Since then there has been no study on this scale. Heston and Shields (1968) found in the case of four out of seven pairs of monozygotic twins that both were homosexual. In the case of seven pairs of dizygotic twins this was true of only one pair.[117] These

116. In cases of anomalies like XO, XXY, or XXX, etc. homosexuality does not occur less or more often than average (the normal constitution of the male is XY, the female XX). For an overview, see J. Money (1980).

117. Monozygotic twins with different sexual preference are rare. In general, no hormonal differences are found between members of such pairs (R.C. Friedman et al. 1976). For an elaborate description of one such pair, see R. Green (1987: 320ff.).

data strongly suggest a genetic component. However, one may readily doubt the quality of Kallmann's research. Further, both studies concern twins who were reared together. Under those circumstances, the influences of the genetic and the environmental component cannot be distinguished.[118] "It's in the family" is no argument for the existence of hereditary variation in differences in sexual behavior. Finally, there is nothing to suggest grounds for differences between the heterosexual members of families with and without homosexual members, as the model of heterozygote advantage predicts.[119] Hence this model is incorrect.

Are homosexuals more altruistic and does their altruism serve the advantage of their relatives? Ruse and Wilson[120] do not get

118. For objections to Kallmann's research, see D. J. Futuyuma and S. J. Risch (1983). In the final analysis, only adoption-studies of monozygotic twins who have grown up separately in sufficiently different milieus can resolve the issue of the influence of the genetic component. But such twins are statistically rare.

119. See, for example, A. P. Bell et al. (1981: 70). Correlations between homosexuality in men and the mother's age at their birth (older mothers more frequently have homosexual sons) and between homosexuality and the birth order (younger sons are more frequently homosexual) found in certain older studies were not confirmed here.

120. E. O. Wilson (1975, 1978); M. Ruse (1979, 1981b). In some cultures "homosexuals" — or men fulfilling a female role — occupy important positions that benefit all of society. That could imply "altruism." In our culture homosexuals are considered artistically more gifted. Some studies show a higher-than-average intelligence in homosexuals. That is said to point in the same direction. There are indications that homosexuals, by comparison with heterosexuals, show slight differences in physical structure. They weigh less, are less inclined to physical violence, and the like. This is the kind of information that is expected if the model of parental manipulation is correct. Thus writes Ruse. Futuyuma et al. (1983) object that (1) the idea that on average homosexuals contribute less to reproduction, though this is likely, has not been definitely demonstrated; (2) in numerous societies homosexuals do not occupy honorable positions; and (3) greater artistic talent or higher IQs have never been proven and, if true, it is to be explained rather as a reaction to society, hence as a consequence instead of a cause. The same applies to differences in body weight and violence. Meyer-Bahlburg (1980) mentions a number of studies that show the existence of anthropometric differences.

beyond summing up a type of evidence that may indicate that homosexuals are more altruistic, assuming that the models of kin-selection and parental manipulation are applicable to humans. Accordingly, their purpose is not to *test* explanations of homosexuality but to show by the example of homosexuality that the sociobiological approach to human behavior yields verifiable scientific hypotheses. Hence they are talking about the *testability* of sociobiological models and that is something else. Testable models may, upon examination, prove to be incorrect but the correctness of untestable models can never be established.[121] Let us assume the correctness of the claim made by sociobiology that its models are testable. This of course in no way answers the question to which altruism of which homosexuals the sociobiological models relate.

Philosophers and ethicists have repeatedly pointed out that in sociobiology "altruistic" behavior refers exclusively to behavior that increases the reproductive potential of others at the expense of its own reproductive success.[122] That is a definition in terms of the *effects* of the behavior. In ordinary usage and morality, however, "altruism" refers to conscious motivation and intentions. A person who acts altruistically in the ordinary sense and "egoistic" in a biological sense (from now on "bioaltruistically") may very well act from egoistic motives. The sociobiological models permit this. Conversely, a person may, with the most noble intentions, help get another into worse trouble than he was in before or unwittingly benefit himself. In that case he is acting "altruistically" in the biological sense. Accordingly, bioaltruism and human altruism are concepts derived from different worlds whose interconnection may not be immediately clear.[123] This means that no inferences about bioaltruism in humans can be drawn from data relating to altruism practiced by humans.

121. For that reason M. Ruse (1984) makes no attempt to refute the criticism of Futuyuma et al. (1983) and that of others of his sociobiological explanations of homosexuality (Ruse 1979, 1981b) but defends the biological approach to behavior: "Why take biology seriously?"

122. See, e.g., B. Voorzanger (1983).

123. R. C. Solomon et al. (1978), A. W. Musschenga (1981). Intentions cannot be reformulated into empirical concepts without loss of meaning.

Again the question of the definition of homosexuality plays an important role here. The sociobiological models explain the requisite non-reproduction phenomena. Only on the assumption that homosexuality is an example of this do the models serve to explain homosexuality. Although the assumption of lessened reproduction among homosexual men is not unlikely, for homosexual women it is much less likely or even incorrect. Secondly, sociobiologists fail to make plausible why non-reproduction and bioaltruism are associated with homosexuality and not, say, with sexual apathy and extreme chastity. In the West, homosexuals appear to spend at least as much energy on their sexual life as heterosexuals invest in reproduction (sociobiologists conduct cost-benefit analysis in terms of energy-investment). It therefore seems justified to suspect the influence of stereotypes in the background of the sociobiological models ("really they are such nice boys; such neat neighbors!" etc.). In short, what sociobiologists explain is non-reproduction in bioaltruists. As explanations of human homosexuality their models fall short.

The question is whether, by virtue of a lack of evidence for the biological explanations we have considered in this and the preceding section, we must now a priori reject them. The answer is no; we must not. Although up until now we have not been furnished unambiguous data that favor a separate genetic basis for homosexuality, nor clear data that suggest the evolution of homosexuality as a separate trait, this does not of course mean that human sexual behavior lacks a genetic basis. In distinction from animals human sexual behavior is enormously flexible. That is a biological fact about this "naked ape" (Desmond Morris). By ignoring biological in favor of social-scientific explanations we deprive ourselves of the possibility of decoding the "program" that underlies human behavior (§ E). Must we know this program? Are social-scientific explanations not enough for us? If that is what we want, yes. But since all behavior is rooted in the interplay between "nature" and "nurture," it at all times makes sense to search for biological explanations. They may be incorrect or caught up in societal prejudices. But that is an argument against ignorance and prejudice, not against biology. This is also what Ruse (1984) has

184

in mind when he states that, though the enterprise of human socio-biology may end in failure, there is nothing to be afraid of in doing biology. The same is true for the so-called genetic determinism that is, in fact, a constituent in popular notions of heredity.[124]

Determinism and indeterminism are venerable philosophical doctrines. This means that, though they are not falsifiable, they can only be made acceptable by arguments pro and con. Sometimes determinism and indeterminism are couched in the form of a dilemma: either a thing is determined and then there is no freedom, or there is freedom of choice and then determinism cannot be true. Either homosexuality is (genetically, hormonally) determined or being homosexual is a choice. An example of this either-or thinking occurs in J. Kessels when he wonders whether girls can be held morally accountable for "tomboy behavior" caused by hormonal abnormality. He thinks the answer depends on which viewpoint deserves priority, the scientific or the moral. This produces "the paradox of the free will." "In the first case we have an explanation without morality, in the second a morality without an explanation. Which deserves preference?"[125]

Here science is linked with determinism and morality with indeterminism and freedom.

A second point of view is that of "partly determined, partly free." J. A. van der Ven, for example, says:

> Freedom lies in the field of tension between determinacy and indeterminacy. It is neither absolute determinacy, nor absolute indeterminacy. . . . Absolute determinacy or absolute unfreedom would deprive humans of their humanness: a human being would be no more than a collection of responses to a collection of stimuli. Absolute indeterminacy or absolute freedom would equally rob

124. In the "naturalism" of turn-of-the-century literature, for example: the heredity that, along with dramatic circumstances, enacts an inescapable fate. A fine Dutch example is *Juffrouw Lina* by Marcellus Emant (1888). A clear American example is *Sister Carrie* by Theodore Dreiser, written in the late 1890s.

125. J. Kessels (1984).

humans of their humanness: a human being would be exempt from all situatedness whatever.[126]

This bipolarity, says van der Ven, is of the essence of man. Humans are simultaneously free and unfree. However much he is determined by internal and external factors, he is not totally immersed in this determinacy but transcends it over and over.[127] Here, in my opinion, two concepts of freedom are confused: freedom from determinacy and the freedom (capacity) to transcend a situation. That is not right.

It is not my intention to discuss the many concepts of freedom. They are surely bound up with a person's view of what (in)determinacy entails. Kessels defines determinism as "the position that everything that happens, including human thoughts, feelings, and actions, is the result of specific causes, so that every event is determined" (p. 20).

Van der Ven, though he stops short of giving a definition, suggests the same thing. We will find that Kessel's definition is incorrect.

(1) To begin with, a distinction has to be made between the explicability and the predictability of human conduct.[128] Human conduct, thinks MacIntyre, has a number of fundamentally unpredictable aspects. Thus, in the development of science, radical conceptual innovations (such as the introduction of the theory of relativity) are unpredictable. Second, the social conduct of humans has a "game theoretical" character: every person tries to make his own conduct as unpredictable as possible for another but that of others as predictable as possible, knowing all along that everyone else does the same thing. Finally, there are chance events: if Cleopatra's nose had, by chance, been a bit longer. . . . But unpredictability does not exclude explicability. Unpredictability is even compatible with determinism (as defined by Kessels).

126. J. A. van der Ven (1985: 61).
127. J. A. van der Ven (1985: 62–66).
128. For the following, see A. MacIntyre (1981: 84ff.).

Conversely, the predictability of human conduct does not imply that its causes are known. People allow themselves to be guided in their conduct by predictable expectations regarding others. Without this they could not make rational choices. But one can have these expectations without any knowledge or with faulty knowledge (stereotypes, for example) about the causes of the behavior of others. It is self-evident that causal knowledge of behavior also plays a role in taking decisions and making plans. Not this, however, but the fact that social life constitutes an intrinsic combination of predictable and unpredictable elements is typical for human social conduct. Without predictability, planning is impossible and human life would be formless. Without unpredictability, humans would become products of the desires and plans of others.[129]

If we now put unpredictability under the heading of human freedom and determinism under that of explicability, then freedom and determinism are not mutually exclusive entities (Kessels) or opposites (van der Ven).

Popper advances a similar point when he says there are no laws of history comparable to the laws of nature. Such laws would be "laws of succession" and they do not exist. There are no laws that link together chains of events. Historical laws are (merely) tendencies that last as long as people want them to.[130]

(2) A second point is that not every causal explanation is a deterministic one. By "determinism" we mean as follows:

> the thesis that whatever occurs under conditions given which nothing else could occur. Indeterminism is simply the minimum denial

129. From this it follows that a model of scientific explanation like the symmetry thesis of Hempel and Oppenheim (every explanation is a potential prediction and every prediction is a potential explanation) does not, at least on MacIntyre's view, hold water for the social behavior of humans.

130. K. R. Popper (1971: ch. 27). The apple falls from the tree (a), lands on the ground (b), and fatally hits a mouse (c). The chain of events that leads to (a) is to be explained in terms of physiological regularities, those leading to (b) in terms of physical, and an ethological or ecological explanation will account for the presence of the mouse. But there are no regularities that link (a) with (b) and the latter with (c)!

of this, viz., that at least some things occur under conditions given which something else could occur instead.[131]

For some people such determinism is inconsistent with the idea of moral responsibility ("hard determinism"). Others think that we are responsible not for intentions, which are determined, but only for our deeds ("soft determinism"). That, too, is unsatisfactory because it means that we cannot be held responsible for our choices and that is not the intention of moral language. As a consequence of the truth of determinism we would, at the very least, have to revise our moral language game.

However, that is not necessary because there is a relatively simple solution: a distinction can be made between determinism as (1) theoretically universal predictability and (2) theoretically universal explicability.[132]

The first version was the thesis of the eighteenth-century mechanist Laplace: that everything is determined by the operation of the laws of nature; that man can track these down and, if he knows the starting conditions, precisely predict what will happen and when. This thesis presupposes that all processes operate in a way that is analogous to those of mechanics. The second version of determinism is very different (this eludes Kessels); it is the simple thesis that every event has a cause and an effect.

Now the ability to point out a cause is not the same as giving an explanation in a scientific sense. We can speak of an explanation only if an event can be brought into relation with a regularity of sequence such that an event of type x is one that conforms to the formula $(x) P(x) \rightarrow Q(x)$ (of every x it is true that if P then Q). Q and P are respectively the necessary and the sufficient conditions for the occurrence of x. One can, therefore, only speak of an explanation in a real sense if the *necessary and the sufficient conditions* are known.

131. R. Taylor (1958: 224) who then proceeds to give a precise elaboration of this definition.

132. C. J. Ducasse (1958: 160ff.).

However, in many cases the term "to explain" is used in a weaker sense because an explanation in the real sense is impossible. Consider this model:

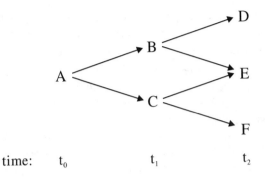

time: t_0 t_1 t_2

From "A at t_0" we cannot predict "D at t_2." But if D occurs at t_2 we can infer "A at t_0." That is an explanation of the form: "if D at t_n then A at t_{n-2}." Such an explanation is called a deductive retrodiction. The occurrence of D is the *sufficient condition* here for the presence of A at an earlier point in time. But the possibility of an explanation of this type does not imply the possibility of an explanation in the form of $(x)\ A(x) \rightarrow D(x)$ (hence in terms of *necessary and sufficient conditions*). In other words: a causal factor is not necessarily a determining factor.[133]

The confusing feature here is that the existence of a deterministic factor is often inferred from the existence of a causal factor — a strictly binding connection, therefore, between a factor and an observed effect. This may happen when one forgets that a causal relation is never a dyadic relation between cause and effect but alway a triadic: a cause-effect relation *under certain circumstances*.[134] But frequently the precise circumstances involved are not known. So if Mr. X is sick and carries a virus, while Mr. Y who is not sick does not carry that virus, it is said that the virus is the cause of the sickness on the assumption that all the boundary conditions have been met.

133. W. J. van der Steen (1973).
134. C. J. Ducasse (1958: 164).

189

By assertion "A is the cause of D" the speaker therefore means: A is *a* cause of D and *the* cause of D under (known or unknown) circumstances *x*. Under other circumstances *y* (or from another viewpoint) the occurrence of D would presumably have a cause other than A. This means that alternative explanations for the occurrence of D could also be furnished. In brief: the statement "A causes D" looks like the logically necessary statement $(x) A(x) \rightarrow D(x)$ but need not be more than a retrodiction: if D, then A at an earlier point in time. In that case one may look for strictly binding connections. But then the determinism in question is no more than a heuristic principle. Also, if such a necessary connection were found, it would still apply only under certain circumstances (which are perhaps unknown); under other circumstances other connections might be found. Implied here is the possibility of alternative explanations (from the perspective of different scientific disciplines).

To round off the argument: when determinism is conceived as we have just described it, there is no reason to consider it in conflict with moral responsibility. The moral consideration of human conduct in terms of intentions arises from a different viewpoint than the explanation of human behavior by biology and other disciplines. This remains true even when intentions, in terms of psychological desires or needs, prove to be explicable (as in the case of the tomboy behavior of girls discussed by Kessels). And human action in freedom is similarly bound up with and limited by natural laws. But the central point is that there is no strictly binding connection between a series of events that result from a rational choice based on intentions and a preceding series caused by congenital, innate, or instilled, or whatever factors. That is Popper's opinion, and MacIntyre means the same thing: human behavior, however predictable it may sometimes be, is not predictable because it is also explicable. Accordingly, the freedom that is morally at issue can better be localized in the tension-field between "authenticity" and pure "role-conformity" than in that of determinism as a state of being conditioned versus a state of being unconditioned (van der Ven).[135]

135. Cf. J. P. Sartre's "mauvaise foi." See R. S. Downie (1971: 62ff., 123ff.). This in the final analysis is also what van der Ven intends to say.

These comments fully apply also to genetic determinism. If biologists believe that homosexuality is genetically determined, they do not mean that homosexuals are programmed to act that way in all circumstances but that some individuals act that way in certain circumstances and others not (contrary to what popularized sociobiological literature may make one believe).[136] Nevertheless, the notion of "genetic determinacy" carries a powerful emotional charge because of its association with inevitability. This may in part be the result of additional confusion. Genetics is simply an account of mechanisms of information-transfer via genes from one generation to another. But there is a semantic difference between a statement like "the structure of proteins is genetically determined" and the statement "physical height is mainly genetically determined." In the first case the reference is to gene-products in an individual (*molecular* genetics); in the second, to differences between (groups of) individuals (*population* genetics).[137] The statement "physical height is genetically determined" means that in all circumstances in which, up until now, physical height has been explored, a greater correlation between height and genetic factors than between height and environmental factors invariably emerged. The stronger the correlation, the greater the genetic determinacy. This is expressed in percentages and designated with the term "heritability." A high heritability (e.g., 0.6 for physical height) means that the descendants of tall parents are on the average taller than those of small parents if parents and children live under the same conditions. For lefthandedness the heritability is low; this characteristic is barely heritable. But heritability says nothing about the changeability or moldability of the characteristic, i.e., about the influence of environmental conditions. Physical height can be influenced by better nutrition; lefthandedness is hard to change. Conversely, from the degree of changeability no con-

136. Thus, correctly, A. A. W. Kirsch and J. E. Rodman (1982: 186). Compare, however, E. O. Wilson (1978: 19): "The question of interest is no longer whether human social behavior is genetically determined; it is to what extent. The accumulated evidence for a large heredity component . . . already is decisive."
137. B. Voorzanger (1982, 1986).

clusions can be drawn with respect to heritability, the degree of "genetic determinacy."

A second source of confusion is that of heritability *within* groups with that *between* groups.[138] The degree of heritability is determined by comparing biological relatives and adopted children. On this basis the heritability of a trait can be assessed *within* a group of, say, white Netherlanders. If these on an average would be taller than Netherlanders in Curaçao, there is a strong temptation to suppose that this difference (*between* groups) is also genetic. That would be incorrect: Netherlanders in Curaçao *may* have a greater genetic potential for physical height than white Netherlanders; but that could only come to expression if, for some generations, they had lived under the same, obviously optimal, conditions. Accordingly, greater heritability does not only not say anything about the degree of changeability but neither does it say anything about the nature of differences between groups that live in different circumstances.

The above is also true for the genetic and sociobiological explanations of homosexuality. When sociobiologists express the belief that genetic factors play a role in it, we must link this information with the population-genetic gene-concept, not with genes that produce homosexuality in the way a gene produces a protein. Such a notion of genetic determinacy is good for a naturalistic novel. Important for population-genetics, as stated earlier, is which groups are compared under which conditions. Western homosexuals and western heterosexuals? That is done by sexology. Biologists compare humans with animals. Given increased knowledge, we might find that differences in sexual behavior do not correlate with genetic differences while biologists would, nevertheless, maintain that homosexuality among humans is a genetically determined adaptive phenomenon. That only means that, in distinction from other primates, humans have a genetic program that, under certain conditions, leads to exclusive homosexuality and, under other conditions, to exclusive heterosexuality. It is worthwhile, therefore, to examine how the two — this program

138. The "hereditarian fallacy," as S. J. Gould (1984: 156ff.) calls it.

and the circumstances — interact. In actual fact, scarcely anything is known about these matters. Add this to the logical and methodological criticism I have made in this and the preceding section of the biological explanations of homosexuality. But this is no reason to stigmatize biological research as such. Biological determinism is a (limiting) philosophy, it is not biology. In biology there is indeed nothing to be afraid of.

G. Social-scientific explanations: constructivism

In this section we will explore the modern social-scientific approach to homosexuality known as "constructivism." I will first present a brief overview of (the origin of) constructivism. After that I will especially focus on the relation constructivists build between biology (depicted as "deterministic") and the suppression of homosexuality on the one hand and between "indeterministic" sociology and gay-liberation on the other. Here again I am particularly interested in knowing what normative viewpoints lie concealed behind constructivist approaches.

Social-scientific research in homosexuality is not new (think of Kinsey, 1948) but it mainly concerned research among homosexual individuals. In that context the homosexual societal role was interpreted as the outflow of an abnormal sexual orientation.[139] In the post-sixties this dominant psychopathological approach has been gradually replaced by a psychosocial one in which homosexuality is studied as a phenomenon that is situated in a specific societal context and undergoes the influences of this context.[140] This does not yet imply a specifically sociological *view* of homosexuality. W. Simon and J. H. Gagnon (1967) formulated a "sociological perspective on homosexuality." They pointed out that, up until now, the emphasis was put on what separates ho-

139. H. Schelsky (1957), for example.
140. G. Sanders (1980[2]: 16). His study of the differences between homosexual and heterosexual boys is an example of this.

mosexuals from heterosexuals, namely the object-choice but that not all the differences between homo- and heterosexual lifestyles can be explained from this perspective. Also the homosexual has to find solutions for the problems posed to him by society: work, living with or without a family, leisure time activities, politics, friends, etc. When these aspects are also involved in the research, there turns out to be no such thing as "the" homosexual.[141]

In the Netherlands, particularly in the sixties, research was aimed toward the prevention of social rejection. Duyves (1985) called this "preventive sociology," the premise of which is that if a homosexual does not deviate too far from prevailing norms ("he is normal but not the same"), society will not reject him. This sociology, says he, does not disengage itself from the sociology of deviant behavior and tends to stress the insignificance rather than the full dignity of sexual variants. Although this approach has contributed to significant societal renewal,[142] it has paralyzed the attempt to broaden the sociological orientation on homosexuality.[143] The rise, since 1978, of "homo-studies" at various universities (e.g., Utrecht, Amsterdam) has furnished a new impulse.

141. W. Simon and W. H. Gagnon (1967: 185) say: "The aims, then, of a sociological approach of homosexuality are to begin to define the factors — both individual and situational — that predispose a homosexual to follow one homosexual path as against others; to spell out the contingencies that will shape the career that has been embarked upon; and to trace out the patterns of living in both their pedestrian and their seemingly exotic aspects. Only then we begin to understand the homosexual." Important descriptive studies are the Kinsey report (1978) mentioned earlier and that of Dannecker and Reicke (1974).

142. This approach, therefore, had a strong liberationist orientation. R. Tielman (1981) is the most important example in the Netherlands. Liberationist efforts in our country, he says, are strongly influenced by circumstances in society. At the time when theological thinking was predominant, an attempt was made to reinterpret the biblical texts. When biological thinking was in vogue, great value was attached to the dissemination of scientific insights. And in a period when insights from the social sciences predominate, the human-rights aspects of gay liberation will be stressed (p. 287).

143. That is also the view of K. Plummers (1981: 27): "it remains overwhelmingly true that homosexuality is largely hidden from sight."

These studies follow a "constructivist" approach that has been developed also in England and America in connection especially with the work of Foucault and symbolic interactionism.[144]

What is constructivism? In my opinion we are for now dealing with a mostly *theoretical* perspective that cannot (yet) be defined with precision. J. Weeks, British leader in the field of homo-studies, mentioned the following characteristics:

(1) rejection of the notion that sexuality is a naturally given and autonomous area of reality that is subject to social control; (2) a focus on the social origin of definitions of sexuality; (3) the opinion that in the West (homo)sexuality is constituted by definition (language) rather than by the repression of a natural capacity; (4) interest in the historical origin of definitions of sexuality: sexuality is a "historical construction," i.e., the product of a certain culture in a specific historical period. In short, constructivism is the belief that

> the meanings we give to sexuality in general, and homosexuality in particular, are socially organized, but contradictory, sustained by a variety of languages, which seek to tell us what sex is, what it ought to be and what it could be.[145]

In contrast, there is the "essentialist" approach rejected by constructivists, the belief that

> behaviors that share an outward similarity can be assumed to share an underlying essence and meaning.[146]

144. Symbolic interactionism is the sociological theory that explains human behavior in terms of the meaning people ascribe to the conduct and speech of others and themselves. Behavior is not determined by the situation but by the way in which people define it. This movement originated in reaction to the rigid determinism of behaviorism. In opposition to this it holds to the theory that processes of meaning-bestowal by actors always play a mediating role between situation (stimulus) and ultimate conduct.

145. J. Weeks (1989: 208).

146. C. S. Vance (1989: 14); cf. J. Weeks (1989: 208). I have opted here for what seem to me the clearest definitions of "constructivism" and "essentialism." The controversy certainly involves a false contrast if the

This view often conceives sexuality as "a basic biological mandate,"[147] an autonomous instinct that precedes social definitions. According to constructivists such an approach automatically leads to the restriction of sociological research to biological and biographical facts concerning homosexual individuals instead of to the study of (homo)sexuality.[148]

The question is whether the essentialist-constructivist antithesis is a fruitful way to frame the problem. I see a number of objections.

(1) In the first place, constructivism relates to different levels of research that are not clearly distinguished: that of *concept-formation* and that of the *explanation* or *clarification* of the behavior. The question how sexuality must be defined belongs to the first level. According to constructivists, all the conceptualizations that define sexuality in terms of a biological given, of sexual behavior, sexual desire, or of sexual identity have in common an assumption: viz., the existence of a biological "essence" that is anchored in the individual, because the biological sex of the partners always constitutes the point of reference. Instead, say the constructivists, what should be central in a well-formulated concept of "sexuality" is the attitudes and expectations of partners-in-relations and their structure. In a given relation, then, "sexual" is what the partners themselves understand by it. In this manner one could escape the ideological and normative character of the biological definitions of homosexuality.[149]

concepts relate to different levels of explanation: the level of the meanings the actor attaches to his actions, or that of sexual identify, or that of the cultural and historical definitions of sexuality. Cf. C. S. Vance, op. cit.

147. J. H. Gagnon and W. Simon (1973: 11).

148. J. Weeks (1981). Symbolic interactionism has little interest in the historical dimension, the reason why M. Duyves (1985: 343) also places this movement under the heading of "essentialism." This in contrast with R. Tielman (1983), K. Plummer (1989), some authors in J. P. de Cecco and M. Shively (eds. 1985), and J. Weeks. A recent historic-constructivist approach in the Netherlands is that of G. Hekma (1987) on the "doctoring" of homosexuality and the "production" of homosexuals. The approaches of Kinsey, Freud, and their followers, as also in general the biological approach of homosexuality, are called "essentialist."

149. M. G. Shively and J. P. de Cecco (1977). Cf. § B of this chapter.

To my mind this reasoning is not coherent. In a single breath it is stated that (1) sexuality, as a rule, is not defined well, something that could in principle be done properly (viz., in terms of a person's self-concept); and that (2) sexuality cannot be defined (in terms of necessary and sufficient conditions), because "sexual" is what the actors understand by it.[150] In the background of this inconsistency lies confusion between terminological and factual issues. The question "Is act *x* a sexual one?" can be taken as (1) "Does *x* satisfy the definition of sexual?" or "Must the word 'sexual' be defined so that *x* is covered by it?"; but also (2) "Does *x* have the characteristics of a sexual act?" The first question concerns a *concept;* the second an *issue.* The confusion is rooted in the equivocal word "meaning,"[151] which here stands for (1) "having meaning" (= definition) and (2) "assigning meaning" (= the intention of the actor). Accordingly, the phrase "the meaning of an act" may mean: the description or identification of an act as being of a certain type *or* the assignment of a meaning to it. The two are totally unrelated. Granted, someone may believe that only the actor himself can indicate the intent (the peculiar meaning) of his act and that he alone can adequately describe the act. But he cannot think that the act can only be *described* (defined) in terms of the meaning he assigns to it. Acts, after all, are also events in the world (§ A) and can always also be described in general terms and, if desired, explained causally.

This also applies to the "sexual" or whatever one wants to call

---

150. F. Suppe (1985: 9): "In short, we are told that issues of sexual identity can be conceptualized in a scientific manner, in ways that avoid illegitimate incorporation of social or other normative values, and still take into account the personal and social meanings that are crucial to understanding the phenomena." He thinks that in this way the rule of formulating concepts in terms of necessary and sufficient conditions is being swept aside. Although the aspect of self-definitions constitutes a part of a person's identity, that is not sufficient: "Social constructionist views of sexual identity, at best, tap only the dimension of self-concept . . ." (p. 13).

151. "Meaning" can be understood inter alia as (1) the communicative aspect of language; (2) intention, reason; (3) effect, influence; (4) consequence; and (5) logical implication (W. D. Hudson 1983: 37ff.).

it. Various constructivists posit: "nothing *is* sexual; we *make* it so."[152] If this means that the word "sexual" could be defined by every individual actor in his own way, this statement is incorrect. The idea that every act can become a part of a context of sexual meaning is correct. Then what does "sexual" mean? We can keep the answer simple and say: sexual is every act (including fantasy) that tends toward an orgasm.[153] That is an objective description of human sexuality. The coming-into-being of such an act can in principle be explained causally. But how and why actions are placed by actors in a context of sexual meaning is indeed something very different. That is not something that can be captured in causal explanations.

Constructivists speak of "homosexuality as a historical construction" and of "the origination of homosexuality" (cf. § D). Homosexuals, they say, are not born as such but are labeled as such or denominate themselves as such.[154] True, "homosexuality" is a concept with a specific content that originated in the nineteenth century; since then westerners have interpreted others and themselves in terms of being "hetero-," "bi-" or "homosexual." There could be no homosexuals if the concept "homosexuality" did not exist. But would not the thing itself, i.e., same-sex orientation, have existed without the label?

Some appear to have adopted this view[155] but in the case of other sociologists this question lies outside their sphere of interest.[156] In any case "the image of the homosexual as thus constituted

---

152. See inter alii K. Plummer (1975) and various essays in *Homojaarboek* 2 (1983).

153. W. J. Lengers (1969: 30); see § B of this chapter.

154. R. Tielman (1983: 35).

155. Th. F. Hoult (1983) and J. P. de Cecco/M.G. Shively (1983), for example. Cf. the editorial essay in *Homojaarboek* 1 (1981: 13): "If it should be the case that homosexuality has a nature of its own, it lies in a special relation between sex and power instead of in something biological, individual, or normal."

156. K. Plummer (1975: 29) says: Symbolic interaction assumes that man is an open-ended being, only "marginally restrained in his daily life by the tyranny of biological processes." And on p. 94: "The interactionist concern is with viewing homosexuality as a process emerging through interactive encounters (part of which will include a potentially hostile reaction) in an

by natural necessity was replaced by the conception of a choice for the homosexual lifestyle, homosexuality as a political choice."[157]

What constructivists rightly stress is that homosexuality cannot be understood apart from the meaning the actors themselves assign to their behavior. By "its meaning for the actors themselves" is then meant the entire complex of meaning-bestowals, ideas, (political) ideals, images, and desires that individuals, in or outside of the homosexual subculture ("gay scene"), have come to entertain or hold. Constructivists also make clear that the changing historic relationship between society, homosexuality, and homosexuals must not only be understood in terms of the oppression and liberation of homosexuals but also in terms of the changing shapes of "homosexuality." That is their strong point. The seventeenth-century "sodomite," the nineteenth-century "urning" or "homosexual," the twentieth-century "homophile" are not the historic manifestations of a Platonic essence called "homosexuality" but represent essentially diverse conceptualizations. The lines of demarcation between the sexual and the non-sexual are not only vague but also variable.

However, though it is true that for the actors themselves acts may have another meaning than observers attribute to them, one may not conclude from this that they can only be explained in terms of those meanings (and therefore not causally).[158] From the fact that the *concept* "homosexuality" has proven to be a biologistic construction, i.e., is defined in terms derived from the medical-biological sciences, it does not follow that homosexuality as *be-*

---

intersubjective world." Interactionism does not concern itself with primary but with secondary deviancy. Plummer does ask (p. 75): "does the category [of homosexuality] mirror or construct the phenomena?" Cf. J. Weeks (1981: 103) who likewise considers important the question: "What were and are the factors which define the individual acceptance or rejection of categorizations?"

157. R. Tielman (1983: 35).

158. J. Harry (1984: 112): "To assume that sexual orientation is the same as its label is to accept the social constructionist position without the supporting evidence."

havior only originates as a result of labeling. Of course, there is nothing against examining the influence of labeling processes in the coming-into-being of sexual behavior. But homosexuality as phenomenon is not synonymous with the labels pinned on it, except in cases where the term and the matter itself are equated.

(2) This brings us to a second objection against constructivism: the antithesis constructivism-essentialism does not coincide with the difference between sociological and biological explanation,[159] as constructivists suggest, but rather with that between determinism and indeterminism and, therefore, concerns a philosophical question.

Sociology yields a different kind of knowledge than the natural sciences. Sociology of religion, for example, is not practiced with a view to discovering the causes behind a person's being religious or non-religious but with a view to finding out what the intentional and unintentional, the foreseen and unforeseen consequences are of conduct that is in accord with a certain type of rules. Thus Weber's concept of "innerworldly asceticism" does not establish a causal connection between the lifestyle of Calvinists and the rise of capitalism but demonstrates a connection between two very different phenomena, a connection of which the actors themselves were not conscious. That can be *explained* to the actors and that explanation may then lead to a change of behavior. The latter may be a goal of emancipatory sociology.[160] So a sociology of homosexuality can bring to light connections between the content of role-patterns and lines of social demarcation between the sexes, between notions of deviance and the nature of the western family structure.[161]

159. Hence between explanations of "conduct" and "behavior" and not between explanations in terms of social factors ("nurture") and biological factors ("nature"). R. Klos (1987) denies that the controversy between constructivism and essentialism relates to the question whether homosexuality is a "natural constant" or a "social and historical product." Here he is right. The issue, in his opinion, is whether homosexuality is a natural or cultural *constant* (essentialism), or the product of a *certain* culture in a *certain* historical situation (constructivism). But why should the one exclude the other? And in saying this what would one have said about the type of explanatory factors?

160. Th. de Boer (1980: 154).

161. K. Plummer (1975: 128ff.).

Sociology (also the Weberian kind) is based on the premise of man as acting being, of his behavior-as-conduct, and is not (in the first place) interested in the psychological motives or biological factors that influence the behavior but in the *reasons* of acting persons. And because a person's reasons for his or her behavior are never only hyper-individual but are often congealed in rule-guided patterns of action, they can be subjected to scientific study. The result is explanation of a kind other than causal, viz., rational explanations in terms of the intentions of the actors; and another kind of knowledge: not of the natural laws of a social sort but of empirical generalizations and societal tendencies.[162]

It is important once again to underscore that reasons are not causes.[163] For that reason causal biological and psychological explanations of behavior stand alongside of, and not in competition with, rational explanations of conduct. The question of how *meaningful* certain explanations are is another matter. On *normative* rather than scientific grounds one may prefer a rational to a causal explanation, when in a given case, say, a causal explanation was intended to explain reasons away.[164] But a question concerning the meaning of an act must be carefully distinguished from one concerning the *correctness* of a causal explanation. The latter is a question for the scholarly discipline involved.

Problems arise, however, when reasons are presented as a kind of causes, i.e., when consciously chosen reasons are made to fill up the gaps in a deterministically conceived causal scheme. This confusion is not so strange when we recall that actions, like causally-determined events, change states of affairs in the world. Causes have consequences and so do the intentional implementa-

---

162. Th. de Boer (1980: 104) calls intentionality "a hoministic postulate": i.e., humans cannot help interpreting their own behavior and that of others in terms of intentions. One finds comparable positions in A. Rosenberg (1980: 93ff., 206) and L. W. Nauta (1973: 35ff., spec. 40–41). See also the preceding section (A. MacIntyre and K. R. Popper).

163. According to A. van de Beld (1982: 76) reasons are sui generis; cf. Th. de Boer (1980: 75).

164. Th. de Boer (1980: 129–30) says that causal explanation serves the interest of understanding: explain if you must; understand if you can.

tion of reasons. But that does not make reasons into causes; they respectively relate to different levels of human behavior. An example of confusion between them, for example, occurs in the work of the interactionists W. Gagnon and J. Simon (1967). They think sexuality is subject to "sociocultural moulding to a degree surpassed by few other forms of human behavior." On that point they may be correct. But from this they infer that

> the social meaning given to physical acts releases biological events. . . . The sources of arousal, passion or excitement . . . as well as the way the event is experienced derive from a complicated set of layered symbolic meanings that are not only difficult to comprehend from the observed behavior, but may also not be shared by the participants. (pp. 22–23)

Here sociology is opposed to biology, social factors (symbolic meanings) to biological ones, culture to nature. The fact that this is fundamentally incorrect and presents a caricature of biology I have shown in § E; here I merely want to point out the phenomenon that meanings — i.e., reasons — are designated as causes that set biological processes in motion. Why? Because, according to the authors, biology is "deterministic" whereas sociology is on the side of freedom and emancipation. It is not biological factors that determine humans; they opt in freedom for a certain lifestyle for reasons of their own, on grounds of their own. Simon and Gagnon are not alone in this position.[165] In my view, though it presents an attractive picture, it is incorrect if for no other reason than that it finds freedom of choice in the absence of causal connections rather than in determination by reasons. And that, in my opinion, is not the way to go; cf. what was said in § F. Of course, we can and — stronger — *must* view homosexual lifestyles as a societal (political) choice (Tielman), as a voluntarily adopted form of existence (Jellema). In § B I already gave expression to this view in my definition. But it is an unrealistic notion of choice to think that every human being has to choose everything.

165. See R. Tielman (1983).

If that is what the essentialists mean, then they and not the constructivists are right. Essentialism is wrong, however, if it is merely another word for determinism.

(3) The constructivist position that sociology stands for freedom and emancipation takes us to a third objection, one that concerns the *moral consequences.* While sociology is an empirical science, the popularity of a specific kind of sociology may be linked with normative ideas in society, just as that was the case earlier with the biological-medical approach.

Under point (1) we observed that constructivists see a close connection between the names assigned to things (labeling) and acting. Now making assertions is also a form of acting: speech-acts. In these speech-acts language-philosophers distinguish three aspects: the locution, the illocution, and the perlocution. The first is the act of saying something; the second, what we do when we say something; and the third, the effects of what has been said on the hearer.[166] Illocutions are done in the locution and perlocutions through the locution. Now the question is: in which of these aspects is the actual meaning of assertions located? The answer depends on the meaning-theory one uses. The meaning of terms lies not only in the state of affairs to which they refer. Words do not refer; people do. Consequently, the meaning cannot be isolated from the use we make of language. C. L. Stevenson thinks that the meaning of an assertion lies on the effect it has on its hearers. The meaning of an assertion equals its dispositional character. A disposition is the tendency of someone or something to conduct oneself or itself in a certain way under certain circumstances or to effect a certain kind of behavior or reaction in someone or something else.[167] Therefore, in order to know the meaning of a word, it is not enough to

166. See V. Brümmer (1975: 19ff.). Consider this example: "Are you by any chance a homo?" The locution is the fundamental aspect: calling someone a "homo." The illocution is the conventional aspect: by conventional rules the proposition "are you by any chance a homo?" is considered a suggestive question. The perlocution is the causal aspect: the reaction (fear, anger, affirmation) on the part of the listener.

167. V. Brümmer (1975: 49; 55ff.).

know the thing to which the term refers; one must also consider the way in which it refers: the "influence" of it.

Such a causal or psychological theory of meaning is usually rejected today precisely because it cannot distinguish between understanding as the logical effect of an assertion and the reaction to it as its causal effect.[168] But suppose we assume that this theory of meaning is employed by constructivists (at least by the interactionists among them). That would yield a hypothetical explanation for (1) the close relation they posit between the definition of a situation and the consequent behavior and (2) their idea that reasons are a kind of causes.

The import of this reconstruction goes beyond noting the language-philosophical assumptions underlying a sociological theory. For if "sexual meanings are constructed, modified, negotiated, negated, and constrained in conjoint action with others,"[169] that takes us, inter alia, directly to the domain of morality. Is it also true that here, in this case the domain of sexual morality, each person has to decide for himself what is acceptable and what is not?

The ethicist A. MacIntyre believes that he can, in fact, demonstrate the presence of a relation. He believes contemporary moral discourse is marked by a radical form of subjectivism and links this situation with the theory of emotivism, which claims that rational justification of moral judgments is impossible. Thus the theory constitutes the philosophical underpinning of the present crisis in ethics.

> Emotivism is the (meta)ethical theory according to which moral-value judgments must be interpreted as emotions. Emotivism is based on the psychological theory of meaning described above. Of moral language it says that it differs from other language by its emotive meaning.[170] According to emotivists moral-value terms

168. W. D. Hudson (1983: 40, 44): "Stevenson . . . failed to distinguish between the causal, and the logical, aspect of language. He recognized that the question to ask is: how is moral language used? But he confused the causes of, with the reasons for, the use to which moral discourse is put."

169. K. Plummer (1975: 29).

170. G. J. Warnock (1974: 448ff.); W. D. Hudson (1983: 123ff.).

are not descriptions of the properties of acts but express the emotions of the speaker — they give vent to his feelings. Stevenson adds: . . . with the intention of producing the same "attitude" in the audience. "X is good" then means: "I approve of X; do so as well!"[171] According to him, therefore, the major use of moral discourse is "not to indicate facts but to create influence."

According to MacIntyre, not a single moral philosophy can be understood apart from the views held on the social reality of the time in which it functions. Every philosophy has a "social content." This is also true of emotivism; and it views reality as it has been pictured by modern sociology since Weber. In it the social world is nothing other than the meeting-place of individual wills each of which has its own attitudes and preferences and views the world as the arena for gaining one's own ends. The modern "self" is the emotive self. It finds no limit imposed on the possible issues on which it can entertain its own opinion because rational criteria for evaluation are missing.

Over against this democratized "self" that has no necessary social content whatever stands the scientized social world in which managers and therapists predominate. The absence of rational criteria in normative issues is extolled as "pluralism." In matters of ends and values rational knowledge offers no foothold. One simply has to choose between conflicting values (Weber's *Entscheidung*). Alongside of this is rational science. But science views ends as "given" and the solution of value-conflicts as lying outside of its competence.[172]

I will refrain from discussing in how far MacIntyre is right

171. To Stevenson, though it is possible to advance reasons for moral judgments, he maintains that the basal criteria are expressions of feelings. When two disputants differ on the question whether fuel-efficient cars are better than fast ones (a *general* value judgment) no rational arguments exist to determine who is right. The disputants differ in attitude. Rational arguments can be adduced when the question is whether car A is better than car B from the viewpoint of fuel-efficiency (a particular value judgment). See D. D. Raphael (1981: 24–33).

172. A. MacIntyre (1981: 22ff., 30).

to assign such far-reaching implications to emotivism. Let us simply follow him for a moment and assume that a connection exists between the moral theory of emotivism and the appearance of certain — popular — forms of sociology. The question can then be asked: does this connection also exist with constructivism? The answer is yes; there is indeed similarity between MacIntyre's picture of the "emotivistic self" and the image of man depicted by symbolic interactionism as represented by K. Plummer. According to him, man is an "open-ended" being continually occupied with role-construction, "performance," and meaning-bestowal on a world without meaning in a never-completed process. Granted, Plummer intends this image of man as a methodological, not a normative principle. According to interactionism, "bestowing meaning" is what humans do; it does not say that, morally speaking, this is what they ought to do. It seems to me impossible for interactionism, given its premises, to deny that the warrant (justification) for a given choice lies in something other than one's own meaning-bestowal. Accordingly, a rational discussion about its correctness is precluded. And with that, interactionist sociology implicitly assumes the emotivist claim that a rational justification of normative judgments is impossible. The same is true for all constructivism. One can ask how constructs originated and how they work but not whether they are true or valid.[173]

So, in fact, there is a demonstrable relation between constructivism and emotivism. And what have we gained by this? It explains, to my mind, why in the gay-liberation movement there is such strong interest in this constructivist type of sociology. It uses this sociology as a means of undergirding the liberation movement. There is no objection to this, but from an ethical viewpoint it is interesting to ask how sociology can be used in the service of liberation. I want to make three comments.

First, constructivists believe that a biological approach to

173. Cf. M. Foucault's low confidence in rational discussion: do not pronounce yourself against power but diffuse and undermine it (1976). See M. v.d. Heyden (1983). Foucault analyzes the construction "sexuality," not in terms of its soundness but in terms of effectiveness.

homosexuality is unsound because, say they, biology is deterministic. And, indeed, conceptions of homosexuality based on the medical model proved to discount a homosexual's freedom-to-act: there are no reasons, only determining causes. However, the sociological approach to homosexuality, which seeks to show that the freedom of homosexuals to act is greater than these (still popular) conceptions allow, runs the risk, first, of overestimating the homosexual's freedom of choice, as we saw under point (2) of this section. But in the second place, from a liberationist viewpoint, this freedom of choice, which is the freedom-to-act, is really not very interesting. Gay-liberationists see the justification of homosexual lifestyles as lying in the meaning-bestowals of the homosexuals themselves: to promote emancipation is to champion the meaning one has conferred on one's own orientation. The freedom at issue, in this connection, is freedom of choice in its quality as freedom-to-decide. The freedom-to-act depends on internal and external "determining" factors. They fall within the domain of biology, psychology, and sociology. But in the freedom-to-decide, the issue is autonomy, the *right* to define one's freedom himself; it is the question of who decides what is good for homosexuals — society or they themselves? That is a moral issue. Sociology cannot resolve it. Precisely in that way the paramount question, that of the freedom-to-decide, is in danger of being overlooked.

Second, sociology cannot justify any behavior; and if gay-liberationists think it can, they end up in the same naturalistic pitfall as earlier generations who appealed to biological nature. The object of sociology is to make clear *that* people have reasons and *what* they are. But from the fact that a person has reasons, one can never infer that they are morally good reasons. The fact that someone assigns meanings to his behavior does not mean he is, therefore, morally justified. It seems constructivism implies this: a self-assigned meaning names the behavior, explains it, and subjectively justifies it. This leads to the remarkable conclusion that then the sociological construct of "meaning-bestowal" fulfills the same double function as the medical-biological concept of "nature." It has the function both to *explain* and to *justify* the behavior. "Meaning-bestowal" is then the sociological analogue of "nature"! The only difference is that the warrant for the behavior is now found in subjective human nature rather than in "objective" (biological) nature. Here, too, we have ended up in the naturalistic pitfall because I can no more derive norms from what I myself view as my nature than from biological data concerning myself.

This brings us to the third point: the appeal to subjective self-justification is an act of desperation in which the influence of emotivism on constructivist sociology comes most clearly to the fore. Says MacIntyre: "to a large degree people now think, talk, and act *as if* emotivism were true."[174] But why can one's own meaning-bestowal not be sufficient justification? Indeed, the ultima ratio of rational conduct is a subjectivity that cannot be grounded anymore deeply: it is the cry, "Here I stand: I cannot do otherwise."[175] But before a person retreats to this final subjectivity there is usually a great deal that can be said. The belief that everyone has to decide for himself is indispensable in allowing everyone to determine his position in freedom (= autonomy), but if that is one's only guideline, the consequence is that one cannot hold another person accountable for anything.[176] MacIntyre goes a step further when he says that emotivism causes the distinction between manipulative and non-manipulative relations to disappear.[177] What remains is a striving for political power that is solely based on the power of numbers instead of arguments. Political power is certainly important if one is not to be dependent on "the soft forces within ancient powers," and homosexuals rightly fear that their newly won freedom will be hedged in and placed under new forms of supervision and control.[178] Autonomy as such, however, is empty. But why should homosexuals give up on moral argumentation in support of their desire for friendship and self-determination and, therefore, give up arguments? Emotivism may, as MacIntyre claims, have deep roots in our

174. A. MacIntyre (1981: 21).
175. Th. de Boer (1980: 76).
176. H. M. Kuitert (1981: 12–13).
177. A. MacIntyre (op. cit., 22–23).
178. Thus the editors in *Homojaarboek* 1 (1980: 15).

culture; as ethical theory it is almost unanimously rejected by philosophers. It is, therefore, of no avail to the gay-liberation movement (unwittingly) to ground the justification of its efforts in an obsolete theory.

We may now summarize what we have found: (a) Constructivist sociologists, in their approach to homosexuality, posit as central the basing of conduct on reasons. Compared to earlier scientific approaches, which were interested only in the causes of behavior, this is a gain.

(b) But constructivism is wrong to reject biological explanations. The reason is that it neglects to distinguish between the explanation of "behavior" in terms of causes and of "conduct" in terms of reasons or rules.

(c) This rejection is not based on scientific but on a priori grounds. Constructivists mistakenly assume that freedom, though not compatible with "deterministic" biology, is compatible with "indeterministic" sociology.

(d) The freedom at stake for gay liberationists oriented to sociology is seemingly the freedom-to-act. That freedom can be examined by empirical methods. In reality the issue is freedom of choice, autonomy. Sociology must limit itself to the former.

(e) In fact this does not happen: the preference for a constructivist-sociological approach serves the cause of autonomy and liberation or emancipation. Under these conditions one can no longer distinguish prescription from description and vice versa, and constructivist gay-liberationists end up in the pitfall of the naturalist fallacy.

(f) Gay liberation that gives up on moral argumentation confirms the emotivist prejudice that a rational accounting for norms is precluded.

H. Explanation and evaluation

I will use the concluding section of this chapter to bring together a number of conclusions from preceding sections with the aid of the question what explanation and (moral) evaluation have to do with each other.

The central question in this chapter arose from a dilemma: on the one hand, no moral norms can be inferred from biological data about man; on the other, the lack of any relation between given reality and the morally good is not conceivable. So what *is* the relation between empirical reality and moral norms? One cannot conduct a moral discussion without having factual information at one's disposal. The sciences are important sources of factual information. The question, then, is how this information relates to moral norms, particularly in the context of the assessment of homosexuality. In this connection we have to distinguish between moral and non-moral value judgments. The latter are judgments stated in terms of health and sickness, of maleness and femaleness, or of choice versus being conditioned.

Because all knowledge is assembled on the basis of a certain selective viewpoint, engagement in any given scientific discipline always brings with it certain assessments of reality. Accordingly, every science rests on specific normative premises. When homosexuality is made an object of study in a specific discipline, a certain "view" and assessment of homosexuality is thereby implied. Such assessments are inevitable. The question is now: precisely what are they? Only those value judgments that are given with the pursuit of a given scientific discipline can be justified from within the perspective of the discipline concerned; in other cases we are dealing with the personal opinions of the practitioners of a given discipline. Accordingly, with a focus on the occurrence of value judgments we have examined the various scientific explanations of homosexuality in order to determine which connection can be justified in terms of the nature of the discipline in question and which cannot. We will now use the results of our inquiry to answer the question concerning the relation between scientific information and moral norms.

Sciences furnish explanations but these are always restricted to certain aspects of a phenomenon. Let me begin with the second point. Given the interest of different disciplines in different aspects of human behavior, different conceptualizations can exist side-by-side and, therefore, also different definitions of homosexuality. Medical professionals define it in terms of "predisposition" and sociologists in terms of "sexual identity." To this there can be no objection; it is the good right of every science to make homosexuality a subject of study. It is first of all the business of the discipline concerned to determine in how far its conceptualization is correct. It is a scientific issue that has nothing to do with moral assessment.

Quite another matter, however, is that from the fact that homosexuality is examined in the context of science x one can never infer that, therefore, the phenomenon is x-like in nature. In the case of homosexuality we are specifically faced with such a misunderstanding because the definitions that have come down in popular usage are medical in nature. The notion that homosexuality is a medical phenomenon constitutes a judgment. In order to evaluate homosexuality, however, we must start not with a (pre)judgment but with a description. The fact that historically this is not what happened in no way detracts from the correctness of this statement.

The starting point in homosexuality has to be that, like any other form of human behavior, it is described in terms of *intentions*, hence as a form of conduct. The premise of intentionality is a fundamental postulate for human communication (§ G). That is always true unless the contrary is evident. At this point the scientific data become relevant because they may evince proof that the premise does not hold water (§ B).

We have found that the different accounts of homosexual behavior have given us no reason to doubt this premise. Measured by rational criteria for disease, homosexual behavior is not a disease; here the distinction between "motion" (*actus hominis*) and "moving" (*actus humanus;* intentional act) proved fundamental (§ C). Neither did the theory that homosexual conduct represents a form of biologically dysfunctional behavior prove tenable because it confuses a biological criterion of function that relates to behavior (descriptive) with a criterion of function as meaning-bestowal that concerns human behavior as "conduct" (intentional action, § D). From this — again — one is not entitled to draw the conclusion that, therefore, biological accounts of homosexual behavior are precluded. Objections to this are, as a rule, based not on knowledge of biology but on certain presuppositions, viz., that of the deterministic character of biological explanations and/or that of the opposition between "nature" and "nurture." Both are incorrect. The philosophical issue of determinism versus indeterminism has nothing to do with the question concerning the biological causes of behavior. The "nature-nurture" polarity is a false construal of the matter. It assumes that whereas biology studies the "nature" side of man, the human sciences study the "nurture" side, and that biological statements are assertions about biologically determined traits. Along with the "nature-nurture" issue, the popular representation of homosexuality as a "natural predisposition" that "determines" the behavior has to be rejected as an unbiological way of thinking. We did note that the comparability of human with animal homosexual behavior — in which biologists are interested — is low, so that results can only be expected from comparisons between different groups of people (§§ E and F).

The misunderstandings referred to also play a role in the debate between "essentialists" and "constructivists" over the question whether homosexuality is a transhistorical "given" or a variable historic "construct." Constructivists view "homosexuality" as the variable resultant of processes of socialization among members of the same sex as they are enacted between groups, individuals, and society and serve as the basis of identity and role formation. In this context the biological approach to sexual behavior is viewed as a certain phase in this historical process. In the case of numerous constructivist sociologists, liberationist goals are central, their starting point being that homosexuality is a choice. This causes confusion because the question concerning the measure of freedom of action in the sphere of sexual behavior (a scientific matter) is replaced by the question concerning freedom of choice (a normative matter), a reason why constructivism acquires naturalistic traits (§ G).

The conclusion has to be that explanation and evaluation differ and that the sciences have to limit themselves to the first. That is their purpose: to furnish trustworthy information about reality. Value judgments, on the other hand, other than those given with the choice of the manner of inquiry, do not come from within the sciences but from another source.

212

However, all this does not mean that in order to judge we can dispense with explanations — quite the contrary. Here the distinction between causal and rational explanations is essential. We saw (§ G) that some constructivist sociologists believe that homosexuality must be explained in terms of the meanings actors themselves ascribe to their actions rather than in terms of causal, such as biological, factors. Such so-called rational explanations are necessary when the evaluation of behavior is at issue. Rational explanations — answers to the question why a person does something — explain actions, according to a teleological scheme, in terms of the intentions (convictions, meaning-bestowals, wishes, desires) that are couched in the reasons of the actors themselves. As a rule, however, the giving of reasons is intended not only to explain but also to justify one's own behavior. Accordingly, for the purpose of evaluation we need to know the reasons for the behavior in question.

Reasons are not causes.[179] A rational explanation yields an end-means relation; a causal explanation a cause-effect relation. Are the two totally unrelated? No — to conceive an action as a means to reach a stated end (intention) implies the existence of a cause-effect relation between the means and the end chosen. Although causal explanation is something other than rational explanation, the latter implies the possibility of the former. Consequently, besides rational explanations causal ones are needed for an evaluation: to check whether the link between action and intention that is presupposed in the reason cited is in fact valid.

In sum: reasons are not causes; causal explanations do not concern intentions, but a rational explanation does presuppose knowledge of causal connections on the part of the actor.[180] The question "Why do you do that?" meaning "How do you justify that behavior?" requires from the actor an answer that presupposes his familiarity with the causal relation between the action and its

179. Although (hidden) wishes may occur as causes of behavior (Freud!), they do not explain it in terms of intentions (rationality). In that case we are dealing with causal explanation. Cf. A. v.d. Beld (op. cit.: 74–75).

180. Th. de Boer (op. cit.: 36) says: "strong arguments exist for the view that we do not understand the concept of action if we do not already know what causation is."

effect. This familiarity is always assumed in our making a moral assessment of his action.

This is at least one, perhaps the primary, reason why we need scientific information in moral discussions. It is needed in the form of causal explanations, which, if advanced with an eye to evaluation, serve as *a check on* the consequences of the evaluation. It serves to check the tenability of a *consequentialist* ethical argument, not to take the place of explanations in terms of reasons. Accordingly, if on scientific grounds it can be demonstrated that the assumptions about consequences are *not* true, the moral evaluation also can turn out differently.

The traditional condemnation of homosexuality viewed heterosexual intercourse as a practical necessity, i.e., as a compelling reason for achieving what people saw as the purpose of sexuality: reproduction. They found confirmation for this view in what they took to be the appropriate functioning of nature (in a biological sense). For that reason they called homosexual intercourse "unnatural": there is never a good reason for it. Later generations, with nineteenth-century physicians in the lead, interpreted practical necessity as biological necessity, i.e., physical necessity. But practical necessity, something that has to do with reasons, is very different from physical necessity, which has to do with determining causes.[181] By that process people ended up in the naturalistic pitfall. The underlying idea — an idea that as such is valid — here was always that when it concerns consequences, moral norms are not arbitrary but ultimately rest on a "must" and, therefore, have to do with regularities (cause-effect relations) in nature. The naturalistic argument concerning homosexuality has, therefore, consistently been also a consequentialist argument!

Now, the scientific study of homosexuality has demonstrated — rather: homosexuals themselves have shown — that such a "must" on which the prohibition of homosexual behavior was said to be based no longer exists. Therefore homosexuality is not "unnatural" in the biological sense of the word.

---

181. A. v.d. Beld (op. cit.: 72ff.).

Chapter III

Against Nature?
"Nature" and Ethics

A. Introduction: framing the question

In the last section of the previous chapter I concluded that, to the extent tradition used the word "unnatural" to mean that the moral condemnation of homosexuality is rooted in a necessity that is given with our humanity as such, it was mistaken. In this biological sense homosexuality is not unnatural.

But this conclusion, however weighty, is not enough to refute the moral judgments concerning homosexual relations we reviewed in Chapter I. After all, even the tolerant position that holds that homosexual relations are morally permissible insofar and because they are conducted in love and faithfulness already assumes that, biologically speaking, homosexuality is natural (there is that specific biological "predisposition"). But this only underscores the fact that biology is not the problem. The problem, as we saw in Chapter I, was that the words "natural" and "unnatural" are used in different senses, the biological, the moral, and the religious sense, and that indiscriminately. This would seem to take care of the biological meaning, but that still leaves the moral and the religious.

We must begin by distinguishing the moral from the religious

215

meaning. To that end, I wish to recall the condemnation pronounced by Barth, who believed he could base his judgment on purely religious grounds. Barth, as we saw, condemned homosexual behavior as "humanity without the fellow-man" (*C.D.* III. 4, p. 166) in his description of "unnatural" (I. C). How did Barth know that this is so? From the "Word of God," he answered. But that proved to be more complex than he bargained for. After all, he gave us what he considered *the reasons* for the biblical condemnation. Among other things it was the fact that with homosexual partners the sexual organs do not match and for that reason homosexuality is sickness and perversion. Hence, for Barth, homosexual intercourse is wrong because of certain biological *characteristics* of this behavior. However, one who infers a moral judgment from biological *characteristics* commits a naturalistic fallacy. Barth commits this fallacy, and it comes neither from the Bible nor from the "Word of God," but from the pen of Barth. That he focuses especially on the *biological* characteristics of homosexual relations, however, is due to the fact that, like his contemporaries, he employs the naturalistic static-mechanical model of sexuality (I. D), something he derived, not from the Bible, but from his culture. This line of thinking *pre*cedes (and is independent of) Barth's notion that because of the "one Word of God" heterosexual relations are "natural" (in the moral sense), i.e., they alone *can* be the bearers of "humanity," something homosexual relations can never be, since it is bearer only of "humanity without one's fellow-man": unnatural.

For his position on homosexuality Barth appeals to the authority of the "Word of God," against which human reasons do not amount to anything. Evidently this does not keep his human and cultural presuppositions from playing a dominant role. In the following chapter I will advance arguments to show that this is always, and even necessarily, the case. At this point I must be content to point out that, if our presuppositions have not first been critically examined, we will all too easily advance as arguments from the biblical authors or from the "Word of God" what in reality are our own positions. For that reason alone the first question we must now answer is: What do we mean when we employ the term "(un)natural" in order by this means to pronounce a moral judgment?

A person may think that this question, because it was the question of the tradition, is now obsolete. Now that it has become clear that, biologically, homosexuality is not unnatural, it is no longer apropos to pay attention to a moral judgment that is formulated in terms of a natural/unnatural distinction. Is that true? In the first place, even if it were true, this conclusion still needs further clarification. After all, when the tradition spoke of a thing as being "(un)natural," it had in mind something other than what today falls within the category of biological information. The classic concept of "natural" had a moral flavor, a relation to the dimension of the good, which is lacking in modern concepts of it. It was a normative concept of nature, grounded in a concept of being that included the idea of moral goodness. If we do not take this into account, we will fail to plumb the traditional assessment at a sufficiently deep level.

In the second place, though to modern ears the terminology of "(un)natural" understood as conveying a moral judgment sounds dated, the view that underlies it — and that is the pivotal issue — is still very much alive. *It is the opinion that homosexual relations require special moral justification.* For even where the same norms are observed by homosexuals and heterosexuals, many people do not unqualifiedly regard homosexual lifestyles as being equivalent to the heterosexual. This comes out in their attitude: "no objections — but preferably not!" It is also evinced by the common division of homosexual yearning into a (homophile) predisposition and (homosexual) behavior. The background here is a moral judgment, the judgment that the behavior is permissible because of the presence of a specific condition. Consequently a homosexual's "coming out" still consistently has the character of a confession. The statement "I am a homosexual" is not only the assertion of a fact but the expression of an attitude, hence of a value judgment: I am in favor, I approve of it. Accordingly, the qualification "homosexual" evokes moral reactions, reactions of approval or disapproval. In contrast with heterosexuality, homosexuality is still considered from a moral viewpoint. Thus contemporary societal tolerance toward homosexuals at the same time embraces a moral judgment by society concerning homosexuality.

Today, of course, many people have fully accepted homosexuality, that is, for them the moral problem has been solved. Besides, numerous people deliberately choose to avoid moral judgments because they are not interested in them. But this does not mean they have no position on homosexuality; they do, even a moral position. The notion that everyone has to decide for himself how to shape his sex life, for example, is a moral position. Especially within the churches homosexuality is still officially a subject of moral discussion. See Chapter I. But this does not, by any means, imply that outside the churches people possess the better arguments. Homosexuals themselves experience existing societal tolerance as unstable, shaky. In practice this tolerance more often springs from indifference than from considerations of equal moral dignity. In general it arises from thinking in terms of a special "condition": "that's the way they are." Now in that regard popular opinion does not differ from that in the churches where it surfaces in the form of an "ethic of exoneration." Behind both lurks the same *moral* premise: heterosexuality is a moral step up from homosexuality. It is better, *morally* better, to be hetero- than to be homosexual. Heterosexuality is the norm and homosexuality is acceptable to the degree it meets the norms held by and among heterosexuals. In my opinion, this position can be interpreted only as the modern variant of the traditional view that heterosexuality is natural and homosexuality is not. Therefore, the fact that the old terminology has lost its appeal does not mean that the underlying assessment has changed! It is definitely worth our time to check out the traditional condemnation ("it is unnatural") in terms of its normative premises. These were already present in the classic concept of nature. In this chapter I will reinterpret the normative component of this ancient concept. From this vantage point I want to answer the question whether the fact that homosexuality in our society still consistently occasions moral interest is justified from a moral viewpoint.

First I wish to examine the fundamental shift in the nature concept that took effect in the scientific revolution of the seventeenth century. This shift is very important for the manner in which, still today, we can connect the term "(un)natural," as expressive of moral judgment, with the causality and regularity characteristic for the modern view of nature (§ B). The result of this analysis will then be applied with a view to correcting the moral assessment of (homo)sexuality in terms of the "natural/unnatural" distinction (§§ C and D).

B. Nature as normative entity?

Does it make sense to speak of "nature" as a normative entity, specifically as morally normative, and if so, how? The concept of nature, as stated earlier, is vague in all of its senses. Further, they often have almost nothing to do with each other. Applied to man, "nature" is sometimes used to refer to the typically human and then again to exclude that very thing. Also, in one and the same author it can mean both one and the other. That is the case, for example, in Thomas Aquinas.[1] That is certainly troublesome. As a result of this confusion, we no longer know precisely how to take the words "natural" and "unnatural" in a moral sense. To pick one of the many meanings of "nature" would be rather arbitrary. Not everyone would have to share my selection and might, therefore, reject as my subjective opinion that conclusion based on it in the argumentation that follows. Add to this that we need a definition of "nature" in the moral sense; how can we find that without ending up in the pitfall of the naturalistic fallacy?[2]

However, the matter is less complex than it would appear at first sight. Terms often get their meaning from being defined in

1. See Chapter I § C. Every philosopher uses a nature-concept more or less his own. Researchers have found as many as sixty different ones, H. de Vos (1970:7).

2. Cf. Chapter I § B. One can, for example, choose as one's definition of nature "that which corresponds to the organism's biological potentialities." But does "natural" in this sense mean "good"?

the context of a theory, scientific or otherwise;[3] or, more generally, in the light of certain assumptions about the nature of reality. That is also true of "nature." Accordingly, we have to know something about the context within which the word "(un)natural" was originally used in a moral sense. That was in the period prior to the seventeenth century. Comparison of that nature-concept with that of the modern period will show why earlier, when people spoke of "nature" in connection with man, they sometimes used it as a descriptive term (man as he is) and then again as norm (man as he ought to be). The question we must now address is whether today we can still do this in that way.

There is a great difference between the ancient and medieval finalistic understanding of nature and the organistic worldview that is based on it[4] on the one hand and on the other hand the causal view of nature and the mechanistic world image that have been dominant since the scientific revolution of the seventeenth century. Although twentieth-century science differs in many respects from the classic science originated by Copernicus, Galileo, and Newton, the real break lies in its difference from the ancient natural science of the time before Copernicus.[5]

The ancient concept of nature[6] *(phusis)* relates to *the true being* of man, animal, or thing. In Plato it comes close to the notion of "idea." But in and through this notion plays the residual pre-Platonic idea that *phusis* refers to the original, the result of a process of becoming, and hence describes the *original* constitution of man, animal, or thing. Hence "being" *(phusis)* is not the result of empirical investigation but is determined speculatively. That is certainly true for Plato who does not hold to a fixed concept of *phusis*. Also in Aristotle we find both meanings of *phusis*. Although he is more empirical in orientation than Plato, in his work *phusis* is determined

3. Cf. what was said in Chapter II § B about extensional and intentional definitions.

4. R. Hooykaas (1972: 29ff.; 98ff.).

5. "The big gap, after all, yawns between the last two (i.e. the Aristotelian science of nature and the classic), not between the classic and the modern" (E. J. Dijksterhuis (1950: v; 9).

6. Cf. H. Köster, art. on *phusis* in *Th.D.N.T.* IX, pp. 251–77.

speculatively insofar as it denotes the essential being of man, animal, or thing. Insofar as *phusis* relates to origin and the process of becoming, Aristotle introduces the concept of "entelechy," i.e., the power of becoming inherent in the "natural." This in distinction from "causes," which constitute the origin of things made (artifacts). Aristotle even attempts to include both meanings in his definition of nature:

> Nature in the primary and chief sense is the primary being of those things which have in them their own source of movement; for a material is called a "nature" because it is capable of receiving it, and the processes of becoming and growing are natural because they are movements proceeding from it. And in this sense nature is the source of movement in things, which are natural because this source is inherent in them, either potentially or completely.[7]

This sketchy description will have to suffice. The essential features of Aristotle's nature-concept are as follows:

1. It introduces a *teleological* concept of nature. Nature is the being of things that have in them a principle of movement or non-movement. "Movement" here stands for change.
2. It is, however, a *static* concept. Being is determined by matter and form. "Nature" can, therefore, also acquire the meaning of "essence," as the unique being of every thing that exists.
3. A third element is the idea of *entelechy,* the notion that the starting point determines the end point as well as the manner of attaining it.
4. Finally, it is a *normative* concept: the goal of nature is the good, and the naturally good is the basis of *natural law* for society (originally the *polis*).

This concept of nature, in rough outline, persists throughout the Middle Ages, albeit in a Christianly adapted form. Thomas adds to it the notion of a natural tendency toward the good present in man (cf. Chapter I § C).

7. In *Metaphysics,* Delta, 4, Translation by Richard Hope, New York, 1952. The quotation is from A. G. M. van Melsen (1983b: 56).

I will now present an equally sketchy description of classic scientific thought (since Newton). The difference consists in a shift away from speculations about nature *(phusis)* as the essence of things and toward empirical observation, toward *mêchanê* and *technê* (the art of experimentation of Renaissance engineers). Phenomena were no longer viewed as individual expressions of the essence of things but as instances of *nature's laws*. Accordingly, causal relations were no longer interpreted within a teleological model. Teleology does not exclude causality, but includes it within a deductive-nomological model. Man can deduce the laws of nature from the phenomena, says Newton: "I frame no hypotheses. . . ." Thus nature becomes the world of visible phenomena controlled by natural laws and not a world that lies behind them (Galileo: the book of nature "is written in the language of mathematics"). Because these laws are not obvious, experiment is necessary. In this way complex natural systems can be studied under simplified conditions. Whereas for Aristotle mechanics was the theory of counter-natural movements (*mêchanê* means: "clever conniving") it now became natural science *par excellence!*[8] The mechanistic world-picture or view that thus arose became dominant, first in physics and last — not until the twentieth century — in biology. Also the *mutability* of nature (evolution, the great discovery of the nineteenth century) proved conceivable in mechanistic terms (Darwin's theory of natural selection and, in this century, genetics).

Western culture never abandoned this mechanistic world-picture or view. The metaphors used for nature continually change: clockwork in the eighteenth, the steam engine in the nineteenth, telephone, radio, and computer in the twentieth century. This world-image also began to shape theorizing about man. While the ancients pictured the world on the analogy of man, i.e., as an organism governed by vital forces (entelechies), after the eighteenth century human nature was increasingly viewed as a mech-

8. This was already Francis Bacon's view; see e.g. S. Mason (1972: 141ff.).

anism on the analogy of machines.[9] The idea of a determined nature, including that of man, was not far behind.

Therefore, comparing the modern understanding of nature with the Aristotelian, we find that (1) the teleology has dropped out; (2) the static element has been replaced by the idea of mutability; (3) the moral element disappeared.

As a result, by contrast with the classic conception, the door was now open for the conception of the natural and the typically human, the factual and the normative, the natural and the cultural, *construed as sets of opposites.* "Control of nature" and "the emancipation of man" from his natural state now became the slogans. R. Spaemann, a Catholic philosopher, has pointed out that the relation between the freedom of man and nature can no longer be construed in the manner of the teleological nature-concept of antiquity. To Aristotle and his disciples natural law made sense only in the context of the *polis,* the community of free men. Today however, says Spaemann, natural law has broken up into two parts: as freedom rights that vary depending on the prevailing cultural circumstances on the one hand and as the entire complex of biological and psychological conditions that precede human action, on the other. He argues that the two should be brought more into mutual relation: freedom needs to be conceived as "remembered nature" in order thus to restrain the despoticized will to freedom.[10]

Spaemann's diagnosis, in my opinion, is correct and I will return to it. The core issue is that the term "(un)natural" in its moral sense presupposes the ancient teleological understanding of nature in which it originated and in which alone it can be understood and *not* on the assumption of a mechanistic view of nature.

This seems more obvious than it is. For within the context of this mechanistic world-image teleological thought and language have maintained themselves as meaningful in especially one context, the sphere of human action. It is meaningful because it is simply a fact that (western) people understand themselves as acting persons

9. See, e.g., P. Vroon and D. Draaisma (1985).
10. R. Spaemann (1973).

and relate to each other as such. In this context we are dealing with intentions, goals, motives. Here we ask what it is that "moves" people, suggesting in the process a principle of movement operating from within, à la Aristotle. Reasons, however, are often described in language derived from precisely this mechanistic thought (such as "turning the clock back," the mainspring of an action, "blowing off steam," being "on the same wavelength," etc.). The language is mechanistic. The idea behind it teleological.

The idea that nature works toward a goal, however, is itself not a fact of nature. It is a norm of human origin that has been added to the facts of nature. And nature is being measured by it: it is nature as desired by man. Consequently, the goal of a human act, i.e., the result an actor aims at, can be described either as a "natural end" or not. Accordingly, nothing can be said about the moral desirability of the fact apart from the norms that, as we said, have been added. And here lies the rule: people use the word "(un)natural" as though speaking in terms of the nature-concept of antiquity, hence as a moral judgment. "Nature" serves as a means of saying something normative. But the content of the idea of the "unnatural" is an empirical given described in terms of the mechanistic concept of nature. In other words, to empirical data ("nature" in the modern, mechanistic sense) people add a norm but act as if they get it *from* nature (in the premodern sense).

To introduce my argument that is designed to show why the latter is not feasible, I will discuss the views of three authors who speak of nature in a normative sense: the ethicist Richards, the Catholic philosopher Van Melsen, and the Protestant theologian Bonhoeffer.

Writes D. A. J. Richards:

> The unnatural, as a concept, implies that the operation of a thing, as explained by a theory of proper process for that thing, has gone awry — and has been impaired, frustrated, or corrupted so radically that we have difficulty in understanding how the thing can operate.[11]

11. D. A. J. Richards (1980: 44).

Unnatural, says Richards, is not the same as "occurring infrequently" or "unusual" or "statistically divergent." Even if, say, matricide or infanticide should occur with some regularity (as in the animal world! P.P.), that would still be an unnatural act; that is, if it is regarded as a departure from correct human functioning. Accordingly we need a theory of appropriate human functioning that tells us what capacities, inclinations, and goals are fundamental for our humanity, i.e., which goods are primary human goods. Now one who deliberately robs us of the possibility of experiencing those goods acts unnaturally. Depending on the capacities made central in a given theory of human nature, different conceptions of the unnatural arise. To Shakespeare, for example, it was regicide; to him the hereditary monarchy was a primary human good.

Hence Richards applies the word "natural," in a normative sense, to certain capacities that man possesses "by nature" and that he is under obligation to develop or to goals he can pursue and ought always to pursue. Unnatural are the capacities, goals, and inclinations a human being can but ought never to pursue. Which these are, however, depends on a *preceding* theory concerning what is *necessary* to being human, i.e., a preceding normative view of man.

A. G. M. van Melsen, wondering how in our day nature can still imply a norm, answers his own question very much in line with the thought of Thomas Aquinas. In thinking about what a human being ought to be, we must inescapably listen to the pointers nature furnishes. The fact that man is a part of nature is an elementary datum that comes to expression in the double meaning of the term "natural law," a scientific and a moral meaning. The term conveys the fact that nature and culture belong to a common order. On the other hand, because of man's freedom to choose, there is also a sharp distinction between the two. A person's action does not exclusively proceed from his nature but is also based on his current knowledge and ideas. Thomas, thoroughly aware of this, defined the moral natural law in very general terms ("the good must be done and evil avoided"), at the same time showing restraint in furnishing specifics.

However, in responding to the question of how this general principle can be concretized, Thomas nevertheless displays a confidence we no longer share. According to him, it is possible to arrive at insightful first principles, and, by way of abstraction from observation, to learn the essence of a thing with its corresponding finality, and by definition to capture it in concepts. With the rise of natural science this conviction disappeared. Science no longer knows of first principles in the sense Thomas understood them. Beside the material principles that emerged from research, there are *constitutive* principles that regulate the research. They have philosophical content (e.g., the falsification principle), not factual. They are ideas that serve to guide the research; they do not tell us what concrete reality looks like. Natural law is such a constitutive principle. It makes assertions about how man *ought* to act on the basis of what man *is*. That is how Thomas meant it and for that reason he held back from detailed interpretation: to act in a concrete situation requires knowledge of that situation and cannot be based only on principle. That, according to van Melsen, is the idea underlying natural law.[12]

Just what principles does van Melsen have in mind? Speaking of sexuality he says that the drives, because they are so strong, require personal and social ordering.

> Natural law judges all sexual behavior by one elementary datum that becomes a principle: sexual intercourse is oriented to reproduction. . . . If one abandons this principle it does not clearly seem possible to order sexual behavior. . . . It seems to be the only possible ordering principle. (p. 73)

This does not yet, however, say whether the pointers of nature in the matter of sexuality are also morally normative. That depends on the value the physical act in question has in human life (p. 75). It is clear, thinks van Melsen, that nature gives signals here. The physical structures involved furnish indications for the behavior that fits them. This is what lifts their use above mere human

12. A. G. M. van Melsen (1983b: 61ff.).

226

arbitrariness. And what is arbitrariness here? Not, in his opinion, the disjunction of the sexual act from reproduction(!) because nature has furnished more egg and sperm cells than are needed for reproduction and, in addition, endowed humans with more love-craving than is necessary for that purpose. Also homosexuality is a natural variant. But whether it may be cultivated is a question van Melsen cannot answer. Although in his eyes the homosexual act is "deficient," it is not, therefore, "morally impermissible." The reproductive principle is not universal enough to serve as natural law and takes too little account of the data of experience (p. 78).

My conclusion is that, though van Melsen has reservations about the traditional interpretation of natural law in the area of sex, as a believing Catholic he wants to retain the idea. We observe, however, that his reasoning is not coherent. No wonder. For if natural law is formally defined as "the evaluation of behavior on the basis of an elementary *datum* that becomes a *principle*," this already implies that the norm is added to rather than deduced from nature. Van Melsen attempts to avoid this conclusion by saying that nature gives pointers, indications. That is misleading. What nature does "teach" — to put it that way — is what humans can, or cannot, do; not what they ought to do. The first is an empirical issue; the second a normative one.

For a Protestant theologian it is relatively exceptional to accord normative significance to nature, but Bonhoeffer does it. He wants to escape the predicament of having to say that everything is either sin or grace.[13] In a fallen creation relative differences remain. It continues to make a difference whether or not a human is reduced to a means or a machine, also in relation to Christ. Bonhoeffer reasons from a rigorous Christological viewpoint. In this sense, too, "the natural" exists. It not only has as its opposite the Word of God but also the unnatural. After the Fall the natural has retained a certain independence, a relative freedom. Man himself has to distinguish the natural from the unnatural.[14]

13. H. M. Kuitert (1985: 113).
14. See F. de Lange (1985: 259).

The natural is the form of life preserved by God for the fallen world and directed toward justification, redemption, and renewal through Christ. . . . Natural life is formed life. The natural is form, immanent in life and serving it. If life detaches itself from this form, if it seeks to break free and to assert itself in isolation from this form, if it is unwilling to allow itself to be served by the form of the natural, then it destroys itself to the very roots.[15]

The natural preserves life for the unnatural. Life itself tends toward the natural and resists the unnatural. It is its own physician. Life is both an end in itself and a means. Natural life stands between two extremes as both the one and the other.

In relation to Jesus Christ the status of life as an end in itself is understood as creaturehood, and its status as a means to an end is understood as participation in the kingdom of God; while, within the framework of the natural life, the fact that life is an end in itself finds expression in the rights with which life is endowed, and the fact that life is a means to an end finds expression in the duties which are imposed on it. (p. 107)

Bonhoeffer is concerned to legitimatize the appeal to nature. In this connection he simply assumes that nature can imply a norm. How the rights and duties that, according to him, are given with the natural life can be inferred from it — our problem — is not an issue for him. The natural can be grasped by the human mind even though it participates in sin, says Bonhoeffer. It is that which the human race has in common. "Natural" is that which is objectively there, exempt from subjectivity. For that reason Bonhoeffer, like van Melsen, grounds rights and duties in nature: the regulation of behavior must not be left to subjective caprice. Bonhoeffer's intent is clear: the natural is the human as governed by built-in norms. But what is natural and how we can distinguish it from the unnatural remains unclear.[16]

15. D. Bonhoeffer (1955: 103, 106).
16. Unless we follow W. Trillhaas (1970: 190–91), who cites Bonhoeffer with approval but reads "nature" in a biological-descriptive sense:

What is it these three illustrations make clear? The problem is that two different conceptions of reality are designated with the same term: nature. Why a problem? Because in our everyday dealings with reality we assume the mechanistic concept of nature but in reference to human action use the word "(un)natural" as a moral value judgment that, as stated earlier, presupposes the concept of nature held by antiquity. Now in the previous chapter we noted that (1) actions have reasons and (2) reasons must not be viewed as the causes of the actions. In other words, the preferences, wishes, convictions, in short the *mental* states that the actor expresses in the form of reasons are not the causes of the act. On the other hand, consideration of a person's reasons are necessary precisely in order to render a moral judgment. Acts are morally judged on the basis of the actor's reasons. Hence the term "(un)natural" as a moral judgment relates to reasons, not causes. "Natural," intended in a moral sense, then implies a further determination of such reasons.

Question: Can the gap between "natural" as it concerns nomological-causal relations and "natural" as it relates to ends be bridged? Answer: Only by assuming that the relation between a certain mental state and a subsequent action is *identical* with a causal relation between a state of the brain and a physical movement that can be described by reference to a biochemical or neurophysiological law. If that were possible, we would indeed have to abandon the notion that reasons explain actions. But it is not. To use an argument employed by A. Rosenberg:[17] terms like "wish," "preference," and "act" are not "natural kinds" but "human

---

"Also in Paul's use of the word nature is that which we find in and for ourselves as given before we reflect on it, before we take a position and act. It is that which we have inherited, which is 'there' as the material and simultaneously vital base of our existence with which we have to come to terms. This nature sustains us but at the same time it has for us an unmistakable character which challenges and beckons us." Here the biological data, including genetics, acquire a normative character. Trillhaas commits the naturalistic fallacy, as we observed in Ch. I § D, and so leaves the problem unsolved.

17. A. Rosenberg (1980: esp. 92–118).

kinds"; they do not refer to causally homogeneous categories. By this I am only saying what I said earlier: explaining behavior within a nomological interpretive model, as the biological sciences do, is something totally different from explaining conduct in terms of reasons. Add to this the fact that the two ways of viewing things cannot be linked by the concept of nature. The difference between the modern and the ancient concept of nature is that between relations in a *law*-like context and relations in a *rule*-like context. Regularity does not exclude law and vice versa, but it is not the same. Regularity still presupposes rules and hence norms satisfied by a relation between variables.[18] This implies that one can ask about their validity or desirability: do the rules serve their purpose or do they not? But with respect to the laws of nature the question of desirability is absurd. One can, however, study the (necessary and/or sufficient) conditions under which they occur. Rules can change, say, because they have proven to be redundant. Laws do not. Admittedly, however, man can in numerous cases so manipulate circumstances as to prevent or promote the occurrence of a nomological event.

Accordingly, Spaemann's remarks about the breakup of natural law are only partly right. He says the freedom of man needs to be "remembered nature," meaning that freedom has to remain conscious of the biological foundations of human existence. But the expression "biological foundations" fails to make sufficiently clear the distinction between *laws* to which he is bound and *rules* he considers desirable. Fertilization requires the conjunction of an egg cell and a sperm cell. This has to do with biological laws. Contraceptives affect fertility. That has to do with norms and human ends. But from the existence of the biological law one cannot infer that people will wish, let alone ought to wish, the event to occur.

In the following section we will, at some length, discuss the concept of nature in the context of (homo)sexuality. Here I will

18. The so-called "laws of history" are regularities (tendencies, cf. Ch. II § G). In nature, too, there are regularities that do not have a causal character, e.g., ecological succession.

make a few concluding remarks. As stated, the phrase "against nature" can only (still) apply to actions, more precisely to the goals the actor wishes to reach with his action and articulates in his reasons. Therefore the question with which this section began, viz., in what way it is meaningful to speak of "nature" in a normative sense, can be answered as follows. In the first place, where a human being acts he manifests himself "naturally," i.e., in accordance with his nature. That is hardly debatable. But, secondly, he acts unnaturally if he pursues ends he cannot reach because they are intrinsically unattainable: if he necessarily bumps up against natural laws. Thirdly, because reasons are linked, not causally, but conceptually with acts,[19] a condition is that the actor can make his actions intelligible; i.e., he can demonstrate a conceptual link between his reason and his action. That condition lies enclosed in the concept "natural" in a normative sense. Otherwise, he acts unnaturally.

In the following sections these three aspects will be further worked out in relation to homosexuality.

Finally, "natural" in a normative sense cannot be equated with "morally good." But "unnatural" *is* morally wrong, even morally perverse. Now at this point nineteenth-century physicians sought to take over from moral philosophers their concern with sexuality by replacing moral condemnation in terms of the designation "unnatural" with a causal explanation in terms of the modern concept of nature. "Unnatural" now became "sick."

C. Why homosexuality is not unnatural

In the first section of this chapter it was stated that the tolerant popular position on homosexuality ("that's how they are" and variations on this theme) must be viewed as a *moral* position rather than as merely a factual observation. It is a modern variation on the traditional theme: the assessment of sexual behavior in terms

19. See Ch. II §§ G and H.

of its being (un)natural. This, therefore, means that for many people the way the tradition framed the issue is still determinative today. Granted, the answers today diverge in opposite directions. But one can place both the traditional negative viewpoint like that of the Catholic church and the tolerant attitude of society in the western world within this one single framework. That is interesting because in the intervening centuries a fundamental change *did* occur in the western concept of nature (§ B). That, then, also explains why in the moral discussion of homosexuality — whether or not conducted explicitly — biological and other causal explanations began to play the role they still play today: namely (as Chapter I showed) as naturalistic arguments in favor of or against its moral acceptability. And — equally important — conversely: when public opinion raises objections to biological research done on homosexuality, these objections are inspired more by normative considerations than by factual criticism or by criticism of the research methods used.

In preceding chapters I repeatedly stated that no moral norm can be inferred from a biological datum ("natural" in the biological sense): no morality can be built on (biological) nature. This applies to *pro* as well as *contra* arguments; both are naturalistic (I will pass over the difficulty of precisely defining what "biologically natural" means). Meanwhile, the ethical tradition of the West did use "natural" in a normative sense. That which is natural is (by that very fact) morally acceptable or even required. And the unnatural is morally wrong, even morally perverse. Now there is an obvious tendency to argue the acceptability of homosexuality in terms of natural or unnatural on the understanding that today people want to substitute the word "natural," as a positive *moral* judgment, for the qualification "unnatural." What I will show in this section is that the application of the terms natural and unnatural in the classic sense is bound to choices that are not tenable as argument.

I will first describe the theory behind the natural/unnatural distinction (in its moral sense). In part that comes down to a repetition of what was said earlier. "Natural" in this sense is another concept than "morally good," although nature and morality are related concepts. But they are not the same. There must be another

232

demonstrable quality that is the reason why the natural is morally good and the unnatural morally wrong.[20] What is it? Answer: animate nature's natural orientation to the good. The core of the ancient concept of nature — in Aristotle, and adopted by Thomas — is the idea of finality. "Nature works toward an end and that end is nature itself." The notion that nature does not work toward an end is contrary to the logic of nature *(contra rationem naturae).* The end or goal is the form, the essence, which is good as such. Nature always marches forward, in an orderly manner, toward fixed ends. It does not do anything that is meaningless. Possible abnormalities are *peccata naturae,* sins of nature; they are "sins" because nature is directed toward the good. The things of nature are not conscious of this finality, as man is; but every thing has in it a natural principle by which it strives toward its end ("all things naturally seek the good"). Only man knows this end and strives toward it. Accordingly, this finality exists in two ways: the way of the natural principle of movement God has created in every creature or this finality as intention, as in the case of man, in whom *ratio* (reason) is created.[21] Now the right use of reason tells man that in all his actions he ought to follow his natural inclination toward the good. Thus he orders his life toward its end, says Thomas.

It is this argument (that the use of "right reason" brings us to the ordering of our lives) that (the more conservative wing of) Catholic ethics keeps repeating. "Right reason" endorses natural inclination and natural inclinations are those that are directed toward the realization of our nature, i.e., toward our natural end. With regard to sexuality the Catholic Magisterium says: "There can be no true promotion of man's dignity unless the order of his nature is respected." Homosexual acts are acts "which lack an essential and indispensable finality."[22]

20. Cf. B. M. Leiser (1979: 58ff.).
21. See A. J. Aertsen (1982: 341–49).
22. So says the Declaration of the Sacred Congregation for the Doctrine of the Faith, in *Persona Humana* (1975). Here the notion of order has since Vatican II been augmented with a more personalistic approach but was not replaced by it (Th. Beemer, 1983; cf. R. Burggraeve, 1985).

Underlying this statement is a view of man that prescribes what is essential to humanity. For man as a sexual being *reproduction* is the natural end, the ordering principle for sexuality.

We find a similar type of thought, although it is argued differently, in many Protestant authors (cf. Chapter I). Brillenburg Wurth, Douma, etc. all take as their starting point the (divinely instituted) order of the sexual life, which homosexuality is said to violate. Man has been created heterosexually, says Douma, and

> One who violates the order God has ordained for the sexual life creates chaos. . . . The homosexual uses his body in a manner for which it has not been created.[23]

For the tolerant positions on homosexuality it is also true that they are based on the notion of order. This is the reason why homosexual relations are described as "inferior" or "deficient." I mention in passing, as a recent spokesman for this view, de Knijff who describes the relation between marriage and sexuality as "entelechy," hence with the Aristotelian term for the inherent finality of sexual intercourse. On this basis he regards fertility and the will to reproduction as "an implicate of the act of coitus." Where the possibility of reproduction is absent, there is a "deficiency." It is not necessarily a moral defect — the homophile also may experience his orientation as "an opportunity for humanity," it is nevertheless a defect.

In the sexual domain, therefore, what Catholic and other authors consider the natural order is what answers to the finality of the sexual act, and that is reproduction. Reproduction is considered the ordering principle for sexuality and for that reason the intention to reproduce is the criterion for the moral quality of the act; it serves as the criterion for what is "natural" in the moral sense. And because homosexual acts do not satisfy that criterion they are (morally) unnatural.

The next question is: How valid is this argument (reproduction as criterion for what is natural)? Allow me to make a few

23. J. Douma (1987: 32–33).

preliminary comments. In the first place, societies commonly take the anatomical differences between man and woman as the starting point for the social differences between men and women, hence for their social concept of "man" and "woman." It is also common for the sexual differentiation to serve as the peg on which to hang the moral order in the domain of sexuality. See, for instance, the relations G. Rubin (II § D) establishes between the prohibition of incest, the requirement of exogamy, and the taboo on homosexuality. And indeed, without order in the sexual domain societies cannot function, if for no other reason than the need to regulate reproduction. Accordingly, every culture has moral rules — i.e., societal principles of order designed not to leave everything to personal whim — that determine the sexual order.

This is also true for western society. Add to this — second comment — that its sexual moral tradition has been strongly shaped by the motif of opposition between pleasure (lust) and reason. It is pleasure, says Augustine,[24] especially sexual pleasure, that, as it moves man with passion, "suspends all mental activity." Thomas makes more room for sexual pleasure, on condition, however, that it be subordinated to order. "Orderly" is that which agrees with reason, i.e., where man consciously follows the inner teleology of the sexual act. Thus, the contrast people stressed — in modern terms — was that between *behavior,* which proceeds from the (biologically determined) inclination or pleasure, and intentional sexual *action (conduct).*

As a result, the intention to reproduce became the condition for the moral acceptability of the sexual behavior. Always, when people engage in sexual intercourse, this intention has to be present and only thus lust is restrained.

But is this reasoning correct? As we saw, both anthropologically and from the viewpoint of the sexual history of the West, reproduction considered as ordering principle is understandable. A very different question is whether the orientation of the sex act toward reproduction is acceptable as moral *duty.* The regulation of reproduction is necessary with a view to the importance of

24. Augustine, *The City of God,* Bk. XIV, 16–18.

children and the importance to society of its survival. But from this one cannot infer the existence of an unconditional duty incumbent on everyone to procreate or bear children. Even factually it does not hold: not all people have the intention to reproduce themselves. Nor does it hold ethically: the notion that people ought to have this intention would amount to inferring an ethical norm from a biological given, which is the naturalistic fallacy. However, without committing this fallacy, one could argue such an obligation via the intermediary of a view of man in which such a norm were already built in. That is done by a view of man that states what is essential to being human (hence: to being "natural") and how that can be known. Now then: can biology, perhaps, furnish the building blocks for such a view of man?

True: biology describes and explains the characteristics and behavior of species, including the human. But the concept of species in biology applied to man differs from what is usually understood by "the view of man." Earlier, in the eighteenth and nineteenth centuries, that was different. Biology then held a typological concept of species. That humans belonged to the species called man then meant they display all the characteristics of this type. But according to modern biology, it is precisely the occurrence of variation that characterizes species. The "nature" of man can no longer be — typologically — conceived as a series of characteristics that all individuals have in common. For that reason not much can be done in biology with the notion of the "nature" of a species.[25] Nor, therefore, does biology teach anything about the "nature of man" in the sense of an order that is supposed to exist among humans. Biology is not concerned with order in this sense; but normative views of man are. Biology can only contribute to these views in the form of corrections of what in them does not correspond with observed reality. But the fact that man is an intentional being and acts on the basis of reasons does not belong to the field of biological

25. See B. Voorzanger (1987: 87ff.): "Evolutionary considerations lead to the conclusion that 'species' need not have a 'nature' if one conceives the nature of a species to be a series of properties held in common by all the members of that species."

research. Therefore, though normative views of man, as a rule, are also grounded in empirical data, one cannot construct a normative view of man with the data of biology.

Now one might object that "natural order" need not refer to a biological order but to the social order. That was already the argument advanced against Kinsey's recommendations by the sociologist H. Schelsky (1955).[26] Kinsey had pleaded, on the basis of his statistical data, for the moral acceptance of a range of socially condemned sexual variants (including homosexuality), citing frequency of occurrence. By doing this, said Schelsky, Kinsey was denying that "natural" means "socially accepted." In Schelsky's opinion there is nothing against calling a range of variants in the sexual domain biologically "natural" instead of viewing them as pathological. But one must not forget that the appeal to biology is never more than a secondary rationalization.

> The decisive aspect of a norm is the determination of a culture that these groups [— the deviants in society, including homosexuals, P. P. —] are unable to attain to the higher levels of the individual and society in this culture. (p. 70)

As a result of (what a culture considers) normal human sexuality, it becomes the foundation of societal security, which is determinative for the societal and personal self-consciousness of the individual. Thus his behavior and moral awareness are fortified and stabilized. Without that institutionalization and channeling a person is doomed to social isolation and loneliness, says Schelsky (pp. 80ff.).

> The homosexual relation is a failure to achieve a heterosexual choice of partner (p. 83), for the processing of the sex drive in the social achievement of a heterosexual partnership belongs to the socialization of the personality. (p. 76)

Schelsky's evaluative diction ("failure," "achievement") indicates where, for him, the rub lies. The order of society is at risk when the "pleasure-principle" (lust) is not restrained, and for him that

26. Cf. Ch. I § B.

means: if the sex drive is not molded in the direction of heterosexuality. Schelsky knows no order other than the heterosexual.
And though, in the situation in which he wrote, the period following World War II, his position is understandable as an expression
of concern over the breakup of traditional patterns of living in
postwar society, it by no means follows that this order can only
be one in which homosexuality is forbidden. Schelsky thinks it
does follow because he reasons that "natural" means "socially
accepted," and that means "morally acceptable." But that is no
argument; it is a mistaken assumption.

Reasoning from a normative view of man is also what we
saw Thomas doing (Chapter I). It is not that as is often asserted,
he derived a norm from biological data. What he does do is define
what is good for an individual in terms of a preconceived normative view of man. However, Thomas no more establishes that the
intention to reproduce ought to be present than Schelsky establishes an obligation to be heterosexual in one's behavior. He simply
assumes it, as the summary of natural inclinations in his treatment
of natural law shows (see I § C).

In contemporary non-progressive Catholic authors the situation is no different. I will give one example. R. Burggraeve
believes that the sexual act cannot be approached solely in terms
of an objective biological procreative finality. That would stand
in the way of integrating the act in the relationship. However,

> in the present climate of relational inflation it is not imaginary for
> people to leave behind the stable ground of biological reality. . . .
> The human relational dimension can only unfold integrally and
> soundly if it is solidly rooted in the sustaining biological substruc-
> ture. . . . A sexual encounter is not fully human unless it includes
> — at least as a positive possibility and value — procreative fruit-
> fulness.[27]

That is clear language — but again an instance of naturalistic
reasoning. What is meant is: the *right* sustaining biological sub-

27. R. Burggraeve (1985: 160–61).

structure; sexuality cannot even be imagined without a biological substructure. Hence the author is assuming a norm for which no grounds are furnished. It is simply posited.

Accordingly, Schelsky as well as Thomas construe a *contrast* between (biological) drive and (social) order or between sexual pleasure and reason. They are not alone. De Knijff, whom I mentioned a moment ago, construes a related contrast between *nature* and *spirit*. Is that right? It is certainly incorrect if he means to set "nature" against "culture." This contrast does not exist, as was demonstrated at length in the previous chapter. Further, this pair of concepts is related to the category of "behavior," not to conduct based on reasons. The contrast is tenable only if by it we mean a distinction on the level of "culture," i.e., in human action. Then we mean that not everything can be done for pleasure alone. One's impact on a necessary order is also a consideration. Pleasure must, therefore, be properly channeled. That only means: there have to be reasons other than pleasure alone. There is in addition the necessity to regulate reproduction in the interest of the care of offspring. These, however, are different issues. It does not now follow that the goal of reproduction is the only possible criterion for the sexual order — hence as a sign that sexual pleasure is subject to order. That would indeed imply that the intention to direct the sexual act toward reproduction is a moral obligation for those engaged in sexual intercourse.

Back to the main question: can such an obligation be defended? Let me simply answer this question with a series of brief comments. First, there is obviously no obligation to engage in sexual intercourse. Most people prefer sexual intercourse to being robbed of it, but that is no more than an empirical datum. One cannot derive a norm from it; abstinence from sexual intercourse is also permitted. The idea of an obligation for every individual to have sex is absurd. Second, it is simply a fact that reproduction is necessary for the preservation of the human species. Does not society then have a rightful claim on my reproductive potential? Not unless the value of a person is exhausted by his value to society, and that is not the case. This is also acknowledged by the Catholic Magisterium when, in opposing the imposition of contraceptive measures by public authorities, it states that the curtailment of the parents' freedom of choice must be regarded as a "grave offense against human dignity."[28] This constitutes an implicit admission that the rights of society are not absolute (in comparison with the obligation to follow the natural finality of the sex act). But then one cannot defend either an obligatory readiness to reproduce oneself based on societal rights. Third, we do have duties related to the future of mankind; for example, the duty to make the earth inhabitable. Those who will live after us have a right to reasonable living conditions, and we, therefore, have a duty to preserve them. But that does not include a duty to contribute to their existence via biological transmission. From the principle that a person, once he exists, has the right to a decent life one cannot infer a duty on my part to help that life come into being. Fourth, though we appreciate the conscious desire for children and regard this as a humane enterprise, such desires are empirical data and from them one can never infer an obligation. Conversely, I grant there are no conceivable obligations that do not stem from preferences, but this must be understood in the sense that duties exist to protect a person's preferences from infringement by others. Duties, therefore, arise from the fact that people want to see their preferences protected, but from a preference one cannot derive a duty.[29] So from the fact — if it is a fact — that most people are eager to have children, no duty can be derived. But this implies at the same time that no one violates his obligations if, for whatever reason, he does not desire to have children.

If there is no obligation to reproduce oneself it is senseless to be compelled to restrict the intention to engage in sexual intercourse to the intention to reproduce oneself. And with that we have come to the core of the issue. For, as we have seen, the intention to reproduce oneself is presented as an obligation with a view to guaranteeing order in the sexual domain. In the classical perspective on nature that order is defined by the natural finality of the sexual

28. *On the Family, Familiaris Consortio,* Apostolic Exhortation, Dec. 15, 1981, p. 27.
29. H. M. Kuitert (1983: 115).

240

act. That is the ultimate standard. But how do we know that natural order? People pretend it emerges from nature itself. But, as we saw earlier, it cannot be read from the biological data. Hence the norm is added from without. It never comes from biology because biology knows of no nature-teleology, only causality. Accordingly, in biology the notion of a nature-teleology is not a tenable one. But it is precisely the norm we are discussing: the obligatory finality toward reproduction of that, it's alleged, is derived from nature. In reality it stems from a normative view of man that is prior to the interpretation of the biological data. The criterion of reproduction as criterion for order, therefore, hangs in the air.

Moreover, it is too broad; it leaves out too much. Intentions, dispositions, motives, acts, etc. are the object of moral judgment, but empirical data and nomological causal relations cannot be. Fertilization is simply a biological consequence of copulation and, therefore, morally neutral. Certainly, the conscious intention to reproduce oneself is to be valued positively, but that cannot be done with the argument that this intention accords with the inner teleology of the sexual act and that agreement with this finality is morally requisite. Otherwise it automatically brings with it that every heterosexual act, apart from any intention, already gets something like a moral pat on the back. After all, as "a matter of fact," it is "oriented" to reproduction. This is how the pope views it (and many non-Catholics eagerly chime in with him): Sexuality derives its *human* dignity from reproduction (while it is, of course, precisely characteristic for sexuality in plant and *animal*).

With this criterion (the intention to reproduce oneself) one, therefore, overshoots one's goal: to distinguish order (reason) from disorder (the "lusts"). The assumption underlying the criterion is, of course, that reproduction is the only possible legitimation for an order. The decisive objection to it is that, if sexuality derives its human dignity from reproduction (the pope's position) instead of vice versa, reproduction deriving its dignity from the possibility of being a choice,[30] then sexuality is re-biologized: the intention becomes secondary and is, therefore, dehumanized instead of humanized.

30. So C. E. M. Struyker Boudier (1983: 92).

241

To sum up: the starting point of the argument discussed above that the pursuit of nature's end brings man to his destiny (a). Therefore, this pursuit also constitutes the criterion for the orderliness of the sex act (b) and the sign that the biological drives are being channeled (c). The natural end of sexuality is reproduction (d) and the intention to reproduce oneself is, therefore, a moral obligation (e). Therefore, heterosexuality is a moral obligation. The crucial step in this line of argument (d) is not valid because, as we saw, it already presupposes the norm (e). On other grounds, too, an obligation to reproduce oneself proved untenable. If a duty to reproduce oneself does not exist, everyone has the right not to reproduce himself. What are the implications of this conclusion for homosexual intercourse? In any case, a duty to be heterosexual based on a duty to reproduce oneself does not exist.

With this also the argument for heterosexuality that is based on the man-woman polarity as biological complementarity loses its cogency.[31] However, in his discussion of the question whether homosexuality is a perversion, the philosopher R. Scruton comments that man-woman complementarity does not reflect a natural order but is a careful social construction — the reason why homosexuality has always met with hostility. That, however, he says, can never be a ground for moral condemnation.

> At best the argument from complementarity shows the presence of a fault in the content of homosexual desire — an imbalance which, if left uncorrected, threatens the course of love. Homosexuality could be shown perverted only if the homosexual act were shown to be intrinsically depersonalized or intrinsically obscene.[32]

Is this last statement true? Scruton argues that the homosexual relation does not involve the same level of mystery and consequent need to risk oneself as is required in a heterosexual relationship. It lacks the strangeness of the other sex, he says.

31. So, correctly, R. Radford Ruether (1989: 24–25).
32. R. Scruton (1986: 310).

It is not possible to assume that the radical revision of gender perception required by the homosexual act will leave the act unchanged, and in particular that it will leave unchanged the perceived relation of the participants to their bodies.[33]

But this fact, as such, is insufficient ground for concluding that an obscene perception of the body is, therefore, involved, as is the case, for example, in necrophilia, according to Scruton. He offers no criterion for what he calls the mystery of a (hetero)sexual relation. Accordingly, one can properly object that the strangeness of the other plays a role in every love-relationship and contributes to the mystery of the relation.[34] If the "strangeness" of the other sex is indistinguishable from the "strangeness" of the love-partner, the argument from man-woman complementarity also fully loses its cogency (cf. Barth: "a man is only a man in relation to a woman and a woman is only a woman in relation to a man").

Nor can such a duty be based on the necessity of reproduction. Reproduction is, indeed, necessary for the preservation of the species, but from this it does not follow that everyone is morally obligated to participate in the order of reproduction. Participation in that order by everyone is not necessary for the preservation of the human species. Nor is it necessary, as we saw in Chapter II, for the personal happiness of everyone.

These arguments do not adequately address the issue of a *right* to engage in homosexual intercourse. I will come to that in the following section. After all, from the biological and sociological data one can no more deduce that right than one can establish a duty to be heterosexual. What does follow from them, in combination with the fact that one's intention to engage in sexual intercourse need not include the intention to reproduce oneself, is that the pope is wrong when he says that the homosexual disposition is "an objective disorder" (*Letter to the Bishops On the Pastoral Care of Homosexual Persons,* point 3). That opinion is based on the mistaken sickness model of homosexuality. Still we have

33. R. Scruton (1986: 311).
34. Cf. M. Ruse (1988: 270).

not sufficiently detached ourselves from the model when a right to homosexual intercourse is made dependent on a right not to reproduce oneself. That is a heterosexual bias that keeps alive the notion that heterosexuality is the paradigm of normal, healthy sexuality. Accordingly, other arguments are needed to establish a right to engage in homosexual intercourse (see the next section).

But our basic concern was to examine the content of the words "natural" and "unnatural" understood in their moral sense and their utility as moral qualifications of sexual behavior. This utility has been proven not to exist. "Naturalness" in a moral sense depends on the prior acceptance of a normative view of man in which reproduction is regarded as the purpose of sexuality. It is this view of man, not the naturalness of it, that makes the intention to reproduce oneself a moral obligation. Now, if naturalness in a moral sense is not applicable to heterosexual behavior because of reproduction, then the counter-notion of "unnaturalness" is not applicable to homosexuality because of non-reproduction. Therefore, the concepts "natural"/"unnatural" have no discriminating value and we cannot do anything with them in our ethical reflection.

Why is this? Let me further illustrate this point with a bit of theory. Many concepts in our language are so-called "open-textured" concepts of which the range of meaning is not precisely fixed. Only about a hard core is there agreement within a culture. Take, for example, a concept like "bureau," even if we limit ourselves to its (British English) meaning of "writing desk." To say that you are sitting writing at your "bureau" is to make an easily intelligible statement even if one does not know how big it is or of what material it is made. We can use such concepts without being able to give a detailed explanation of their range of application. This is precisely why statements containing them are intelligible even when we do not know precisely what the thing referred to looks like. That is, at the same time, their flexibility; time and again one can subsume new "specimens" under the same concept. Such "open-textured" concepts also exist in morality. There they are called "moral species terms" (D'Arcy) or "moral concepts" (Brennan), concepts like "murder," "theft," "lying."

Their specifically normative aspect is that in them facts are bound up with values. They are descriptive terms that simultaneously imply a moral judgment. These concepts, too, have a hard core. "Murder," for example, means "unjustified killing," "killing without good reason." All language-users subscribe to that meaning. But precisely which actions are "murder" and precisely which reasons are not good reasons for killing are matters for discussion. Thus people use the word "murder" in the same sense ("killing without good reason") but apply it in very different ways (abortion is, or is not, murder). Such an application of the word is not arbitrary but is made from within a certain selective moral viewpoint. It is these moral viewpoints on which groups and cultures differ. In the case of "murder" the selective viewpoint has to do with the value attributed to life; this is the reason why a person might call abortion murder but not the killing of seal pups. Brennan calls such a basic criterion of selection, in terms of which the same concept is supplied with a different content, the "rationale" behind the concept. He shows that the rationality of moral discussions is embedded in these rationales because concrete rules of behavior have their source here (rules are "explications" of the rationale). Typical for all "open-textured" concepts, including moral concepts, is that the explication of the rationale is a never-ending process. Consensus in moral discussions can, therefore, be reached only when there is consensus about the rationales behind the pivotal concepts used.[35]

Now at first sight the statement "*x* is morally natural" resembles a judgment of the type "*x* is murder." "Natural" is a descriptive term intended at the same time to convey a moral judgment. And since "naturalness" is the key term in the moral discussion about homosexuality (cf. § A) only agreement about the rationale behind this concept could lead to a moral consensus. We have to conclude, however, that this rationale does not exist. In a concept like "murder" a norm and a description (killing) are

35. J. M. Brennan (1977: 38ff.; 57ff.; 63ff.; 130ff.). Cf. H. M. Kuitert (1983: 25). The use of terms that simultaneously imply a value judgment, such as "murder," presupposes a certain unity in life-style.

bound together in a logical relation: murder means "unjustified killing." But "naturalness" lacks such a hard core. There is, as we saw, no logical relation between "natural" (in the context of sexuality) and the norm of reproduction, but we have a norm that precedes the interpretation of the word "natural." Now an attempt is made to establish such a relation. What happens is that a value judgment ("natural") is applied to morally neutral facts (reproduction as a biologically natural datum) and that does not hold water.[36]

D. Wants and reasons

We have seen, then, that society uses biological arguments to pronounce a — now generally positive — *moral* judgment about homosexuality (§ A). The fact that this involved a naturalistic fallacy was discussed in Chapter I. The reason for using especially biological arguments is that the moral assessment of homosexuality is expressed, in line with the tradition, in terms of the words "natural" or "unnatural." But from the analysis of the previous section we discovered that it is a pseudo-concept. "Nature" as a concept is too ambiguous and vague to derive from it criteria for the determination of moral goods. A prior choice rooted in a normative view of man determines what is natural and what is not. The idea behind the term "natural" in its application to sexuality is that the intention to reproduce oneself makes the sexual act natural and is, therefore, a moral obligation. That obligation proved implausible unless one assumed it. Therefore, from an ethical viewpoint, the appeal to "nature," has no value as argument.

But this also implies that the word "unnatural" is not useful. A person does not shirk a moral duty if he chooses not to reproduce himself. Non-participation in the order of reproduction does not make an act unnatural and, therefore, the term is not applicable — because of the intention not to reproduce oneself — to homosex-

36. Cf. J. M. Brennan (op. cit.: 31).

uality. But, conversely, every attempt to argue the acceptability of homosexuality in terms of its being "natural" will likewise come to nothing.

Still, we have not finished with the question of the naturalness of homosexuality. In classical thought the concept of nature had the double function of justification (making morally acceptable; furnishing moral warrant for) and explanation. "Nature" was the criterion for finality toward the good, but at the same time the presence of this finality explained *why* something exists, viz., as natural inclination. All this is packed into the nature-concept of antiquity: only by following the *ordo naturae,* knowable by *ratio,* does one act morally correct; but because man has a natural inclination toward the good, the doing of the good — conversely — also explains a thing as being a natural inclination. Therefore, the fact that a thing is natural (in the classic sense) explains why people do it. "Explain" here does not (just) mean: indicate the conditions under which something does or does not occur — as modern science does — but refers to the actor's reasons for action; it, therefore, concerns what we earlier called a rational explanation.

Without understanding an act one cannot judge it. Understanding is a necessary condition for evaluation. To make understandable is to explain, but that can be done in two ways, as we saw earlier: by uncovering the causes of someone's behavior and/or by someone explaining his own behavior in terms of the reasons he has for it. In the case of causes one need not be conscious of them; in the case of reasons the opposite is true. The latter is the normal explanation for a person's behavior. The fact that at times explanation entails indicating why someone's reasons do *not* explain his behavior (e.g., in the case of unconscious motives or mental illness) suggests that normally it *is* a person's reasons that explain his behavior. We explain our behavior by giving reasons for it: the idea is to make it intelligible to others. Conversely, this is something that may be asked of everyone else, too. And only when there are grounds for doubting a person's competence or capacity to act may a causal explanation *take the place of* the actor's own explanation. Therefore, to be content with a causal explanation generally means that someone's reasons are not taken seriously.[37]

Now then, in addition to regarding it as a moral question, we can also view the question "Is homosexuality natural?" as a question seeking a rational explanation for homosexual behavior, hence as the question: Do their reasons explain their behavior? After all, by "natural" the tradition not only intended a moral judgment but also the explanatory ground.[38]

The fact that the term "natural" as applied to homosexuality also refers to its explanation can be demonstrated with the example of those who use the distinction between homophile disposition and homosexual behavior. They argue somewhat as follows: the disposition or inclination as such is a (biological) given; people so inclined are not responsible for it; but *what right* to homosexual practice does this give them? In my view, this question can be variously interpreted. In the first place, as the (correct) observation that there is no straight line running from a biological explanation to a moral judgment; from a biological datum one can no more derive a right than a duty. A second explanation is the view that *only* causal or biological explanations adequately explain homosexual behavior, and this is because there are no reasons for it, let alone good ones, and therefore no rights to it. We have to reject, as we have done, the notion that there are no reasons because homosexuality is not a sickness; and, therefore, we may not deny to homosexual intercourse the status of acts.

Another matter is — and that in the third place — whether we understand the behavior on the basis of reasons we know or were given. Accordingly, the question "By what right?" can be taken as a request for further explanation: "Why is what you want a reason for acting at all?" It is, after all, very common for a person

37. Rational explanation of actions does not, of course, exclude causal explanation (cf. behavior), Ch. II.

38. M. Ruse also tends to go in this direction (1988: 199ff.). He says the unnaturalness of an act lies precisely in the fact that we do not understand it: not in a causal sense but in the sense that we do not "feel an empathy with a fellow human being."

to explain his actions in terms of rights and duties. In that case the right or the duty constitutes the explanation for his action. In that way reasons stated in terms of obligation or right are reasons for action: one cannot very well subscribe to an obligation and, at the same time, not have a certain disposition to fulfill it. Therefore, the inquiry concerning a "right" can also be construed as one asking for a further explanation, one that precedes evaluation. Then the question is *when* can a person's reason (the reason he presents) count as a reason for action (a reason everyone could possibly have) and hence his act as a form of rational action. Therefore, when can a person claim to have explained his behavior as intelligible action on the basis of his reasons? That is the first question.

As stated earlier, without understanding an act we cannot judge it. That statement is not reversible, as though behavior could not be intelligible without being morally approved. The grounds for the intelligibility of behavior differ from the grounds for its moral correctness. Intelligible action is rational action. Not every rational act is morally responsible; a morally responsible act *is* rational. We must, therefore, distinguish understanding from judging (even though in practice reasons are very often simultaneously intended to explain and to justify an act). However, in the approach to human behavior in terms of the nature-concept of antiquity that we discussed, there is a close connection between the two. For an act that is directed toward a good is "natural," and this finality toward the good is the criterion for its naturalness. That would imply that moral acceptance is a condition for the intelligibility of an act; i.e., that actions have been made intelligible only when a person's reasons are good moral reasons. Behind this, as stated earlier, lay the theory that only action that is directed toward the good is in accord with reason; otherwise it is a matter of lustful desire. Now earlier I stated that an appeal to duties and rights can very well function as a sufficient explanation of a person's behavior; duties and rights constitute reasons for action. But whether that is *necessary* in order for a person to have an intelligible reason for action, hence to *explain* the behavior, is a very different matter. That is the second question.

The simplest answer to the second question is: reasons for

action are psychological motives that guide one's behavior or wants one wishes to satisfy. But when are these rational? Not everything can be done to satisfy sexual desire. Reason must guide it; it is simply the case that society demands the restraint of the natural desires. This is the basis of natural law. But this does not mean that only actions rooted in a sense of duty are in accord with reason. The opposite of action motivated by sexual desire is not action arising from a sense of duty. Now it is not so simple to picture precisely what it is to act from sexual desire. In any case, Augustine's idea of the sexual as lust, i.e., as a drive that suspends the activity of reason, is mistaken. People can, if necessary, defer the gratification of sexual "need" throughout their whole life, and sexual behavior like any other behavior is subject to the control of reasons.[39]

An intention (reason) has reference solely to a want.[40] Accordingly, one can say that if someone intentionally performs an act, he wants to perform it.[41] The want then explains the act, hence constitutes the reason for action.

G. E. M. Anscombe has given us an extensive analysis of the notion of "intention." She makes a distinction between "desire" and "want." The difference, briefly, lies in the element of rationality and choice. According to Anscombe, the two fundamental characteristics of wanting are "trying to get" and "knowledge." One can speak of wanting only if the speaker makes an effort to get the thing wanted and has knowledge that the thing wanted exists and is available. Hence that is different from having a wish or expressing a hope. Wanting something also distinguishes itself, says Anscombe, from acting out of desire. The latter is what Aristotle called *epithumia* (desire). Wanting always has an aspect of *calculation*.[42] On the level of practical reasoning the issue is intentions and they decide, according to Anscombe, whether we

39. D. A. J. Richards (1980: 49).
40. See the analysis of "want" in G. E. M. Anscombe (1976).
41. R. Norman (1971: 19).
42. "Calculation with a view to an end," G. E. M. Anscombe (op. cit.: 65; 81).

are dealing with desires or with wants that are the ultimate reasons for acting.[43] Hence reasons (intentions) are the decisive criterion. How?

They have to lead to what Anscombe calls a "desirability characterization" of the want in order thus to explain it. Not everything can reasonably be wanted even though there are no logical boundaries to what humans can want; hence we need a more precise characterization of the want.

When are we dealing with such a characterization? As stated, the use of "wanting," according to Anscombe, is bound to rules. Simply saying "I just want it" without any further characterization is to rob the word of its meaning (p. 71). When someone says, "I want . . . ," according to Anscombe, he invites the question "What for?" The answer can, again, give rise to the same question, etc., until a point has been reached where there is no room anymore for a further "What for?" Descriptions that have the effect of bringing a chain of questions to a stop Anscombe calls "desirability characterizations." As examples she mentions the expressions "it gives pleasure," "it is pleasant," "it suits me," "I like it," etc.

With this presentation by Anscombe, our first question has, at least provisionally, been answered. In her opinion, "wants" are "the reasons for action." But to make clear the object of wanting something one has to furnish a "desirability characterization." The ability to provide one decides whether or not we are dealing with a rational want. Hence the desirability characterization is needed to make clear the relation between a want and an action. *That* the relation exists is Anscombe's premise, one she derives from Aristotle: the *archê* (starting point) is *to orekton* (the thing wanted).[44] Desirability characterizations are needed to make the thing wanted intelligible as object of wanting and that occurs by presenting it as *desirable*. But the fact that the thing is wanted is the reason for action. Accordingly, we can say that desirability characterizations clarify mental states (choices, attitudes, or dispositions), and when they do that, they are logically good reasons for a person's choice.

43. G. E. M. Anscombe (op. cit.: 65–70).
44. G. E. M. Anscombe (op. cit.: 63).

Now — to return to our subject — the question is whether homosexuality is to be regarded as a *want* that deserves a desirability characterization or must be viewed merely as *desire*. The latter is what the tradition and also many tolerant ethicists have always asserted. Basic to this position is the question we criticized earlier: Is it reason — something that can be ordered; or sexual desire — a biological drive?[45] But just as in Anscombe, so here also, the assumption is that wants constitute the ultimate reason for action and that desirability characterizations are needed to make the *want* intelligible. The premise is, therefore, that reasons proceed from wants *as mental states* in the individual. They constitute the Archimedean point of the argument. It is they that give to facts the status of reasons.[46] Wants, therefore, have logical priority over reasons. Whether that is correct, hence whether wants are the ultimate reasons for action, we will consider in what follows.

At first sight it is not hard to say yes to the question of whether homosexuality is to be viewed as a want. It satisfies Anscombe's definition of a want; and in answer to the question "What do you want it for?" homosexuals advance precisely the same reasons as heterosexuals, e.g., for pleasure, relaxation, or security.

In my opinion, this is an adequate answer, but this will be clear only at the end of this section. Because someone may object: "Your reasons are reasons for an unusual want; what suits you is not what would suit most people; your want is, therefore, an unusual one, and if desirability is to be attributed to it, that applies only to you and the members of your group but not to society as a whole." This argument, therefore, comes down to saying: no desirability characterization can be given for homosexuality because only the yearnings that all people have in common can count as wants. Hence a desirability characterization here comes down to a description of a preference such that it is clear that the want is a specimen of what all people want. And that has been done only if the thing wanted has been shown to be desirable for all, for that which is desirable is that

45. See, e.g., the positions of Thielicke and Trillhaas in Ch. I.
46. R. Norman (op. cit.: 5–6).

which is desired by all, which is what is *natural,* according to this argument. This means that even when homosexuals have the same reasons as heterosexuals, there nevertheless remains room for the question: "But why is this reason a reason for *homo*sexual intercourse?" The want is, therefore, not understood as rational but as one that is only intelligible for *themselves,* because this want is not everybody's want. That is the reason why it still has to be explained, and why, for this purpose, the causal explanations of biology and psychology are pressed into service.

Is this argument not absurd? Surely not all people want the same thing? One likes peas, another beans. No — but the two can equally well be characterized as "appetizing food." This desirability characterization is adequate; the question "Why do you want appetizing food?" is pointless. And society finds the difference in preference for peas or beans of too little importance to ask for a further reason: "You want appetizing food but why is that a reason for eating beans?" That could be the case if in society, say, eating a certain food were linked with special situations. With respect to eating meat such a question would already sound less absurd. So which wants or preferences are accepted as reasons for action, and which are not, obviously has in part to do with a *judgment* of society.

But now we face a difficulty because "appetizing" means good-tasting. "Appetizing" as accepted desirability characterization, therefore, means that the thing wanted or desired — beans — are presented as being desirable, namely, for eating. A desirability characterization presents the thing wanted as *desirable.* "Desirable" means "worthy of being desired," not "is" or "can be" desired. The fact that something is wanted or desired can never support the inference that it is desirable. The reverse, however, does hold true: to call something desirable does have the logical implication that someone has at least a disposition to want it. To furnish a desirability characterization for homosexuality, therefore, also implies presenting this preference as desirable. Now suppose someone offers as his reason for homosexual intercourse the statement: "It relaxes me" (I will stick with this example in this section). But does this serve to present homosexuality as being desirable?

Has a desirability characterization been furnished by it? After all, one can say that such a person is saying words without meaning: he is giving the word "relaxation" a meaning that differs from what most people in society would give it.

We find one answer in the position of R. M. Hare. Concepts like "appetizing" and "relaxing" are divisible into two elements, a descriptive and a prescriptive one. Hare works this out with the example of pain.[47] "Painful" as a descriptive term refers to the presence of certain physical sensations. But "painful" usually means: such sensations (pain [1]) plus the experience of "unpleasantness," "dislike," etc. (pain [2]). Then a negative value judgment enters the picture. According to Hare there is no logical connection between what is painful in sense [1] and what is painful in sense [2]. Between the two lies someone's choice, decision. This *turns* the first into the second, viz., because someone subscribes to the principle that pain [1] experiences are painful [2]. Granted that most people call painful [2] what is painful [1]. But a question of contingent fact must not be confused with a *logical* connection between [1] and [2]; it does not exist.[48] No logical objection can be raised against someone ascribing positive value to pain [1] experiences.

From this perspective one can understand that Hare finds Anscombe's "desirability characterization" notion ambiguous. It allows for two interpretations, each of which is, as such, valid but which must not be confused with each other. It can take the form of (1) giving a description of the *aspect* that makes a thing an object of a want, say, a certain flavor x and of (2) using a *word* that is logically linked with wants, say, "it tastes good" or "it is pleasant." Between (1) and (2) there is no logical connection. Version (1) expresses the fact that when we prefer a thing or regard it as good, we always do it because of some aspect of the object. But (1) does not say anything about what can and what cannot be the object of a desirability characterization. A generally appre-

47. R. M. Hare (1972b: 76ff.).
48. Hence "the relation between choice and reasons for choice is not a logical relation," R. M. Hare (1972: 74).

ciated taste can, for a given person, mean an *un*desirability characterization; that depends on that person's choice.[49] It may perhaps be hard to imagine that someone should choose (want, prefer) the characteristics that for most people are precisely the reason why they disapprove of a thing, but logically there can be no objection to them.

Nor is there a logical objection against finding something relaxing — e.g., homosexual intercourse — that other people cannot associate with relaxation. Not everyone can appreciate the triathlon or lazing away a day on the beach as relaxation. It is a person's decision to value as relaxing the sensations produced by a given activity. By this decision desirability is assigned to the sensation and so it gains the status of a reason for action (for what is desirable is a reason for acting). Accordingly, I choose what is relaxing or recreational *for me*. And this, of course, is what homosexuals consistently advance: homosexuality is a choice. On Hare's position, one cannot say a word against it: there is no logical relation between what a person prefers (i.e., homosexuality) and what relaxes him. Logic tells us, says Hare, that when a person says he wants something there are certain *words* (namely, those that convey undesirability) he must not use; but it does not tell us what *things* he can, or cannot, want.[50]

---

49. R. M. Hare (1972: 73): "In short, our disposition to call only a certain range of things good (and to choose and desire them) can be explained . . . without bringing in logic; and therefore the explanation contributes nothing to logic either and, specifically, tells us nothing about the meanings of uses of the evaluative words, except that they have certain common descriptive meanings."

50. The concept of "wanting" is, therefore, connected with the idea of the good. In this connection Anscombe raises the question whether, given the necessity of a desirability characterization to explain an action, finally only characterizations that point to the morally good — that which is desirable to all — succeed in this. It is a question whether a desirability characterization ultimately has to be an ethical characterization. She denies this, as does Hare (1972: 67), because: "*Bonum est multiplex*: good is multiform, and all that is required for our concept of wanting is that a man should see what he wants under the aspect of some good."

Let me add a comment here. Does not the use of the word "desirable"

What have we now gained? A great deal, because with this we have come to the core of the issue. If there is no logical relation between the statements "I prefer x" and "because x has property p," anymore than between "I find x desirable as relaxation" and "x has property p," then the desirability of something to somebody does not depend on whether the thing desired is, or is not, desired by all humans. And because the latter was precisely the criterion for the "naturalness" of a want, the non-utility of the term "natural" again, as in the preceding section, becomes evident. A logical relation between what all people desire and what is desirable does not exist.[51]

Therefore, if we follow Hare's position, by means of the word "relaxing" or similar expressions, a person certainly furnishes a desirability characterization for his homosexual preference. Another matter is whether society agrees with it. In the final analysis, what homosexuals find relaxing differs from what most people find relaxing. All Hare demonstrates is that a person does not act in violation of logic, hence is *not irrational,* when he does it. But is that not too limited a criterion for rationality? In other words, does this really answer the objection that the reasons of homosexuals are only *their* reasons for their wants, i.e., *intelligible* to them but not to society? I think not. The fact that also on the basis of Hare's position there is still room for the same objection is no wonder: both Hare and the advocates of natural law ground desirability in wants as their final reasons for action. Wants have

---

or "good" imply the notion of "good for anyone"? Yes, but "good for anyone" is not always the same as "good for everyone." The negation makes that plain: "not good for everyone" = good for some; "not good for anyone" = good for nobody = bad. Cf. A. Quinton (op. cit.: 67). Similarly: if in situation y I pursue doing x or consider x desirable because of property p, then p is my reason for x. "Reason" implies that p is a reason for everyone to pursue x in situation y. But it is possible that p is not a reason for someone else to do x. That only means that p is not a reason for everyone (but only for some) but not that p is not a reason for anybody (is not a reason).

51. Nor in relation to so-called "fundamental human needs." The word "need" is logically connected with desirability but not with things that are desired as such. See R. M. Hare (1972: 72).

logical priority over reasons; the difference is only that in natural law this priority is due to wants all humans have in common whereas in Hare it is due to individual choice. At precisely this point R. Norman enters his criticism.

He thinks that the idea of wants as the ultimate reasons for action has no more than a certain plausibility in its favor. It is plausible because a person can cite as a reason for his doing *x:* "It is right to do *x*," and that is unquestionably a reason for action; the aim of a desirability characterization has been reached. However, there *is* room for the question of how he knows that *x* is right. And then in fact no other answer can ultimately be given than "Because I want *x*." The reason is that "I want" simultaneously implies a description and an evaluation ("he wants," on the other hand, is purely a description). That, accordingly, is also the reason wants are regarded as a person's ultimate reasons for action.[52] Norman, however, takes issue with this viewpoint. He agrees with Anscombe that the statement "I just want *x*" as it stands is not always intelligible or rational and that what Anscombe calls a desirability characterization is then needed. But in his opinion the function of reasons is a very different one than she — and Hare — thinks: to show what you want it for, in order thus to make clear that the concept of "want" rather than "desire" is appropriate. Over against this Norman states that it is the function of reasons — like "It relaxes me" — to make wants intelligible. In support of this viewpoint he refers to the parallelism between language and wants. Just as there is no private language that is not based on public language, as Wittgenstein has demonstrated, so there are no private wants. The members of a society share a common public language and in the use of words people always refer to suprapersonal, public standards of meaning. Therefore, one cannot maintain that a want is intelligible to "them" and not to "us" when it is described in public language. In speaking of a private reason Norman does not mean a personal want. Of course, people have and pursue their own interests. But these, too, can be described in terms of public reasons and that precisely is the ground for their

52. R. Norman (1970: 23–24).

acceptability as private interest.[53] Private reasons in the sense of reasons intelligible only to me are no reasons. It is impossible for a language-using being to withdraw from the meanings of public language and the criteria for correct usage embodied in it. Hence he writes:

> We can now begin to see why the theory of 'wants as reasons' breaks down. . . . Not all wants are intrinsically rational or intelligible. Those which are not can be made intelligible only if the thing wanted can be further described by means of some desirability characterization. In other words, some further *reason* has to be given. Wants have to be backed up by reasons. Therefore, not just any assertion of the form 'I just want x' can provide an ultimate reason-for-action. If it does so, this will be because the description 'x' characterizes the thing wanted in such a way that no further reason is necessary. And in that case, it is the fact that the thing is describable as 'x,' not the fact that the thing is wanted, that constitutes the reason-for-acting. The notion of 'wanting' can be allowed to fall out altogether.[54]

This is so because reasons have logical priority over wants instead of vice versa, as Hare and Anscombe assert (and is also, I may add, assumed in natural law). Therefore, to be intelligible, a want has to be described in terms of a public reason; that applies also to personal wants (e.g., sexual preferences). Accordingly, wants are public reasons for an action.

But what counts as a public reason? Not every description can serve as such, thinks Norman, and indeed what is then needed is something like what Anscombe calls a desirability characterization. But that term suggests a connection between desire and act, precisely something Norman opposes. In this he is not deny-

---

53. For example, a person may oppose the construction of an expressway for environmental reasons (a social concern) but also because his own living comfort and quiet would be affected (a personal interest). "Quiet" and "comfort," however, though personal, are nevertheless public reasons. "Private" reasons need to be distinguished from "personal" reasons. (Cf. also Ch. I § B-4).

54. R. Norman (op. cit.: 63).

ing that wants have a psychological basis but that this is the reason why a want is intelligible. Reasons, i.e., public reasons, are not intelligible because they refer to wants that most people have. In that case reasons would indeed be ultimately rooted in basic wants or needs. Then public reasons are as such basic want statements and as desirability characterization they make a connection between want and act. Norman states, however, that, on the contrary, reasons logically precede wants. By this he means that reasons do not refer to what all people want but to the normative and evaluative *concepts* of public language. Such a concept — Norman cites as examples the words "just," "peace and quiet," "spontaneous" — is not only a word in a normative vocabulary but also encapsules how people *act* in relation to the concept. And because people do not always (want to) act justly, a reference to such concepts does not imply a simple identification with what most people want.[55] Reference to this type of concept furnishes the public reasons for rational action; the norms encapsulated in them are the criteria for its intelligibility. These concepts precede wants not only logically but also chronologically. And that is because we *learn* the intelligible use of the word "wanting." A growing child learns to use it and does so in inseparable connection with rational action. When, for example, we attribute wanting to a baby — say, to be held close — that is because it displays behavior that bears superficial resemblance to what, on a later rational level, is called "wanting." True, Hare may be correct in saying that from a *logical* point of view the choice or decision has priority, but what counts as a want, even on the biological level, depends on the rational norms operative in a culture.[56] The relation between a want and an act is, therefore, a cultural fact rather than a reason being a psychic motive for an

55. R. Norman (op. cit.: 66).

56. R. Norman (op. cit.: 76–77) says: "That what counts as a want, even at the biological level, is determined by the system of rational norms within a culture, and that one is able to ascribe wants to a baby at all is only because one can see its actions as potentially those of a rational agent. Our paradigm of wanting is not wanting at the biological level of stimulus and response, but wanting at the level of rational reflection and assessment."

259

act.[57] Therefore — to put it that way — wanting is always a "social construct" (cf. II-6).

Now back to "relaxing" (as a reason for homosexual intercourse) as a way of summarizing what we have found. In natural law the criterion for the distinction between a "desire" (indulging a craving) and a want is the moral desirability of a thing. Therefore, a preference has only been presented as a want and made intelligible when the moral desirability has been established (and then the preference is called "natural"). For that reason it is necessary to show that the thing wanted corresponds with a right or a duty. In other words, a desirability characterization has to be an ethical characterization. That is incorrect because it assumes a logical connection between the thing wanted and its desirability. That, as Hare demonstrated, is impossible. There is something in between the two, namely, "choice." Granted, most people choose the same things for the same reasons. That is a contingent fact but not a logical relation. But, says Norman, reasons (which explain) are similarly reasons for wanting.[58] The reason why a person wants something is explained by his psychic state. This explains why one person prefers a different form of relaxation for another. But the fact that the relaxation is *wanted* makes it a reason for action and not the fact that it is *relaxation* that someone wants. This idea, says Norman, is incorrect. Hare thinks this because he believes he can split up concepts like "relaxation" into a descriptive and a prescriptive component. This, however, is only an imaginary possibility because our language has no separate words for the two components.[59] The correct use of language is not based on a preceding decision and, therefore, wants do not precede reasons. Therefore, it is not, as is the case

57. R. Norman (op. cit.: 76).

58. And that is the case for Hare as well as in natural law. In Hare, however, they are individual wants and in natural law they are wants shared by all people.

59. Cf. how Hare believes he can do this with respect to "a good father" by distinguishing between a prescriptive element "good" and a descriptive element (for which he coins the word) "doog." For criticism, see J. M. Brennan (op. cit.: 51).

in natural law and in Hare, the being thus constituted — hence the knowledge of *causes* — that is the ultimate explanation of a want. According to Norman, it is the reasons a person advances that determine whether an act is rational (intelligible) or not. And to describe an act as "relaxing" is undoubtedly to refer to the kind of evaluative concept Norman has in mind, which furnish reasons for action.

But what if society insists: What relaxes you is not what we understand by relaxation and so you have not really made your want intelligible? Well, society may say this, but grounds for it are lacking. Certainly, one man's relaxation is not that of another and no one is logically obligated to appreciate as relaxation for himself what someone else describes as relaxation for himself. But when someone explains *his own* behavior in terms of being "relaxing" and in so doing describes his choice in public terms, others, though they can indeed insist that the behavior is not something they can *appreciate* as relaxing, cannot maintain that it is not for that reason relaxing, at least not insofar as that person shows the signs society considers the signs of relaxation. But *that* is an empirical matter, and in the case of homosexuality that is no longer an issue. So one can make a distinction between "what relaxes them" and "what relaxes us" — which convey the difference in appreciation — but not between "what they call relaxation" and "what is relaxation to us," nor, therefore, between what is "intelligible to them" and what is "intelligible to us." And just as with other wants, so here, too, the learning process plays an important role. It does this for the individual homosexual (the "coming out" process) and for society as a whole. In principle I see no difference between this and the "coming out" of new sports or new technologies or of other religions as openings for new developments in an open society.

And with that we have reached a conclusion. By saying, "It relaxes me," a homosexual offers an intelligible — because public — reason. And that he can give this reason is based on the obvious given that people are so constituted that also homosexual intercourse can relax them. Therefore, not the (existing or non-existing biological or psychological) constitution as such (homosexual desire) explains the act and constitutes the reason for it — as would be the case in Hare and in natural law — but the fact that the want can be described in public terms.

What I have done here for the stated reason of "relaxation" can be done in the same way for other reasons advanced by homosexuals. These are, as I said earlier, the same reasons heterosexuals advance. These reasons explain homosexual behavior in the same way they explain heterosexual behavior. Apart from these reasons it is superfluous to appeal to a (possible) biological given for purposes of explanation; it is also a sign that someone's reasons are not being taken seriously.

With what has just been said, we have not yet entered the field of moral assessment. Understanding is necessary before one can assess a thing morally, as I said. One can, of course, refuse to make his act intelligible and fasten on strictly individual meanings. Then he leaves himself open to the condemnation of society. But because homosexual behavior — at least certain forms of it — can be made intelligible, the implication is that the reasons that are considered (morally) good reasons for heterosexual intercourse are also good reasons for homosexual behavior. Homosexuals not only describe their sexual behavior in the same terms as heterosexuals; they *have* the same reasons, both good and bad ones. Homosexuality is, in the same way, susceptible and subject to good and evil as heterosexuality. The accent here lies on "in the same way." From this it follows that the sex of the partner is morally irrelevant and, therefore, that sexual acts must be assessed by some reference point other than the sex of the partner. That itself is a moral judgment. It means that, from a moral viewpoint, the sex of the partner is not (no longer) a relevant datum. No longer. But that conclusion has nothing to do with the fact that today we know more about the causes of homosexuality than in the past. It is separate from the question whether homosexuality is a biological datum (explained by biological factors) or can be better described as a choice (in the way constructivist sociologists do). Of course, biological data are morally neutral: with them we do not enter upon the domain of morality. Not that, however, is the reason why, from a moral viewpoint, the sex of the partner is unimportant, but the fact that homosexuality clearly carries with it the same potentialities for humanity or inhumanity as heterosexuality. And for no other reason than that the sex of the partner is morally irrelevant.

In the previous section we concluded that one does not shirk a moral obligation if he does not want to reproduce himself. This means that one has the right not to participate in the order of reproduction. Right in the sense of a freedom right.[60] But a freedom right not to reproduce oneself does not as such imply a right to homosexual intercourse. That right, we can now say, does exist. It follows from the right not to reproduce oneself in combination with the datum that the sex of the partner is morally irrelevant.

A right can be used or misused. In that way morality once more enters in. Who decides? Here I would merely say that in the first place this is a matter for the person(s) involved. Undoubtedly, for a good morality they can get help from tried-and-tested morality, but this morality was tried and tested within an exclusively heterosexual society. Not everything that is needed for a good heterosexual morality is needed in homosexual contexts. What is needed in these contexts falls outside the scope of this book.[61]

60. In distinction from so-called claim rights. To have freedom to do x means: there is no duty to do x nor a duty to refrain from doing x. A claim right means that a person has a right to x (say, respect) because others have a duty to show x. See R. Veldhuis (1985).

61. This will not be simple because the social and historical processes that have made possible the now existing, strongly divergent homosexual identities are also the reason why homosexuals lack a common language and hence a basis for working out an ethics, according to J. Weeks (1989: 208–12).

Chapter IV

Homosexuality and the Will of God

A. Introduction: framing the question

In discussions among Christians, particularly Christians in the Reformed and Presbyterian tradition, the appeal to Scripture traditionally and self-evidently plays a large role. With regard to homosexuality this appeal is always to the same textual data. The majority of exegetes come to the same conclusion: these texts unanimously reject homosexual behavior. In light of this, is it possible for Christians to arrive at a positive assessment of homosexual relations? That is the main question addressed in this chapter.

Now the results of exegesis alone clearly do not settle the issue for anyone — witness the steady stream of publications that have appeared on the subject since the fifties. This ought not to surprise us because exegesis, as such, furnishes no answer to the question of what weight has to be attributed to the textual data involved. That answer comes from another source. An interpretive framework is needed. The question is now in how far that perspective is a factor in shaping the results of the exegesis. This is for us a reason for beginning with the well-known biblical texts. One can conceive of two possibilities (which are not mutually exclusive): first, that theological presuppositions (which I will later describe as models of revelation) determine the outcome of the exegetical process; and second, that a position on homosexuality determines a person's attitude in exegesis, hence that a person's position on the role of Scripture depends in turn on his prior position on homosexuality, so that a specific viewpoint is carried into the exegetical process.

At this point I will not yet make a choice for either one. First, analysis has to furnish clarity. Let me begin by making a comment. On the one hand, a reconstruction of the theological presuppositions would seem most desirable. For mainline Protestant churches in Europe and North America, after all, the difficulty of arriving at a unanimous decision has in recent years been demonstrated with ever increasing clarity. In that respect recent publications show a marked difference from those of the sixties and seventies, which, at least, arrived at a position pro or con. Thus, after thorough exegesis, the GKN report "Homophilia" (1982) came out with an articulation of four conflicting positions, euphemistically described as "nuances." After less careful exegesis the parallel NHK report "Confusion and Recognition" (1984) arrived at seven strongly divergent positions and defended this result as encouragement to further dialogue within the church. Such a dialogue is, in fact, conducted within the pages of the report. It remains stuck, however, in a juxtaposition of a motley variety of viewpoints — some of them heartrending — without choosing a position. British and North American reports, as we saw in Chapter I, mirror a similar diversity. This unsatisfactory result raises doubt about whether the road taken is really traversable: in the GKN report it is called "the use of the Scriptural data"; in the NHK report it is described as "listening to the texts — in dialogue with each other."

On the other hand, a reconstruction of theological presuppositions is virtually unfeasible. After all, they relate potentially to the entire field of (systematic) theology. The focus, then, easily shifts from a theological discussion of homosexuality to homosexuality as an occasion for theological discussion. In some cases one's position on homosexuality even becomes the criterion for judging the quality of his theology.[1] The discussion has, therefore, dead-ended over differences in theological position. But agreement on this level is not easily attained. Hence the standoff.

The following reflection, as will become apparent in § D, may help us to move forward. Christians appeal to Scripture because they think that, for a resolution of moral issues, they are so obligated. They also believe it leads to resolution. But what, really, do they do when they appeal to the Bible as document of revelation? That question is not one of a materially theological kind but one of a scientific-theoretical nature, a preliminary question that can be put to the discipline of Christian ethics. We will find that the answer to it will enable us to answer in the affirmative the question whether it is possible for Christians to approve of homosexuality, without necessarily having to dwell at length on the material content of theological issues.

In brief: there are good reasons for starting with a discussion of the textual biblical data on homosexuality. We will do this in § B. Then we will examine how theological arguments function in the moral discussion of homosexuality. That will offer us ground for doubting the sense of an appeal to the scriptural data in the context of a moral discussion (§ C). In § D I will, therefore, explore the theoretical backgrounds of the appeal to revelation with a view to finding out whether some way other than the direct appeal to Scripture cannot be considered more suitable also for Christians.

B. Bible texts: their exegesis and interpretation

The texts mainly at issue are these:

(a) Genesis 19:1–11 with Judges 19 as parallel;

---

1. The ultimate consequence being a split in the Reformed Ecumenical Synod (now Reformed Ecumenical Council) in June 1988 (see Ch. I § E.4) because of the liberal position of the *Gereformeerde Kerken in Nederland* (GKN).

(b) Leviticus 18:22 and 20:13;
(c) 1 Corinthians 6:9 and 10;
(d) 1 Timothy 1:8–10;
(e) Romans 1:26 and 27.

I will restrict myself to the points that prompt the (more or less professional) exegetes[2] to engage in discussion.

(a) The sin of Sodom, Genesis 19:1–11. The Christian tradition has always used this passage as prooftext against homosexual acts. This goes back to Philo and Flavius Josephus — Hellenistic Judaism, therefore — and can be found already in Clement and Tertullian. Still, it was never said that the sin of Sodom amounted to just this transgression. Reference is consistently made to the violation of the rights of hospitality.

In addressing the question whether the Sodom-story in fact (also) relates to same-sex acts, the discussion has focused on the meaning of *yādha* (vs. 5), "becoming acquainted" or "knowing" in a sexual sense. In the parallel text (Judg. 19), the outrage at Gibeah involving heterosexual rape, verse 22, produces the same problem. Tradition unanimously offers the sexual interpretation. Bailey (1955) is the first to present the interpretation of "becoming acquainted" as meaning "to make an inquiry into someone's credentials." Most exegetes have not followed him in this interpretation, using as their main argument that the same word in Genesis 19:8 and Judges 19:25 is clearly intended in a sexual sense. Zuurmond reads *yādha* as specifically expressing the aspect of violence, the element of sexual rape including, in his opinion, homosexual rape.

2. My Dutch sources: J. Bonda (1981), J. Douma (1973/84), the GKN report on "Homophilia" (1982), J. van Hooydonk (1981), C. J. Labuschagne (1970), S. W. R. Polman (1972), H. N. Ridderbos (1959), S. J. Ridderbos (1959, 1961), J. van Veen (1977), J. Vlaardingerbroek (1972), R. Zuurmond (1984). My non-Dutch sources: D. S. Bailey (1955), J. Becker (1987), J. Boswell (1980), P. Coleman (1980, 1989), R. B. Hayes (1986), H. D. Lance (1989), G. Ménard (1982), R. Scroggs (1983), A. M. J. H. van de Spijker (1968), K. Wengst (1987), H. G. Wiedemann (1983b). Further, the most important commentaries.

A few exegetes think that the Sodom-story exclusively has in view the violation of the law of hospitality (Labuschagne). For where Sodom is mentioned elsewhere in Scripture[3] there is never any connection with sexual sins. Some scholars, therefore, believe that two Sodom-traditions existed, a sexual and a non-sexual interpretation (Von Rad). That argument has little weight. Hellenistic Jews stressed one thing (homosexuality) and Palestinian Jews another (hospitality rights) (Becker). Sodom everywhere stands for a place of lawlessness and injustice, and sexual license is a part of this. The people of Sodom were as "hungry as hyenas for a piece of meat" (S. J. Ridderbos). Some exegetes arrive at a less pronounced conclusion. Coleman (1980), for example, believes that, in any case, one cannot derive any form of approval of homosexual behavior from the story. Zuurmond states that the threats of the Sodomites can, at most, have raised the suspicion they had homosexual rape in mind but the *desire* for it was simply part of a total actual assault on life (is the component of violence really that prominent? P. P.).[4] Vlaardingerbroek presents the most nuanced view: the sin of Sodom is not homosexual intercourse as such, nor only rape and the violation of the law of hospitality; the city simply displayed a homosexual aspect that possibly further accentuated its overall degradation.

If we accept this, the question remains in how far these texts, which bear on same-sex acts, apply also to every behavior that is covered by the modern term "homosexuality." Some writers deny this (van Veen): in Sodom we are dealing with homosexual acts committed by otherwise heterosexual men (cf. Gen. 19:4: "all the people to the last man," *NRSV*). This consideration is only relevant, however, if one assumes the existence of a specific "disposition," as van Veen does. But the text does not permit us to make a distinction between different forms of homosexual conduct (Vlaardingerbroek). If, however, "homosexual" is simply used as

3. Cf. Isaiah 1; Jeremiah 23; Lamentations 4:6; Ezekiel 16:46; Matthew 10:15; 11:23; Luke 10:12; 17:29.

4. Lot's daughters would undoubtedly have suffered a similar fate but the story makes no mention of it.

the modern word for something that has been known from ancient times, there is no objection to using it in connection with Sodom.

(b) The Leviticus texts as part of the Holiness Code condemn sexual relations ("as with a woman") between men as an abomination and prescribe the death penalty for it (Lev. 20:13). The Hebrew word *(toëbah)* can apply to cultic as well as to non-cultic acts. In the Holiness Code it is further used only in the summary of Leviticus 18:26–30. According to all exegetes, what is condemned is homosexual anal coitus.

The discussion relates to whether these texts require a cultic (ceremonial) or an ethical interpretation. The idea in the background is that cultic prohibitions are no longer binding on us while ethical prohibitions are. That equation is too simple (Vlaardingerbroek). According to some scholars (Labuschagne, Menard), the texts are aimed against the homosexual temple prostitution that was prevalent in the Ancient East. The issue at stake, then, is the antithesis between Israel and paganism. Many authors question this interpretation. In Israel *cult* and *ethos* cannot be thus separated. Numerous ethical commands also have a cultic aspect (S. J. Ridderbos; Wiedemann) and most other regulations in Leviticus 18 have no cultic background but concern marriage, chastity, and incest (Vlaardingerbroek). (In Leviticus 20 these matters are construed somewhat differently, see vss. 6, 25–27.) Leviticus offers no rationale. One can think in this connection of a common "homophobic" reaction (Coleman, who also advances the following arguments), preventive opposition to the undermining of the family (Douma), the rejection of pagan practices (GKN "Homophilia" Report), or of the fact that only the man-woman polarity is in view, or of the value attached to fertility (idem.). The text, however, is silent on the underlying reasons. The intent, meanwhile, is crystal-clear: "One who approves of homosexual relations must first have passed through the dread of Leviticus" (S. J. Ridderbos). But dread of what? The feminist theologian Ruether Radford offers an interpretation: dread that a man will be reduced to the inferior status of a woman.

Homosexual acts are mentioned in no other Old Testament texts. For an interpretation in this direction of the relations between

Naomi and Ruth, or of Jonathan and David, these texts offer no support.[5] Our conclusion, therefore, has to be that the Old Testament pronounces itself very rarely, but then exclusively with disapproval, on homosexual acts and nowhere provides points of contact for a more positive attitude. This does not surprise us because homosexuality did not constitute a live problem in Palestinian Judaism (Becker; Scroggs).

Disapproval is indirectly evident also from Genesis 1:26–27, which tells of the creation of man in the image of God, and from Genesis 2:18–24, which presents an aetiology of the normal sexual behavior of man and woman. This is not only explained here but also presented as normative (Douma, Vlaardingerbrook, "Homophilia" report; contra: Wiedemann). In the appeal to Scripture and, therefore, in their application to the contemporary situation, these texts consistently play a role but also already in the Bible itself, e.g., in Romans 1 and, therefore, in New Testament Judaism. "Genesis 1:27 is the fundamental pronouncement underlying the entire problematic; what else could the fuss be about?" thinks S. J. Ridderbos. Granted: one need not go so far as K. Barth who sees the image of God, "almost in the manner of a definition,"[6] exclusively expressed in the man-woman relation in order to arrive at no other conclusion than that the view of man in Genesis 1 and 2 is exclusively and virtually self-evidently heterosexual. This, too, is the import of Genesis 2:18 ("It is not good that man should be alone").

As for the New Testament, references to homosexuality are

---

5. Not that, therefore, an interpretation in this direction would be forbidden. "Where the Bible seems to speak of love from man to man, as in the relationship between David and Jonathan . . . , it sings its greatest song," H. J. Schoeps (1962: 373).

6. Cf. J. van Veen, op. cit., who cites at length G. C. Berkouwer's criticism (1957: 72–73) of Barth's interpretation of Genesis 1:26–27. Cf. the opinion of H. Berkhof (1985: 192): "This definition of P is, however, the reflection of only one witness. Even though there are hardly any other definitions in the Bible besides it, this does not mean that therefore it can be declared the dogmatic foundation." J. Vlaardingerbroek (op. cit.) states: though one cannot equate the image of God with the man-woman relation, the biblical authors regard this polarity essential for being human.

lacking in the Synoptics and the Johannine literature. Further, it is not accidental that Paul's admonitions occur in the letters to the churches at Rome and Corinth, centers of the Hellenistic world (the letter to Timothy is of a later date). In all three letters the condemnation is part of a catalog of vices.

(c) and (d) 1 Corinthians 6:9-10; 1 Timothy 8-10. Both passages speak of *arsenokoitai* ("those who lie with males" or "sodomites" — NRSV) and 1 Corinthians 6:10 also has *malakoi*, "weaklings" or "boy-prostitutes." In both cases, condemnation is strong. 1 Timothy calls such behavior contrary to sound teaching (vs. 10) and 1 Corinthians excludes those guilty of it from the kingdom of God. The meaning of the Greek words is not entirely clear. Most exegetes (and most Bible translations; see, e.g., Lance and Coleman) relate them to homosexual acts. *Arsenokoitai* may be the technical term for the active partners in homosexual anal intercourse; *malakoi* for the passive partners. That is how the words were understood in the secular Greek (Coleman, 1980). Scroggs thinks that *arsenokoites* is the Greek translation (possibly originating with Paul) of the Hebrew expression with which Leviticus 18:22 condemns homosexual intercourse ("lying with a male"). Some interpreters present a non-homosexual explanation: it is said *malakos* could mean "morally weak, immoral" and *arsenokoitai* applies to anal coitus in general, hence both hetero- and homosexual (van Hooydonk). Others view *arsenokoitai* as male prostitutes. That also comes through in both the NIV and NRSV. Labuschagne again thinks here particularly of cultic prostitution. According to him the *malakoi* are the same as the *qᵉdešim*, boys devoted to temple prostitution in the Old Testament, and *arsenokoitai* are men who have sex with young boys: pederasts. Coleman furnishes the most arguments. The *Theological Dictionary of the New Testament (Th.D.N.T.)* does not discuss the terms. In short, it is probable that these texts condemn homosexual behavior both in and apart from the cult. Scroggs points out that they (only) condemn a certain form of homosexual intercourse, a form (viz., pederasty) also condemned by the Greeks, hence by the culture of those days in general.

(e) The condemnation in the letter to the Romans forms part

of a larger whole (ending with Romans 3:20), in which Paul argues that neither Jews nor Gentiles are to be excused for their sins. Although the latter do not have the Law they could still have known better, for they had received the revelation of God in his works: the creation points to the Creator (Rom. 1:20). Him they have not seen fit to acknowledge and in the place of the immortal Creator they have worshiped mortal creatures: men, birds, and other animals. For this reason — the exchange of one for the other — God has punished them by giving them up to unnatural passions. In that way they received in their own person the due penalty for their error (vs. 27). As punishment for their rejection of God they were given up to a debased mind and immoral behavior (vss. 28ff.). They could have known that such behavior is deserving of death but they even applaud those who do such things (vs. 32, the climax).

The discussion concerns especially two things: the meaning of *exchanging, metellaxan* (vss. 25 and 26), and *giving up, aphentes* (vs. 27), on the one hand, and of *against nature, para phusin*. Some exegetes conclude from "exchanging" that verse 26 speaks of heterosexuals, so that the condemnation is not applicable to people with a homosexual orientation (Boswell, van Veen, Wengst). Scroggs thinks that here, too, the condemnation is aimed at pederasty. S. J. Ridderbos writes that Paul's judgment certainly comes down on homosexual intercourse as such, but he still thinks that the accent lies on the deliberate act of one who is apparently still able to "exchange" something. This, in my opinion, is not how one should read these words. However well-intended, a distinction in judging the sexual behavior of "real" homosexuals and other homosexual behavior is condescending and, therefore, morally objectionable. On top of this, the text does not permit a distinction between the "act" and the "condition." Bonda rightly comments that the issue is not whether the people Paul had in mind earlier followed a different lifestyle but that, in his view, they had drifted away from God's intent. That is the context: idolatry irrevocably leads to moral decay (the "Homophilia" Report). The "exchange" in verse 26 and the "giving up" in verse 27, therefore, have to be read in the passive sense as meaning: "having come in the place of" in contrast to the active meaning of the word in verse 25 (the exchange of God's truth for a lie). Similarly Hays: Paul's condemnation is based, not on the assumption that the homosexual behavior was voluntary, but on the assumption of the universality of sin, which drives humans into disobedient actions, which, though involuntary, still render them culpable.

The meaning of *para phusin* is harder to determine. Does "nature" here have normative significance? It could refer to (a) conformity with the social conventions of Paul's day, or (b) to the biologically natural, or (c) to the normative creation order, or, finally, to a combination of these meanings. Van Hooydonk, Coleman (1980), and Zuurmond think that Paul had especially (a) in mind; Polman and the "Homophilia" Report think of (a) and (c); Ridderbos and van Veen (b) and (c); Douma and Bonda (c). Scroggs believes that the word "unnatural" was the contemporary judgment applied to pederasty, so that Paul's view cannot be applied to the modern discussion.

In the Greek world the *phusis* concept passed through various developments.[7] It already came up in § B of the previous chapter, but in this connection we have to take a closer look. The oldest meaning stemmed from *phuein:* to grow, develop (1); in addition it meant "the external form of nature" (2). Somewhat later the term occurred in the sense of birth, (3), e.g., in *kata phusin,* "according to nature," meaning "by birth."

Besides these purely descriptive meanings *phusis* has the general meaning of something that, by its constitution, is a given, the "true" nature. Applied to humans it describes their character, gifts, or attributes, such as the upbringing of children. When a person does something that he knows is wrong, he deserts his nature, i.e., his true nature. In Ionian nature-philosophy the concept acquired a scientific meaning; *phusis* is everything that cannot be attributed to human or divine causes. Aristotle adopts this meaning; in his works *phusis* is the final form, the end product, of a development. This *phusis* can be scientifically established.

7. For the following, cf. esp. H. Köster's art. on *phusis* in *Th.D.N.T.* IX, pp. 251–77.

In tension with this stands "nature" as related to the origin of all things. In Aristotle it also occurs in this sense: nature is the principle of movement inherent in things that takes them to their *telos.* This nature is a non-empirical force. In classical Greek thought it is still distinguished from the deity but in Hellenism the two are equated.

In Greek thought *nomos,* law, was originally antithetical to *phusis.* The two were separate spheres; to each of these man was subject in a unique way. Later, in order to safeguard positive law from arbitrariness, Plato and Aristotle sought to ground it in the *phusis* of the *polis,* the city-state. Man, by his true nature, is political. But one does not find in them the idea of a moral natural law, a *nomos phuseôs.* Granted, *phusis* is also related to moral nurture, but then as the condition for ethical conduct, as a natural disposition, especially in the form of the *logos,* for man has received this from nature. *Logos,* according to Aristotle, may even bring a person to action that is "against custom and nature." The virtues themselves are neither natural *(phusei),* nor against nature *(para phusin)* because one acquires them by acting in accordance with insights made possible by *logos.*

The expressions *kata phusin,* "according to nature," and *para phusin,* "against nature," were, however, also used in moral judgments, particularly with reference to sexual vices. Thus Plato could call death at an advanced age *kata phusin,* normal; and for his disapproval of pederasty (in *The Laws*) use the expression *para phusin,* abnormal, to that end referring to the animal world, hence to empirical observation.[8]

The expressions *kata/para phusin* acquire a more comprehensive meaning in the Stoa. For Stoicism nature is a cosmic principle. The cosmos is *logos*-permeated, and the World Spirit manifests itself in the spirit of man. Man can discover this *logos*

8. J. Boswell (1980: 13ff.) regards this idea of Plato as a "chance remark" (cf., e.g., Plato's very different position in his *Symposium*). He, too, rejects the idea that by *para phusin* Plato means "unnatural" in the sense of: in conflict with a moral law. He translates the phrase by "unrelated to birth" or "non-procreative."

and live in accordance with it. Thus, what nature demands has already been given to man as a basic impulse in his *logos*. Living *kata phusin,* in harmony with nature, therefore, is an abstract, non-empirical principle that represents the goal of life. However, what *in concreto* corresponds to this is, in fact, that which corresponds to the existing order and common sense. Health, strength, and perfection of the sense organs are *kata phusin,* while sickness, weakness, etc. are *para phusin.* Still, because of the old *nomos-phusis* (law-nature) antithesis, the notion of a moral natural law scarcely occurs even among the Greek-speaking Stoics. It does, however, occur among the Romans (Cicero: the *lex naturalis* is what nature teaches all living beings) and among the Hellenistic Jews Philo and Josephus *(nomos phuseoos).* For Philo the law of nature is the Torah by which God made the world, hence the *moral* law. Specifically the sexual vices are deviations from the law of nature, *para phusin,* unnatural. For the rest, the term *phusis* was used very generally in the idiom of Hellenism.

It is all the more striking that in the New Testament, as for that matter in the Septuagint, this term occurs only sporadically. Paul, moreover, employs the term in clearly different senses,[9] a fact that makes implausible an interpretation in the direction of Stoic or Jewish-Hellenistic natural-law thinking.[10] Paul indeed uses "nature" in the normative sense in 1 Corinthians 11, where hair style is the subject. Hair style and sexuality were already related to each other in antiquity. But while it is already out of the question that Paul should recognize another authority center alongside of divine revelation — all nature is created nature — also in 1 Corinthians 11 the reference is not to the moral law of nature but to a bit of popular

9. For the sake of completeness, I will list the texts: Romans 11:21, 24; 2:27; Galatians 4:8; 1 Corinthians 11:14; Ephesians 2:3; and Romans 2:14; 1:26.

10. According to H. Köster in *Th.D.N.T.,* this is also the case in Romans 2:14, the text that most clearly betrays Greek influences. Here *nomos* and *phusis* occur side by side: The Gentiles do by nature *(phusei)* the works of the law *(nomos).* For the same view see inter alii G. C. Berkouwer (1951: 150) and H. N. Ridderbos (1966: 112). But cf. G. Th. Rothuizen (1962: 152ff.).

philosophy, to a standard of public propriety rather than to a moral law. The best proof for this is in fact Romans 1, for when Paul speaks of knowing God from the works of the Creator — a normative setting — the term *phusis* is lacking. In *this* context occur verses 26 and 27, where homosexual acts are said to be in conflict with "natural use" and "against nature" *(para phusin)*.

Paul indeed illustrates the wrath of God upon the Gentile world with the example of homosexuality. But this does not mean that the *reason* for God's wrath consists in its unnatural character. If that were the case the word "natural" *would* have been intended normatively (i.e., as created nature = nature as God intended = the original nature of Genesis 1 = the creation order), and that, as is evident from the context, is not likely. It is more likely that Paul viewed homosexual behavior as a typical sign, a classic example, of *paganism* for which he did not have to present any special arguments. *That* is his religious-moral judgment. And he further illustrates this by referring to the nature known to him and all men in its normal functioning,[11] hence to empirical observation. Paul regards this being-given-up to the non-self-evident, the non-normal — the unnatural — as a consequence of God's wrath. Not because the non-normal is morally unnatural but because the unnatural is a sign of *unbelief.* The thrust of Paul's argument, therefore, is directed not against "nature" but against "unbelief."

Hence Paul calls homosexual behavior "unnatural" in order to furnish factual information. That homosexuality is unnatural is a reason — for Paul — to view it as a form of unbelief. This means that the rationale[12] behind Paul's reasoning is the concept of unbelief. The tradition, by contrast, has always inquired about the rationale behind the word "natural" ("Nature" in the sense of the moral law) and hung the discussion about homosexuality up on disputes about natural theology and general revelation.

I, therefore, conclude that, seeing Paul does not equate creation (= normative creation order) and nature, the word "unnatural" in Romans 1 cannot without qualification be taken as referring to

11. Cf. G. Th. Rothuizen (1962: 157).
12. For this term, see Ch. III § C.

Genesis 1. We, therefore, have to reject view (c) (see above) concerning the meaning of *para phusin*. The expression is not charged with the heavy import that the tradition, following the line of natural law thinking, has assigned to it. For the rest, Paul's condemnation is no less sharp for all that.

Armed with this conclusion we can now dismiss a number of interpretations as incorrect. The GKN "Homophilia" report states that, in line with his Jewish upbringing, Paul sharply condemns homosexuality and regards heterosexual relations within marriage as the only legitimate form of sexuality.

> In light of the context in which Paul uses the word 'natural' it is likely that, again like the Old Testament, he views the normal as the creation order which must therefore be considered normative for every human being.[13]

Paul indeed regards the normal as the natural and the natural as God-created nature, but the idea that the natural or normal is normative because it expresses the creation order is not his line of reasoning.

For that reason, in my opinion, R. B. Hays goes too far when he says concerning Paul:

> Though he offers no explicit reflection on the concept of 'nature,' it is clear that in this passage Paul identifies 'nature' with the created order. The understanding of 'nature' in this conventional language does not rest on empirical observation of what actually exists; instead, it appeals to an intuitive conception of what ought to be, of the world as designed by God.[14]

Even further out of line is the position of K. Barth. His "humanity without one's fellow-man," though it is a fine description of "unnatural" in its moral sense, does not well convey the sense of *para phusin* in Romans 1.

Still a few other New Testament passages are sometimes

13. "Homophilia" (1982: 19).
14. R. B. Hays (1986: 194).

linked with homosexuality: Ephesians 5:11–12; 2 Peter 2:6–8; Jude 6, 7; Revelation 21:8; 22:15. It is not that this meaning is explicitly present in or required by the texts, but neither is this interpretation impossible. If it is correct, these texts also confirm the negative assessment of homosexuality (van de Spijker, Coleman, Douma).

To sum up: wherever homosexual intercourse is mentioned in Scripture, it is condemned. With reference to it the New Testament adds no new arguments to those of the Old. Rejection is a foregone conclusion; the assessment of it nowhere constitutes a problem. It obviously has to be repeated from time to time, but the phenomenon as such nowhere becomes the focus of moral attention. It is never condemned in isolation but always in association with other major sins: unchastity, violence, moral corruption, and idolatry.

Now how should Christians deal with this material? It seems so simple: if it says that it is wrong, then it *is* wrong, and therefore forbidden. In fact many ethicists-exegetes take this biblicist road, also the tolerant ones because they, in turn, attempt to read *into* these texts that they do *not* say that it is wrong. The *decision,* however, does not fall in exegesis but in hermeneutics. Between the text and its interpretation stands the believer as user and meaning-bestower: he decides on the weight to be attributed to the text. This is not done arbitrarily but depends on a person's theological "viewpoint," hence with his fundamental faith assumptions. Theologically these assumptions are accounted for in the dogmatic system of the theologian. The claim is made that this system is derived from the Bible but it is equally decisive for the way in which the Bible is read. Not so much with regard to what it says — which is something exegesis and historical research can more or less reliably recover — but with respect to what series of texts are deemed applicable and which are not. Accordingly, there is, always and inevitably, reciprocity between reading the Bible and the reader's (naive or reasoned) interpretative system. That has nothing to do with the nature of faith — though as believers we may think that this reciprocity is integral to Scripture's intent[15] — but is apparently given with the nature of

15. E.g., H. Berkhof (op. cit.: 95) on the authority of Scripture: "first, with an authoritative voice Scripture refers us to the revelation; next, on the

human knowing. As humans, we always interpret reality through the grids we impose on it and that also applies to the reality that is the content of revelation.

In the natural sciences the fundamental normative grids that determine the mode of human observation are called *paradigms,* a concept also used nowadays in theology.[16] Paradigms have a legitimating function with regard to the way issues are framed and are characterized, among other things by the fact that they cannot possibly be precisely defined and delimited. The presuppositions of faith — what people understand by revelation — are ordered within such paradigms. Examples are Barthian theology ("the one Word of God"), liberation theology, neo-Calvinism, the Lutheran two-Kingdoms doctrine, or the Catholic nature-supranature scheme. They serve to help us in resolving new issues. That is their function. They, therefore, also contribute to the formation of new insights.

Because observation (including that of revelation) and theoretical interpretative frameworks are so closely intertwined, ethical positions taken in the church also tend to mirror much broader theological positions embraced by the paradigms. Accordingly, discussions of positions pertaining to homosexuality also bring out the distinctive features of the paradigms adhered to. The reason is that the value of a given paradigm partly depends on its capacity to furnish answers to new questions. (This explains why the influence of, say, Barthianism seems to be waning and simultaneously that of theologies of liberation and experience is rising).

A possible analogy between paradigms in the natural sciences and those in theology need not be examined here. An interesting point in the case of paradigms is the connection between the way knowledge is obtained and what is known. In the following section we will examine whether such a connection can in fact be found in the

---

authority of what we have understood of the revelation we evaluate the testimonies of Scripture, and so there arises an interaction between the two. The concept of the 'authority of Scripture' is part of this process and is qualified by it."

16. Th. Kuhn (1970); H. Koningsweld (1976). H. M. Kuitert used the concept of paradigm in a theological context already in 1972. See also A. van de Beek (1990: 222–23).

theological discussions of homosexuality (hence: different paradigms yield different positions) or whether discussions of homosexuality are used (especially) to characterize and confirm the paradigm. In the latter case, the point at issue is no longer a position on homosexuality but the rightness of the theological paradigm adhered to.

C. The role of revelational models of interpretation in theological-ethical discussion

The positions described in this section have largely been discussed already in Chapter I. There, however, the focus was ethical; here it is theological. According to the statement of affairs given in the GKN "Homophilia" report, in the mainline Protestant churches[17] the following theological-ethical positions can be distinguished. I will simply restate them without comment; they are divided into two groupings, arguments con and arguments pro.

CON:

(1) The texts in question have *always* been interpreted as prohibiting homosexual intercourse. Could the church have been mistaken all these years?

(2) Some prohibitions have lost their validity for us. The prohibition of homosexuality, however, is an expression of *God's eternal will.*

(3) Homosexuality is a sign of the *brokenness of the world* after the Fall; accordingly, it is a sinful inclination against which one must struggle.

(4) The Bible pictures homosexuality as *unchastity and lawlessness.*

(5) One may not reduce God's commands to that of loving one's neighbor.

17. Cf. "Verwarring an Herkenning" (1984: 46ff.). Even by comparison with non-Dutch literature (e.g., The Osborne Report; Coleman 1989; Müller 1986; Scroggs 1983) this list of positions is the most complete.

(6) Homosexual conduct is in conflict with the normative creation order of marriage.

(7) To think that sometimes we can or should know better than Paul is to leave the door open to arbitrariness in the use of Scripture.

(8) Despite this rejection the church should nevertheless support the homosexual in his struggle (the pastoral approach).

PRO:

(9) There is good warrant for homosexual practice in the context of love and faithfulness.

(10) Heterosexuals, too, live in a broken world. It is, therefore, *arbitrary* to approve of marital relations but not of homosexual relations.

(11) The church must reappraise and redefine its morality because it recommends as the will of God what is actually the morality of the heterosexual majority.

(12) In this context, just as was done in the case of slavery and the position of women, we must oppose the *letter* of the Bible because at bottom the love-command is at stake.

(13) The biblical writers were not acquainted with the homosexual condition; they condemned only certain homosexual practices.

(14) The pastoral approach is *condescending*. Consequently the individual has to bear the burden of a decision the church as a whole avoids.

I will assume that these fourteen positions are representative, also for the situation outside the Netherlands. One can draw three conclusions from them.

(a) The existence of a specific homosexual orientation is assumed in most of these positions (see Chapter I[18]);

18. Where the appeal to a specific orientation or predisposition is rejected as a valid argument in ethics, viz., as a naturalistic fallacy.

282

(b) Isolated biblical texts play a predominant role, except where an appeal is made to the love-command and the creation order. This puts the appeal to Scripture on a broader theological foundation.

(c) All positions except (11) and possibly (12) proceed on the assumption that the morality found in the Bible is normative for us. Revelation here means: God's disclosure of his will (command). For the Christian tradition I am here discussing, revelation and Bible coincide. Consequently the question concerning the relation between revelation and ethics is that concerning the relation between the Bible (here: biblical morality) and ethics.

This last point (c) is the most interesting because it is the most far-reaching. Accordingly, this is the relation we will discuss further. Naturally the positions on homosexuality reproduced here do not stand by themselves. They can be viewed as having been derived by deduction from *a number of different theological positions bearing on the relation between revelation and ethics.* They are the positions that are to furnish a criterion for handling the data of Scripture. The following statement of these positions is to be regarded as an idealized and greatly simplified account of more comprehensive theological paradigms. I, therefore, call these theological positions models, *models of revelation.* I believe that this schematic approach[19] will prove adequate.

(1) Moral guidelines (norms) can and must be *deduced* from the Bible as the revealed Word of God:

variant (a): they can be deduced directly because Revelation = Word = Scripture = text;

variant (b): they can be deduced directly but not without taking account of the *historical distance* between the biblical writers and our time. This is done by factoring the difference in situation into the formation of a judgment;

variant (c): they can be deduced *indirectly* by way of an appeal to central biblical motifs (covenant, view of man, view of the body, the love-command, etc.).

(2) One can indeed deduce guidelines for action from the

19. Cf. — less schematically — H. M. Kuitert (1981b) and A. Dulles, *Models of Revelation,* New York (1985).

Bible, not primarily because their moral validity is rooted in the fact that they are laid down in Scripture, but because, from an ethical viewpoint, they are good for people. Consequently we find them also in the Bible. To "deduce" means one can also trace them to Scripture. In the Bible, though morality often turns out to be crucial in the end, it is not the central issue. God's design is to continue to teach us even through a fallen nature, culture, and history.

(3) Central to our agenda must be the doing of God's will. That does not consist in following rules but is discovered in seeing what God is concretely doing in history. The church has found that God's action is liberating. The Bible is the story of liberation from oppression. For that reason we must not automatically do the same today as what God's people did in earlier times. The church must understand the Bible in light of its concrete experience with liberation and oppression.

Again, these models nowhere occur in pure form. Nor is it my concern to press anybody's theology into such a system. No theology can be adequately represented by models; they are expressly designed as (in part deliberately untrue) simplifications of reality, in this case of theological reality. My purpose in this connection is only to show that *types* of theological views play an important role in theological-ethical discussions about homosexuality.

Now my thesis is that the existence of such different types of moral argumentation, despite their intent, actually makes moral discussion insoluble. The reason is that the grounds for a person's attachment to model 1, 2, or 3 have nothing to do with (in this case) the issue of homosexuality. I will illustrate this with the aid of four somewhat detailed examples. They are derived from the Dutch situation, but I also relate them to the situation existing elsewhere.

J. Douma vs. S. J. Ridderbos on Romans 1[20]

Ridderbos concludes that the biblical texts in question signal the danger of homosexual intercourse but that this is not the last word.

20. J. Douma (1973, 1984); S. J. Ridderbos (1961, 1973a, 1973b).

One must consider the total structure of the biblical ethos, a structure marked by the double love-command. On that basis one cannot permanently demand that homosexuals abstain. Ridderbos's main argument, however, is that God's will also comes to us through nature and human existence. Granted, one then still has to say that all homosexual intercourse is contrary to the will of God but only *insofar* as a person acts, or is treated, unnaturally. Now when a person's physical structure does not correspond with his psychic structure, the love of neighbor has to take account of this. While *contra naturam* concerns all homosexual intercourse, including that of the constitutional homosexual, the argument can also be used *in defense of* sexual intercourse between homosexuals. Ridderbos thus theologically lays the groundwork for an "ethic of compromise."

This is going too far for J. Douma. If we say that an abnormal deviant psychic structure may be factored into our ethics, we are saying that we know better than Paul. Paul takes no account of what a given person, given his nature, can live "with," but refers to the divinely intended nature of Genesis 1. Homosexual intercourse is always a sign of departure from God. The texts must not be exegeted in light of modern distinctions (constitutional and pseudohomosexuality), even though these distinctions may be ethically and pastorally significant (viz., for accepting the homophile orientation).

Douma, therefore, considers the texts that speak of homosexuality decisive. He can be classified under model (1a). Not so Ridderbos. According to him, one can and may in ethics work with the "obviousness of nature," understood by him as "the consistent orientation of the basic structure." According to him, this is also what Paul does in Romans 1. There, after all, Paul speaks from a sense of what is obvious, not in virtue of a special revelation. This does not mean that this obviousness can serve as an independent source of knowledge for what God wills, but it does mean that it is wrong to derive all sorts of data from Scripture apart from the gospel; these elements may be in the text but it is not intended that they should be presented as normative.[21] Both the Bible and

21. S. J. Ridderbos (1973b: 151).

285

human experience are critical standards. The yearning for a partner is integral to the basic structure of human beings. For that reason it is unnatural not to take account of the psychic structure of the homosexual.

Accordingly, Ridderbos has a different notion of the relation between Bible and ethics than Douma.[22] He can be classified under model (2). The opposing conclusions of the two, however, have nothing to do with a different model of homosexuality. Both use the "predisposition" model. Nor is there a difference in exegesis. The difference is theological. They differ about the relation among ethics, biblical morality, and revelation, specifically about the role assignable to human experience ("natural obviousness"). Still, one has to wonder whether it is, in fact, this difference that, for them, has the last word. There is perhaps a possibility that their divergent theological position is the *result* of their differing view of homosexuality. That this hypothesis is by no means imaginary can be illustrated from the report of the Christian Reformed Church in North America discussed in Chapter I § 5.3. Its judgment is comparable to Douma's but in theological position it is closer to Ridderbos when it states that also the sciences can teach us about creation. Accordingly, its difference with Ridderbos does not lie in theology but in the evaluation of the scientific data: for this American church homosexuality is "disorder," "unnatural," something that is not true for Ridderbos. To test the hypothesis we need to discuss still other examples.

J. van Veen vs. K. Barth on Genesis 1[23]

Van Veen responds to the question of what the Bible says about homosexuality by answering: nothing. He, too, considers exegesis decisive but, in contrast with Douma, attributes so much weight

22. Ridderbos (1973b: 149) favors a concept of revelation that takes as its point of departure the revelation in Christ but at the same time wants to recognize general revelation in the reality of man and the world.

23. J. van Veen (1977). On K. Barth, see Ch. I § B.

to the divergent orientation of homosexuals that, to his mind, the biblical texts in question are not applicable. The church must stop "whining about sodomy" and read the "abomination texts" of Leviticus (terms used by van Veen) against the cultic background of the time of the writer. At the same time it should factor in Paul's unfamiliarity with the phenomenon of the divergent predisposition. In other words, though van Veen takes account of the historical distance, the exegesis is still what clinches it for him. He can, therefore, be classified under model (1b). From the perspective of exegesis he makes much of Barth's rejection of homosexuality, which, in his opinion, is based on Barth's self-contradictory exegesis of Genesis 1:26–27. Barth found the image of God in man's existence as man and woman, better: in *their* relation. But he is not consistent in this because he also says that the image of God consists in the distinction and relation between one human being and another. Van Veen views the assertions of Genesis as "theological rationales" for the heterosexual relation that was deemed self-evident at the time. To us that is no longer the case and, therefore, Genesis 2:18 ("It is not good that the man should be alone") is also applicable to homosexual relations.

True, there is an "unresolved problematic"[24] lurking in Barth's exposition. But it is not the exegesis of this text (alone) that causes Barth to reject homosexuality, nor is this rejection based on it; the reason for it is much deeper, rooted as it is in his theology (the Christologically based anthropology, see Chapter I). In light of his revelational model (1b), van Veen suggests that if Barth had been consistent he would not have come to his condemnation of homosexuality. That is an oversimple interpretation of Barth, but from van Veen's perspective only Barth's exegesis is relevant.

We must, he thinks, read the Bible without dogmatic bias. Only then will its basic intent emerge clearly, the message of liberation. That is correct. But this thesis is misleading because no one can read the Bible without an interpretive framework. Van Veen says exegesis is the only issue, but in fact it is only his way

24. G. C. Berkouwer (1962: 73), whom van Veen cites.

of demonstrating the incomparability of biblical same-sex relations with the present ones. That intent is wrapped up in a view of revelation (Bible). And from this angle — the requirement of un-biased exegesis — he then criticizes Barth. The statement "Barth's exegesis is wrong," therefore, really means: "arguments other than exegetical or biblical ones may also be advanced." Evidently van Veen is afraid to say that because he presents his conclusion (the Bible says nothing about homosexuality) as a result of exegesis. For that reason I classify him under model (1b).

But is there a possibility that actually the reverse process occurred: that exegesis had to confirm the position van Veen had held long before? Then his reasoning is as follows. Homosexual intercourse is not wrong and *therefore* not a sin. That view should then be traceable to Scripture, read: to the texts in question. That is possible only, however, if the texts in question refer to a different "kind" of homosexuality. This van Veen, therefore, has to *read into* the texts. A comparable viewpoint occurs in Boswell (1980). Wiedemann (1983b) furnishes examples of the practice of reading things into the texts from the German situation. But, as with the previous example, I will defer judgment.

Do We Know Better Than Paul?

Exegetically more nuanced, but struggling with the same problem, are the two GKN reports (1972, 1982). On the ethical-hermeneutic section of the first, citing van Ruler, G. Th. Rothuizen comments that, in some things, the church may and must know better than the apostle. This statement triggered a strong reaction: in this matter is not the will of Christ the highest law for Rothuizen? When the reference is to biological knowledge one can and may speak as Rothuizen does but not when it concerns what God requires of us.[25]

Actually this intense reaction is remarkable. Was it because it concerned homosexuality? In the fifties, speaking of morality in

25. Report on Synod in: *Kerkinformatie* 1, 11 (1972): 27–30.

general, R. Schippers, professor of New Testament and ethics at the Free University, felt free to use virtually the same words:

> . . . for some of our rules of living we love to appeal to the Bible saints, but on other issues we often have another, and better, view than they did.[26]

In any case the 1982 report did not wish to repeat Rothuizen's words but restricted itself to the relation between the Command and the commandments, between Christ and the law. On that subject it makes some good theological comments:

> To insure the ethical integrity of the church we must not resort to pleas for rules and good works but continually call the church to self examination — and dialogue! — with regard to the sincerity of our love for Christ. . . . In the tension of approaching judgment . . . an important radicalization of the norms occurs: we cannot be too holy! On the other hand, it also means a certain relativization of the norms: they must be helpful! . . . In the light of approaching judgment there is a strikingly broad margin of freedom of conscience. . . . 'An ethic of the last hour' therefore calls for strict watchfulness to insure that these norms have a dynamic and positive, rather than a stultifying or evaporative effect. (pp. 37, 43, 45)

So the cry is for an eschatological ethos. But such an ethos puts pressure on *all* the rules for living. Was there a reason for saying this especially in the context of homosexuality? Was this said perhaps to avoid asserting either that homosexual intercourse is not a good work or that there is no objection to it? Can an eschatological ethos really be expected to yield rules in relation to (homo)sexual intercourse? In the *eschaton,* after all, there is no such thing as marriage either. In plain fact the authors of the report do not derive their conclusions concerning homosexuality from an eschatological ethos. The chapter from which the quotations are taken is silent on homosexuality. But the last chapter again proves to view homosexuals as patients: "those who are different against

26. R. Schippers (1955: 24; see also, e.g., 54ff.).

their own will"; those who "after much struggle" believe "they are justified in entering upon a relationship," etc. Accordingly, the report does not get past the so-called "shadings" that describe contrary positions.

From a pastoral-ethical point of view it is not unimportant for the *church* to arrive at consensus regarding an eschatological ethos. But does it help *homosexuals* when opinions diverge in all directions over the moral translation of this ethos?[27] An eschatological ethos — in the sense of: "now comes the crunch" — can hardly be helpful when the issue concerns the value of homosexual lifestyles, simply because the *moral* answer is left to the individual. Make room for the homosexual, sure, but also for the traditionalist. Or are the authors implying that, in the matter of morality, the church and theology have no special wisdom so that in some things individuals may differ with, or know better than, Paul? In that case the revelational view behind the two GKN reports can be classified as model (2). If this is not the case, the more recent report can be best described in terms of model (1c).

Outside the Netherlands I have found no parallel to Rothuizen's position. Rather general, however, is the view that the sexual ethics of the churches is too much dominated by tradition. This is reflected in the reports of the Church of England and the Presbyterian Church (U.S.A.) (see Chapter I § E.3). But precisely here an attempt is made to get Paul on one's side. The theological views of the GKN "Homophilia" report are virtually without analogy elsewhere. The report to the Synod of Westphalia (I 5.2) comes closest.

On the basis of analysis of these three examples a cautious conclusion can now be drawn. A difference in one's position regarding homosexuality proves to be linked with a difference in one's view of revelation. The authors discussed themselves attribute their difference on the former to a difference in relation to the latter. That emerges clearly from the first two cases. But this link is assumed

---

27. Cf. the humiliating treatment often accorded homosexual candidates for the ministry when they apply for a church position; see S. Rozendal (ed.) 1987. "The church is not ready for it." K. A. Schippers correctly asks whether the church has a right to raise this objection.

rather than argued (this is especially noticeable in the discussion on Genesis) because even after careful theological analysis (as in the third example) and despite theological consensus, mutually contradictory moral viewpoints prove to be possible! How is that possible? We will return to it later. This conclusion can be even more clearly illustrated with the following — our last — example.

Liberation Theology vs. Natural Theology

F. J. Hirs and R. Reeling Brouwer offer a form of liberation theology that expressly "counters natural theology." Their contribution to the theological discussion[28] is undoubtedly the most cheerful (the gayest?) to appear in the Netherlands. Following in the footsteps of K. Barth they oppose natural theology, which they[29] describe as follows:

> There is no room for an attempt to infer information as to who God is, what he does, and what he wants from us from the state of affairs we think we can naturally see surrounding us. (p. 23)

Ethics must be theological ethics; natural science (the biological argumentation regarding homosexuality) must not be the deciding factor: "Theological ethics, also when it deals with homosexuals, has to . . . remain theology and decisions have to be made theologically" (p. 9).

Actually the concern of the authors is to refute the notion that homosexuality is unnatural. That is done in a way that is very different from that of Chapter III.

> We think . . . that the church debate on the question whether it is permissible, regardless of whether the discussion is carried on

28. F. J. Hirs and R. Reeling Brouwer (1985).

29. Not even Barth, however, defines natural theology in that way. For him it is everything that cannot be deduced from Christology, all prior knowledge of God that has not yet become knowledge of God as the Father of Jesus Christ.

exegetically, ethically, or pastorally, has to come to nothing. After all, in the church we know that the right to judge another's life has not been given us. . . . (p. 10)

The reasoning here is as follows.

(a) God is looking "for fruit apart from what is natural" (they appeal to Mark 11:11–26, the story of the withered fig tree);

(b) Man is the image of God; i.e., he has no specific nature, no natural disposition, only a destiny: his nature consists in being suited for God's history with humans;

(c) What people call the "natural" is in fact the "cultural," hence changeable. What people consider "sexually natural," as the social sciences have demonstrated, is "phallocracy." Theologically this must be considered *phallolatry,* or phallicism, the worship of images;

(d) Against this idolatry homosexuality is a protest (the authors cite Gal. 3:28). Not homosexual intercourse is idolatry but opposition to homosexuality is because that is "phallolatry" (pp. 21–33).

Thus, both naturalness and unnaturalness are theologically defined. To act naturally is to follow one's God-given destiny; that implies opposition to what *people* commonly call natural but which is actually phallicism. And resistance to this phallicism means being homosexual. But how can homosexuals be certain that it is they who stand in the tradition of Scripture? They know this from experience, which they can interpret as Exodus-experience. Is it permissible to speak of it in those words? Yes — in the church there is no other way. The one constant in Scripture is the Name:

> The Name which constitutes the unity and center of Scripture teaches us that we must be attentive to the present to see and hear who God is and how he acts, and that we cannot simply derive this knowledge from the past. The history of this God with his people tells of his trustworthiness, true enough; but it does not furnish the data in terms of which we can predict the future. (pp. 41–42)

Biblical stories must be read as a whole, and isolated texts must not be put into battle position like cannons. Read correctly, they can illumine the historical situation of people living today. One has to become part of the story as one reads it to discover that the issue of the story is liberation. To that event he must himself make an active contribution and so "respond to God's redemptive will." "Thus liberation theology is a 'political' reading of Scripture and a 'biblical' reading of politics" (p. 44). Homosexuals have discussed God's liberating action in their own lives. Their "coming out" is to be considered their conversion. To this conversion they need to witness in the church. By doing so they are being faithful to their call and election (1 Cor. 1:26–28) (pp. 70ff.).

The type of appeal to Scripture here is very different from what we encountered in the previous examples. Hirs and Reeling Brouwer are clearly classifiable under model (3). The background is the experience of being homosexual. They legitimate their appeal to Scripture in terms of their belief that the Scriptural narrative demonstrates the collective experience of liberation from the house of bondage. This means that when a person can portray his experiences as part of a collective Exodus-experience, this legitimates his actions theologically and ethically.

Is this a possibility? Hirs and Brouwer appeal in clear terms to the experience of their own group. Of course theologians like Douma and van Veen do the same thing but they do not say it. For that reason the fact that the authors start with experience feels refreshing. It is a witness, not an attempt to persuade. And that is, think the authors, as it ought to be. That seems to me a question. In my opinion, their reasoning makes their position on homosexuality needlessly vulnerable. They are right in seeking to prevent a situation in which homosexuals continually have to enter a discussion of the same texts — texts in which they do not recognize themselves and which, to them, do not seem to have anything to do with the Gospel. But a position that does not validate itself by argument vis-à-vis other positions is vulnerable. This fact is in no way altered by presenting the position as one of faith. The matter is all the more pressing because such arguments are readily available. We can put it more strongly — and that touches the core of the issue — Hirs and Brouwer even presuppose them though they do not articulate them. They knew very well — before they read Scripture on the subject — that homosexual intercourse is not unnatural. Consequently, noting Barth's strong condemnation, they commented that "even Barth, admittedly the clear-eyed warrior against natural theology, proved himself myopic here." But saying that they failed to recognize the problem, that in his argument Barth committed a naturalistic fallacy, as we saw in Chapter I. The reason they do not see this is that they want to work in the same way. This means that while officially they refrain from engaging in ethical argumentation as ethicists (for them that is "natural theology"), they still more or less subtly consult extrabiblical norms, the norms of nature and culture. For Barth, in keeping with his time, that was the medical-biological model of illness; for Hirs and Brouwer it is social science.[30] This furnishes them — as naturalistically as Barth — a norm that is subsequently accorded theological legitimation.[31] The result is a theological ethic that abstains from rational, universally human argumentation but does not escape making naturalistic assumptions. Leveling the charge of "natural theology," they dismiss all forms of argumentative ethics as useless to Christians. But in doing this one cannot, of course, render theological ethics invulnerable to the type of logical fallacies ethicists are trained to point out.[32] And all this happens while the authors' intention is precisely to present an alternative to naturalistic thinking! The fact they do not succeed is due to their premise that the decisions have to be made theologically. Consequently, for these authors, too, the difference in position on homosexual intercourse relates to a difference in revelational

30. On naturalistic reasons based on material from the social sciences, see Ch. II § G.

31. Cf. the objections of H. M. Kuitert (1981b; 1985: § 9) to this kind of liberation theology. It replaces moral argumentation with religious arguments. In this manner problems are covered up with "God-talk." Similarly, H. W. Vijver (1985).

32. I can agree with the norm Hirs and Brouwer propose (unnatural sexual conduct is phallocracy = phallolatry = idolatry). But why is male homosexual behavior, in distinction from heterosexual behavior, not phallocracy? The authors neglect to demonstrate this.

model: (3) (liberation) versus (2) and (1) ("natural theology," oppression). In reality the difference is rooted in moral presuppositions.

Other liberation theologians as well refrain from explicitly raising the question concerning the ethical value of homosexual intercourse. The criterion is their own experience of liberation. Still in each case the moral issue does play a role, as was the case in Hirs and Brouwer. Take the German theologian D. Sölle for example.[33] For her, creation in God's image as man and wife implies no reference to procreation but to the fact that we are created as sexual beings. Only humans are sexual beings, i.e., have a capacity for relations. The connection of our sexuality with our creation in the image of God has to become the starting point for the redefinition of our sexuality. We must become "lovers like God." That is a part of what she calls the ontological project of creation that we realize in the historical project of liberation. "Creation" is "liberation" therefore; in other words, it is to bring about the transition from nature to history. Naturalness does not relate to the biological aspect of sexuality, nor to being homo- or heterosexual, but to participation in the project of liberation. Conservative Christians who see the image of God in the link between sexuality and procreation have not yet made the transition from a naturalistic idea of sexuality to a historical one, which is the biblical view, she says. She works this out in the four dimensions of love: as participation in the ecstasy of life, in trust, and solidarity, and toward wholeness.

Accordingly, naturalness or creatureliness (naturalness in the religious sense) is liberation. In the Bible the reference is not to naturalness in the biological sense, she says, nor, therefore, to the distinction between sexual preferences. Homosexuals no less than heterosexuals are aware of the love stirring in them when they talk about God in connection with their sexuality; that is the issue.

Is that true? Sölle's viewpoints are most reminiscent of the relational ethics of van Gennep, less radical than those of Hirs and Reeling Brouwer. But her mode of reasoning is the same as that

33. D. Sölle/S. A. Cloyes (1984, spec. Ch. XI).

295

of the latter two. The things she considers morally reprehensible like, say, heterosexism, she calls natural in the biological-naturalistic sense; the things that are morally required according to her are "natural," i.e., liberating. But she already held that view before she started reading the Bible. Theology here serves to legitimate Sölle's own otherwise respectable positions. But this theology does not argue; it merely seeks to persuade. For the grounding of an ethics that is not enough. Related to Sölle's approach is that of the Presbyterian Church (U.S.A.), the most radical report discussed in Chapter I.

We encounter the same thing — a theology that does not argue but simply makes assertions (or preaches) — in the Catholic American author J. McNeill, who wrote a liberation theology for gays.[34] In the terms of liberation theology it is intended to encourage homosexual Christians to find a healthy self-image, become conscious of oppressive structures, and to start their own gay communities in the churches. McNeill does this by interpreting Scripture and theology from the perspective of homosexuals. His starting point is that "every human being has a God-given right to sexual love and intimacy. Anyone who would deny that right to any individual must prove beyond all doubt the grounds for this denial" (1988: xvi), a position he had already developed in an earlier book.[35] In that book McNeill criticized the traditional Roman Catholic natural-law approach, which posits the centrality of reproduction over interpersonal love. McNeill, for his part, views the latter as the typically human dimension of sexuality (1976: 102–3). The reasoning, in its reference to human nature, is typical for McNeill. He is true to form when he asserts that sexual expression comes most fully into its own in a stable relationship. In this way the conditions are present for the development of the fundamental human need for trust and love (1988: 134–35). McNeill relates such needs to God's creation-plan (Gen. 2:18). He blames the tradition for conceiving human nature as uniformly heterosexual, counterposing that God created human beings with

34. J. J. McNeill (1988).
35. J. J. McNeill (1976).

a great variety in sexual preferences. That is part of his creative plan. For that reason homosexual identity has been endowed with special gifts that enable especially homosexuals to make a positive contribution to the humanization of society. They constitute a corrective to a one-sidedly heterosexual society that was not intended by God. Their love is a sign of God's presence in the world.

How does McNeill arrive at this "celebration of homosexuality"? He repeatedly affirms that the homosexual object-choice is based on a given orientation that is not voluntary, that occurred in every period of history and in all cultures (McNeill is an essentialist, therefore), and is unchangeable. Biblical condemnation of homosexuality concerns people who are not "genuinely" homosexual (1976: 37ff.). The unchangeable orientation is so important to him because he presupposes the same nature-concept as his own Catholic tradition, according to which the notion of the "natural" is normative. He seeks to show that homosexuality is not unnatural but natural (in the moral sense of the word). This is how he arrives at his moral right to sexual expression. That in turn is grounded in the plan of creation ("natural" in the religious sense) as a God-given right. This order, he says, is known from nature as empirical datum (the data of the sciences). So, though he arrives at the opposite conclusion from that of the Catholic tradition, he operates with the same logic, a scheme we rejected in Ch. I § B. In other words, basic also to his liberation theology is the confusion of the different meanings of the word "natural."[36]

Accordingly, within the camp of liberation theology one encounters a rather wide variety of ethical viewpoints. In the case of Hirs and Reeling Brouwer homosexuality is itself the medium of liberation; for Sölle a person's sexual preference is ethically irrelevant, and McNeill exonerates the homosexual who is "that way." Here, too, the link between theological starting point (model 3) and ethical position is less strong than the authors think.

So what is going on? Church and theology tie their positions on homosexuality to their more comprehensive faith perspectives,

36. So, correctly, J. van Hooydonk (1981: 199–209).

297

to what I have called models of revelation. Among Christians this seems to be the thing to do. The result was that discussions on homosexuality became discussions about these faith perspectives (and vice versa!). So the issue itself, a position on homosexuality, gets snowed under.

We can, however, now put our finger on the weak spot of the churches' approach. The relation between one's position on homosexuality and one's model of revelation (or "view of Scripture") is, in fact, much less solid than the individual authors pretend. This is not clear when these positions are evaluated separately but emerges vividly when they are compared with each other, as I did. Our conclusion was that, on the basis of approximately the same view of revelation, people may arrive at antithetical positions. The opposite is equally true: on the basis of divergent views of revelation people actually arrive at similar positions. That is the first conclusion.[37] From this emerges a second: one's moral position is clearly antecedent to one's theological view. This would mean that it is impossible to resolve moral issues, to arrive at, in this case, a position on homosexuality, by "faith" arguments alone.

Why is this? In answer, we can link up with the ethical theory of J. M. Brennan briefly referred to in the previous chapter. Although the arguments of a Christian ethics may differ materially from a non-Christian ethics, the former still needs to meet the formal standards of the discipline called ethics. Consequently, we are right to use Brennan's theory. He states that in every moral

---

37. This conclusion gains an even sharper profile when one looks at the work of W. Müller (1986). He presents a lengthy overview of personal and church positions gathered from around the world and divides them into three groups: (1) "No" to the homosexual orientation and to homosexual intercourse; (2) "Yes" to the homosexual orientation, "No" to homosexual intercourse; (3) "Yes" to both the homosexual orientation and to homosexual intercourse. He then attempts to classify each of these groups under a certain type of theology. He does not succeed in this: in all three groups, for example, he finds adherents of a theology of creation-ordinances. So a given position on homosexuality can no more be traced to a certain type of theology than a certain type of theology is likely to produce a given position on homosexuality.

discussion certain normative concepts play a key role. These concepts are "open-textured." Although they have the same formal meaning for all, they are given different contents by different groups. The process of supplying this content is mediated by a basic criterion of selection: the rationale underlying the concept. Brennan posits that agreement in moral discussions can be reached only through agreement on the level of the rationale. The goal of moral discussion is to reach this agreement. In this context he distinguishes four types of moral discussion. One can differ about what the relevant facts are. That is the simplest type of problem (Level I). A difference of opinion can also be due to a lack of clarity about the meaning each of the partners in discussion assigns to the central normative concepts. That situation requires clarification of the underlying rationale(s) (Level II). A new difference of opinion can then arise concerning what — given agreement on the rationale — follows from the rationale in the way of concrete rules of conduct. This leads to — what Brennan calls — a renewed explication of the rationale (Level III). And finally the disputants can reciprocally reject each other's rationales. That is the most fundamental form of difference (Level IV).[38]

Now let us, for the moment, place the discussion on homosexuality in the context of Brennan's problem types. The central normative concept in the discussion was "naturalness" or "unnaturalness." At the end of the fifties the discussion began with the discovery that homosexuality is a different phenomenon from what people for centuries had thought. With that discovery came the question whether the traditional condemnation of it could any longer be applicable. That is Brennan's Level I, that of factual information. That led to a critical examination of the arguments that were always advanced in Christian circles against homosexual intercourse, the arguments derived from the biblical texts we have discussed. That is Level II: the question concerning the reason for the prohibition. The pivotal point is Paul's condemnation: *against nature*. Christians define "unnatural" as that in which love toward God and neighbor is lacking. That is Brennan's Level III: the

38. J. M. Brennan (1977: 134–49).

explication of the rationale. Consequently, where love *is* present one can no longer reasonably use the word "unnatural." Logically speaking, then, when it was found that homophiles, too, can fulfill the love-command, the issue was settled.[39] That should have ended the matter for the churches; the fact that alongside of arguments derived from the Bible still other — naturalistic — arguments played a role in the discussion (see Chapter I) is not pertinent for theological argumentation.

But the discussion was not over for the churches because now another problem emerged: one would have to accept that Israel and Paul were obviously wrong. How can that be squared with the fact that it is the Bible, the word of God, that condemns homosexual intercourse as sinful? With that the issue of the authority of Scripture became central.[40] But, logically speaking, this issue has nothing to do with the question whether homosexuality is natural. For that reason different views of revelation or Scripture proved compatible with the same position on homosexuality and vice versa. This can be clarified as follows. The appeal to the love-command is a valid and, for Christians, a decisive argument when the issue is whether a given action *x* is natural or unnatural. The rationale underlying the word "(un)natural" then becomes the context of the discussion. In that way a rational argument becomes the deciding factor. That is how *ethical* discussions are conducted. But the same argument — the appeal to the love-command — has another meaning when the question becomes: "How does this command relate to the other commandments?" For then the rationale underlying the issue of biblical authority becomes the context of the discussion. The appeal to love can, therefore, be a valid argument in different contexts. But in order to achieve moral consensus, agreement on the level of

39. Hence it could have been settled with Ridderbos's conclusion: "Love your neighbor as yourself and for the rest find your own way" (see Ch. I § D).

40. An example of this way of framing the issue is the synodical discussion of Rothuizen's chapter in the GKN report of 1972. Van Veen's question: "What does the Bible say about homosexuality?" and his answer: "nothing!" belong in this framework.

the rationale is needed (Brennan's Level IV). Accordingly, the position that an action x is wrong because the *Bible* calls it "unnatural" has a different status than the position that x is "unnatural" because it lacks love. The first position presupposed a Christian view: one has to be a Christian to share it. It requires *theological* discussion. For the second position, by contrast, rational arguments and empirical data are decisive; one need not be a Christian to share it.

If in this manner we can distinguish a theological discussion from an ethical one, a necessary consequence is that people have their moral positions even before theology enters the picture. I want to defend that statement. But there is a complication, one that explains why for numerous Christians the two discussions coincide. It is simply the case that for Christians moral judgments are always normative assertions of faith; for them nothing else counts but doing the will of God.[41] Now, many Christians link this indisputable principle with the conclusion that, for the validation of moral positions, the appeal to revelation, in this case Scripture, is indispensable. Given this position, one can readily see why moral discussion of homosexuality became a discussion of the authority of Scripture. But is this correct? In the next section we will discuss the value of appealing to Scripture in ethical discussions.

D. Ethics and the appeal to revelation

In this section I will discuss the question of what the appeal to Scripture really amounts to as argument. From there we can draw conclusions about the use of theological arguments in ethical discussions.

To begin with, I want to introduce a simplification. I will restrict myself to theologians for whom the appeal to revelation

41. He thus reinforces his moral choice with his religion and makes it a "hard" position, H. M. Kuitert (1974: 34; 1975: 182).

practically coincides with the appeal to Scripture. The Reformed ethicists J. Douma and W. H. Velema can serve as models. Both, moreover, are contemporary representatives of the traditional condemnation of homosexuality. To enter on a discussion of their arguments, therefore, implies entering on a discussion of the grounds for the churches' condemnation of it. I will again briefly summarize Douma's reasoning as we encountered it earlier. The character of the "unnaturalness" of which Paul speaks, says he, may not be defined in light of biological science but must be judged in accordance with God's creation plan. This we only know from Scripture. Romans 1 must, therefore, be read in the light of Genesis 1 and 2: man and woman — those two — will be one flesh. That is God's revelation and, therefore, homosexuality must be termed unnatural, says Douma.[42]

So his reasoning runs as follows:

(a) the only norm is God's will;

(b) this is revealed in Scripture;

(c) therefore Scripture is the only norm and ethics is obligated to adhere to it;

(d) accordingly, Romans 1 and Genesis 1–2 must be considered as a sufficient and conclusive argument against homosexual intercourse.

In saying this Douma achieves two things. On the one hand, he immunizes his position from the criticism that this can no longer be maintained on rational, universal grounds. On the other, in this way he makes plausible the idea that Christians must and can derive from Scripture a specifically Christian understanding of the term "natural" and conclude on this basis that homosexual intercourse is unnatural.

Now my conclusion was that Douma's moral position is antecedent to his appeal to Scripture. Implied is that his antecedent position determines his choice of the texts that are used for what he considers a biblical view of homosexuality. By contrast Douma asserts that he does the reverse and derives his position from the Bible. That is rather a striking difference. In what follows we will

42. J. Douma (1984: 96).

see that this is connected with Douma's idea of the way in which moral positions have to be validated. That is done, in his opinion, by testing them in the light of Scripture. The appeal to Scripture has the character of a test for normative positions. For Christians a norm has authority only when it can be demonstrated that it is rooted in Scripture. Conversely: if it proves to be rooted in Scripture, it has authority. Therefore testing for Douma means checking by Scripture, the latter playing the role of a "body of knowledge." For that reason arguments derived from biblical texts are indispensable in ethical discussions. That is the argumentative value of the appeal to revelation. Let us see if he is right.

Douma's reasoning can be reconstructed and restated in three related theses:

(1) Christians appeal to Scripture as God's revelation in order thus to learn to know the will of God;

(2) God's will alone must be done because it is the ground and foundation of all our moral obligations; and

(3) apart from the knowledge of God we know nothing about the good. Therefore the validation of normative positions comes down to testing them by the Scriptures. This view not only raises theological but also logical and epistemological questions. That makes it complicated. Let me first briefly sketch the complex of problems involved in this view in order later to return to it at greater length.

(1) *God's Will.* For Christians the duty to do the will of God is self-evident. That is their ultimate moral ideal. Accordingly, it seems obvious that the validation of a moral position occurs in accordance with the following scheme:

- Christians are obligated to do the will of God;
- The Bible prohibits action *x*;
- Therefore *x* is contrary to the will of God and hence wrong.

This reasoning seems logically correct: it has a normative premise, a factual premise, and a normative conclusion. Even non-Christians are familiar with this argument: if the Bible forbids homosexual intercourse, then how could it ever be permissible for

Christians? The problem, of course, is situated in the second premise. It looks purely descriptive, meaning: the Bible says it; but it is
intended as a normative statement, meaning: it is binding for us.
Even for the most faithful Bible-believing Christian, not everything
written in the Bible is "biblical" in this normative sense. Only the
latter can be equated with the will of God. Accordingly, one always
needs a *criterion* for distinguishing what is from what is not "biblical," what is really the will of God from what people think is the will
of God. What determines the choice of criterion? That is the *theological* problem: giving an account of one's choice of criterion. At
this point we can already make the sober observation that various
criteria are being used. Also the different ecclesiastical positions on
homosexuality[43] demonstrate this: some apply the double love-
command, others the eternal, unchangeable will of God. We note,
therefore, that the difference in normative positions proves to go
hand in hand with difference in the appeal to Scripture.

(2) *God's will and the good.* "To validate" means to give a
materially and logically satisfying answer to the question why
the good is good.[44] Is it *logically* possible and/or necessary to
validate our standards of action in terms of the will of God? On
this level we face many difficult questions,[45] but fundamentally
the issue would seem to be whether the good is good because
God wills it or whether, conversely, the good is God's will because it is good. That is the so-called Euthyphro-problem, named
after Plato's dialogue by that name that deals with an analogous
question. Various answers are given to the question. Most philosophers, however, and also some theologians, take the second
position. Logically, they say, the concept of good and evil is
antecedent to the concept of God's will because if it were not so
we could not call God "good." A consequence of this position is
the autonomy of morality vis-à-vis religion.[46] Many theologians

43. See the beginning of the previous section.
44. H. M. Kuitert (1975: 183).
45. See W. K. Frankena (1973: 295–314).
46. For the variations on the thesis that morality is autonomous —
which in this form goes back to Kant — see D. E. de Villiers (1978). For a

cling to the first position because otherwise one would be proceeding from a standard that is more fundamental than the will of God, and such a standard does not exist for Christians. For them the will of God is the ground of our obligations and they consequently reject the idea of an autonomous morality. Douma and Velema belong to this group. A third group considers both positions defensible. This, in fact, seems to me to be the right position — as we will see later — but to validate it I think we need not only logic but also epistemology.

(3) *Our insight and God's will.* The reason why I made that last statement is that Douma and Velema represent the problem of validation as an epistemological problem. Douma asks:

> Is it possible for humans to find their own way in their relationship to God or . . . are they clearly shown a way in Scripture which they must follow for God's sake?[47]

similarly Velema:

> Do we owe our knowledge of the good to Revelation or to the Enlightenment? . . . Revelation means: man does not know the truth from within himself. . . . The Enlightenment means: man has the truth at his disposal. He knows it from his own being.[48]

Their objection against an autonomous morality, therefore, has to do with their idea of the way one gets knowledge: man knows the good only from revelation. I want to show that there is a misunderstanding here. Their appeal to God's will presupposes a certain view of man and a certain epistemology. For this view of man there are good grounds that have been enlarged upon by Protestantism: profound distrust of man's natural inclinations. But tacitly linked up with this view is a very specific epistemology. It says that man by nature does wrong because he takes his cues from the

---

critical discussion of Kuitert's view of this autonomy, see A. Houtepen (1989).

47. J. Douma (1983[4]: 30).

48. W. H. Velema.

wrong authority but would find the truth if he sought out the right source of knowledge, viz., God. Man does not know the good from within his own nature but from God. So this epistemology asserts that we will know the truth if we consult the right source. Over against this stands another epistemology that says that man, even when he has the right sources at his disposal, is nevertheless often in error because he is fallible or deceives himself. Both epistemologies presuppose the existence of absolute truth but they differ in the way it is known. For the first the truth consists in revealed knowledge (revealed truths). It can, therefore, be known with certainty. According to the second, even when we are convinced of the truth, we can only approximate it because knowledge is not revealed and we only know the truth, including the truth that comes from God, in the form of what people in a given period consider it to be. Hence knowledge of it is fallible and therefore needs constant testing.

In short: in moral issues Christians appeal to the will of God. That is their right, but what do they mean by it? If they intend to lodge their normative positions "in the realm of God" (Kuitert), that is a self-evident matter. If they think they are thus testing their positions, they proceed from the assumption that the good is good because God wills it to be. From within logic objections have been advanced against this view. Even if one does not find these objections convincing, the question still remains: How do we know God's will? At this point we have to make a choice, say Douma and Velema; our knowledge of God's will is either from Revelation or from the Enlightenment. In what follows I want to show first that (a) this dilemma is based on a mistaken epistemology. Next that (b) in fact nobody, including Douma and Velema, can successfully work on that basis. Finally that (c) from a theological perspective this dilemma is completely unnecessary but (d) is meanwhile responsible for the fact that church discussion on homosexuality, while touching on numerous theological topics, no longer concerns homosexuality.

(a) *Testing.* In our time especially the philosopher K. R. Popper directed his attention to epistemology. I first want to explore his views in general in order then to discuss their relevance for the appeal to revelation. As is rather well-known,[49] he regards testing as an effort to falsify rather to verify representation of reality. Falsifiability or refutability is the criterion of demarcation between scientific and non-scientific forms of knowledge.[50] Herewith he opposes the neo-positivist philosophers who viewed verification as the characteristic feature of empirical science. He also applied his philosophy-of-science insights to the social and political world. There, too, criticism has to be central. Testing is criticizing, the elimination of errors, instead of justification by positive reasons that have to prove that one's theories are correct. Why does Popper think this? This is linked with his view that human knowledge is necessarily fallible. He does not deny that in our daily life and also in science we ordinarily attempt to corroborate our views and theories. But the characteristic feature of a scientific theory is that it has stood up under the attempt to falsify it. For every theory, even the most senseless, grounds can usually be found. Theories that later proved untenable were sometimes corroborated for centuries by the evidence (e.g., the geocentric worldview). Consequently, it is not the degree to which a theory has been corroborated but the fact that it has stood up under testing that constitutes the standard for its scientific character. Is such a theory, which was corroborated in an attempt to falsify it, therefore true? No; but it is accepted provisionally. The more critical the test, the better the theory. But scientific truth is always provisional truth. Theories are conjectures that have stood up under criticism. The implication is that the time may come when it will not be able to stand up under new criticism.

Science does consistently get better, thinks Popper ("the growth of knowledge"). But this is not by an increase of positive evidence but by way of the modification of earlier knowledge through the elimination of untruth. The fact that a theory has been frequently corroborated does not make it true.[51]

49. K. R. Popper (1972: 34ff.; 1974: 3ff., 37ff.).

50. More modern philosophers of science regard the criterion of falsifiability as criterion of demarcation inadequate. But refutability is certainly always a necessary feature. See, e.g., A. A. Derksen (1985: 32, 47).

51. K. R. Popper (1972) points out that truth and corroboration (by

In the background of the notion that corroboration makes a theory true, according to Popper, is a false conception of human knowledge. The question "How do you know that?" is often mistakenly conceived as "Where do you get your knowledge; what are the sources of your assertion?" Behind this lies the idea that a person can arrive at certain knowledge *(epistêmê)* provided he consults the right source (*interpretatio* originally meant "spelling out" rather than the subjective kind of "reading" — Popper, *Conjectures and Refutations,* p. 13), hence that man can arrive at truth by appealing to the right external authority. An assertion would then be true if it stemmed from the right authority. For antiquity and the middle ages, that was God and Aristotle; after the Renaissance they were replaced by reason (Descartes) and the senses (Bacon). Accordingly, despite its anti-traditionalism the Enlightenment remained faithful to the same epistemology: that of *a revelation model of human knowledge.* It is wrong, thinks Popper, because human knowledge is never *epistêmê* (knowledge in terms of Plato) but always *doxa* (uncertain opinion). we must inquire after truth but always in the awareness that it always transcends human knowing. The sources of our knowledge are many, the most important being tradition, but none has absolute authority. The epistemology of the ultimate sources of our knowledge — God, nature, or reason — is mistaken because all knowledge is fallible and every source is open to critical investigation. The question "How do you know that; what are the sources of your knowledge?" necessarily results in an authoritarian answer. The right question is therefore: "How can we hope to detect and eliminate error?"

---

empirical evidence) are absolutely different concepts. One can never say that something that was correct yesterday is incorrect today. If a person denies today what he affirmed yesterday, he was [probably] wrong yesterday: he wrongly accepted an assertion as true yesterday. "Truth" is a timeless, non-empirical, and logical concept. "Corroboration" is not. One can very well say that up until yesterday an assertion was confirmed but no longer stands up today. Corroboration always applies to a system of basic assertions or propositions that were accepted at a given time. "Corroboration is therefore not 'a truth value'; that is, it cannot be placed on a par with the concepts 'true' and 'false' (which are free from temporal subscripts)" (p. 275).

(p. 25). That can be achieved only by criticizing our assertions, says Popper. He, therefore, has no objections to faith in authorities *behind* knowledge: on the contrary, knowledge does not originate in a vacuum and all knowledge builds on earlier knowledge, and faith in absolute truth safeguards the interests of knowledge. But he denies that we can arrive at reliable knowledge in any way other than by critical inquiry.

Popper also demonstrates[52] that the epistemology of the ultimate sources of our knowledge rests on a logical error. Its fundamental idea, viz., that the truth of an assertion can be decided by examining its source, is based on a confusion between the meaning of words (terms) and the truth of assertions. The meaning of terms does depend on their origin, i.e., with the situation in which they were originally defined or learned by us. The meaning of terms has to do with the truth of the assertions in which they occur insofar as an assertion can only be understood when the terms in it have meaning. But meaningful, intelligible assertions need not be true. It may even be impossible to demonstrate their truth. Definitions of terms *(meaning)* have nothing to do with the truth of assertions because they add nothing to our factual knowledge. Defining does not equal testing. One can, therefore, say that the theory of the ultimate sources of our knowledge mistakenly conceives a criterion of testing as a criterion of meaning.[53]

Now back to the appeal to revelation. There can be no doubt that the testing criteria in theology and philosophy are different from those in the empirical sciences. But this does not detract in any way from Popper's basic idea that testing does not occur by reference to the source of the knowledge in question. By testing I mean the examination of positions in light of logical and material criteria that all people share. That is done by employing

52. K. R. Popper (1972/1963: 35ff.).
53. The verificationists conceive verification, their criterion of testing, at the same time as their criterion of meaning. Only assertions that can be verified are said to be meaningful. According to Popper non-testable assertions, say religious assertions, may very well be meaningful. An example of a non-sensical assertion is "Socrates is not identical." K. J. Popper (1972: 67, note 6).

arguments that do not need an appeal to external authorities to be true. And conversely, appeal to authorities alone is not a fully satisfactory form of argumentation.[54] We are exclusively dependent on the sources only for historical knowledge. To the degree religious knowledge is of a historical nature, the appeal to the source, which is Scripture, is therefore a valid test. But when it concerns knowing what God's will for us is, such an appeal will not suffice. The intent of our appealing to Scripture in ethics is to appeal to revelation. But revelation is always a criterion for the origin of knowledge. And because in all matters of a non-historical nature (also in moral matters, therefore) our reference to the source is not a test but an appeal to an external authority, only one conclusion is possible: also in moral issues an appeal to revelation does not mean the kind of test that could serve as a substitute for moral deliberation in the human community. And, therefore, the fact that the Bible forbids homosexual intercourse is not the whole story.

(b) *The indispensability of testing* (in the Popperian sense). It is true that the prohibition of homosexuality has always been viewed as part of the knowledge of faith; it was a part of the *fides quae creditur* (the faith that is believed). And Christians regarded it as the fruit of revelation. That is a confessional statement. But those who view the appeal to Scripture as the test of moral positions take a further step. They view faith-inspired positions as the knowledge of a set of revealed truths. Thereby they adopt the epistemologically untenable revelation model of knowledge. Knowledge, however, is never revealed but always consists in the form of fallible assertions that have stood up under the test of the best knowledge available. That also applies to faith-inspired assertions: if the concept of "knowledge" is applicable, they are true, not because of their supposed "revealedness" but as a result of having stood up under testing and their truth is provisional. Accordingly, the dilemma posed by Velema, "Enlightenment or Revelation," is not correct. That dilemma is based on the presupposi-

54. Cf. H. M. Kuitert (1977: 58ff.); esp. for ethical argumentation, G. Manenschijn (1985: 42ff.).

tion that *either* man *or* God is the source of knowledge of good and evil. My position is that it is not contradictory to view God as the ultimate source of all good and at the same time to underscore the necessity of checking out normative positions against the reality known to us. I will come back to this position under (c). In any case, the dilemma "Enlightenment vs. Revelation" relates to the question concerning the sources of knowledge. That was the problem advanced by the Enlightenment, but the dilemma thus posed now no longer structures our epistemology.

Linked up with this is a second point. An appeal to revelation, therefore, implies designating the source of our knowledge but not the fact of its having been tested. But how convincing is this argument from the theory of science to those who appeal to the divine authority of Scripture? On their view, we meet there the self-revealing God who has made known his eternal will. This then describes the source of knowledge, Scripture and its truth. Now it is obvious that an argument from the theory of science cannot be refuted with a theological argument. But one can, therefore, still view it as irrelevant: for the knowledge of God's will we need only the Scriptures, not the philosophy of science. We can easily refute that argument, however, by showing that one does not come out well without testing in the Popperian sense, not even when this is explicitly denied.

For a demonstration of this, consider Douma's use of Scripture. He wants to avoid the "atomistic" use of Scripture — no biblicism.[55] Even though the boundary between what can and what cannot function can never be precisely indicated, he says, we are not without a criterion: the ability, given with the maturity we have in Christ, to discern what is best (Phil. 1:10). The following examples furnished by Douma show how this criterion functions. Many agrarian and civil laws, apart from their time and place in Israel, no longer apply to us. They are outdated, even though as the once-spoken word of God they do retain their "substance" (p. 63). On the other hand the agrarian laws of ancient Israel might possibly function again in our day but only after the environmental

55. J. Douma (1983: 60).

crisis has forced us to deal more sensitively with these passages (p. 61). Among Christians slavery was not abolished until late, not because Scripture is unclear, but because we were lacking in discernment (p. 65). About the relation between authorities and subjects, master and servant, husband and wife we think differently than Paul because the forms have changed, not however the structures (p. 68). But homosexuality remains wrong: it is impermissible to appeal to the biblical theme of love where one no longer knows what to do with the individual biblical texts.

This is hardly consistent and that is significant. The conclusion can only be that it depends on our insight whether a stipulation is antiquated. When this insight is lacking, so will sensitivity, and vice versa. In other words the only conceivable criterion by which to judge whether a biblical stipulation has to do with God's will for us is our insight into good and evil. Why? Because logically there is always a criterion at stake between the assertion "this is what the Bible says" and the judgment "that is God's will for us." And where does it come from? We frame it ourselves, even when the criterion is, in turn, derived from the Bible.[56] That criterion decides which passages can and which cannot be considered suitable for a "biblical" view.[57] Although there are grounds for the choice of criterion, those grounds must first be justified before we can equate the observation "this is what the Bible says" with the normative statement "that is God's will." Those grounds can be no other than our insight into good and evil, granted that in our western tradition this insight has also been shaped by Scripture.

Indeed, for Christians the ultimate and only guarantee of the truth of their assertions about God and his will is its origin in God. But we cannot discover this truth without testing it by generally acceptable logical and objective criteria. Neither can Douma. The only difference is that he proceeds from a prior position without justifying it. The reason for that is that his view of testing as checking against Scripture prevents him from seeing the necessity of justification.

56. Cf. H. M. Kuitert (1977: 62–63).
57. Cf. H. M. Kuitert (1981a: 72, 79).

This conclusion can be further highlighted with the aid of Velema's position. Whereas Douma stresses that we often lack the sensitivity to discern in Scripture what is best in a given situation, in Velema it is even clearer that no one arrives at a solution without testing his ideas *by the world of experience.* True, he denies this: he firmly rejects the idea that one does not have to be a Christian to know what is permissible and what is not.[58] However, this does not alter the fact, he says, that Christians also often wonder whether and when their action is in accord with the will of God. But there is a way out. A Christian can test whether a given action accords with the will of God by putting God's commandment alongside his situation and by then taking a decision in full personal responsibility. So the belief that a given action is the will of God is a person's own conclusion and, therefore, there is indeed a possibility of being mistaken, of passing off as the will of God something that, in retrospect, proves to have been our own will. But this does not take a person back to square one. For God's commandment, known in the light of Christ, is characterized, among other things, by the well-being it envisages. Certainly one may not determine what is good by worldly standards, i.e., from a self-centered perspective. What *God* commands is by definition good for people, not vice versa. One can only see the good of the commandment if one follows Jesus. But then [obedience to] the commandment results in happiness, whereas disobedience results in ruin, according to Velema.[59]

In brief, what he says is that a Christian must test his situation by the will of God. In this process, as may be evident in retrospect, he may err. The question is: By what evidence must one conclude there was a mistake? The key is Velema's comment[60] that the commandment results in happiness, whereas disobedience produces ruin. As examples of the latter, Velema mentions the con-

58. W. H. Velema (1987: 23) incorrectly suggests that the consequence of saying that one need not be a Christian to know what is good is that we cannot say anything meaningful about the will of God.

59. W. H. Velema (1983, and esp. 1987: 22–34).

60. W. H. Velema (1987: 30).

sequences of divorce, alcohol, and drug abuse. That is interesting. Because, first, we now have to do with ordinary teleological-ethical reasoning in terms of the consequences of one's actions: doing God's will results in good, and when the consequences are bad, a person can conclude he was not dealing with the commandment of God. Velema, it turns out, therefore regards the testing of God's commandment by the world of experience both possible and necessary! The reason is that, though we know the will of God with certainty (from Scripture), we can err in applying it to our situation. But, second, and now it gets really interesting: Suppose it says a divorce — which is forbidden in Scripture — in certain cases proved not to be ruinous at all. If, from the consequences, one can deduce whether or not we have to do with the will of God, Velema's reasoning that we know it only from Scripture (hence: no divorce) completely hangs in the air. In any case, if Velema concedes that we recognize God's will by the good that follows from it, he must at the same time admit that a person must, therefore, first know what (a) good or (an) evil is before he says: this is, or is not, the will of God!

Now let us for a moment apply this conclusion to Douma's and Velema's condemnation of homosexual intercourse. If there is a chance we are lacking in sensitivity or if we can err, why could that not be the case when we deem the biblical condemnation applicable to the modern situation? According to Velema the answer is: because the Bible prohibits homosexuality (a) and we recognize God's prohibition by the fact that homosexuality is an evil (b). But how does he know the latter? Because he proceeds from it as his point of departure. But why does he proceed from it and why does he not test his position? Because his epistemology will not let him: testing, to Velema, is testing the situation by the standard of revelation. He, therefore, has no room in which to unfold the arguments he subscribes to for the position he already held before the testing began. In this manner, what are actually two questions are reduced to one: the question "How do you know what is good?" On the one hand, that is to ask about the origin of the knowledge of the good; for Christians that is God and to demonstrate this is what Douma and Velema call testing. On the other hand, it is to ask "How do you know that something is really good; how do you avoid passing off as good (and as the will of God!) what is not good?" That is what Popper calls testing. But this latter question does not come into its own in the work of the two theologians. And precisely there lies the crucial point in the ecclesiastical discussion on homosexuality. People appeal to the Bible to reinforce the very position they were convinced of before making the appeal, *First, however, we must test these positions by moral deliberation in the human community as a whole.*

The mode of thinking I have criticized is not necessarily linked with conservative ethics: the liberation theologians Hirs and Brouwer do the same thing. There is no objection to viewing "coming out" as an Exodus-experience (and, therefore, as the will of God) and being gay as a calling in the church, as they do, but only after it has been determined by testing in accordance with the instruments of ethics that gay liberation is a good thing. But they condemn that procedure as reprehensible "natural theology."

We have now found the following. (1) Epistemologically, testing is something other than asking about the origin of knowledge. (2) An appeal to revelation means asking about that origin. (3) There is no objection to this but, as we saw, it does not produce a final answer. A criterion is needed for distinguishing between the statement "in Scripture x is forbidden" and the assertion "x is against God's will." We find that only by testing in terms of our moral awareness of good and evil. The premise "x is wrong" is inescapable, therefore, if we are to conclude that "x is against God's will." Or "x is wrong" is a necessary condition for "x is against God's will." Accordingly, that is the reason moral positions are prior to the appeal to revelation.

From the above only one conclusion can be drawn: for the knowledge of good and evil knowledge of God is not necessary, and, conversely, for the determination of whether or not we are dealing with God's will our insight into good and evil is the only criterion. In saying this we have simultaneously made our choice in the Euthyphro-dilemma. A thing is God's will because it is good: that is the unavoidable conclusion. And therefore, to discover the will of God, we just need to follow the path of moral deliberation in the human community as a whole, as we did in Chapter III. However, this is not to say that the other position, viz., that a thing is good because God wills it, is incorrect;[61] for that reason I hold to an intermediate position with regard to that dilemma. I will return to it in a moment. But in the meantime we can say here that in taking that second position we are talking about another question than that of testing normative positions: the question concerning the origin of the good. According to the Christian confession, all that is good derives from God. That insight, however, does not make moral argumentation unnecessary; on the contrary, it underscores the necessity of moral deliberation.

(c) *The knowledge of God's will.* To many Christians this conclusion is unacceptable. They object to it on religious grounds. They think that for Christians the question concerning right action is always an issue of faith (James 1) and, therefore, normative assertions are assertions of faith. From this it follows, in their opinion, that norms, in order to be acceptable to Christians, have to be justified on religious grounds (i.e., with arguments derived from biblical texts). Where this is not done God is left outside the knowledge of good and evil.

Here, in my opinion, we face the most basic reason for resistance to the grounding of norms via moral deliberation in the human community as a whole. But such Christians are mistaken, as we will see. It is true: for Christians normative positions are statements of faith, but this does not mean that such positions have to be justified in religious *terms.*

The first misconception that may be involved is of a logical kind. First let us get our definitions straight. There are norms stated in religious or theological terms (concepts), like "we should do the will of God"; "we ought to follow Jesus"; "it is our duty to proclaim the gospel to everyone," etc. There are also norms stated without such terms, such as "killing is wrong." I will not discuss here the difference between moral and religious norms; all assertions mentioned that have the words "should," "ought," or "good"

---

61. Cf. H. M. Kuitert (1987: 44): "For Christians the moral problem therefore is not knowing (non-Christians know it too) but doing."

in them can be regarded as morally normative assertions. Now the logical misconception is that a norm "*x* is right" is already justified when it is legitimated by means of theological premises and can, e.g., be stated in terms of "the Bible says . . . ." In this option theological or "biblical" arguments constitute sufficient justification. Why is this a misconception? Well, undoubtedly, for the justification of norms containing theological *terms* theological premises are needed. After all, such terms are defined in theology and they have their meaning in the framework of religion. But from this it does not follow that theological terms by themselves are adequate for the justification of norms. It is simply the case that fundamental ethical terms, such as "ought," "duty," or "good," cannot be defined in terms of God's will,[62] unless the concept "God" has been described so as to include the good as a component,[63] but then we end up with a tautology: good is what is good. Fundamental ethical concepts cannot be reduced to concepts of another kind. Accordingly, Christians and non-Christians alike use them in the same sense: for purposes of prescription, recommendation, etc. The respect in which they differ concerns the content of what is prescribed or recommended in them: doing God's will or something else.[64] This does not mean more, however, than that the rationale underlying the norms stated in religious terms differs from those without these terms; but not that then the concrete guidelines-for-action (explications) of believers and non-believers will differ.[65] And it is these that must be justified, and that by appraisal of their being good, which is what occurs in moral

62. Such definitions are refuted by what G. E. Moore called the "open question test"; see H. G. Hubbeling (1971: 34–35).

63. The Christian tradition speaks of God as the Perfectly Good One. For an elaboration, see D. E. Villiers (op. cit.: 135ff.).

64. G. Outka (1973: 233): "The believer has antecedently a meaning in using the word duty which he shares with non-believers, and which he continues to use for the purpose of commendation. His criterion of application differs in this instance. He is in agreement about the general public meaning of the word, and he uses it in the same way as non-believers. It is what he commends that is distinctive."

65. For the terminology, see Ch. III § D.

317

deliberation. From this it follows that norms not stated in religious terms can certainly not be justified with theological premises alone. While religious convictions do play a role in the formation of moral judgments,[66] ethical judgments are not logically dependent on them.[67]

The rationale underlying the norms that Christians endorse, therefore, differs from that of non-Christians. For them a moral demand is a demand from God. Hence for Christians there is always the additional context of the will of God. But is it true that therefore further objective differences between Christians and non-Christians will naturally follow? The answer depends on the theological question: How do we know God's will? The prior position of Christians is always: We know God's will and on that basis we prescribe, recommend, etc. The question can also be stated as follows: Is a normative assertion a faith-assertion only when and because it can be stated in religious terms ("the Bible says . . .")? (It then necessarily follows that normative questions are questions that must be solved by theology.) Many Christians answer in the affirmative — and I will repeat their reasoning: We do not start by asking what is good or evil but by asking what is or is not the will of God (a); we can only know God's will from his revelation in Scripture (b); therefore, we have to do what Scripture tells us. In this option theological premises constitute a *necessary* condition for justifying the assertion "*x* is God's will." The crucial link here is premise (b). It states that we can only know the will of God if we know God. Knowing God is the condition for knowing the will of God. From this it follows that in order to know the will of God, *a distinct way of obtaining knowledge (Du: een aparte kenweg) is* needed.

But is that true? I want to address this issue in two ways: (1) in terms of the testability of assertions about God and (2) in terms of testing assertions about the will of God.

(1) *Testability.* I grant that to have knowledge of God's will is to have knowledge of God. Knowledge of God naturally assumes

---

66. H. M. Kuitert (1984: 211ff.).
67. That is the conclusion of W. K. Frankena (1973, spec. 302–6).

the existence of God and that of a God who makes himself known. All (true) knowledge of God has its origin in God. Without God, even without God's initiative, knowledge of God is impossible. The fact that God has made himself known is expressed in theology by the concept of "revelation." That term conveys the condition for, and possibility of, the knowledge of God, i.e., God is antecedent to our faith and our discourse about God. God's act of revealing himself means that he is the source or cause of our faith. God's act of revealing himself in Jesus means there is a ground, a cognitive reason, for believing in him.[68] From this it follows that the concept of "revelation" deserves the status of a criterion of meaning in the sense indicated earlier: given this "revelation," speaking about God is meaningful in our language and assertions about God are meaningful assertions. But precisely *because* they are meaningful assertions they depend for their truth on being tested (in the Popperian sense): by human experience of the world of nature and history. Accordingly, we have to choose. One cannot, on the one hand, use the appeal to revelation to make clear that God is knowable — thereby implying that assertions about God are testable — and on the other that God can only be known via the way of revelation because this implies that assertions about God are *not* testable; this would come down to the model of revealed truths, or "propositional truths" (a model considered refuted in theology[69]). Not only is this logically contradictory but it overlooks the fact that revelation is by definition what people consider to be such. Not God, but our assertions about God, are subjected to appraisal by testing of the Popperian kind.[70] That is what Douma and Velema overlook. The problem with a distinct way of knowing, therefore, again comes down to the fact that the answer to the question concerning the origin of the knowledge of God is equated with the answer to the question concerning the testing of our assertions about God. The notion of a

68. See H. M. Kuitert (1977: 95–96), who relates this distinction between cause and source or ground of faith to H. Bavinck's distinction between *principium internum* (the Spirit) and *principium externum* (Scripture).

69. See J. A. Montsma (1985: 77; cf. also pp. 113ff., spec. 121–23) about "the right to be convinced."

70. See the arguments of H. M. Kuitert (1977: 108).

distinct way of knowing — revelation — is a product of a mistaken epistemology concerning the ultimate sources of knowledge.

(2) *Testing.* God is, therefore, knowable but assertions about God require testing. God's will is the norm for our assertions about God's will. But how do we know God's will? From the Scriptures, say Douma and Velema, because God has revealed himself in his Word and that, therefore, is the touchstone. But now we must make a careful distinction. There is a big difference between knowing *of* God's will (because we have the Scriptures) and knowing *what* God's will is in a concrete situation; in short, between knowing the *that* and knowing the *what.* Knowledge of the Scriptures and the Christian tradition is a condition for knowing that we have grounds for speaking of *God's* will, but not, once we have learned to know God, for knowing what God's will is in a specific situation. To cite a simple example: we daily have to do with the laws of nature even if we do not know they have been formulated in physics. One does not have to know physics to know, i.e., to experience, the laws of nature, and ignorance of physics does not cancel out our being subject to the laws of nature. Knowing has its own order, which differs from the order of being.[71] Believing that God is the creator of all trees does not mean that we can only know a tree if we know God. In the same way we can also know the good (God's will) without knowing God; one does not need to know God to know the will of God. Unfamiliarity with God, i.e., not knowing God, does not imply not knowing the will of God. Accordingly the former does not exclude the possibility that people do God's will without knowing God. For that reason one does not need theology to know the will of God.

This conclusion is further highlighted by the following argument. The belief that God has revealed himself does not imply that everything he has revealed can be expressed in theological premises.[72] Theology is a discipline, one among others, with limited expertise, like every other field of knowledge; it is the

71. H. M. Kuitert (1985: 36–40); H. G. Hubbeling (1971: 41).
72. W. K. Frankena (1973: 308ff.) who also furnishes the first argument.

discipline that judges what people say, or refrain from saying, about God. Admittedly God has to do with all aspects of reality; he is, according to the Christian confession, the Power over all things. But in the investigation of reality the subject of God does not always and everywhere come up. Only to the extent that he does come up for discussion is theology competent to speak. However, if God does not or cannot come up for discussion, this in no way means that God is not involved. Physics, philosophy, and ethics are also "creations of God" (Schillebeeckx). The fact that God need not come up in moral deliberation in which right and wrong are defined, accordingly, does not mean that God is uninvolved in the knowledge of good and evil but only that for the knowledge of good and evil the appeal to God's will (= Scripture) is not necessary. There is, therefore, nothing unchristian about believing that God makes his will (= the good) known by way of moral deliberation.

Linked with this is the following point. As we saw earlier, between "the Bible says" and "it is the will of God" there is always an interpretation that yields a criterion. It is a fact of experience that ours often differs from that of earlier generations. The reason is that interpretation is necessarily a human activity by which, via whatever reasoning process, norms are indicated in Scripture that are subsequently elevated to the status of the divine will. Accordingly, it is totally arbitrary to regard this human activity (by which we find answers in Scripture to *our* questions) in keeping with the will of God but not the results of moral deliberation in the human community as a whole.[73] In the process we do indeed frequently, at least sometimes, come into conflict with the letter of certain biblical texts. But this is also true, as we saw, for Douma and Velema. It is true that in Scripture homosexual intercourse is prohibited. But is it against God's will? Gay liberation theology has shown us how we can read the Bible differently. Only without supplementary ethical argumentation its use of Scripture no more constitutes justification for its normative positions than that of

73. Cf. D. E. de Villiers' criticism (op. cit.: 166–74) of Barth's position on knowing the will of God.

Douma for his position. And, as we saw, this argumentation was also lacking there.

Meanwhile, the idea that knowledge of God — and hence of the Christian tradition — is not necessary for the knowledge of God's will is also a theological position. Theology accounts for it with the classic conception of General and Special Revelation, in the confession of God as Creator in distinction from God as Redeemer. Thereby it refers to two distinct ways in which, in different matters, man can know God.[74] It, therefore, takes theology to make clear that ethics does not need theology. Knowing what is permissible and what is not does not need the appeal to Scripture for it to be from God. Normative positions need generally recognized moral premises to be valid, but this does not mean God is not involved. In other words there is no necessary opposition between what people, in their best judgment, consider good and the will of God. That is a theological position. So theology is involved, not as the epistemological source of the knowledge of good and evil, but to make clear that morality is the will of God. For the *what* of morality more is needed than theology: moral education, a capacity for critical thinking, rational argumentation, etc.

This conclusion, viz., that theologically speaking the appeal to revelation (Scripture) is not necessary for the knowledge of good and evil, corresponds with the earlier conclusion that, epistemologically speaking, the appeal to revelation, which implies an appeal to the origin of our knowledge, is insufficient for the justification of normative positions. But this does not make theological discussion redundant. The fact that something is good is the only conceivable criterion for determining whether we have to do with God's will, but this does not mean that the assertion "*x* is good" exhausts the meaning of "*x* is God's will." For Christians the designation "God" carries a larger meaning than the word "good." It includes trust, hope, final ground, etc. Precisely what the word "God" covers is the meat of theological discussion, a discussion about models of revelation. But it never takes the place of moral argumentation.

74. To say it with Calvin (*Institutes* II, II, § 13): in earthly and heavenly things.

(d) *Homosexuality and faith in God.* Christians, as a matter of course, appeal to the Bible for their position on homosexuality, be it pro or con. It is for them a faith position, after all, and people are eager to see it supported by the Bible. In this case that support is lacking. But a divergent viewpoint does not, for that reason, cease to be a faith-position; it need not, by every possible means, e.g., by a twisted exegesis, find its legitimation in the Bible. Theologically speaking, for the knowledge of the good, hence of the content of the will of God, no distinct way of knowing (viz., Revelation vs. our experience) is needed. Nor is there a revealed, uniquely Christian concept of what is "against nature," on the basis of which Christians condemn homosexual intercourse. The issue of homosexuality cannot be settled one way or another on the level of the different models of revelation, of views on the authority of Scripture, or of exegesis and hermeneutics — in short, by theological discussion — but only by deliberation in the human community as a whole. This conclusion may be a problem for those Christians who think they get their position from the Bible instead of — as is actually the case — finding in the Bible a position handed down to them by tradition. Such Christians, as we have seen, are mistaken. Among Christians there is indeed much difference about how homosexual intercourse should be assessed. This difference stems, not primarily from differences in theological position — though they may contribute to it — but from differences in acquaintance with the phenomenon of homosexuality as well as the phenomenon of morality. As soon as this is clear, the formulation by the churches of a positive position on homosexual intercourse need no longer present problems. In summarizing this chapter I will once more list the theological arguments for such a position.

Chapter III demonstrated that the moral objections to homosexual intercourse do not stand up. This leaves the religious objections. What if someone believes from the bottom of his heart that God himself has forbidden it? Our discussion of the "proofs" for this belief yielded the following. True: for the authors of Scripture homosexuality is sin. Moreover, the Bible nowhere suggests a more positive viewpoint (§ B). Now the issue is not decided for any Christian by exegesis alone. The understanding of texts is always mediated by interpretive frameworks. I called them models of revelation, the different theological conceptions of how we know God. It turned out that theologians with roughly the same model arrive at opposing ethical conclusions regarding homosexuality and that scholars having different models defended the same ethical position. This permits only one conclusion: in reality moral positions are antecedent to the appeal to revelation (§ C). There is a compelling reason for this, as we saw. A well-founded moral judgment requires testing (1). Epistemologically speaking, testing is something other than an appeal to the origin of knowledge (2). But an appeal to revelation always means an appeal to its origin: God (3). This does not yield a final conclusion, however, because in order to distinguish between what the Bible says and what is really the will of God for us (= "biblical" in the normative sense) a criterion is always needed (4). That criterion can be no other than testing what is good and what is bad by the world of experience. Accordingly, this is how theologians work, even conservative ones like Douma and Velema (5). Thus our best judgment of what constitutes good and evil is the criterion by which to tell what is and what is not the will of God (6). The Bible is not, therefore, a necessary condition for knowing what good and evil is. Accordingly, that is why moral positions are antecedent to the appeal to revelation (7). In taking this position we are not placing human insight above divine Revelation: the fact that the Bible is not indispensable for knowing what good and evil is does not mean that God is uninvolved in the knowledge of good and evil. But one does not need to know God by way of the Scriptures in order to know his will (which is the good). In classic theology this is accounted for by the distinction between General and Special Revelation (8).

Our conclusion, therefore, has to be that theology does not need to play a role in the formulation of moral guidelines (that is the task of ethics, the discipline in which systematic reflection on morality takes place) without ethical assertions thereby ceasing to be assertions of faith. The function of an appeal to Scripture is to reinforce the position one finds convincing before making that appeal. There is no objection to making such an appeal provided one's position has first been tested in moral deliberation within the human community as a whole. When this is omitted, one's position remains untested and continues to be a pre-judgment or a prejudice. This is what has happened in the church's discussions on homosexuality: they touch on a wide assortment of theological issues but the real question, a well-grounded position on homosexuality, has disappeared behind the horizon (§ D).

In short: there is every reason to remove the homosexuality issue permanently from the church's agendas as a moral and religious, i.e., as a *scientific,* problem. And then? As Wittgenstein put it toward the end of his *Tractatus:* "We feel that even if *all possible* scientific questions can be answered, the problems of life have still not been touched at all" (6.52).

Bibliography

Aalders, W. J., Handboek der ethiek. Amsterdam, 1947².

Aardweg, G. J. M. van den, Homofilie, neurose en dwangzelfbeklag. Een psychologische theorie over homofilie, toegelicht met een analyse van leven en werk van André Gide. Amsterdam, 1967.

——, Geaardheid of scheefgroei? Een psychologische kijk op homofilie. Brugge, 1984.

——, Das Drama des gewöhnlichen Homosexuellen. Analyse und Therapie. Neuhausen/Stuttgart, 1985.

Aardweg, G. J. M. van den, en J. Bonda, Een netelig vraagstuk. Nykerk, 1981.

Achterhuis, H., De markt van welzijn en geluk. Baarn 1979.

Acton, H. B., Kant's Moral Philosophy. In: W. D. Hudson (1974): 305–78.

Aertsen, J. A., Natura en creatura. De denkweg van Thomas van Aquino. Amsterdam, 1982.

Altman, D., C. Vance, M. Vicinus, J. Weeks, et al., Homosexuality, Which Homosexuality? London/Amsterdam, 1989.

Anscombe, G. E. M., Intention. Oxford, 1976².

Arntz, J. Th. C., Die Entwicklung des naturrechtlichen Denkens innerhalb des Thomismus. In: F. Böckle (Hrgb.) (1966): 87–122.

Asperen, G. M., De goede maatschappij. Inleiding in de sociale filosofie. Assen, 1978.

Augustine, A., The City of God. New York, 1983.

Baerends, G. P. (red.), Ethologie, de biologie van gedrag. Wageningen, 1973, 1980.

————, Geprogrammeerd leren, seksuele identiteit en partnerkeuze. In: Tijdschrift voor psychiatrie 22, 7/8 (1980): 447–62.

Bailey, D. S., Homosexuality and the Western Christian Tradition. London, 1955.

Barnhoorn, J. A. J., Het vraagstuk der homosexualiteit, beschouwingen samengevoegd vanwege de R. K. Artsenvereniging naar aanleiding van het congres 1939 te Nijmegen. Roermond, 1941.

Barth, K., Church Dogmatics III.1, III.2, III.4. Edinburgh.

Batchelor, E. (ed.), Homosexuality and Ethics. New York, 1980.

Becker, J., Zum Problem der Homosexualität in der Bibel. In: Zeitschrift für Evangelische Ethik 31, 1 (1987): 36–59.

Beach, F. A. (ed.), Human Sexuality in Four Perspectives. London, 1976.

————, Cross-species Comparisons and the Human Heritage. In: Archives of Sexual Behavior 5, 5 (1976): 469–85.

————, Animal Models for Human Sexuality. In: Ciba Foundation (1979): 113–31.

Beek, A. Van de, Why? On Suffering, Guilt, and God. Grand Rapids, 1990.

Beemer, Th., Sodomie in de geschiedenis van de kerkelijke zedenleer. In: Tenminste 4 (1982): 41–56.

————, De fundering van de seksuele moraal in een door God ingestelde morele orde. Analyse en commentaar op grond van enkele recente kerkelijke documenten. In: Th. Beemer, A. G. M. van Melsen, C. E. M. Struyker Boudier, P. Voestermans, J. Heyke, M. Christiaens, E. Schillebeeckx, Het kerkelijk spreken over seksualiteit en huwelijk. Nijmegen/Baarn (1983): 15–52.

Beld, A. van den, Filosofie van het menselijk handelen. Assen, 1982.

Bell, A. P., en M. S. Weinberg, Het Kinsey-rapport over vrouwelijke en mannelijke homoseksualiteit. Amsterdam/Brussel, 1979 (= Titel: Homosexualities 1978).

Bell, A. P., M. S. Weinberg, and S. K. Hammersmith, Sexual Preference: Its Development in Men and Women. Bloomington, 1981.

Berkhof, H., Christelijk geloof. Inleiding in de geloofsleer. Nijkerk, 1985[5].

Berkouwer, G. C., General Revelation. Grand Rapids, 1962. Dogmatische studien. Kampen.

——, Man: The Image of God. Grand Rapids, 1955. Dogmatische studien. Kampen.

Bieber, I., Clinical aspects of Male Homosexuality. In: J. Marmor (ed.) (1965): 248–67.

Birke, L. I. A., Is Homosexuality Hormonally Determined? In: Journal of Homosexuality 6, 4 (1981): 35–49.

Böckle, F. (Hrgb.), Das Naturrecht im Disput. Düsseldorff, 1966.

——, Fundamentalmoral. München, 1977.

Bockmühl, K., Die Diskussion über Homosexualität in theologischer Sicht. In: Homosexualität in evangelischer Sicht. Wuppertal, 1965.

Bolewski, H., Homosexualität als Problem der evangelischen Ethik. In: T. Brocher et al. (1966): 73–108.

Boer, Th. de, Grondslagen van een kritische psychologie. Baarn, 1980.

Bonhoeffer, D., Ethics. New York, 1962.

Bontekoe, E. H. M., Criminaliteit en geslacht. In: Tijdschrift voor Criminologie 1 (1984): 18–31.

Boswell, J., Christianity, Social Tolerance and Homosexuality. Chicago, London, 1980.

——, Concepts, Experience and Sexuality. In: E. Stein (ed.) (1990): 133–74.

Bovet, Th., Sinnerfültes Anderssein. Seelsorgerliche Gespräche mit Homophilen. Tübingen, 1959.

Brennan, J. M., The Open-texture of Moral Concepts. London/Basingstoke, 1977.

Brillenburg Wurth, G., Het christelijk leven in huwelijk en gezin. Kampen, 1951.

——, Noodlot of schuld. Horizon 16 (1953): 289–94.

Brocher, T. e.a., Plädoyer für die Abschaffung des § 175. Frankfurt, 1966.

Brümmer, V., Wijsgerige begripsanalyse. Eeen inleiding voor theologen en andere belangstellenden. Kampen, 1975.

Burggraeve, R., Zinvolle seksualiteit. 1. Antropologische en bij-belstheologische horizon. Leuven/Amersfoort, 1985.

Calvin, J., Institutes (translated by Ford Lewis Battles). Philadelphia, 1967.

Cecco, J. P. de, Definition and Meaning of Sexual Orientation. In: Journal of Homosexuality 6, 4 (1981): 51–67.

Cecco, J. P. de, and M. G. Shively, From Sexual Identity to Sexual Relationships: a contextual shift. In: Journal of Homosexuality 9, 2/3 (1984): 1–26.

———— (eds.), Origins of Sexuality and Homosexuality. (Reprint of J. of Homosexuality 9, 2/3 (1984).) New York/London, 1985.

Ciba Foundation, Sex, Hormones and Behaviour (symposium). Amsterdam/Oxford/New York, 1979.

Coleman, P., Christian Attitudes to Homosexuality. London, 1980.

————, Gay Christians. A Moral Dilemma. London/Philadelphia, 1989.

Commutator, Homosexualiteit. Amsterdam, 1927.

Congregation for the Doctrine of Faith, Letter to Bishops. The Pastoral Care of Homosexual Persons, 1986. Origins, NC Documentary Service 1986 *16* 22: 378 e.v.

Dannecker, M., Theories of Homosexuality. London, 1981.

Dannecker, M. en R. Reiche, Der gewöhnliche Homosexuelle. Frankfurt, 1974.

D'Arcy, E., "Worthy of worship." A catholic contribution. In: G. Outka and J. P. Reeder (ed.), Religion and morality. New York, 1973.

Dekker, A., Van tolerantie naar acceptatie. De ontwikkeling in het gesprek over homofilie. In: Liefde, lust en leven, Tenminste 4 (1982): 81–93.

Derksen, A. A., Wetenschap of willekeur? Wat is wetenschap. Muiderberg, 1985.

Denniston, R. H., Ambisexuality in Animals. In: J. Marmor (ed.) (1980): 25–40.

Devlin, P., The Enforcement of Morals. Maccabean Lecture in Jurisprudence, 1959.

Diamond, M., Human Sexual Development: Biological Foundations for Social Development. In: F. A. Beach (ed.) (1976): 22–62.

————, Sexual identity, Monozygotic twins reared in discordant sex roles and a BBC follow-up. In: Archives of Sexual Behavior 11, 2 (1982): 181–86.

Dijksterhuis, E. J., De mechanisering van het wereldbeeld. Amsterdam, 1985 (1950).

Dörner, G., Hormones and sexual differentiation of the brain. In: Ciba Foundation (1979): 81–102.

Douma, J., Homofilie. Amsterdam, 1973.

―――, Voorbeeld of gebod? Enkele opmerkingen over het schriftberoep in de ethiek. Kampen, 1983[4].

―――, Homofilie. Kampen, 1984[5].

―――, Aids, meer dan een ziekte. Kampen, 1987.

Downie, R. S., Roles and Values. An Introduction to Social Ethics. London, 1971.

Drayer, N., Seksueel geweld en heteroseksualiteit. Ontwikkelingen in onderzoek vanaf 1968. Onderzoek verricht in opdracht van het ministerie van Sociale zaken en Werkgelegenheid, Directie Coördinatie Emancipatiebeleid, 1984.

Ducasse, C. J., Determinism, freedom and responsibility. In: S. Hook (ed.) (1958): 160–69.

Duintjer, O., Moderne wetenschap en waardevrijheid. In: Th. de Boer en A. J. F. Köbben (red.), Waarden en wetenschap. Polemische opstellen over de plaats van het waardeoordeel in de sociale wetenschappen. Bilthoven, 1974.

Dullaart, L. (samenst.), Interviews met Michel Foucault. Den Haage, 1983[2].

Dulles, A., Models of Revelation. New York, 1983, 1985.

Duyves, M., Bij de meerderjarigheid van homostudies: Nederlandse sociologen over homoseksualiteit 1965–1985. In: Sociologische Gids 32, 5/6 (1985): 332–51.

Duyves, M., G. Hekma, en P. Koelemij (red.), Onder mannen, onder vrouwen. Studies van homosociale emancipatie. Amsterdam, 1984.

Eichrodt, W. Homosexualität-Andersartigkeit oder Perversion? In: Reformatio 12 (1963): 67–82.

Ehrhardt, A. A., and H. F. L. Meyer-Bahlburg, Psychosexual Development: An Examination of the Role of Prenatal Hormones. In: Ciba Foundation (1979): 41–50.

331

————, Effects of Prenatal Hormones on Gender-related Behavior. In: Science 211 (1981): 1312–18.

Emants, Marcellus, Juffrouw Lina. Amsterdam, 1982 (1888).

Enden, H. van Enden, Jos van Ussel als moralist en ethicus. In: J. Kruithof en I. Geurts (red.) (1979): 221–54.

Epstein, S., Gay Politics, Ethnic Identity: The Limits of Social Constructionism. In: E. Stein (ed.) (1990): 239–93.

Familiaris Consortio, 22.10.1981. In: Verlautbarungen des Apostolischen Stule 33 (1981).

Feyerabend, P., Against Method. London, 1975.

Fagothey, A., Right and Reason: Ethics in Theory and Practice. Saint Louis, 1972[5].

Flew, A., Crime or disease? London/Basingstoke, 1973.

Ford, C. S., en F. A. Beach, Vormen van sexueel gedrag. Utrecht/Antwerpen, 1970 (1951).

Foucault, M., History of Sexuality Vol. I. An introduction. New York, 1978.

————, Geschiedenis van de seksualiteit. II. Het gebruik van de lust. Nijmegen, 1984 (oorspr. l'Usage des plaisirs Galimard, 1984).

Frankena, W. K., Is Morality Logically Dependent on Religion? In: G. Outka and J. P. Reeder (eds.), Religion and Morality. New York (1973): 295–317.

————, Ethics. London, 1963, 1973.

Friedman, R. C., F. Wollesen, en R. Tendler, Psychological Development and Blood Levels of Sex Steroids in Male Identical Twins of Divergent Sexual Orientation. In: The Journal of Nervous and Mental Disease 163, 4 (1976): 282–88.

Freud, S., The Standard Edition of the Complete Psychological Works of Sigmund Freud, Vol. VII, "Three Essays on the Theory St. Sexuality, pp. 135–243.

————, Die 'kulturelle' Sexualmoral und die moderne Nervosität. In: S. Freud (1938): 120–39.

————, General Introduction to Psychoanalysis. New York, 1938.

————, Letter to an American mother. 1935. In: M. Ruse (1981): 271.

Futuyuma, D. J., and S. J. Risch, Sexual Orientation, Sociobiology and Evolution. In: Journal of Homosexuality 9, 2/3 (1984): 157–68.

Bibliography

Galagher, J. (ed.), Homosexuality and the Magisterium. Documents from the Vatican and U.S. Bishops 1975–1985. Maryland, 1985.

Gagnon, J. H., and W. Simon, Sexual Deviance. New York/Evanston/London, 1967.

————, Sexual Conduct: The Social Sources of Human Sexuality. Chicago, 1973.

Gartrell, N. K., Hormones and Homosexuality. In: W. Paul e.a. (eds.) (1982): 169–82.

Gedanken und Masstäbe zum Dienst von Homophilen in der Kirche, Vereinigte Evangelisch-Lutherische Kirche Deutschland 1980. In: H. Kentler (Hrsg.) (1983): 62–79.

Gennep, F. O. van, Mensen hebben mensen nodig. Een studie over seksualiteit en nieuwe moraal. Baarn, 1972.

Gezondheidsraad, Advies van de gezondheidsraad inzake homoseksuele relaties met minderjarigen, in het bijzonder met betrekking tot artikel 248bis van het Wetboek van Strafrecht (1969). In: DIC-mappen Homofilie, informatie, onderderzoek en herwaardering. Amersfoort, 1973.

Gonsiorek, J. C., Results of Psychological Testing on Homosexual Populations. In: W. Paul e.a. (eds.) (1982): 71–81.

Gooren, L., The Neuroendocrine Response of Luteinizing Hormone to Estrogen Administration in the Human Is Not Sex-specific but Dependent on the Hormonal Environment. In: Journal of Clinical Endocrinology and Metabolism 63.3 (1986): 589–93.

Gooren, L. J. G., Biomedizinische Theorien zur Entstehung der Homosexualität: eine Kritik. In: Zeitschrift für Sexualforschung 1 (1988a): 132–45.

————, An Appraisal of Endocrine Theories of Homosexuality and Gender Dysphoria. In: Handbook of Sexology. Vol. 6: The Pharmacology and Endocrinology of Sexual Function. Elsevier (1988b): 410–24.

Goossensen, J., en M. Sleutjes, "De homosexuele naaste." In: Homojaarboek 3 (1985): 25–38.

Gould, S. J., The Mismeasure of Man. Harmondsworth, 1984 (1981).

Graaf, J. de, Elementair begrip van de ethiek. Amsterdam, 1974.

Gramick, J. (ed.), Homosexuality in the Priesthood and the Religious Life. New York, 1989.

Green, R., Sex-dimorphic Behaviour Development in the Human: Prenatale Hormone Administration and Postnatal Socialization. In: Ciba Foundation (1979): 59–68.

————, The Sissy Boy Syndrome and the Development of Homosexuality. New Haven/London, 1987.

Greenberg, D. F., The Construction of Homosexuality. Chicago/London, 1988.

Groenewegen, H. Y., Het Donkere Vraagstuk der Sexueele Ethiek. Leiden, 1923.

————, Schijn-wetenschap en schijn-moraal in den strijd over het donker vraagstuk der sexueele ethiek. Leiden, 1928.

Habermas, J., Techniek en wetenschap als ideologie. In: Een keuze uit het werk van Jürgen Habermas. Deventer, 1973 (1968).

————, Erkenntnis und Interesse. Frankfurt am Main, 1975³ (1968).

Hare, R. M., Freedom and Reason. Oxford, 1963.

————, Descriptivism. In: Essays on the Moral Concepts: 55–75. London/Basingstoke, 1972.

————, Pain and evil. In: Essays on the moral concepts. London/Basingstoke, 1972 (= 1972b).

————, Moral Thinking: Its Levels, Method and Point. Oxford, 1981.

Harry, J., Sexual Orientation as Destiny. In: Journal of Homosexuality 10, 3/4 (1985): 111–24.

Hart, H. L. A., Law, Liberty and Morality. Oxford/New York, 1962.

Hays, R. B., Relations Natural and Unnatural: a Response to John Boswell's Exegesis of Romans 1. In: The Journal of Religious Ethics 1 (1986): 184–215.

Hekma, G., De medische fundering van een luchtkasteel. In: Homojaarboek (1981): 49–73.

————, Geschiedenis der seksuologie, sociologie van de seksualiteit. In: Sociologische Gids 32, 5/6 (1985): 352–70.

————, Homoseksualiteit, een medische reputatie. De uitdoktering van de homoseksueel in negentiende-eeuws Nederland. Amsterdam, 1987.

Hempel, C. G., Philosophy of Natural Science. Englewood Cliffs, N.J., 1966.

Hencken, J. D., Homosexuality and Psychoanalysis: Toward a Mutual Understanding. In: W. Paul e.a. (eds.): 121–49.

Hertz, A., W. Korff, T. Rendtorff, en H. Ringeling, Handbuch der christlichen Ethik II. Freiburg/Basel/Wien, 1978.

Heyden, M. van der, De homo is dood, leve de homo. Opvattingen over de identiteit in de homobeweging van de jaren zevetnig. In: Hoojaarboek 2 (1983): 129–49.

Hiltner, S., Homosexuality and the Churches. In: J. Marmor (ed.) 1980: 219–31.

Hinde, R. A., Biological Bases of Human Social Behavior. New York, 1974.

Hirs, F. J., Boekenrubriek. Homosexualiteit en theologie: een overzicht over de afgelopen tien jaar. In: Tijdschrift voor Theologie 22, 2 (1982): 178–93.

Hirs, F. J., en R. Reeling Brouwer, De verlossing van ons lichaam. Tegen natuurlijke theologie. Gravenhage, 1985.

Hirschfield, M., Geschlechtskunde. I. Die körper-seelischen Grundlagen. Stuttgart, 1926.

Hirschler, H., Homosexualität und Pfarrerberuf. Hannover, 1985.

Homofilie, Rapport over gebruik van Schriftgegevens bij vragen rondom homofilie van deputaten kerk en Theologie aan de Generale Synode van de Gereformeerde Kerken in Nederland van Bentheim, 1981. Leusden, 1982.

Homojaarboek 1. Artikelen over emancipatie en homoseksualiteit. Amsterdam, 1981.

Homojaarboek 2. Artikelen over emancipatie en homoseksualiteit. Amsterdam, 1983.

Homojaarboek 3. Artikelen over emancipatie en homoseksualiteit. Amsterdam, 1985.

Homosexualiteit. Nederlands Gesprekcentrum. Publicatie nr. 31. Kampen, 1966.

Homosexualität kirchlicher Mitarbeiter. Bericht des Sonderausschusses für Fragen der Lebensführung kirchlicher Mitarbeiter. In: Niederschrift der Verhandlungen der 19. Landessynode der Ev.-Luth. Landeskirche Hannovers vom 2. bis 5. März 1983, Aktenstück 179:549–63.

Homosexuelle in der Kirche? Ein Text der Theologischen Studienabteilung beim Bund der Evangelkischen Kirchen in der DDR. Berlin, 1985.

Homosexual relationships. A Contribution to Discussion. General Synod Board for Social Responsibility of the Anglican Church (= Gloucester Report). London, 1979.

Homosexuelle und Kirche (HuK), Materialsammlung zu Schwulenpolitischen Themen. Dezember, 1988.

Hoof, J. J. B. M., Symbolisch interactionisme. In: L. Rademaker en H. Bergman (red.), Sociologische stromingen. Utrecht, 1977: 116–45.

Hook, S. (ed.), Determinism and Freedom in the Age of Modern Science. New York/London, 1958.

Hooker, E., Male Homosexuals and Their "Worlds." In: J. Marmor (ed.) (1965): 83–107.

Hooydonk, J. van, De homoseksualiteit voorbij? Eindscriptie Agogischetheologische opleiding van de Katholieke Theologische Hogeschool Utrecht, z.j. (= 1981).

Hooykaas, R., Religion and the Rise of Modern Science. Grand Rapids, 1972.

Houdijk, R., Kerk en homoseksualiteit. In: Tijdscrift voor Theologie 26 (1986): 259–81.

Hoult, Th.F., Human Sexuality in Biological Perspective: Theoretical and Methodological Considerations. In: Journal of Homosexuality 9, 2/3 (1984): 137–55.

Houtepen, A., Toch een christelijke moraal? In: K. U. Gäbler (red.), Geloof dat te denken geeft. Festschrift for Prof. Dr. H. M. Kuitert. Baarn (1989): 102–18.

Hubbeling, H. G., Language, Logic and Criterion. Amsterdam, 1971.

Hudson, W. D. (ed.), New Studies in Ethics. Volume I, Classical Theories. Volume II, Modern theories. London/Basingstoke, 1974.

Hudson, W. D., Modern Moral Philosophy. Second edition. London/Basingstoke, 1983.

Huwelijk, Het., Herderlijk schrijven van de Generale Synode der Nederlandse Hervormde Kerk. Den Haag, 1952.

Huxley, A., Het menselijk bestaan. Amsterdam, 1978 (oorspr. The Human Stituation, London, 1977).

Iersel, J. J. A. van, Veroorzaking van gedrag, ethologisch bezien. In: G. P. Baerends (red.) (1973): 39–78.

Bibliography

Illich, I., Man-vrouw; geslacht en sekse. Baarn, 1984.

Imperato-McGinley, J., L. Guerrero, T. Gautier, en R. E. Peterson, Steroid 5α-reductase Deficiency in Man: An Inherited Form of Male Pseudo-hermaphroditism. In: Science 186 (1974): 1213–15.

In liefde trouw zijn. Pastorale handreiking. Driebergen, 1983.

Instaan voor elkaar. Werkgroep Pastoraat. Dienstencentrum, Leusden, 1982.

Janse de Jonge, A. L. (red.), De homosexuele naaste. Baarn, 1961.

Jellema, C. O., Homoseksualiteit als gekozen bestaansvorm. In: Een mens hoeft niet alleen te blijven. Eeen evangelische visie op homofilie, Baarn (1977): 71–89.

Kallmann, F. J., Twin and Sibship Study of Overt Male Homosexuality. In: American Journal of Human Genetics 4 (1952): 136–46.

Kant, I., Grundlegung zur Metaphysik der Sitten. In: W. Weischedel (ed.), Immanuel Kant, Werke in sechs Bänden, deel IV. Darmstadt, 1957.

———, Kritik der Urteilskraft. In: W. Weischedel (ed.), Vol. V. Darmstadt, 1957.

———, Der Metaphysik der Sitten. In: W. Weischedel (ed.), Vol. IV. Darmstadt, 1957.

Katholieke Raad voor Kerk en Samenleving, Homofielen in de samenleving. Utrecht, 1979.

Keeping Body and Soul Together: Sexuality, Spirituality, and Social Justice. A document prepared for the 203rd General Assembly (1991), by the General Assembly Special Committee on Human Sexuality of the Presbyterian Church (U.S.A.), 1991.

Keil, Rechtfertigung ist aller Ethik Grund. Theologisch-ethische Beurteilung der Homosexualität. In: Ev. Akademie Iserlohn, Homosexualität-Information-Diskussion-Beurteilung. Tagung, (1986): 68–77.

Kentler, H. (Hrsg.), Die Menschlichkeit der Sexualität. München, 1983.

Kempe, G. Th., Maatschappelijke aspecten van homophile. In: A. F. C. Overing (red.) (1961): 45–62.

Kessels, J., De paradox van de vrije wil. In: Filosofie en Praktijk 5, 1 (1984): 19–29.

Kimball-Jones, H., Towards a Christian Understanding of the Homosexual. London, 1967.

Kinsey, A. C., W. B. Pomeroy, and C. E. Martin, Sexual Behavior in the Human Male. Niederteufen, 1948.

Kirsch, J. A. W., and J. E. Rodman, Selection and Sexuality: The Darwinian View of Homosexuality. In: W. Paul e.a. (eds.) (1982): 183–97.

Klos, R., Essentialisme Versus Constructivisme. In: Homologie 9, 6 (1987): 10.

Knijff, H. W. de, Venus aan de leiband. Kampen, 1987.

Koertge, N. (ed.), Philosophy and Homosexuality. Overdruk van J. of Homosexuality 6, 4 (1981). New York/Binghamton, 1985.

Kosnik, A. (ed.), Human Sexuality — New Directions in Catholic Thought. New York-Paramus-Toronto, 1977.

Köster, H., *Phusis*. In: Theological Dictionary of the New Testament. Volume IX. Grand Rapids 1974: 251–77.

Kruithof, J., en I. Geurts (red.), De seksualiteit herzien. Het werk van Jos van Ussel. Deventer, 1979.

Kuhn, T. S., The Structure of Scientific Revolutions. Chicago, 1970[2].

Kuiper, P. C., Neurosenleer. Arnhem, 1968.

―――, Nieuwe neurosenleer. Deventer, 1984.

Kuitert, H. M., Anders gezegd. Een bundel theologische opstellen voor de welwillende lezer. Kampen, 1970.

―――, The Necessity of Faith. Grand Rapids, 1976.

―――, De wil van God doen. In: Ad Interim. Opstellen over eschatologie, apocalyptiek en ethiek, aangeboden aan R. Schippers. Kampen, 1975.

―――, Wat heet geloven? Structuur en herkomst van de christelijke geloofsuitspraken. Baarn, 1977.

―――, Een gewenste dood. Euthanasie en zelfbeschikking als moreel en godsdienstig probleem. Baarn, 1981 (= 1981a).

―――, De rol van de bijbel in de protestantse theologische ethiek. In: Gereformeerd Theologisch Tijdschrift 6 (1981): 65–82 (= 1981b).

―――, Suicide: wat is er tegen? Zelfdoding in moreel perspectief. Baarn, 1983.

―――, Mogelijkheden en onmogelijkheden ten aanzien van homoseksualiteit in de reformatorische kerken. In: Kultuurleven 51, 2 (1984): 76–86.

Kuitert, H. M., Everything is Politics but Politics is not Everything. Grand Rapids, 1986.

Labuschagne, C. J., De bijbel en het probleem van de homofilie. In: Tijdschrift Kerk en Theologie 21, 1 (1970).

Lance, H. D., The Bible und homosexuality. In: American Bapist Quarterly (1989): 140–51.

Lange, F. de, Grond onder de voeten. Burgerlijkheid bij Dietrich Bonhoeffer. Kampen, 1985.

Leiser, B. M., Liberty, Justice and Morals. Contemporary Value Conflicts. Second edition. New York/London, 1979.

Lever, J., Geintegreerde biologie. Utrecht, 1973.

Liefde en sexualiteit. Pastorale handreiking, aanvaard door de Generale Synode der Nederlands Hervormde Kerk. Den Haag, 1972.

Lieshout, M. van, Geen backroom, wel aids: de emancipatie van de Dikke Van Dale. In: Homologie 7, 4 (1985): 8–9.

Little, D., en S. B. Twiss, Basic terms in the study of religious ethics. In: G. Outka en J. P. Reeder (eds.), Religion and Morality. New York (1973): 35–77.

Luykx, P., De veranderde houding van de Nederlandse Katholieken inzake homoseksualiteit, 1930–1980. In: Groniek 6 (1980): 63–75.

Maccoby, E. E., en C. M. Jacklin, The Psychology of Sex Differences. Stanford, 1974.

Macourt, M. (ed.), Towards a Theology of Gay Liberation. London, 1977.

MacIntyre, A., After Virtue. Notre Dame, Ind., 1981.

Manenschijn, G., Spanningen rond christelijk handelen. Sociaal-filosofische benadering van pluraliteit in de ethiek. In: Tijdschrift voor Theologie 23, 2 (1983): 381–402.

———, Reasoning in Science and Ethics. In: B. Musschenga en D. Gosling (eds.), Science Education and Ethical Values. Washington (1985): 37–54.

Marcuse, H., Eros and Civilization. A Philosophical Inquiry into Freud. Boston, 1955.

Maris, C. W., Filosofie en praktijk in de ethiek van Hare. In: Fiolosofie en Praktijk 6, 3 (1985): 137–67.

Marmor, J. (ed.), Sexual Inversion: The Multiple Roots of Homosexuality. New York/London, 1965.

———— (ed.), Homosexual Behavior: A Modern Reappraisal. New York, 1980.

————, Overview: The Multiple Roots of Homosexuality. In: J. Marmor (ed.) (1980): 3–24.

Marshall, J., Pansies, Perverts and Macho Men: Changing Conceptions of Male Homosexuality. In: K. Plummer (ed.) (1981): 133–54.

Mason, S., A History of the Sciences. New York, 1972[12].

Masters, W. H., and V. E. Johnson, Human Sexual Response. Boston, 1966.

Maynard Smith, J., The Concepts of Sociobiology. In: G. S. Stent (ed.) (1978): 23–34.

McIntosh, M., The Homosexual Role. In: K. Plummer (ed.) (1981): 30–33.

McNeill, J. J., The Church and the Homosexual. Kansas City, 1978[3].

————, Taking a Chance on God: Liberating Theology for Gays, Lesbians and Their Lovers, Families and Friends. Boston, 1988.

Melsen, A. G. M. van, Natur und Moral. In: F. Böckle (Hrgb.) (1966): 61–86.

————, Natuurwetenschap en natuur. Nijmegen/Baarn, 1983a.

————, Natuur en norm. Beschouwingen over de natuurwet als zedelijke norm. In: Th. Beemer e.a., Het kerkelijk spreken over seksualiteit en huwelijk. Nijmegen/Baarn, 1983b.

Ménard, G., De Sodom à l'exode. Jalons pour une theologie de la liberation gaie. Québec, 1982.

————, Gay Theology, Which Gay Theology? In: D. Altman et al. (1989): 127–38.

Meyer-Bahlburg, H. F. L., Sex Hormones and Male Homosexuality in Comparative Perspective. In: Archives of Sexual Behavior 6, 4 (1977): 297–325.

————, Homosexual Orientation in Women and Men: a Hormonal Basis? In: J. E. Parsons (ed.) (1980): 105–30.

Mieth, D., Christliche Sexualethik. In: W. Ernst (Hrsg.), Grundlagen und Probleme der heutigen Moraltheologie. Würzburg, 1989.

Mitchell, J., Psychoanalysis and Feminism. Harmondsworth, 1974.

Moberly, E., Homosexuality: a New Christian Ethic. Cambridge, 1983.

Money, J., Genetic and Chromosomal Aspects of Homosexual Etiology. In: J. Marmor (ed.) (1980): 59–74.

⸻, Gender-transposition Theory and Homosexual Genesis. In: Journal of Sex & Marital Therapy 10, 2 (1984): 75–82.

⸻, and A. A. Ehrhardt, Man & Woman, Boy & Girl: Differentiation and Dimorphism of Gender Identity from Conception to Maturity. Baltimore/London, 1982[8] (1972).

⸻, and Ch. Ogunro, Behavorial Sexology: Ten Cases of Genetic Male Intersexuality with Impaired Prenatal and Pubertal Androgenization. In: Archives of Sexual Behavior 3:3 (1974): 181–205.

Montsma, J. A., De Exterritoriale Openbaring. De Openbaringsopvatting achter de fundamentalistische Schriftbeschouwing. Amsterdam, 1985.

Mooy, A., Taal en verlangen. Lacan's theorie van de psychoanalyse. Meppel, 1975.

Müller, W., Homosexualität, eine Herausforderung für Theologie und Seelsorge. Mainz, 1986.

Murphy, J. G., Evolution, Morality, and the Meaning of Life. Totowa, N. J., 1982.

Musschenga, A. W., Noodzakelijkheid en mogelijkheid van moraal. Assen, 1980.

⸻, De bijdrage van de sociobiologie aan moraalwetenschap en ethiek. In: F. B. M. de Waal (red.) (1981): 157–74.

⸻, Relativisme, pluralisme en het gevaar van indoctrinatie. In: A. W. Musschenga (red.), Onderwijs in de natuurwetenschappen en morele vorming. Baarn (1984): 185–205.

Nagel, E., The Structure of Science: Problems in the Logic of Scientific Explanation. London, 1961.

Nagel, Th., Sexual Perversion. In: J. Rachels (ed.), Moral Problems: A Collection of Philosophical Essays. London (1971): 70–83.

Nauta, L. W. (red.), Het neopositivisme in de sociale wetenschappen. Analyse, kritiek, alternatieven. Amsterdam, 1973.

Niebuhr, R., Sexualiteit en godsdienst in het Kinsey-rapport. In: Wending 5/6 (1954): 408–16.

Niesink, R., Bestaat er een biologische basis voor homoseksueel gedrag? In: Homojaarboek 3 (1985): 159–75.

Norman, R., Reasons for Action: A Critique of Utilitarian Rationality. Oxford, 1971.

Over mensen die homofiel zijn. Rapport aan de Generale Synode van Dordrecht 1971/2. Kerkinformatie 1 (1972).

O'Connor, D. J., Aquinas and Natural Law. In: W. D. Hudson (ed.) (1974): I. 79–173.

O'Donovan, O., Discussing Homosexuality with St. Paul: A Theological and Pastoral Approach. In: D. O'Leary (ed.), A Crisis of Understanding. Burlington, Ontario (1988): 51–61.

Overing, A. F. C., G. Th. Kempe, J. Vermeulen, en H. Ruygers, Homosexualiteit. Pastorele Cahiers. Hilversum, 1961.

Outka, G., Religious and Moral Duty: Notes on Fear and Trembling. In: G. Outka en J. P. Reeder (eds.), Religion and morality. New York (1973): 204–51.

Oyen, H. van, Pastorale Bemerkungen zur Homophilie. Zeitschrift für evangelische Ethik 8 (1964): 25-34.

Parsons, J. E. (ed.), The Psychobiology of Sex Differences and Sex Roles. Washington/New York/London, 1980.

Paul, W., J. D. Weinrich, J. C. Gonsiorek, en M. Hotvedt (eds.), Homosexuality: Social, Psychological and Social Issues. Beverly Hills/London/New Delhi, 1982.

Persona Humana, Declaration on Certain Questions Concerning Sexual Ethics. Sacred Congregation for the Doctrine of the Faith, Commentaries, Washington D.C., 1977.

Petersen, A. C., Biopsychological Processes in the Development of Sex-related Differences. In: J. E. Parsons (ed.) (1980): 31–56.

Piper, O. A., The Christian Interpretation of Sex. New York, 1941.

Pittenger, N., What It Means to Be Human. In: M. Macourt (ed.) (1977): 83–90.

Plummer, K., Sexual Stigma: An Interactionist Account. London/Boston, 1975.

———— (ed.), The Making of the Modern Homosexual. London/Melbourne, 1981.

————, Building a Sociology of Homosexuality. In: K. Plummer (ed.) (1981): 17–29.

Polman, S. W. R., Nieuwtestamentische gegevens. In: Over mensen die homofiel zijn (1972): 18–20.

Popper, K. R., The Poverty of Historicism. London, 1901[2].

———, The Logic of Scientific Discovery. London, 1972[6].

———, Conjectures and Refutations: The Growth of Scientific Knowledge. London, 1974[5].

Punge, M., Das gebrochene Tabu. Zu Gang und Stand der Homosexualitäts-Debatte in den Kirchen der DDR. In: G. Grau (Hrsg.), Und diese Liebe auch. Berlin-Ost, 1987.

Quinton, A., Utilitarian ethics. In: W. D. Hudson (ed.) (1974) II:1–118.

Rad, G. von, Genesis: A Commentary. 1973. Göttingen, 1972.

Rado, S., A critical examination of the concept of bisexuality. In: J. Marmor (ed.) (1965): 175–89.

Redactie Homojaarboek 1, Welke homoseksualiteit, welke emancipatie? In: Homojaarboek 1 (1981): 7–18.

Reiche, R., and M. Dannecker, Male Homosexuality in West-Germany — a Sociological Investigation. In: The Journal of Sex Research 13, 1 (1977): 33–53.

Report of the Commission on Human Affairs to the General Convention of the Episcopal Church USA, Office of the Bishop. Providence, R. I., 1991.

Report of RES Committee on homophilia to RES Harare. In: Acts of the Reformed Ecumenical Synod Harare, 1988: 263–94.

Report of the Committee to study homosexuality, Acta Synodi of the Christian Reformed Churches USA, Report 42 (1973): 609–33.

Report to the House of Bishops on Homosexuality. The Osborne Report on Homosexuality 1988. Copy Homo documentation Center, Amsterdam.

Resolutions accepted in 1985, National Association of Evangelicals, Carol Stream, Ill.

Richards, D. A. J., Homosexual Acts and the Constitutional Right to Privacy. In: Journal of Homosexuality 5, 1/2 (1980): 43–65.

Ridderbos, H. N., Aan de Romeinen. Kampen, 1959.

Ridderbos, S. J., Bijbel en homosexualiteit. In: A. L. Janse de Jonge (red.) (1961): 27–43.

———, Het theologisch aspect van de homosexualiteit. In S. J. Ridderbos (red.) (1973): 126–35 (= 1973a).

————, Contra naturam? In: S. J. Ridderbos (red.) (1973): 136–56. (= 1973b).

————, (red.), Psychiatrie en theologie in gesprek. Kampen, 1973.

Riess, B. F., Psychological Tests in Homosexuality. In: J. Marmor (ed.) (1980): 296–311.

Ringeling, H., Theologie und Sexualität. Gütersloh, 1968.

————, Homosexualität. Teil I: Zum Ansatz der Problemstellung in der theologischen Ethik. In: Zeitschrift für Evangelische Ethik 31 (1987): 6–35 (= 1987a).

————, Homosexualität. Teil II: Zur ethischen Urteilsfindung. In: Zeitschrift für Evangelische Ethik 31 (1987): 82–102 (= 1987b).

Roos, S. P. de, De ethiek van de ongehuwde staat. Nijkerk, 1964.

Rosenberg, A., Sociobiology and the Preemption of Social Science. Baltimore/London, 1980.

Roscam Abbing, P. J., Zielszorg aan hen die homosexueel zijn. Het pastoraal aspect. In: H. M. Bolkestein e.a. (red.), Zielszorg aan maatschappelijk getypeerde mensen. 's-Gravenhage, 1959.

Rothuizen, G. Th., Primus usus legis. Studie over het burgerlijk gebruik van de wet. Kampen, 1962.

————, Hoe verder? Ethisch-hermeneutische overwegingen. In: Over mensen die homofiel zijn (1972): 21–22.

Rozendal, S. (red.), Wie ben ik dat ik dit niet doen mag? Ervaringen van homo-theologen in de Gereformeerde Kerken. Kampen, 1987.

Rubin, G., The Traffic in Women: Notes on the "Political Economy" of Sex. In: R. Reiter (ed.), Toward an Anthropology of Women. New York (1975): 157–210.

Ruddick, S., On Sexual Morality. In: J. Rachels (ed.), Moral Problems. A Collection of Philosophical Essays. London (1971): 85–105.

Ruether, R. Radford, Homophobia, Heterosexism, and Pastoral. In: J. Gramick (ed.) 1989: 21–35.

Ruiter, L. de, Veroorzaking van gedrag, fysiologisch bezien. In: G. P. Baerends (red.) (1973): 79–114.

Ruse, M., Sociobiology: Sense or Nonsense? Dordrecht/Boston/London, 1979.

————, Is Science Sexist? Dordrecht/Boston/London, 1981.

————, Are There Gay Genes? Sociobiology and Homosexuality. In: Journal of Homosexuality 6, 4 (1981): 5–34 (= 1981b).

Bibliography

Bibliography

————, Nature/nurture: Reflections on Approaches to the Study of Homosexuality. In: Journal of Homosexuality 10, 3/4 (1985): 141–58.

————, Homosexuality: A Philosophical Inquiry. Oxford, 1988.

Sanders, G., Het gewone en het bijzondere van de homoseksuele leefsituatie, Verslag van een vergelijkend onderzoek bij ruim 500 homo- en heteroseksuele jongens en meisjes. Deventer, 1980[2].

Schelsky, H., Sociologie der sexualiteit. Assen/Amsterdam, 1957.

Schippers, K. A., "De gemeente is er niet aan toe." in: S. Rozendal (red.) (1987): 124–32.

Schippers, R., De gereformeerde zede. Kampen, 1955.

Schofield, M., Sociologische aspecten van de homoseksualiteit. Utrecht/Antwerpen, 1970 (Sociological Aspects of Homosexuality. London, 1965).

Schmidt, G., and E. Schorsch, Psychosurgery of Sexual Deviant Patients: Review and Analysis of New Empirical Findings. In: Archives of Sexual Behavior 10, 3 (1981): 301–23.

Schoeps, H. J., Homosexualität und Bible. In: Zeitschrift für evangelischen Ethik 6 (1962): 369–74.

Scroggs, R., The New Testament and Homosexuality. Philadelphia, 1989[6] (1983).

Scruton, R., Sexual desire. A Philosophical Investigation. London, 1986.

Sengers, W. J., Gewoon hetzelfde? Een visie op vragen rond de homofilie. Bussum, 1968.

————, Homoseksualiteit als klacht. Een psychiatrische studie. Bussum, 1969.

Sexualiteit en moraal. Een rapport, aangeboden aan de Britse raad van Kerken. Amsterdam/Hilversum, 1967 (Sexuality and Morality. The British Council of Churches. London, 1966).

Shively, M. G., and J. P. de Cecco, Components of Sexual Identity. In: Journal of Homosexuality 3, 1 (1977): 41–48.

Siegelman, M., Adjustment of Male Homosexuals and Heterosexuals. In: Archives of Sexual Behavior 2, 1 (1972): 9–25.

————, Psychological Adjustment of Homosexual and Heterosexual Men: A Cross-national Replication. In: Archives of Sexual Behavior 7, 1 (1978): 1–11.

Simon, W., and J. H. Gagnon, Homosexuality: The Formulation of a

Sociological Perspective. In: Journal of Health and Social Behavior 8 (1967): 177–85.

Sölle, D., and S. A. Cloyes, To Work and to Love. A Theology of Creation. Philadelphia, 1984.

Solomon, R. C., Group Report: Sociobiology, Morality and Culture. In: G. S. Stent (ed.) (1978): 283–308.

Spaemann, R., Die Aktualität des Naturrechts, In: F. Böckle, E. W. Böckenförde (Hrgb.), Naturrecht in der Kritik. Mainz, 1973.

Speelman, W., "Het christelijk huwelijk" — wat zou dat kunnen zijn? In: Praktische Theologie 1 (1974): 159–67.

Spijker, A. M. J. M. H. van de, Die gleichgeschlechtliche Zuneigung. Homotropie: Homosexualität, Homoerotik, Homophilie — und die katholische Moraltheologie. Olten/Freiburg, 1968.

Steen, W. J. van der, Inleiding tot de wijsbegeerte van de biologie. Utrecht, 1973.

————, Some Comments on "Reduction." In: Acts Biotheoretica 24 (3–4) (1975): 163–67.

————, Algemene methodologie voor biologen. Utrecht/Antwerpen, 1982.

Stein, E. (ed.), Forms of Desire. Sexual Orientation and the Social Constructionist Debate. New York/London, 1990.

————, Conclusion. In: E. Stein (ed.) (1990): 325–53.

Stellungnahme zur Frage der Homosexualität. Vorlage der Kirchenleitung. Ev. Kirche Sachsen, 1984.

Stent, G. S. (ed.), Morality as a Biological Phenomenon. Berlin, 1978.

Stoker, W., De christelijke gosdienst in de filosofie van de Verlichting. Assen, 1980.

Stoller, R., Passing and the Continuum of Gender Identity. In: J. Marmor (ed.) (1965): 191–207.

Struyker Boudier, C. E. M., Het kerkelijk spreken over seksualiteit. Een antropologische interventie. In: Th. Beemer e.a. (1983): 79–94.

Suppe, F., In Defense of a Multidimensional Approach to Sexual Identity. In: Journal of Homosexuality 10, 3/4 (1985): 7–14.

Swaab, D. F., and M. A. Hofman, Sexual Differentiation of the Human Hypothalamus: Ontogeny of the Sexually Dimorhic

Nucleus of the Preoptic Area. In: Developmental Brain Research 44 (1988): 314–18.

———, An Enlarged Suprachiasmatic Nucleus in Homosexual Men. In: Brain Research 537 1/2 (1990): 141–48.

Symons, D., The Evolution of Human Sexuality. New York/Oxford, 1979.

Taylor, R., Determinism and the Theory of Agency. In: S. Hook (ed.) (1958): 224–30.

Terborgh-Dupuis, H., Medische ethiek in perspectief. Eeen onderzoek naar normen en argumentaties in de (medische) ethiek. Leiden, 1976.

Ten Have, H., Geneeskunde en filosofie. Lochem-Poperinge, 1983.

———, Gezondheid in filosofisch perspectief. In: Filosofie en Praktijk 8, 3 (1987): 113–27.

Thielicke, H., The Ethics of Sex. New York/Evanston/London, 1964.

Thomas van Aquino, Summa Theologica. Taurini, 1937.

Tielman, R., Homosexualiteit in Nederland. Meppel, 1982.

———, Homogeschiedschrijving. Een analytisch overzicht. In: Homojaarboek 2 (1983): 31–48.

Tolsma, F. J., Homosexualiteit en homoërotiek. Den Haag, 1948.

———, Homosexualiteit en homoërotiek (2e druk). Den Haag, 1963.

Towards a Quaker View of Sex (1963). In: E. Batchelor (ed.) (1980): 135–38.

Tourney, G., Hormones and Homosexuality. In: J. Marmor (ed.) (1980): 41–58.

Trillhaas, W., Der Dienst der Kirche am Menschen. München, 1950.

———, Sexualethik. Göttingen, 1969.

———, Ethik. Göttingen, 1970[3].

Trimbos, C. J. B. J., Gehuwd en ongehuwd (radio talk). Amsterdam, 1961.

Twee dominees, Ook wij zijn homofiel. Baarn, 1971.

Ussel, J. M. W. van, Geschiedenis van het seksuele probleem. Mennel/Amsterdam, 1982[7] (1968).

Ussel, J. van, Afscheid van de sexualiteit. Deventer, 1974.

———, Intimiteit. Deventer, 1975.

Vance, C., Social Construction Theory: Problems in the History of Sexuality. In: D. Altman et al. (1989): 13–34.

Veen, J. van, Wat zegt de bijbel over homofilie? In: Een mens hoeft niet alleen te blijven. een evangelische visie op homofilie. Baarn (1977): 90–128.

Veen, J. M. van, Sexual Behavior in the Human Male (boekbespreking). In: Wending 3 (1948–49): 377–81.

Veenhof, J., Bijbel en Homosexualiteit. In: S. Rozendal (red.) (1987): 109–23.

Veldhuis, R., Rechten — de moraal van de toekomst? In: H. G. Hubbeling en R. Veldhuis (red.), Ethiek in meervoud. Assen/Maastricht (1985): 81–115.

Velema, W. H., Huwelijk en sexualiteit in de greep van het relatiedenken. In: W. H. Velema, Midden in de maatschappij. Ethiek en samenleving. Kampen, 1979.

————, Hoe christelijk is de christelijke ethiek? Over het eigene van de christelijke ethiek. Kampen, 1983.

————, Zin in het leven. Een boekje voor jongeren. Kampen, 1987.

Ven, J. A. van der, Vorming in waarden en normen. Kampen, 1985.

Verwarring en herkenning. Over gemeente en homoseksualiteit. 's Gravenhage, 1984.

Vijver, H. W., Theologie en bevrijding. Amsterdam, 1985.

Villiers, D. E. de, Die eiesoortigheid van die christelike moraal. Amsterdam, 1978.

Vlaardingerbroek, J., Oudtestamentische gegevens. In: Over mensen die homofiel zijn (1972): 15–17.

Voorzanger, B., Menselijk gedrag in evolutionair perspectief. In: Vakblad voor Biologen 62, 13 (1982): 252–56.

————, Eigenbelang en goede bedoelingen. Het altruïsmebegrip in de sociobiologie. In: Vakblad voor Biologen 63, 6 (1983): 102–4.

————, De mens is een. bijzonder dier. In: Intermediair 22, 34 (1986): 29–33.

————, Woorden, waarden en de evolutie van gedrag. Humane sociobiologie in methodologisch perspectief. Amsterdam, 1987.

Vos, H. de, Beknopte geschiedenis van het begrip natuur. Groningen, 1970.

Bibliography

Vroon, P., en D. Draaisma. De mens als metafoor. Over vergelijkingen van mens en machine in filosofie en psychologie. Baarn, 1985.

Waal, F. B. M. de (red.), Sociobiologie ter discussie. Evolutionaire wortels van menselijk gedrag? Utrecht/Antwerpen, 1981.

Walsh, W. H., Hegelian Ethics. In: W. D. Hudson (ed.) (1974): 379–464.

Warnock, G. J., Kant. In: D. J. O'Connor (ed.), A Critical History of Western Philosophy. London (1964): 296–318.

———, The Object of Morality. London, 1971.

———, Contemporary Moral Philosophy (1967). In: W. D. Hudson (ed.) II (1974): 421–503.

Weeks, J., Discourse, Desire and Sexual Deviance: Some Problems in a History of Homosexuals. In: K. Plummer (ed.) (1981): 76–111.

———, Sex, Politics and Society: The Regulation of Sexuality Since 1800. London/New York, 1981 (= 1981a).

———, Sexuality and Its Discontents. Meaning, Myths and Modern Sexualities. London/Melbourne/Henley, 1985.

———, Against Nature. In: D. Altman et al. (1989): 199–214.

Weinberg, Th. S., Biology, Ideology, and the Reification of Developmental Stages in the Study of Homosexual Identities. In: Journal of Homosexuality 10, 3/4 (1985): 77–84.

Weinrich, J. D., Is Homosexuality Biologically Natural? In: W. Paul e.a. (eds.) (1982): 197–209.

Wengst, K., Paulus und die Homosexualität. In: Zeitschrift für evangelische Ethik 31, 1 (1987): 72–81.

Westermarck, E., The Origin and Development of Moral Ideas. New York, 1971 (1906).

Wiedemann, H., G., Homosexuelle Liebe. Stuttgart, 1982.

———, Die Beurteilung homosexueller Beziehungen in Stellungnahmen der evangelischen Kirchen in der Bundesrepublik Deutschland. In: H. Kentler (Hrsg.), 1983: 81-88 (= 1983a).

———, Homosexualität und Bibel. In: H. Kentler (Hrsg.), 1983: 89–105 (= 1983b).

Wilson, E. O., Sociobiology: The New Synthesis. Cambridge, Mass., 1975.

———, On Human Nature. Cambridge, Mass./New York, 1978.

Windelband, W., Die Geschichte der neueren Philosophie. Deel II. Leipzig, 1880.

Wit, J. de, en G. van der Veer, Psychologie van de adolescentie. Nijkerk, 1984[9].

Wolfenden-rapport (Report of the Committee on Homosexual Offences and Prostitution). London, 1957.

Zur Situation homosexueller Menschen in Kirche und Gesellschaft. Bericht der Arbeitsgruppe in der Kirche. In: Verhandlungen der 2. Tagung der 11. Westfalischen Landessynode vom 13. bis 17. November, 1989.

Zuurmond, R., Sodom: de geschiedenis van een vooroordeel. In: Amsterdamse cahiers voor exegese en Bijbelse theologie 5 (1984): 27–40.